DANIEL WEBSTE

"The Completest Man"

+ 0 -

DANIEL WEBSTER
"The Completest Man"

———◆———

Kenneth E. Shewmaker, Editor

Foreword by William H. Rehnquist

Essays by Richard N. Current, Irving H. Bartlett,
Maurice G. Baxter, and Howard Jones

Documents from The Papers of Daniel Webster
Charles M. Wiltse, Editor-in-Chief

Dartmouth College
Published by University Press of New England
Hanover and London

The University Press of New England

is a consortium of universities in New England dedicated to publishing scholarly and trade works by authors from member campuses and elsewhere. The New England imprint signifies uniform standards for publication excellence maintained without exception by the consortium members. A joint imprint of University Press of New England and a sponsoring member acknowledges the publishing mission of that university and its support for the dissemination of scholarship throughout the world. Cited by the American Council of Learned Societies as a model to be followed, University Press of New England publishes books under its own imprint and the imprints of

Brandeis University	University of New Hampshire
Brown University	University of Rhode Island
Clark University	Tufts University
University of Connecticut	University of Vermont
Dartmouth College	Wesleyan University

© 1990 by Trustees of Dartmouth College

Printed in the United States of America

∞

5   4   3   2   1

Library of Congress Cataloging-in-Publication Data

Webster, Daniel, 1782–1852.
    Daniel Webster, "the completest man" / Kenneth E. Shewmaker, editor ; foreword by William H. Rehnquist ; essays by Richard N. Current . . . [et al.].
        p.   cm.
    "Documents from The papers of Daniel Webster, Charles M. Wiltse, editor-in-chief."
    Includes bibliographical references and index.
    ISBN 0-87451-528-9
    1. Webster, Daniel, 1782–1852.   2. United States—Politics and government—1815–1861.   I. Shewmaker, Kenneth E., 1936–   .
II. Current, Richard Nelson.   III. Webster, Daniel, 1782–1852.
Papers of Daniel Webster.   IV. Title.
E337.8.W242   1990
973.5′092—dc20
[B]   90–13057
                                                                            CIP

CONTENTS

FOREWORD
Daniel Webster and the Oratorical Tradition

IT IS A GREAT PLEASURE to join with you today to celebrate the completion of the publication of the Papers of Daniel Webster. I am sure that these volumes represent a major contribution to our efforts to understand and appreciate one of the giants of the nineteenth century. And surely no more fitting institution of higher learning could be imagined as a place for this celebration than Dartmouth College.

As many of you know, Daniel Webster was born and raised in the Merrimack Valley of New Hampshire. He was born in the town of Salisbury in 1782—just as the Revolutionary War was ending. His father farmed and kept a tavern in Salisbury, which was then on the northern edge of the American frontier. When young Daniel was a few years old, his father moved the family to a larger farm about fifteen miles north of Concord, just off of present-day I-93.

Webster was unusual in appearance even as a child—he had a particularly large head topped with jet black hair, and large black eyes. He was called "little Black Dan." At the age of fifteen, he set off on horseback for Hanover to enter Dartmouth. At this time, 1797, Dartmouth was one of the larger colleges in the United States, but its setting was bucolic. Cows grazed on the college common. One of Webster's biographers says that he and his classmates got so tired of picking dung off their shoes that one night a group of them rebelled and chased the cows across the Connecticut River into Vermont.

Although Webster was about four years younger than most of his classmates, he managed to distinguish himself at the college. He was admitted into one of the two leading literary societies on the campus as a freshman and became one of its leading lights. He was elected to Phi Beta Kappa as a junior and was recognized even then for his oratorical abilities. He was also showing some indication of the spendthrift qualities that would dog him later in life: By the end of his senior year he had run up one of the largest accounts of any student at the General Store in Hanover. He graduated from Dartmouth in 1801 at the age of nineteen.

In a manner typical of the time, he taught school for a while, read

Delivered at the Daniel Webster Symposium, Dartmouth College, Hanover, New Hampshire, May 12, 1989.

ix

law for a while, and was admitted to practice law in New Hampshire in 1805. In 1807, he moved to Portsmouth, which was then the largest city in the state, searching out greener fields for the practice of law. He married a local Salisbury woman, Grace Fletcher, and the young couple settled down in Portsmouth. Webster was elected to the United States House of Representatives in 1812, and served two terms there. But once again he began looking for greener pastures for his law practice, and in 1816 he and his family moved to Boston. It was in the Boston area that Webster spent the rest of his life. He was elected to the House of Representatives from Massachusetts in 1822, and to the United States Senate in 1827. He was a leading figure on the nation's political stage from that date until the time of his death twenty-five years later in 1852.

We merely need to look around us at the automobile, the airplane, radio, television—to name only obvious material differences—to realize how different the twentieth century is from the nineteenth. One of the many ways in which the nineteenth century differed from the twentieth century was that its public figures wrote their own speeches. Both the ability to speak publicly and the ability to say something worth listening to were considered qualifications for public office. Not all public officials possessed these qualifications, but those who did were listened to with marked attention.

At first blush we may feel that we cannot truly appreciate Webster's orations, when they are reduced to writing, in the same way that we could have had we been present to hear them delivered. In a way, of course, that is true; but most of the people who knew these orations in his time learned of them in the same way that we do today. Only the relatively few spectators who could crowd into the Senate gallery when he spoke actually heard his famous speeches there; only the much more numerous group of spectators actually present at his Bunker Hill Monument dedication or his Plymouth oration heard him speak. But thousands and thousands of reprints of each of these speeches were gobbled up by the public, after considerable editing by Daniel Webster.

Webster was the greatest orator of his day in the United States Senate, and he was also one of the greatest advocates who has ever appeared before the Supreme Court of the United States. Let me first tell you a little bit about his advocacy before the Supreme Court.

Most practicing attorneys today, like those who practiced in Webster's time, never have an opportunity to argue a case before the Supreme Court. And of those who do, most appear there only rarely. Webster, however, argued 170 cases before the Supreme Court over a span of thirty-eight years, an amazing achievement and a record never surpassed. Although he won slightly fewer than half of his cases, this is generally the lot of the lawyer who has a reputation as a great advocate before the Supreme Court. Charles Evans Hughes and John W. Davis, the great advocates before the Court during the first half of this century, were by no means always successful. The reason for their mixed success, and for that of Webster's in the nineteenth century, was that frequently "great advocates" are called in by one of the parties only when the legal situation is roughly equivalent to a baseball game in the last half of the ninth inning when there are two outs and the home team is down by a couple of runs. Even a great batter will hit less than .500, and even the great advocate will not win a majority of these cases. But he will win more of them than the mediocre lawyer.

Oral arguments before the Supreme Court in Webster's time were far different than they are now. Today the Court receives extensive written briefs containing the contentions of the parties well before argument, and each attorney is given only half an hour to present the client's case orally. A red light on the podium dramatically indicates when this time has expired.

In Webster's day, by contrast, the case load of the Supreme Court was far lighter than it is today. In the early days of his advocacy, the Court would sit in Washington for only a few months in the late winter and early spring in order to finish its business, and oral argument was a more leisurely affair. Arguments frequently lasted not merely for hours on end, but in the great cases, sometimes for several days. An attorney with a gift of eloquence, a knowledge of the law, and a good deal of stamina, could hold the attention of justices and spectators for an entire day as he played a leading role on the stage where these great issues were debated.

It is interesting to note that in countries other than the United States that have inherited the English common law tradition, oral advocacy is even today much as it was in Webster's time before our Supreme Court. In the House of Lords in England and in the High Court of Australia, there is no time limit on oral argument; in an important case, it can go on for days. The Supreme Court of Canada only departed from this tradition within the past couple of years.

Among the cases Webster argued are some with which all students of the Constitution are familiar. He was on the winning side in *Gibbons* v. *Ogden* in 1824, when Chief Justice Marshall spoke for the Court in giving a broad interpretation to the Commerce Clause. He was also on the winning side in *McCulloch* v. *Maryland* in 1819, when the Court,

again speaking through Chief Justice Marshall, upheld the authority
of Congress to charter a national bank. The arguments in those cases
lasted five days and nine days, respectively. But surely the most interesting of Webster's cases to the present audience is the case of *Dartmouth College* v. *Woodward*, which he argued before the Supreme Court
of the United States in 1818.

The case arose from a dispute between the president and trustees
of Dartmouth College. The college had received a royal charter from
the Crown before the American Revolution. The charter provided
for twelve trustees to govern the college and authorized them to fill
vacancies occurring among their own number. The trustees had exercised their authority to turn the president of the college out of office,
only to see his cause become a burning political issue in the state of
New Hampshire. In 1818, the state legislature converted Dartmouth
College into Dartmouth University, raised the number of trustees
from twelve to twenty-one, and made other changes in the governance
of the institution. The majority of the old trustees refused to accept
the amendment to the charter and sued in the state court, claiming
that the changes "impaired the obligation of contract" in violation of
the United States Constitution. Meanwhile, they continued to operate
Dartmouth College in makeshift quarters after being evicted from the
"university" buildings.

The New Hampshire state courts ruled against the claims of the old
trustees, and they retained Webster to present their case to the Supreme Court of the United States. He was then thirty-six years old
and had just moved to Boston; he had already argued several cases in
the Supreme Court. But despite the fact that this case presented a
new point of constitutional law—whether a corporate charter was a
"contract"—and that the political infighting which gave rise to the
dispute was a "hot" issue in New Hampshire, the case attracted little
attention or interest from the legal profession or the general public in
other parts of the country.

Arguments were heard in March 1818, in the cramped temporary
quarters to which the Supreme Court had been relegated after its
courtroom in the United States Capitol had been burned by the British
during the War of 1812. Arguments began at 11 o'clock on the morning of March 10, with Webster's argument consuming most of the first
day. The audience consisted of only a few interested lawyers and a
small band of New Englanders, an assemblage that Webster later
described as "small and unsympathetic."

Webster spoke in a calm, deliberate manner. As one observer wrote:

It was hardly eloquence in any strict sense of the term. . . . It was pure reason. Now and then for a sentence, his eyes flashed and his voice swelled into a bolder note as he uttered some emphatic thought, but he instantly fell back into a tone of earnest conversation.

Drawing upon not only prior Supreme Court decisions but also such varied sources as New Hampshire law, the *Federalist Papers,* Blackstone's *Commentaries,* and English precedent dating back to the reign of Queen Elizabeth I, Webster endeavored to persuade the Court that under the United States Constitution the rights and property of private corporations were beyond legislative interference. He argued that if Dartmouth College, his alma mater, could be destroyed by legislative fiat, so could Yale and Harvard.

After four hours of intricate legal reasoning, Webster paused for a moment, then made a dramatic, emotional appeal to the justices' sympathies for the cause of higher education. He stated, according to one surviving account of the oration:

Sir, you may destroy this institution; it is weak; it is in your hands! I know it is one of the lesser lights in the literary horizon of our country. You may put it out! But, if you do so, you must carry through your work! You must extinguish, one after another, all those greater lights of science which, for more than a century, have thrown their radiance over our land!

No doubt there are many in this audience today, as there may have been in the audience who heard Webster in 1818, who would disagree about Dartmouth being a "lesser light" on the literary horizons of our country. But in any event, Webster was just laying the foundation for his next line, which I am sure is known well by many in this audience:

It is, sir, as I have said, a small college. And yet there are those of us who love it—.

It was an extraordinary presentation. Though the peroration appears to have been planned, Webster was overcome with emotion; tears clouded the eyes of the chief justice; the audience and the associate justices sat spellbound. As Justice Joseph Story wrote years later:

[Webster's] whole air and manner . . . gave to his oratory an almost superhuman influence. . . . the whole audience had been wrought up to the highest excitement; many were dissolved in tears; many betrayed the most agitating mental struggles; many were sinking under exhausting efforts to conceal their own emotions.

When the Court met for its 1819 term, it convened for the first time in what one newspaper described as a "splendid room provided for it in the Capitol." The decision in the *Dartmouth College* case was announced at the Court's first session. When Chief Justice John Marshall began to deliver his opinion from the bench it was soon clear that Webster's advocacy had proved persuasive. The chief justice stated that the colonial charter of Dartmouth College was indeed a "contract," which the New Hampshire state legislature could not impair without violating the Constitution. One justice dissented without opinion, and another was absent, but the remaining four of the seven justices who then served on the Court concurred with the chief justice.

Before this audience, it would be tempting to say that the *Dartmouth College* case was in the very first rank of constitutional importance among those cases which Webster argued. That, however, would be something of an overstatement. The principle that a corporate charter issued by the Crown in colonial days was a "contract" within the meaning of the Constitution was an important one, but later decisions of the Supreme Court cut back on some of the language of Chief Justice Marshall concerning what actions by the state would constitute an "impairment" of such a contract. Yet there is no doubt that the case had a tremendous impact on Webster's career, establishing him among the outstanding members of the bar of the Supreme Court.

Webster would be accounted a supporter of the Constitution of the Union throughout his time in the Senate and in his several unsuccessful bids for the presidency. His first great speech on this subject in the Senate occurred in January 1830. The previous day he had walked into the Senate chamber while waiting to argue another case before the Supreme Court (one floor below). Though the topic under consideration was a resolution to restrict the sale of public lands, the debate had begun to encompass other subjects, including the raising of revenues under the national tariff, sectional differences, and even the nature of the Union itself. The political interests of the East, South, and West frequently differed, and Senator Robert Y. Hayne of South Carolina sought to forge an alliance between the southern and western interests.

From the floor of the Senate, Senator Hayne attacked the East as being opposed to the low land prices that would favor the West. He also asserted that eastern exploitation of the protectionist tariff victimized both the South and the West by cheapening southern exports and making imports more expensive. A states' rights proponent, Hayne asserted that the tariff was unconstitutional and that individual states had the power to nullify such national legislation.

Astonished by the virulence of Hayne's remarks, Webster rose the following day to reply. Thus began what has since been described as "the greatest debate in the history of the Senate." At length, Webster aggressively contested Hayne's charge of eastern hostility to the West, then launched into a vigorous defense of the Union. To those politicians who believed that the Union was merely an arrangement of convenience that could easily be dispensed with, Webster proclaimed:

> I deem far otherwise the Union of the States. . . . I believe, fully and sincerely believe, that the union of the States is essential to the prosperity and safety of the States. I am a unionist, and . . . I would strengthen the ties that hold us together.

Hayne's response to Webster was extensive and consumed most of two days. Some believed that his eloquence was so effective that he had demolished Webster's argument. By the time that Webster rose to reply, the debate had aroused unusual interest—perhaps more because of the personalities involved than because of the issues. The ornate Senate chamber was full to overflowing, and as Webster later remembered, he "never spoke in the presence of an audience so eager and so sympathetic." Webster's response ran for three hours the first day and almost as long on the next, as he rose to a level of oratorical excellence that he never exceeded and that few others have attained.

Answering Hayne point by point, Webster eventually turned to the subjects of the Union and the Constitution. He rejected the idea that the Union was merely a creature of the states, whose actions any state could declare to be constitutionally invalid. It was for the Supreme Court, and not the individual states, to decide whether an Act of Congress violated the Constitution. For his peroration, Webster turned directly toward Hayne and proclaimed his belief that the United States could have both liberty and union:

> When my eyes shall be turned to behold for the last time the sun in heaven, may I not see him shining on the broken and dishonored fragments of a once glorious Union; on States dissevered, discordant, belligerent; on a land rent with civil feuds, or drenched, it may be, in fraternal blood! Let their last feeble and lingering glance rather behold the glorious ensign of the republic. . . . Liberty *and* Union, now and forever, one and inseparable!

Webster's speech, by fortunate chance, had been taken down in shorthand by a spectator in the Senate gallery. It soon went through more than twenty printings, and over one hundred thousand copies were distributed throughout the country, particularly to the western states, where Webster's reputation now spread. According to one historian, "The speech touched the craving of the American imagination for the heroic and the fabulous." In later years, Hayne himself acknowledged Webster as "the most consummate orator of either ancient or modern times."

Webster would remain in the Senate for more than twenty years after his Reply to Hayne, but he never gave a better speech there. During these succeeding years he would be known as a member of the "Great Triumvirate," along with John C. Calhoun of South Carolina and Henry Clay of Kentucky. These three would dominate the senatorial horizon for twenty years and would amount to a major force in the nation's government, by reason of their political skills and the force of their personalities. They had come into Congress at the same time, as representatives during the War of 1812. They were last gathered together in the United States Senate during the winter of 1850, when sectional antagonism over the institution of slavery had once more reared its head.

With the end of the Mexican War in 1848, the United States had acquired a huge amount of territory from Mexico—what is now virtually the entire southwestern part of our country. Out of this territory, California wished admission as a free state, but the southerners in Congress demanded concessions from the North in exchange. That body turned to the difficult task of fashioning what would be called the Compromise of 1850. Physically, the Great Triumvirate was on its collective last legs, if I may use that expression. Clay, seventy-three, was frail and constantly coughing, sometimes appearing too ill to climb the steps of the Capitol. Calhoun, sixty-seven and near death, "already seemed a disembodied spirit." Webster, sixty-eight, was far from well, "broken down with labor and anxiety."

In a speech to the Senate in late January 1850, Clay outlined a comprehensive solution that he believed would form a basis upon which the warring factions could get together. In early March, Calhoun undertook to respond on behalf of the die-hard southerners, but he was so infirm that he had to listen to another senator read his speech as he slumped huddled in a blanket. In a matter of months, he would be dead. Against this background, Webster's response was eagerly awaited, and on March 7 he took up the cudgels once more for the Union. But this time he was pleading not only with the southerners but with the northerners to compromise on issues that were very important to them. He spoke for more than three hours, seldom looking at his extensive notes. According to one commentator, "no utterance by an American statesman created more excitement at the time of the delivery or has been more fiercely discussed by historians."

The Compromise of 1850 was passed later that year. Some two years later Webster died at his estate in Marshfield, Massachusetts, at the age of seventy.

Shortly after I began practicing law in Arizona thirty-five years ago, I noticed hanging on the wall of the office of the United States Attorney a lithograph of someone who is obviously Daniel Webster making a speech to a group of people who looked like other senators. I asked the U.S. Attorney what the occasion was, and he said that it depicted Webster's Reply to Hayne. I did not know much more about Webster's Reply to Hayne than the peroration, to which I had been exposed somewhere during my education, and I think the same was true of the U.S. Attorney.

As I was preparing for my remarks for today I thought back to this incident from my past and realized that it took place about a century and a quarter after Webster delivered that speech. Then I asked myself whether it is conceivable that 125 years from now—indeed, 25 years from now—people would have paintings on the wall of a present-day senator or representative delivering a speech in the legislative chamber while colleagues crowded in to hear. The answer is obviously no. In a way, this summarizes the difference between the times of Daniel Webster and our own times. It is easy to make too much of these differences and to exaggerate them often to the benefit of the dead and departed. Webster, Clay, and Calhoun were not consistent in the views they expressed throughout their long lives. Indeed, each of them seemed to exemplify Emerson's maxim that "a foolish consistency is the hobgobblin of little minds." None of them was above reproach in keeping the political bargains he made. Webster was venal even by the standards of his own day, for he encouraged the solicitation of funds from wealthy Bostonian constituents to maintain his lavish life-style in Washington. All three of the Triumvirate—Webster, Clay, and Calhoun—were badly bitten by the presidential bug, and it showed in their conduct.

But when all of this debunking is given its due, there does, it seems to me, remain a difference between these three giants of the first half of the nineteenth century and public figures of more recent times. Calhoun, Clay, and Webster all sat down by themselves on numerous occasions and either wrote out a speech or at least made notes that would be used in delivering a speech on some great issue. By the standards of our times, these speeches were often incredibly long, and reading them today can in places seem incredibly dull. But we must also remember that at the time these speeches were given there were far fewer competing modes of entertainment or enlightenment than there are today. In this the orators of the nineteenth century were fortunate; those exposed to the emotional roller coasters of today's talk shows would hardly be likely to weep at Webster's peroration in the *Dartmouth College* case.

These statesmen were at least willing to stand up and say what they thought about an important public question, and to give the reasons why they thought the way they did. And the speeches or articles or letters that bore their names were more likely than not to be their own work. As a result, people listened when these men spoke; they did not need a "Meet the Press" format to obtain a public hearing. That this is not so today, it seems to me, is a singular loss to our society; but it is all the more reason for celebrating on this happy occasion the completion of the publication of the Papers of Daniel Webster.

WILLIAM H. REHNQUIST
Chief Justice of the United States

INTRODUCTION
"The Legacy"

———◆◆———

IN 1850, BELIEVING that the Union was in peril, Daniel Webster unequivocally supported the Fugitive Slave Law. Ralph Waldo Emerson, along with many other antislavery New Englanders who had previously admired Webster, now likened him to a god that had failed. When Webster died two years later, Emerson stood on the sandy beaches of Plymouth while thousands of his fellow countrymen assembled at Marshfield to pay their last respects to the eminent statesman. "The sea, the rocks, the woods," he wrote in his celebrated journal, "gave no sign that America and the world had lost the completest man. Nature had not in our days, or not since Napoleon, cut out such a masterpiece. He brought the strength of a savage into the height of culture. He was a man *in equilibrio;* a man within and without, the strong and perfect body of the first ages, with the civility and thought of the last. . . . He held undiminished the power and terror of his strength, the majesty of his demeanour."[1]

What is important about Daniel Webster? Why study the man and his career? What, as Maurice G. Baxter framed the question, is Webster's "long-range impact upon history?"[2] In sum, what is Webster's legacy to subsequent generations of Americans?

Historians agree that Webster had a large impact on American history. Along with John C. Calhoun and Henry Clay, he stood out as one of the most important public figures in the second generation of American leadership. In his collective biography of these men, *The Great Triumvirate: Webster, Clay, and Calhoun,* Merrill D. Peterson characterizes them as "the ornaments of American statesmanship in the era between the founding and the Civil War" and as worthy successors to George Washington, John Adams, and Thomas Jefferson.[3] With respect specifically to Webster, Irving H. Bartlett has pointed out that "no American in the first half of the nineteenth century was more visible than Daniel Webster."[4]

Webster's visibility in the second generation of American leadership seems to be rooted in his remarkable versatility and long career in public affairs. From the War of 1812 until his death in 1852, Webster was rarely out of the public eye. Peterson's observation that it is unusual for a person to attain "double fame" is particularly valuable for understanding Webster's prominence in American society, for he achieved quadruple fame as one of the greatest lawyers, orators, politicians, and secretaries of state in American history.[5] As the essays in this volume suggest, Webster had a significant impact on shaping constitutional law in the United States through his legal practice. He argued between 170 to 180 cases before the Supreme Court, and these included most of the landmark constitutional decision made between 1818 and 1852.[6] In an age that valued forensic talents, he gained a reputation as the preeminent orator. Generations of Americans repeated the conclusion of the Second Reply to Hayne—"Liberty *and* Union, now and for ever, one and inseparable!"—and that address of 1830 is still regarded as one of the greatest speeches ever delivered by a United States senator. The importance of Webster's political career, which focused on promoting American nationalism and economic development, is suggested by the fact that in 1957 the United States Senate itself elected him to its gallery of great senators. Webster holds an equally outstanding reputation as a diplomat. During two terms as secretary of state, he registered many achievements, including the Webster-Ashburton Treaty of 1842 that promoted peace between the United States and Great Britain. By almost any standard Webster ranks as one of the most prominent statesmen of nineteenth-century America. What, then, was his legacy?

As an orator and author, Webster offered posterity a model of effective speaking and writing. He was regarded by contemporaries not only as the preeminent public speaker in "an age of great orators," but also as a literary craftsman and giant, a reputation he attained through the carefully edited, published version of his addresses.[7] John Adams, for example, considered the Plymouth oration of 1820 to be a literary classic that should be read every year "for ever and ever," and he told Webster that he had surpassed Edmund Burke as "the most consummate orator of modern times."[8] That address, as Peterson wrote, marked not only Webster's "debut on the stage of literary eminence" but also the "commencement of a remarkable career in commemorative oratory." By following the speech at Plymouth with such memorable discourses as the first Bunker Hill address in 1825 and that on Adams and Jefferson in 1826, Webster became the founder of the school of commemorative oratory in America.[9] In addition to this long-range legacy, Webster also, as Baxter and Richard N. Current observed, inspired such third generation leaders as Abraham Lincoln, whose House Divided speech of 1858 and Gettysburg Address of 1863 borrowed much from the statesman from Massachusetts.[10]

Webster, then, was outstanding not only as a speaker but also as a writer. Unlike many public figures today, as Chief Justice William H.

Rehnquist stated in the Foreword to this book, Webster authored his own speeches and was "willing to stand up and publicly say" what he thought about important issues and to give the reasons why he thought as he did. One has but to reread Webster's discourse on the nature of "true eloquence" in the commemorative address on Adams and Jefferson or to follow the compelling logic of his brilliant argument on the nature of sovereignty under the Constitution in the Second Reply to Hayne to understand why Webster provided a model of effective writing and speaking. His speeches and formal writings, Current observed, were characterized by "clearness, force, and eloquence; he had what it takes."[11]

He also had what it takes as a lawyer, and Webster has become legendary for his courtroom prowess. In Stephen Vincent Benet's famous short story of 1936, "The Devil and Daniel Webster," he convinces a jury of the dead and damned, handpicked by Satan himself, to free a condemned New Hampshire man who has bargained away his soul and understandably has second thoughts. The reality of Webster's ability as a lawyer was not too far removed from that of the mythological hero of Benet's fictional classic. As Baxter wrote, Webster stood at "the front rank of an unusually talented bar" during the "formative era of American legal history."[12] Beginning with *Dartmouth College v Woodward* (1818) and continuing with other landmark cases before the United States Supreme Court, such as *McCulloch v Maryland* (1819), *Gibbons v Ogden* (1824), *Ogden v Saunders* (1827), *Swift v Tyson* (1842), and *Luther v Borden* (1849), Webster helped transform the constitutional and economic direction of the young republic. Although criticized both by contemporaries and historians for being too closely aligned with the rich and the powerful,[13] there is little question about the significance of the legacy. Through his legal practice, Webster strengthened corporate and individual property rights, promoted the growth of free enterprise, and enhanced the power of the federal government in such areas as interstate commerce. In the words of Baxter, when Webster's "contemporaries referred to him as the expounder and defender of the Constitution, they could use the terms correctly, whether applied to the politician or to the lawyer."[14]

It was, however, in the arena of politics, as expounder and defender of the Constitution, that Webster made his greatest impact upon American history. If Daniel Webster stood for anything, it was for an expansive philosophy of constitutional nationalism that centered on the assertion that the Constitution of 1787 provided for the perpetual union of one people. In the Fourth of July address of 1800, he called the Constitution "the greatest approximation towards human perfec-

tion the political world ever yet experienced;" in the Bunker Hill
speech of 1825 he implored Americans to let their great object be "OUR
COUNTRY, OUR WHOLE COUNTRY, AND NOTHING BUT OUR COUNTRY;" in
the Seventh of March oration of 1850 he spoke "not as a Massachusetts
man, nor as a Northern man, but as an American . . . for the preservation of the Union."[15] But Webster most eloquently expressed his essential message in the peroration of the Second Reply to Hayne in 1830:
"Liberty *and* Union, now and for ever, one and inseparable!"[16] In that
compelling equation, as Peterson wrote, Webster identified liberty with
Union, and Union with liberty at a time when the "idea of a supreme
and permanent Union was still something of a novelty."[17]

Charles Francis Adams commented in 1900 that "it was the mission
of Daniel Webster to preach nationality,"[18] and that appraisal has been
endorsed by many scholars. Bartlett, for example, credits Webster
with helping shape a national consciousness in America in the crucial
decades before the Civil War.[19] According to Bartlett, Webster never
wavered "on the great subjects—Constitution, Union, and the American past."[20] Baxter believes that Webster's greatest contribution to
posterity lay in the nationalistic "concept of Union, one and inseparable with liberty," which ultimately triumphed over Calhoun's thesis
that the United States consisted of a "loose compact of sovereign
states."[21] Current emphasizes that while Webster stood for "nationalism and constitutionalism," for "the integrity of the Union," he was
never a jingo. Rather, Webster hoped that the United States "would
serve as an example to the rest of the world as a great, rich, and
powerful republic that was not motivated by a spirit of aggrandize-
ment."[22] With respect to the nationalistic legacy, both Current and
Baxter have pointed to the inspiration Webster provided to Lincoln
and to Union soldiers during the Civil War, and Peterson interprets
Lincoln's defense of the Union as "a confirmation and vindication of
Webster's lifework."[23] If we take Webster's expansive constitutional
nationalism and concept of liberty and union for granted today, it may
be because we are as much a part of Webster's history as he is of our
history.

As the Hülsemann letter of 1850 demonstrates, Webster even occasionally used foreign policy to promote national unity. Assuming that
domestic politics should stop at the water's edge, diplomatic historians
have been almost uniformly critical of Webster's undiplomatic letter
to the Austrian chargé d'affaires.[24] That bombastic note, however, did
not typify Webster's management of American foreign policy, and in
part because of the prudent and thoughtful way in which he normally
conducted affairs during two terms as secretary of state, Webster has

been ranked by scholars among the greatest to hold that office in the history of the United States.[25] He also, as Peter Parish commented, holds the distinction of being one of the few nineteenth-century Americans who gained admiration and respect in Britain.[26]

Howard Jones's high regard for Webster as a diplomatist is based primarily on Webster's realistic approach to international politics. In Jones's words, Webster understood "that meaningful diplomacy derives from carefully balancing the nation's priorities with its means of enforcement."[27] In addition to knowing how to correlate means and ends, Webster also appreciated the importance of good personal relations with foreign statesmen, of compromise when necessary, and of the relationship of domestic to international politics. He also tended to think in terms of overall strategies, such as enhancing America's national interests through a systematic policy of commercial expansion with the countries of East Asia, as reflected in the Cushing mission to China and the Perry expedition to Japan. According to Jones, Webster was farsighted in his views on the constitutional primacy of the federal government in the making of foreign policy, on the importance of congressional authority over the war power, in formulating what has become the generally accepted doctrine of self-defense, and especially on long-term relations with Great Britain.[28] The Webster-Ashburton Treaty of 1842 not only upheld the honor of the United States and possibly averted a third Anglo-American war, it laid the basis for a rapprochement with England that has endured to the present.[29] Webster, then, according to Jones and other scholars, offers Americans a model of realistic and farsighted diplomacy.

According to Bartlett, another "significant legacy of Webster is that he provided us with a model of sensible conservatism."[30] Current thinks that Webster was a more able expounder of that philosophy than either Calhoun or Clay, but he also has pointed out that Webster has become "the forgotten man of American conservatism."[31] Webster was regarded in his own time as a leading spokesman for the establishment and thought of himself as a conservative, but the nature of his conservatism is not well understood today.

Scholars have described Webster's conservatism in different ways. Current emphasizes that in contrast to the more parochial views of Calhoun, Webster's conservatism stressed "Americanism" and was broadly national in its scope.[32] Bartlett calls Webster "the aboriginal patriot" and considers him to be one of the most intelligent and eloquent defenders of the establishment in American history.[33] Peterson sees "an ideological commitment to democratic capitalism" at the center of Webster's philosophy of an orderly promotion of individual liberty and political harmony in the United States, and Baxter underscores Webster's unwavering opposition to extremes of either the left or the right and to abrupt change.[34]

Despite differences in emphasis, these scholars have identified several themes basic to Webster's conservative philosophy. He valued tradition and the patriotic virtues of the past highly, believed in upholding the law and in the fundamentals of Christianity, advocated a kind of elitist republicanism in which political influence would be proportionate to the ownership of property in the context of popular rule and social harmony, and venerated George Washington, the Constitution, and the Union.[35] All of these themes can be illustrated by the speeches reprinted in this book. In the Fourth of July oration of 1800, in addition to praising the perfection of the Constitution, Webster idolized Washington as the national hero "who led us to victory" and "gave us freedom."[36] He argued in the Plymouth address of 1820 that the key to republican government lay in "laws which regulate the descent and transmission of property . . . to [the] interest [of] the great majority in society."[37] In the Bunker Hill speech of 1825, he interpreted the American Revolution as a conservative movement undertaken, unlike other revolutions, not to plunder but to protect property rights.[38] Along similar lines, in "Adams and Jefferson" in 1826, he urged Americans to "preserve" the God-given heritage of liberty transmitted through the founding fathers.[39] The intensely patriotic Second Reply to Hayne of 1830 identified the Constitution as the palladium of that liberty.[40] In the Seventh of March speech of 1850, he denounced both abolitionists and secessionists. Abolitionists were fanatics and perfectionists who dealt "with morals as with mathematics" and ignored the dictum of St. Paul "that we are not to 'do evil that good may come,'" and secessionists were not conservatives but irresponsible reactionaries advocating "an utter impossibility." "Never did there devolve on any generation of men higher trusts than now devolve upon us," he concluded, "for the preservation of this Constitution and the harmony and peace of all who are destined to live under it."[41]

Finally, unlike some of today's conservatives, Webster did not see the federal government as part of the problem but as part of the solution to many of America's difficulties. In contrast to the laissez-faire philosophy of the majority Democratic party, Webster advocated a Hamiltonian or "parental" state that guided and stimulated the economy to promote economic prosperity and social stability. Thus, he supported Clay's so-called American system of protective tariffs, internal improvements, and a sound fiscal management through a centrally operated national bank. He also wanted to make credit readily available to ordinary citizens to enable them to become affluent capitalists.[42] Webster most clearly expressed the underlying principle behind his philosophy on the role of the federal government in a speech of 1838 made in reply to Calhoun's more constricted views. The "very end of government," Webster said, is to "do that for individuals which individuals cannot do for themselves."[43]

Recent scholarship suggests that Webster's legacy to subsequent generations was large and diverse. There were, as Bartlett commented, many arrows to Webster's bow, and there probably is "a legacy for every arrow."[44] With his remarkable versatility, the defender of the Constitution and the Union provided Americans with models for distinction in oratory and formal writing, law, politics, diplomacy, and responsible conservatism. Webster, however, was no saint, and historians like Bartlett have not been reluctant to point out that he made mistakes and had "a character problem."[45] One reason why he never gained a presidential nomination, as Current suggested, was his too close association with the plutocracy and his dependence on wealthy supporters for "copious handouts."[46] For example, in the 1830s Webster was at one and the same time a United States senator from Massachusetts advocating a rechartering of the Bank of the United States, the chief legal counsel to Nicholas Biddle's powerful institution, and heavily indebted to him for substantial loans granted on favorable terms. "Even allowing for the well-known flexibility of public ethics of that day," Baxter wrote, "it is difficult to reconcile Webster's intimate relationship to the BUS with his conduct in Congress."[47] Biddle in effect allowed Webster to become secretary of state by relieving him of a huge debt of approximately $114,000, and Webster immediately continued his extravagant ways by purchasing an expensive home in Washington, D.C., where he entertained on a lavish scale.[48] He also maintained a 1400-acre showplace estate at Marshfield, replete with some thirty buildings, a small army of about twenty-five laborers, several boats and a yacht, and a collection of livestock and birds that included llamas from Peru and peacocks from India. Webster fits the profile of what we call today a "compulsive spender," and he lived most of his life on the brink of financial disaster.[49] Driven by accumulating bills and expensive habits, Current analogized, Webster "came more and more to crave money, as an addict craves the drug, and he was to satisfy that craving in ways that eventually hurt his reputation."[50] With respect to personal financial management and dependence on others for money, Webster does not offer an edifying model; he died approximately $200,000 in debt.

In addition to a self-indulgent lifestyle and involvement in conflict of interest situations, Webster also has been pillored for moral insensitivity on the most important issue of his day, slavery. Especially because of the positions he took in the Seventh of March speech, Webster was roundly denounced by eminent contemporaries like Ralph Waldo Emerson, Theodore Parker, and John Greenleaf Whittier, the latter comparing him to a "fallen angel."[51] Bartlett criticizes Webster for moral insensitivity with respect to slavery and thinks he just did not understand the abolitionist mind.[52] In 1846, Charles Sumner and other so-called Conscience Whigs implored Webster to lead them in a crusade to rid the nation of slavery. To do so, Sumner told him, would be to earn a title greater than that of Defender of the Constitution; posterity would remember him as Defender of Humanity. Webster, however, chose to stand, in his own words, by the Constitution "*as it is*," and it would have been out of character for him to have done otherwise.[53] To him, upholding the Constitution was no less a matter of moral principle than antislavery, but he showed little concern for the plight of those in bondage and may have missed a historic opportunity to lead a crusade on behalf of human rights. Like Lincoln, Webster took the position that although slavery was wrong, it was constitutional and legal. Finally, as Jones points out in his essay, like other statesmen, Webster was capable of serious errors of judgment as demonstrated by the controversy over the Lobos Islands in 1852.[54]

For all his achievements and virtues, then, Webster was not without his faults. The verdict of contemporary historians accordingly is mixed. Bartlett, for example, assesses him as a flawed Goliath, and Baxter sees him as an enormously talented person "culpable of serious impropriety."[55] Nevertheless, those scholars who have recently studied Webster's life and times agree that he contributed much that was beneficial to his country and that he left a large imprint on American history. Perhaps Webster's greatest legacy, as Parish commented, was the forthright way in which he addressed the perennial problem of leadership in America. He tried to reconcile the enormous capacity for growth and development in a dynamic and imperfect society with the need for balance and stability. Whatever one thinks of Webster's solutions to the problems of nineteenth-century America, he recognized the central issues of his times and wrestled with them throughout his life.[56]

The multifaceted career of Daniel Webster opens a window to many aspects of antebellum America, and the purpose of this book is to enhance historical understanding both of the man and of the society in which he lived. *Daniel Webster, "The Completest Man"* will be of value to scholars, but it is directed primarily toward college students and is intended to be useful in courses on American history. The book's organization reflects this purpose. It contains a foreword, four essays accompanied by documents selected mainly from *The Papers of Daniel Webster*, a chronology, and a bibliographical essay.

In the Foreword, Chief Justice William H. Rehnquist offers a thoughtful comparative analysis of the differing roles of public men and lawyers in the nineteenth and twentieth centuries, which raises the important question of how American society has changed over the course of a century. The Foreword is followed by four essays dealing with the life and times of Daniel Webster. In "Daniel Webster The Politician," Richard N. Current, Distinguished Professor Emeritus of the University of North Carolina, provides a broad overview of Webster's activities as a partisan politician and political strategist. Among the questions addressed by Current is the intriguing one of why Webster never received the presidential nomination of the Whig Party. The second essay, on "Daniel Webster The Orator and Writer," by Irving H. Bartlett, John F. Kennedy Professor of American Civilization at the University of Massachusetts, Boston, analyzes Webster's speeches from 1800 until his death. In seeking to understand the extraordinary hold that Webster had over the American mind and imagination, Bartlett focuses on why Webster's contemporaries thought he was such a great man. Maurice Baxter, professor of history at Indiana University and the leading authority on "Daniel Webster The Lawyer," assesses Webster's extensive legal practice at all levels, from the state and lower federal courts to the United States Supreme Court. At the center of Baxter's essay is the question of the nature of the impact Webster had on constitutional and economic developments in antebellum America. In "Daniel Webster The Diplomatist," Howard Jones, professor of history at the University of Alabama and author of a prize-winning study of the Webster-Ashburton Treaty,[57] provides a knowledgeable assessment of Webster's two terms as secretary of state. Jones believes that Webster's contributions to American foreign policy were as significant as those he made to politics and law, and his essay raises the question of what determines greatness in the conduct of international relations. All four of the authors draw extensively on *The Papers of Daniel Webster*, and, taken together, they offer readers a concise but comprehensive account of Webster's influential and versatile career.

Appended to each of the four essays is a set of documents. These primary sources have been coordinated with the essays and are intended to illuminate further Webster's activities as politician, as orator and writer, as lawyer, and as diplomatist. By reading Webster's private letters, great speeches, legal arguments, and diplomatic correspondence, students will gain a deeper understanding of the man and of the historical developments assessed by the scholars in the essays. Taken together, moreover, the documents comprise a kind of "portable Webster" in the sense that they comprise a balanced selection of his most important private and public papers.

The documents have been reproduced in type as true to the original as possible. Misspellings have been retained without the use of the obtrusive "(sic)"; abbreviations and contractions have been allowed to stand unless they would not be readily understood by the modern reader. In such cases, the abbreviations have been expanded, with square brackets enclosing the letters supplied. In general, square brackets have been used to indicate material provided by an editor. Punctuation has been left as Webster and his contemporaries used it. The ampersand, far more frequently employed than the spelled out "and," has been retained. Canceled words or passages that show some change of thought or attitude or have stylistic implications have been included between angled brackets. Foreign words and names have been printed as they appear in the original documents. Footnotes are used to identify persons, places, events, issues, or situations related to specific letters and documents.

To encourage and facilitate further research, the book contains a Bibliographical Essay that highlights the most significant primary sources and secondary works on Webster's life and times. A Chronology is also included to provide the reader with a convenient guide to the milestones in his versatile career. Webster himself, unlike many other statesmen, did not leave posterity an autobiography or memoir. He believed, as he wrote to a friend, that "public men and scholars will be remembered by their works."[58] In effect, he left it to those who followed him to evaluate the nature of his impact upon history, and *Daniel Webster, "The Completest Man,"* is fashioned so that the reader can do just that.

1. Bliss Perry, ed., *The Heart of Emerson's Journals* (Boston and New York, 1926), p. 261.

2. Maurice G. Baxter, *One and Inseparable: Daniel Webster and the Union* (Cambridge, Mass., 1984), p. 507.

3. Merrill D. Peterson, *The Great Triumvirate: Webster, Clay, and Calhoun* (New York and Oxford, 1987), p. 234.

4. Irving H. Bartlett, *Daniel Webster* (New York, 1978), p. 3.

5. Peterson, *The Great Triumvirate*, p. 112.

6. Just how many cases Webster argued before the U.S. Supreme Court is an interesting and complex question, and the answer depends upon how and what one counts. Professor Andrew J. King of the University of Maryland School of Law, the editor of the volume of *Legal Papers* that deals with Webster's practice before the Supreme Court, has provided the following answer to the question:

How many cases did Daniel Webster argue? The question is more easily asked than answered. In *Daniel Webster and the Supreme Court* (Amherst, Mass., 1966), Maurice Baxter counted the 168 Supreme Court cases that name Webster as counsel. However, during an era when rearguments were not uncommon Webster argued several of these reported cases more than once. Should one count these arguments separately? In the *Charles River Bridge* case, for example, Webster's second argument covered new ground and addressed new precedent. For him, it was a new argument. Baxter's count, also includes *Mason v. Haile* in which the court reporter credited Webster with the argument. In fact, Webster permitted his associate Alexander Bliss to stand in his place. In another case, *Hazard's Administrator v. New England Marine Insurance Company*, Webster simply stood up, told the Court his co-counsel had made all the points necessary in the case, and sat down again. Even if we could resolve the problem of the reported cases, we face two more. First, there were at least five cases argued by Webster but never reported in the Supreme Court reports. These were cases in which the Court gave no written opinion. Probably, the reporter saw no utility in publishing the arguments of counsel. Second, Webster often appeared on behalf of litigants in cases that he never argued on the merits. Arguments made on procedural motions were noted in the clerk's minutes but not reported. In still other cases the parties retained Webster as counsel, but dropped the case before argument. There may have been as many as fifteen of these two kinds of cases. This leaves the historian who seeks to give an accurate count of Webster's "cases" in a quandary. The non-historian, however, may not be as troubled by these difficulties. The ordinary reader is more willing to settle for a reasonable estimate of the cases in which Webster acted in the role of advocate for which history remembers him. The term "Webster cases" then includes only his substantive arguments both reported and unreported. Under this criterion, Webster argued between 170 and 180 cases.

Andrew J. King to Kenneth E. Shewmaker, December 6, 1989.

7. Bartlett, *Daniel Webster*, pp. 3–4.
8. Adams quoted in Peterson, *The Great Triumvirate*, p. 107.
9. Ibid., 107–12.
10. Baxter and Current made these observations at a panel discussion on "The Legacy of Daniel Webster" held at Dartmouth College on May 13, 1989. In addition to Professors Baxter and Current, the panelists included Irving H. Bartlett, Howard Jones and Peter Parish, who chaired the session. Statements drawn from the discussion on "The Legacy of Daniel Webster" will be referred to hereafter as Panel discussion, May 13, 1989.
11. Panel discussion, May 13, 1989.
12. Baxter, "Daniel Webster The Lawyer," pp. 143, 150.
13. For example, see Peterson, *The Great Triumvirate*, pp. 103, 245, 391–92.
14. Baxter, "Daniel Webster The Lawyer," p. 151.
15. Document #37, p. 93; Document #39, p. 104; Document #42, p. 121.
16. Document #41, p. 120.
17. Peterson, *The Great Triumvirate*, p. 178.
18. Quoted in ibid., p. 498.
19. Panel discussion, May 13, 1989.
20. Bartlett, *Daniel Webster*, p. 7.
21. Baxter, *One and Inseparable*, p. 511.
22. Panel discussion, May 13, 1989.
23. Comments by Current and Baxter at Panel discussion, May 13, 1989; Peterson, *The Great Triumvirate*, p. 496.
24. For criticisms of the Hülsemann Letter see Kenneth E. Shewmaker, "Daniel Webster and the Politics of Foreign Policy, 1850–1852," *Journal of American History* 63 (September 1976):303–15.
25. See Alexander De Conde, *The American Secretary of State: An Interpretation* (New York, 1962), p. 172, and David L. Porter, "The Ten Best Secretaries of State—And the Five Worst," *American Heritage* 33 (December 1981):78–80.
26. Panel discussion, May 13, 1989.
27. Howard Jones, *To the Webster-Ashburton Treaty: A Study in Anglo-American Relations, 1783–1843* (Chapel Hill, 1977), p. xvi.

28. Panel discussion, May 13, 1989.

29. Jones, *To the Webster-Ashburton Treaty*, pp. 179–80.

30. Panel discussion, May 13, 1989.

31. Richard N. Current, *Daniel Webster and the Rise of National Conservatism* (Boston and Toronto, 1955), p. 202.

32. Current, *Daniel Webster and the Rise of National Conservatism*, pp. 195–99.

33. Bartlett, *Daniel Webster*, p. 295.

34. Peterson, *The Great Triumvirate*, pp. 396–99; Baxter, *One and Inseparable*, p. 19.

35. See Bartlett, *Daniel Webster*, pp. 166–73; *One and Inseparable*, pp. 19, 92–93; Current, *Daniel Webster and the Rise of National Conservatism*, pp. 27–28, 37–38, 196; Peterson, *The Great Triumvirate*, pp. 395–400.

36. Document #37, p. 93.

37. Document #38, pp. 96–97.

38. Document #39, pp. 102–103.

39. Document #40, pp. 112–13.

40. Document #41, p. 120.

41. Document #42, pp. 123, 127–29.

42. On Webster's conception of the "parental" state, see especially Bartlett, *Daniel Webster*, pp. 172–73.

43. Charles M. Wiltse and Alan R. Berolzheimer, eds., *The Papers of Daniel Webster, Speeches and Formal Writings* (2 vols.; Hanover, N.H., and London, England, 1986–88), 2:305.

44. Panel discussion, May 13, 1989.

45. Ibid.

46. Current, "Daniel Webster The Politician," p. 14.

47. Baxter, *One and Inseparable*, p. 204.

48. See Peterson, *The Great Triumvirate*, pp. 298–303.

49. On Marshfield and Webster's almost unbelievable financial irresponsibility see Bartlett, *Daniel Webster*, pp. 207–14.

50. Current, *Daniel Webster and the Rise of National Conservatism*, p. 50.

51. Bartlett, *Daniel Webster*, p. 8.

52. Panel discussion, May 13, 1989.

53. Peterson, *The Great Triumvirate*, pp. 429–30; Webster's comment is in James W. McIntyre, ed., *The National Edition of the Writings and Speeches of Daniel Webster* (18 vols.; Boston, 1903), 4:100.

54. Jones, "Daniel Webster The Diplomat," pp. 222–24.

55. Bartlett, *Daniel Webster*, p. 295; Baxter, *One and Inseparable*, p. 502.

56. Panel discussion, May 13, 1989.

57. *To the Webster-Ashburton Treaty: A Study in Anglo-American Relations, 1783–1843* (Chapel Hill, 1977).

58. Webster to Edward Everett, May 6, 1851, in Fletcher Webster, ed., *The Private Correspondence of Daniel Webster* (2 vols.; Boston, 1857), 2:442.

WEBSTER CHRONOLOGY,
1782–1852

1782   January 18—Daniel Webster born in Salisbury, New Hampshire.

1796   Studied at Phillips Exeter Academy from May to December.

1797   Entered Dartmouth College.

1800   July 4—delivered Independence Day address at Hanover, New Hampshire.

1801   Graduated from Dartmouth near the top of his class and began the study of law in the office of Thomas W. Thompson in Salisbury, New Hampshire.

1802   Taught at Freyburg Academy, Freyeburg, Maine, from January to September, when he resumed legal studies with Thompson.

1804   Entered the law office of Christopher Gore in Boston as a student.

1805   Admitted to the bar and commenced the practice of law in Boscawen, New Hampshire.

1807   Moved to Portsmouth, New Hampshire, and established a law practice there.

1808   Married Grace Fletcher of Hopkinton, New Hampshire; campaigned for Federalist candidates.

1809   Unsuccessful candidate for the New Hampshire state legislature from Portsmouth. In three subsequent attempts from 1810 to 1812, Webster also failed to gain election to the state legislature.

1810   Webster's first child, Grace Fletcher Webster, born.

1812   Congress declared war on Great Britain; Webster prepared the Rockingham Memorial opposing the War of 1812 on behalf of New Hampshire Federalists; Webster elected to Congress on the Federalist ticket in November.

1813   May 24—Webster took his seat in the House of Representatives; June 10—made his first speech in Congress in support of reopening the debate on the origins of the war; July 23—a second child, Daniel Fletcher Webster, born.

1814   Continued to oppose the War of 1812; admitted to practice
        before the Supreme Court of the United States and argued
        his first case before that body; reelected to Congress;
        Treaty of Ghent ending the war with Britain signed on Decem-
        ber 24.

1816   Moved from Portsmouth to Boston; James Monroe elected
        president.

1817   Daughter, Grace Fletcher, died; second term in the House
        of Representatives ended.

1818   Third child, Julia, born; delivered the main argument in
        the *Dartmouth College* case before the Supreme Court.

1819   Supreme Court rule in favor of the plaintiff in *Dartmouth
        College v. Woodward;* argued the case for the Bank of the
        United States in *McCulloch v. Maryland.*

1820   Fourth child, Edward, born; Missouri Compromise,
        opposed by Webster, enacted by Congress; chosen a
        presidential elector for Massachusetts and as a delegate to
        the Massachusetts constitutional convention; December 22—
        delivered Plymouth oration commemorating the
        bicentennial of the landing of the Pilgrims.

1821   Fifth child, Charles, born.

1822   Elected to the Massachusetts General Court, representing a
        Boston district; appeared before the Spanish Claims
        Commission; November 4—elected to the House of
        Representatives from Boston on the Federalist ticket.

1823   Named legal adviser to the Boston branch of the Bank of
        the United States; Monroe Doctrine proclaimed by
        President James Monroe.

1824   Supported the cause of Greek independence and opposed
        the tariff in Congress; argued in the Supreme Court for
        the plaintiff in *Gibbons v. Ogden;* reelected to Congress in
        November; visited Thomas Jefferson and James Madison;
        son, Charles Webster, died.

1825   With Webster's help, John Quincy Adams elected president
        by the House of Representatives over Andrew Jackson;
        supported internal improvements in Congress; June 17—
        delivered oration at the laying of the cornerstone of the
        Bunker Hill monument.

1826   Served as chairman of the House Judiciary Committee;
        delivered a major speech in Congress on April 14 favoring
        the participation of the United States in the Panama

Congress of American Nations and a commemorative address in Boston on August 2 on John Adams and Thomas Jefferson; reelected to the House of Representatives in November.

1827 Supported the protective tariff in Congress; elected a director of the Bank of the United States; argued several important cases before the Supreme Court, including *Ogden v. Saunders* and *Bank of the United States v. Dandridge;* June 8—elected to the United States Senate from Massachusetts.

1828 January 21—Grace Fletcher Webster died; voted for the Tariff of 1828; Andrew Jackson elected president.

1829 December 12—Married Caroline Le Roy of New York.

1830 January 26–27—made the famous "Second Reply" to Robert Y. Hayne in the Senate; appeared for the prosecution in the trial of the Knapp boys charged with killing Captain Joseph White in Salem, Massachusetts.

1831 Argued the Charles River Bridge Case before the Supreme Court; Henry Clay nominated for president by the National Republicans.

1832 Purchased the Marshfield, Massachusetts, property that was thereafter his home; supported the Tariff of 1832; denounced President Jackson's veto of a bill rechartering the Bank of the United States but supported Jackson in the nullification crisis with South Carolina; Jackson reelected President of the United States.

1833 Reelected to the Senate; chaired the Committee on Finance; in a major speech on February 16 opposed John C. Calhoun's doctrine of nullification; supported President Jackson's Force Bill but opposed the Compromise Tariff of 1833; toured New York, Ohio, and Pennsylvania.

1834 Argued the copyright case, *Wheaton v. Peters,* before the Supreme Court; voted with the Senate majority to censure President Jackson.

1835 January 21—nominated for president of the United States by the Massachusetts legislature; William Lloyd Garrison, editor of the *Liberator,* attacked by a mob in Boston.

1836 Speculated heavily in western lands; Roger B. Taney confirmed as chief justice of the Supreme Court; Martin Van Buren elected president over Webster, Hugh Lawson White, and William Henry Harrison.

1837 March 15—delivered speech at Niblo's Garden, New York City, on the principles of the Whig Party; Picnic of 1837 undermined Webster's speculative investments in western lands.

1838   Represented Massachusetts before the Supreme Court in a boundary dispute with Rhode Island.

1839   January 17—reelected to the Senate; argued *Bank of the United States v. Primrose* before the Supreme Court; visited England and France from May to December; William Henry Harrison nominated for president by the Whig Party.

1840   Campaigned extensively for Harrison and John Tyler.

1841   March 6—assumed duties as secretary of state; April 4— Harrison died; April 24—formulated the doctrine of self-defense; September 10–11—except for Webster, all of Tyler's cabinet resigned; Alexander McLeod acquitted on October 12; November 7—slaves seized the *Creole*.

1842   Signed Webster-Ashburton Treaty on August 9; defended his decision to remain in Tyler's cabinet in a speech at Faneuil Hall on September 30; Tyler Doctrine proclaimed by the president on December 30.

1843   May 8—issued instructions to Caleb Cushing for the mission to China and resigned as secretary of state; June 17—delivered the second Bunker Hill address; argued the Girard will case before the Supreme Court in December.

1844   Opposed the annexation of Texas; Henry Clay nominated for president by the Whig Party; James K. Polk elected president.

1845   January 15—reelected to the Senate; argued the "license case" *Thurlow v. Massachusetts* before the Supreme Court; Texas annexed by the United States.

1846   Cleared of charges of misconduct while serving as secretary of state after a congressional investigation; supported the Oregon Partition Treaty with Britain but opposed the war with Mexico as unconstitutional, unnecessary, and unjust.

1847   Toured Virginia, the Carolinas, and Georgia; argued the "passenger cases" in the Supreme Court.

1848   Unsuccessful candidate for the presidency; argued *Luther v. Borden* before the Supreme Court; Webster's son, Edward, died in the Mexican War, and his daughter, Julia, died of tuberculosis; opposed the Treaty of Guadalupe Hidalgo; Zachary Taylor and Millard Fillmore nominated by the Whig Party.

1850   Supported the Compromise of 1850; delivered "Seventh of March" speech; July 9—President Taylor died; July 23—assumed office as secretary of state; December 21—issued the Hülsemann Letter.

1851   Tried to enforce Fugitive Slave Law in Massachusetts; Harriet Beecher Stowe's *Uncle Tom's Cabin* began serial publication in the *National Era;* negotiated a claims convention with Peru; established diplomatic relations with Nicaragua; issued instructions for a mission to Japan; reiterated the Tyler Doctrine in a dispute with France; resolved issues with Spain growing out of Narciso Lopez's invasion of Cuba; presented Louis Kossuth to President Millard Fillmore.

1852   Unsuccessful candidate for the presidency; January 7—delivered Kossuth banquet speech; February 23—delivered lecture on "The Dignity and Importance of History" before the New York Historical Society; upheld Charles Goodyear's patent in *Goodyear v. Day* before the United States Circuit Court for the District of New Jersey; May 8—injured in a serious carriage accident; July 25—made a speech in Marshfield on the fisheries dispute with Great Britain; involved the United States in a dispute with Peru over the Lobos Islands; negotiated an extradition convention with Prussia; Winfield Scott nominated for president by the Whig Party; October 24—died at Marshfield in his seventy-first year.

ABBREVIATIONS

Correspondence	Charles M. Wiltse and others, eds., *The Papers of Daniel Webster, Correspondence* (7 vols.; Hanover, N.H., and London, England, 1974–1986).
Diplomatic Papers	Kenneth E. Shewmaker and others, eds., *The Papers of Daniel Webster, Diplomatic Papers* (2 vols.; Hanover, N.H., and London, England, 1983–1987).
Legal Papers	Alfred S. Konefsky and Andrew J. King, eds., *The Papers of Daniel Webster, Legal Papers* (3 vols.; Hanover, N.H., and London, England, 1982–1989).
Speeches and Formal Writings	Charles M. Wiltse and Alan R. Berolzheimer, eds., *The Papers of Daniel Webster, Speeches and Formal Writings* (2 vols.; Hanover, N.H., and London, England, 1986–1988).
W & S	James W. McIntyre, ed., *The Writings and Speeches of Daniel Webster* (18 vols.; New York, 1903).

DANIEL WEBSTER
"The Completest Man"

Richard N. Current

———◆◆———

DANIEL WEBSTER

The Politician

D ANIEL WEBSTER was not a politician; he was a statesman. So
believed James Bryce, author of *The American Commonwealth*
(1888), which still stands as one of the two most perspicacious studies
that foreigners have written about the American people and their
ways. Before Andrew Jackson, the presidents had all been "statesmen,"
Bryce wrote, but from Jackson's election to the Civil War they were
either "mere politicians" or merely "successful soldiers." "They were
intellectual pigmies beside the real leaders of that generation—Clay,
Calhoun, and Webster."[1]

Webster was indeed a statesman. He achieved greatness as an intellect, an orator, a constitutional lawyer, a legislator, and a diplomat.
But he was also a politician. Throughout most of his career, he served
the interests of a political party as that party went through a series of
transformations. And he was long driven by ambition for political
office, for the highest office in the land.

He did not conceal from himself either his passion for politics or
his identity as a practitioner of it. In mid-career he confided, "My
habits, I must confess, & the nature of my pursuits for some years,
render it more agreeable to me to attend to political than to professional subjects."[2] He once implied he was so much the politician he
could never be chief justice or any other judge—"I have mixed up so
much study of politics with my study of law."[3] Only in moments of
political disappointment or personal despondency did he consider
abandoning public life.

Webster had gone into politics as a zealous partisan. From his father
he had learned to admire George Washington and to favor the Federalist party. But Washington died during Webster's junior year at Dartmouth, and Thomas Jefferson took over the presidency before Webster graduated from college.

1

Henceforth the Federalists constituted a minority in the country as a whole. "Yet," Webster remarked as a young man of twenty-four, "I consider the minority the place where a great politician is made." He hoped a "division in the democratic party" (as he called the Republican party of Jefferson) would "give feds the pleasure of voting with a majority."[4] He certainly did what he could to bring the Federalists back into control of Congress and the presidency. But he and his associates ceased to be Federalists of the George Washington type. In reaction against Jefferson's embargo and James Madison's war, they became rabid advocates of state rights and immediate peace. When the war was at its worst, in 1814, Webster (then in Congress) heard from his brother Ezekiel: "I am confident that the people would support almost any attack that should be made on the administration."[5]

Webster ceased to be a Federalist only when the Federalist party ceased to exist. "I congratulate you on your nomination by the Republican party," Henry Clay wrote him after his renomination for Congress in 1826, "although we really have in this Country no other than a Republican party. Names may be gotten up or kept up in particular States for local or personal purposes, but at this time there are but two parties in the Union, that of the Administration and the Opposition."[6] As long as John Quincy Adams remained in the presidency, Webster and Clay belonged to the Administration party, which became the Opposition after Jackson's election. Anti-Jacksonians such as Clay and Webster thought of themselves as National Republicans in opposition to Democratic Republicans.

By 1830, the year of his famous replies to Senator Robert Y. Hayne, Webster had completed his transition from state-rights Federalism to pro-tariff nationalism—Massachusetts having developed a strong manufacturing interest. He now thought the anti-Jackson party ought to "cultivate a truly national spirit—go for great ends, & hold up the necessity of the Union &c."[7] When some of the anti-Jacksonians turned into Antimasons, he hoped to attract them as National Republicans, but he knew that Antimasonry was much too narrow a basis for a successful political organization. "*If we bring about a change,*" he wrote, and he underlined the words, "*it will be done by us as a Union Party.*"[8] When President Jackson invoked national power against the South Carolina nullifiers, Webster briefly dreamed of winning even Jacksonians over to his own Union cause.

Webster remained a loyal party man after the National Republicans—the believers in his version of the Constitution and the Union—began to call themselves Whigs. He feared that a "complete dismemberment of the Whig party must be the inevitable consequence" of its decision in 1836 to hold no national convention and nominate no presidential candidate but, instead, to let three men (one of them Webster) run pretty much on their own.[9] Looking ahead to the 1840 contest, he stated his conviction, "Nothing but a fair, *deliberative,* & upright Convention, *can save the Whig cause.*"[10]

When the convention candidate, William Henry Harrison, won the 1840 election, Webster rejoiced at having "lived to see a great revolution accomplished"—a revolution "so extensive, so complete, & so over whelming." A dozen years earlier he had been amused at the jubilant way people flocked to the inauguration of that war hero Jackson: "They really seem to think that the Country is rescued from some dreadful danger." Now, at the victory of the war hero Harrison, Webster himself was overjoyed "to contemplate the dangers we have escaped."[11]

After President Harrison's untimely death in 1841, Webster had a decision to make about his duty as a faithful Whig. All the other cabinet members resigned, at Clay's insistence, to protest President John Tyler's veto of Clay's bank bill. Should Webster resign as secretary of state? He liked the job, had important negotiations coming up, and was in no mood to take orders from Clay. The Clayites denounced Tyler as a Democrat, but Webster saw no cause "to weaken the confidence of the Whig Party in President Tyler."[12] Still, before deciding, he inquired of a Boston friend, "Do the Whigs of Mass think I ought to quit—or ought to stay?"[13] He was assured of their "great desire" that he "remain in Office," and the Massachusetts congressmen and senators unanimously agreed with that sentiment.[14] But Congressman Robert C. Winthrop also warned him that his "*disesteem*" among Whigs would be even greater than Tyler's if he should stick too long with the Tyler administration.[15]

Once Webster had signed his treaty with Lord Ashburton in 1842, many of the leading Massachusetts Whigs thought it was time for him to go, but he stayed on for months after the treaty had been ratified. He blamed his critics, not himself, for damaging the party. "It is obvious," he confided to his son Daniel Fletcher, "that the political power in the Country is falling back, into the hands of those who were outnumbered by the Whigs, in 1840. All this was to have been expected, from the violence & injustice which have characterized the conduct of the Whig leaders."[16] And he meant Henry Clay together with those other leaders, in Massachusetts and elsewhere, who went along with Clay in denouncing Tyler.

After finally resigning from the Tyler cabinet in May 1843, Webster needed somehow to restore his standing in the party at home. Nicholas

Biddle gave him some advice. Explain at a public meeting that you are still a "Whig unchangeably," Biddle recommended. Tell the disaffected Whigs, "You separated from me, not I from you."[17] That is essentially what Webster had already told them in his September 30, 1842 speech in Faneuil Hall. He did not ask permission to return to the party; he insisted he had never left it.

By the time of the 1844 election, there was no longer any question about his orthodoxy. He supported the party—if not the candidate—with enthusiasm. Clay needed only five thousand more votes to win New York State and, with it, the presidency. "Any other respectable Whig candidate would have recd. a large majority," Webster thought. "The Whig party is strong, but it wants good direction."[18]

Already the Whigs were confronting challenges from two separate political movements, both of which were ultimately to erode Whig support. One was freesoilism, the other nativism. Clay in 1844 lost votes to the Liberty party candidate, and Clay's Democratic opponent James K. Polk gained votes from ineligible Irish immigrants.

Or so Webster believed. He agreed with Edward Everett, who wrote him from London, "I inferred that they [the Democrats] resolved to make a President at all hazards; and that the defection of the Abolitionists and the indefinite expansibility of the Alien vote would furnish them the means."[19] The alien vote occasioned the rise of the Native American party, and the Natives (forerunners of the Know Nothings) won a striking victory in the Boston elections of 1844. But Webster was not tempted to take up the nativist cause. Though the Natives were "enjoying their municipal triumph," he did not think they would be "troublesome in other & greater things." He hoped to distract them by means of the Texas issue. "This Native American question grows more & more interesting," he said, "& I know nothing better than to direct it, if possible, towards the keeping out of Texas."[20]

Nor was Webster tempted to join the Free Soil party in 1848, even though he thought the Whig choice of Zachary Taylor was a nomination not fit to be made. He intended to speak not for the Whig candidate but only for the Whig cause. "I must not, in consistency, abandon the support of Whig principles," he said.[21]

Even at the end of his career, Webster had no intention of abandoning Whig principles. But he finally concluded there must be "a remodelling of Parties" when Northern Whigs objected to the enforcement of the new Fugitive Slave Law, which he considered the crux of the Compromise of 1850. "There must be a Union Party, & an opposing Party under some name, I know not what, very likely the Party of Liberty."[22] Free Soil Whigs were combining with Free Soil Democrats;

Union Whigs ought to combine with Union Democrats. The 1852 nomination of Winfield Scott, with the backing of such "half abolition Gentlemen" as William H. Seward, meant the end of the Whig party, so far as Webster was concerned.[23] He foresaw that there would never be another Whig administration; hence, when he declined to say a word for Scott in the campaign, he did not think of himself as deserting the Whig party. The party was abandoning its own principles; it was deserting *him*.

A Federalist, a National Republican, a Whig, a proponent of a new Constitutional Union party—Webster had never been a no-party man. All along, he was a partisan, and a fervent one at that. He followed politics closely, not only in New Hampshire and Massachusetts but throughout the country, keeping up an extensive correspondence with other politicians. Something of a political strategist, he played an effective role in several campaigns, and he helped to elect other men to the presidency, even if he could not do the same for himself.

As a strategist and campaigner, he had distinguished himself as early as 1808, when he determined to prevent the election of James Madison. He took the initiative in alerting fellow Federalists in Portsmouth and other New Hampshire towns. This is the kind of advice he gave: "We have felt a good deal of alarm here about the Election—& are taking some pains to wake up our folks. . . . The Federalists must be roused. . . . *You must see to all the Towns around you.*"[24] Worrying about the "Democratic circulars," he proposed counter-propaganda to be distributed "in the Newspapers & in every other possible way." He also saw to the circulation of his own pamphlet condemning the Jefferson embargo.[25]

Though unable to defeat Madison in 1808, or in 1812, Webster helped bring about the victory of John Quincy Adams in 1825. The decision this year was up to the House of Representatives, since no candidate held a majority in the electoral college. Jackson could claim the largest number of popular votes, but Adams had the backing of both Webster and Clay in the House. Adams needed the vote of the Maryland delegation to be sure of winning. One of the Maryland congressmen, an old Federalist like Webster, said he would cast his ballot for Adams if Adams, as president, would not discriminate against "Federals" in his appointments. Webster, after consulting Adams, assured the Marylander that Adams "would administer the Government on liberal principles" and would make appointments on the basis of personal character rather than old party labels.[26] Maryland then went for Adams.

Thus Webster, along with Clay, succeeded as a president-maker in

1825, but he was to do less well when Adams ran for reelection in 1828. The Jacksonians started their presidential campaign as soon as Adams was inaugurated, and Webster took it upon himself to defend the administration against their attacks. Well ahead of election time, he was electioneering in person or by mail not only in Massachusetts but also in New Hampshire, New York, Maryland, Pennsylvania, and other states. Our "friends need to be waked up and excited," he insisted, as in earlier times.[27] Newspapers must be brought to the administration's support; too many of the editors, he complained, were "not willing to *take a side,* & to make their papers political papers."[28] State legislators should "introduce a string of Resolutions, approving the election of Mr. Adams—& of the general measures of the Administration—& characterizing the opposition as groundless."[29] As the election approached, Webster was (for neither the first nor the last time) overoptimistic, and he suffered quite a shock at Jackson's decisive victory.

Webster campaigned most actively in 1840, when the Whigs, offering no platform but only the slogan "Tippecanoe and Tyler too," outdid the Democrats in demagoguery. He reveled in it as he stumped through the Northeast and even into the South as far as Virginia. "Great conventions of the People, as you see, are all the rage," he wrote to a friend in London. "Thus far they have had powerful effect, & there is yet no abatement of spirit & zeal."[30] He was in such demand that—even though he declined to take off four days for a hunting trip—he could by no means accept all the invitations to speak. Some requests were urgent, for he was expected to make the difference between victory and defeat. Thus, from Whigs in a New York congressional district, which the Democrats dominated, he received this appeal: "We believe if you will come & address the people, we can carry the District."[31]

In addressing the people, he dealt seriously with real issues such as the tariff and monetary policy, but he also resorted to the claptrap common to the Whig campaigners that year. They maintained—and so did he—that the so-called Democrats were really the party of the rich, and the Whigs, the party of the common man. Like the others, he made the most out of the log-cabin-and-hard-cider theme. The aristocratic Democrats, he said at Saratoga, betrayed themselves "with an occasional sneer at whatever savors of humble life. Witness the reproach [by a Democratic journalist in an unguarded moment] against a candidate now before the people for their highest honors, that a log cabin, with plenty of hard cider, is good enough for him!"

Many a Whig was now bragging that he himself had been born in a log cabin. "Gentlemen," Webster apologized, "it did not happen to me to be born in a log cabin; but my elder brothers and sisters were born in a log cabin. . . ."[32]

Webster did not have to campaign on his own behalf in order to be elected to Congress. He easily won election to the House of Representatives twice from the Portsmouth district in New Hampshire and three times from the Suffolk district in Massachusetts. The Massachusetts legislature sent him to the Senate four times. In neither the House nor the Senate did he actively seek a place. The office, quite literally, sought him.

Boston Federalists first asked him to run for Congress in 1822. His friends, who had begun to call themselves Republicans, renominated him in 1826 to represent the Suffolk district for a third term. They expected him to run unopposed, since all the politicians were now calling themselves Republicans. But a few Jacksonians, as he complained, became "very industrious *to prevent the re-election of the present incumbent from appearing to be the Act of the Republican Party.*"[33] They put up another Boston lawyer against him, and Webster won in a landslide.

When his friends proposed to make him a senator, he said he would accept election only out of a sense of obligation to them. They had proposed him for the Senate twice before. "On those occasions I was able *to get excused,* without great difficulty, & without giving offence."[34] He though it would be more difficult to refuse a third time, unless he could persuade Levi Lincoln to be the candidate. He urged him to accept, but Lincoln persisted in declining. Webster seemed genuinely reluctant to leave the House. The legislature sent him to the Senate by a large majority in 1827 and reelected him by an almost unanimous vote in 1833.

He remained in the Senate as a favor to his friends, particularly those among the big businessmen of Boston and New York. By 1837 he was ready to leave his senatorial duties and concentrate on his law practice. "Your retirement now would discourage the Whigs of the Union—and probably change Massts.," one of his Boston backers protested to him. "In the State we are now but just alive—the contest for your place would weaken [the party], by souring probably some prominent men."[35] "My desire to relinquish my seat . . . is sincere & strong," Webster averred.[36] He decided not to resign, however, after his friends promised to compensate him for partially neglecting the law. They contributed to a kitty, one of several generous funds they raised for him from time to time.

Massachusetts Whigs were eager to put him back in the Senate after he had offended many of them by staying too long in Tyler's cabinet. An opportunity came when Senator Rufus Choate announced he would resign before the end of his term in 1845. "Your devotion to the true interests of your country, and your readiness to make a personal sacrifice for her welfare, are well known," one of the Boston Whigs wrote, appealing to Webster.[37] He was not yet ready to make that kind of a sacrifice, but preferred to wait until the six-year term was over. "If it should be the wish of friends, that I should enter the next Congress, I should have great regard to their wishes."[38] He did have great regard for their wishes, and he reluctantly retook the Senate seat as soon as Choate abandoned it.

Thus, for a couple of decades, the senatorship was his for the asking—or, rather, his without his even having to ask. But eventually this ceased to be so. Webster's support for the Fugitive Slave Act of 1850 undermined his position in Massachusetts. If, in 1851, he had been a candidate again, his friends would have found it difficult if not impossible to reelect him. They could not prevent the election of Charles Sumner, despite Webster's strenuous opposition to it.

Webster had reconciled himself to staying in Congress the first time his party, under John Quincy Adams, controlled the executive branch. A friend consoled him, "Your situation as an independent member of Congress[,] with the opportunity it leaves for your professional concerns, is better than any situation in the Cabinet."[39] Webster had no choice, since Adams offered him no job—not even that of minister to England, which would have pleased him—though Adams owed him a political debt and had promised not to discriminate against Federalists. But Webster did receive a cabinet appointment the next two times his party was in power. In the number one position as secretary of state, he had an opportunity to handle patronage as well as diplomacy.

Federal jobs were rewards for political service. That was how the Democrats had treated them, and that was how Webster could be expected to treat them. They could not be dispensed entirely as personal favors though. While waiting for the Harrison administration to begin, Webster put off Nicholas Biddle's request for appointment as minister to Austria by saying, "Nothing would be more agreeable to me. . . . The difficulty will be with the *Tobacco* men." They would expect a Marylander or a Virginian to fill the job. "The necessity, real or supposed, of [geographical] *distribution*—somewhat restricts the choice of men."[40] Webster told Edward Everett, "The richer collectorships, & Attorneyships, are subjects of much competition—so are the

Post Offices in the great Cities."[41] Webster and his friends must have been somewhat taken aback when President Harrison announced to all "persons employed under the government" that "partisan interference in popular elections" would be "cause of removal."[42]

Neither Harrison nor his civil service reform lasted very long. Upon Tyler's accession, Webster lost none of his influence in the awarding of jobs. "Among ourselves," he soon wrote regarding his relationship with the new president, "we are quite harmonious, & get on without jarring; but indeed we have done little except settle questions of appointment, & I do not see when we shall find an end to that most disagreeable business."[43] It was disagreeable partly because an appointment, while gratifying to one applicant, might antagonize several others. Webster proposed to reduce the number of applications for a particular job by requiring local bosses to winnow them in advance. As he said, in regard to the Philadelphia collectorship of customs, it would be "expedient to delay; and to signify to the heads of clans, that they must come to some terms, among themselves, before any thing will be done."[44]

In making appointments, Webster needed the approval not only of Tyler but also of Clay. The Clayites in the Senate could, if they wished, prevent the confirmation of any of the high-ranking appointees. Regarding one of these, Biddle admonished Webster, "He is I have no doubt a good officer—& very much your friend—& his rejection would in some quarters be considered as a triumph over your influence."[45] It does not appear that the Senate rejected any of Webster's nominees, and they included several of his closest personal and political friends, among them Edward Curtis as customs collector in New York and Edward Everett as minister to the Court of St. James.

Webster made a few appointments for reasons other than personal or political friendship. For one jobseeker he secured a post as chargé d'affaires in Denmark, and that man lent him money for the down payment on a house. For Washington Irving he obtained a place as minister to Spain, and Irving's wealthy brother-in-law canceled a mortgage on some of Webster's real estate. These two cases led to a rumor that Webster was selling government offices. Then a government clerk publicly accused him of accepting a bribe from his appointee as consul in Brazil. Webster denied the charge and had the clerk who made it fired, while Tyler withdrew the consul's appointment.[46]

Massachusetts Whigs expected Webster to become secretary of state again when the next Whig president took office. "They think that General Taylor will be disposed . . . to follow very much the course of General Harrison . . . & place you, if you desire it, at the head of his administration,"[47] wrote Everett, urging Webster to accept. But Webster said that, having opposed Taylor's nomination, he did not anticipate an offer and could not accept the offer even if it were made (it was not). He gave several reasons: his financial necessities, "the confining and irksome nature of the duties of the office," and the preference in appointments that would be given to Taylor's supporters as distinct from his own anti-Taylor friends.

"Another *general* reason is, that although I would not yield myself to any undue feelings of self-respect, yet it is certain that I am senior, in years, to General Taylor; that I have been thirty years in public civil life, and have had some few friends who have thought that, for the administration of civil and political affairs, my own qualifications entitled me to be considered a candidate for nomination for the office to which General Taylor has been chosen." In short, "I shall best consult my own dignity by declining to fill a subordinate place in the Executive Government."[48]

But Webster's dignity did not stand in the way of his accepting a subordinate place after Taylor died and Millard Fillmore became president. Webster was senior to Taylor by less than three years; he was senior to Fillmore by all of eighteen years. Fillmore was much less famous than Taylor. Still, Fillmore was not a professional soldier, and he had not deprived Webster of the presidential nomination, as Webster thought Taylor had done. "I never did any thing more reluctantly, than taking the office, which I have taken," Webster confided after resuming the position of secretary of state. "I was so much urged, on all hands, that resistance was out of the case. . . ."[49]

Webster proceeded to use the patronage against those who objected to the Fugitive Slave Law and who threw their support to Free Soilers such as Horace Mann. But, as the election year 1852 approached, Webster could not very well exploit the patronage to further his own presidential candidacy, since Fillmore refrained from taking himself out of the running. This Fillmore-Webster standoff was to culminate in the final, terrible shattering of Webster's presidential hopes.

For at least a quarter of a century Webster had been aspiring to the presidency. "As early as 1824 he was behaving like a future candidate, and by 1826 he seems to have been so regarded by friends and foes alike."[50] By 1830, with his replies to Hayne, he had (in the words of one admirer) raised himself "to an elevation, on which he [might] be viewed from all parts of an extensive empire, with an honorable national pride."[51] At the approach of every one of the next six presidential elections, he and his adherents rejoiced at his glorious prospects, then watched them wither and fade away.

Before the 1832 election he originally accepted Clay as the frontrunner of their party, but he changed his mind somewhat after he had gained fame as the Defender of the Constitution. He now began to intimate that the party was giving too much attention to Clay's name. There was "too much of a *personal cast*. We should be both for men & measures."[52] The Jacksonians had a "personal party"; the anti-Jacksonians ought not to imitate them with their own cult of personality. Besides, Webster suggested, Clay could not win. But finally he had to yield as gracefully as he could to Clay.

Once Clay had run and lost, the followers of Webster thought it was *his* turn next. In preparation for 1836 they acquired a newspaper, the *Boston Atlas,* and launched their campaign. "Who . . . should be the candidate of the great WHIG PARTY?" the *Atlas* editorialized. "DANIEL WEBSTER. . . . He stands before the friends of the Constitution, as the ablest expounder and champion of that sacred charter."[53] He fished for Antimasonic support but was unwilling to go so far as to imply that he would appoint only Antimasons to office. In the end he gained a nomination and electoral votes only from Massachusetts.

His hopes for 1840 and for 1844 expired long before election time, but his prospects for 1848 appeared to be good as late as the spring of that year. "The iron seems sufficiently heated," Charles W. March assured him in April, "& all that is necessary for shaping our ends is a succession of well-directed blows."[54] By summer the iron was cold; the Webster boom had fizzled out again.

So, for the ill and aging Webster, 1852 loomed as the last chance. He and his friends assumed the country would "have the discernment & the gratitude to appreciate & recompense the service" he had done in saving the Union through his Seventh of March address and the Compromise of 1850.[55] While he could no longer get the backing of the regular Whig organization, even in Massachusetts, his supporters encouraged him to believe they could sway the state convention by gathering petitions from Whig voters in the various towns. He remained optimistic that Fillmore would eventually make way for him. From James Watson Webb of the *New York Courier and Enquirer,* he received the following assurance in February 1852: "Your election is a near certainty if nominated; & I know . . . that we can secure the nomination if we abandon our timid measures & play a bold game."[56]

But Webb proposed a game that was more timid than bold as far as Webster's role in it was concerned. I "hope," Webb counseled, "that you will not permit any considerations whatever, [to] induce you to *write* or *speak*, until after the nomination; & not then if it can be avoided, as it assuredly can be."[56] In other words, Webb was telling

Webster to avoid all discussion of issues. That was what Taylor had done—Taylor, whose nomination Webster thought not fit to be made—but Webster was now so desperate for the presidency that he was more than ready to follow Webb's advice. "I feel quite obliged to you," he responded, ". . . & shall take good care to regard your prudent & timely suggestions."[57]

After the Whig nomination of Winfield Scott, conservative splinter groups under the name of Native American or Constitutional Union parties were willing to run Webster. Whig leaders in Massachusetts and elsewhere asked him for a "public disclaimer" of any such candidacy.[58] He refused to give one. In a reply he wrote on October 12, just twelve days before he died, he expressed the final bitterness of his long-thwarted ambition. The desired disclaimer, he said, would "gratify" not only his friends "but that great body of implacable enemies, who have prevented me from being elected President of the United States."[59]

Why did he never achieve the presidency? Was he too great a man for the job? James Bryce seemed to think so when undertaking to explain "Why Great Men Are Not Chosen Presidents." Bryce said, "The ordinary American voter does not object to mediocrity." The party looks for a winning candidate, but "the merits of a President are one thing and those of a candidate another thing."[60]

To have a chance to win, a person must of course be the candidate of a major party. Webster never was the nominee of the Whig party except in his own state. The question, then, really is, Why did the national Whigs never nominate him?

They might well have nominated him for vice president if he had been willing. His friends urged him to seek the second place on the ticket with Harrison in 1840 and again with Taylor in 1848. Obviously, he would have succeeded to the presidency if he had run for the vice-presidency either time. But he wanted a Webster-Harrison ticket, not a Harrison-Webster one. It would have been just as much beneath his dignity to be Taylor's subordinate in the campaign as to be Taylor's subordinate in the cabinet.

When Webster blamed his failure on his "implacable enemies," he meant his pretended friends, his fellow Whigs. Repeatedly they had refused to unite behind him and give him the chance he deserved. Most of these faithless Whigs were in the South and West, but as time went by the faithless appeared in growing numbers even in New England. Mainly responsible for misleading them was Henry Clay; at least, that is the way Webster generally looked at the matter.

But the majority of Whig politicians in the country as a whole held a different view. They admired Webster as a public man but could not see him as a presidential candidate. "If Mr. Webster could be elected," the *New York Courier and Enquirer* commented in 1848, "his nomination would give joy to the hearts of the intelligent Whigs of the country, and reflect honor upon our people and our institutions." *If* he could be elected! Too many of the Whigs believed, "He is not available"; that is, they thought him unelectable. They did not agree with Webster's campaign paper, the *Boston Journal*, when it maintained in 1848, "To contend successfully . . . the Whigs must abandon neither their principles nor their men."[61] Well, they chose men instead of principles in 1836, 1840, 1848, and 1852, and they won two of the four elections. They went for principles with Henry Clay in 1832 and 1844, and they lost both times.

Webster was considered unelectable because—for one thing—he had acquired, from his opposition to the War of 1812, a reputation as one of the allegedly disloyal Federalists of that period. An admiring fellow Massachusetts congressman noted in 1826 that Webster stood "upon disadvantageous ground because he was a leading federalist during the war and incurred a hatred which cannot be effaced from the minds of his adversaries."[62] The treason charge became especially worrisome as Webster looked forward to the election of 1836. After Pennsylvania Antimasons had chosen Harrison over Webster, one of them wrote to Webster, "What a farce! All agree, Mr. Webster, is my first choice, but we cannot carry him. Why? . . . Ah, but he was a Federalist? Damning sin! Never to be forgiven: But he was opposed to the war!"[63]

The charge persisted even though Webster again and again pointed out (quite honestly) that he had had nothing to do with the Hartford Convention of 1814, which supposedly had conspired to bring about the secession of New England. In 1835, when a newspaper campaign biography was about to be republished as a pamphlet, Webster suggested that the following patriotic note be added: "In the Summer of 1814, when the whole seaboard was threatened by invasion, Mr W. gave the principal part of his time in cooperating with others for preparing for defence."[64] But he did not suggest adding a reference to his December 1814 speech opposing, as unconstitutional, a bill for conscripting men from the state militia into the United States Army. "It will be the solemn duty of the State Governments," he declared in that speech, "to protect their own authority over their own militia, and to interpose between their citizens and arbitrary power."[65] Here he hinted at nullification. And on the same occasion, he defended the Hartford Convention Federalists by arguing that not they but the Madison administration Republicans were the real disunionists. No wonder a suspicion about his patriotism lingered on long after he had become famous as the Defender of the Constitution and the Union.

Another disadvantage was his reputation as an agent of the plutocracy. This reputation derived from his association with the Bank of the United States, from his closeness to the big businessmen of Boston and New York, and from his dependence on them for their copious handouts. Treasury Secretary Roger B. Taney called him a "pliant instrument" of the Bank. Webster did not help his own case much when he retorted that Taney was a "pliant instrument" of Andrew Jackson.[66] The Jacksonian *Portland Argus* attributed the following quotation to Webster: "Let Congress take care of the Rich, and the Rich will take care of the Poor." This statement was much catchier than his reply. He said he believed "the Laws should favor the distribution of property to the end that the number of the very rich, and the number of the poor, may both be diminished, as far as practicable, consistently with the rights of industry and property."[67] Such a cautious and qualified statement could hardly have enhanced his availability.

His availability was further impaired by sectionalism—by the stands he took on sectional issues. At the beginning, he seemed too much a Northerner, a New Englander, a Massachusetts man to be acceptable to Southerners. At the end, he seemed too pro-Southern for many of his followers even in New England, and yet he could get the support of very few politicians in the South.

After speaking for the North in his debates with Hayne and John C. Calhoun, he sought to appease the South with the following assurance in 1833: "In my opinion, the domestic slavery of the southern states is a subject within the exclusive control of the states themselves; and this, I am sure, is the opinion of the whole north."[68] But he failed to mollify the southern Whigs, who went for Jackson's fellow Tennessean and former ally Hugh Lawson White in 1836. Webster ruefully noted, "The movement of the Southern Whigs (as they call themselves) in Mr. White's favor, has disgusted, deeply, the whole body of our friends in the North."[69]

"No Massachusetts man can ever get the support of a slave-state," the antislavery Kentuckian Cassius M. Clay wrote to Webster in 1845, urging him to oppose the annexation of Texas. "If ever you meet with such reward as becomes the first mind in the nation," Cassius Clay went on, "it must come from a concentrated public sentiment in the free states strong enough to carry you in *spite of the South*."[70] Webster in the Senate did speak and vote against the admission of Texas as a state and also against the war with Mexico.

Nevertheless, as he prepared for 1848, he hoped again for southern support. In 1847 he undertook a politicking tour of the South, only to discover that the popularity of Taylor (a Southerner and a slave-holder) was spreading "like wild fire" through both the South and the West.[71] Still, when the Whig convention met, he wanted the delegates to be told:

> —That if they intend to preserve the integrity and strength of the Whig Party, they must show a disposition to be just towards the North, where the main strength of the party lies;
> —That they must be ready to trust a Northern man, fully disposed, & fully pledged, to maintain all the constitutional rights of the South;
> —That a persistence in the purpose of setting up a Southern Candidate, in the present state of public feeling, cannot but threaten the worst consequence to the Party, and to the Country. . . .[72]

Taylor, though a southern candidate, turned out to be no pro-Southern president. Indeed, he proved less pro-Southern than Webster was in dealing with the 1850 crisis. Taylor opposed any concessions to proslavery Southerners. Webster favored conciliating them with the adoption of a new, tough fugitive-slave law and with the omission of any law against slavery in the territories. That was the gist of his Seventh of March address, which he said he was delivering "not as a Massachusetts man, nor as a Northern man, but as an American."[73]

Just before March 7, Webster had received a report of a conversation between Calhoun and his South Carolina friend James Hamilton. According to the report, "Genl. H. said to Mr. Calhoun suppose that Mr. Webster does interpose and succeed in adjusting the question which is now agitating the country. What shall we of the South do for him. Mr. Calhoun instantly replied make him President Sir—for he will deserve it for that single act."[74] After the speech, Webster received expressions of gratitude and support from other Southerners, one of whom wrote, "It is my ardent hope & opinion that the people of this Country will do that justice to you which you so highly deserve of electing you to the Presidency of the U. States."[75]

Writing from Cambridge, Edward Everett had this to say about the speech: "Its effect at the South, as far as I can judge from the newspapers, appears to be entirely satisfactory. It was almost a necessary consequence of this circumstance, that the North should receive it with some misgiving. The open attacks upon your positions are however made by those whose support you could not expect, avowed abolitionists and free soilers, & whose denunciations will rather aid than impair the effect of the speech with the Conservative portion of the Community."[76]

The Massachusetts conservatives did indeed approve. More than seven hundred prominent men, "representing every major segment of the Boston community and its environs," signed a congratulatory letter, which appeared in a number of newspapers.[77] Webster personally encouraged the printing and circulation of hundreds of thousands of copies of the speech. But this speech certainly did not help with those antislavery people who, like John Greenleaf Whittier, thought his honor gone and his soul dead. The "country" Whigs—as distinct from the Boston Whigs—became less and less willing to forgive him as he proceeded to demand a strict enforcement of the Fugitive Slave Act.

Meanwhile, the gratitude of the southern slaveowners did not materialize in Webster votes at the Whig convention. The southern delegates preferred Fillmore, and even Scott. Webster got the backing of a few Georgia Whigs who talked, optimistically but futilely, of combining with conservative Democrats, forming a Constitutional Union party, and putting up a ticket of Daniel Webster and Alexander H. Stephens. Webster could take what satisfaction he might get from refusing to repudiate even a hopeless candidacy of that kind.

Edward Everett undertook to console him upon his failing to get the regular Whig nomination in 1852. "Assuming that election would have followed nomination, what could the Presidency add to your happiness or fame?" Everett wrote him. "Even before the office had been let down by second rate and wholly incompetent persons, the example of Mr Madison shows that even repeated election to the office is of very little moment to a great constitutional statesman."[78]

To assume, as Everett did, that "election would have followed nomination" was certainly unrealistic in 1852, when Webster was to be dead before election day. Even if he had lived and had been the Whig candidate, he could hardly have won an election that Scott, the military hero, lost. Indeed, he could hardly have won if he had run instead of one of those other military heroes, Harrison and Taylor, in a year when the Whig party was victorious.

But surely Everett was quite correct in pointing to the example of James Madison—an example that ought to have struck Webster forcibly, since he himself had done so much to make Madison's presidential years as miserable and as ineffectual as they were. The Father of the Constitution did not need the presidency to establish his greatness and his fame. Neither did the Defender of the Constitution.

1. James Bryce, *The American Commonwealth* (2 vols.; London and New York, 1889), 1:80.

2. DW to Jeremiah Mason, Feb. 6, 1835, in Charles M. Wiltse and others, eds., *The Correspondence of Daniel Webster* (7 vols.; Hanover, N.H., and London, England, 1974–86), 4:26–27. See Document 15, p. 45. All letters quoted in this paper are to be found in the *Correspondence* and hereinafter will be cited by volume and page only.

3. DW to Hiram Ketchum, Dec. 18, 1840, 5:69–70.

4. DW to Thomas W. Thompson, Mar. 5, 1806, 1:79–80.

5. Ezekiel to DW, Oct. 29, 1814, 1:172–74.

6. Clay to DW, Nov. 10, 1826, 2:140.

7. DW to John H. Pleasants, Mar. 6, 1830, 3:25–26. See Document 9, p. 35.

8. DW to Charles Miner, Aug. 28, 1831, 3:119–20.

9. DW to Edward Everett, Jan. 27, 1836, 4:78–79.

10. DW to Richard Haughton, Feb. 23, 1838, 4:275–76. See Document 19, p. 51.

11. DW to Achsah Pollard Webster, Mar. 4, 1829, 2:405–6; to Nathanial F. Williams, Nov. 7, 1840, 5:61; to John M. Clayton, Nov. 16, 1840, 5:62–63.

12. DW's note, Aug. 16, 1841, regarding Tyler's veto of Clay's bank bill, 5:142–43.

13. DW to Isaac P. Davis, Sept. 10, 1841, 5:149.

14. Isaac P. Davis to DW, Sept. 13, 1841, 5:152.

15. Winthrop to DW, Sept. 13, 1841, 5:152–53.

16. DW to Daniel Fletcher Webster, Oct. 19, 1842, 5:246.

17. Biddle to DW, Apr. 5, 1843, 5:284–86.

18. DW to Edward Everett, Dec. 15, 1844, 6:63–64. See Document 25, pp. 60–61.

19. Everett to DW, Jan. 3, 1845, 6:67–68.

20. DW to Robert C. Winthrop, Dec. 24, 29, 30, 1844, 6:66–67. Webster wrote, for a Whig meeting in Washington on March 15, 1845, the following resolution: "That there is abundant reason to believe, that the late Election of President & Vice President was carried against the Whig Candidates, by fraudulent practices, & illegal votes. . . ." 6:79–80.

21. DW to Daniel Fletcher Webster, June 19, 1848, 6:299. See Document 28, p. 64.

22. DW to Peter Harvey, Oct. 2, 1850, 7:155–56. See Document 32, p. 70.

23. DW to Franklin Haven, July 11, 1850, 7:123–24.

24. DW to Samuel Smith, Mar. 6, 1808, 1:101–2. See Document 1, p. 19.

25. DW to Thomas W. Thompson, July 25, 1808, 1:105; to Stephen Moody, Oct. 21, 1808, 1:106–7.

26. Henry R. Warfield, to DW, Feb. 3, 1825, 2:18; DW to Warfield, Feb. 5, 1825, 2:21–22. For Webster's letter to Warfield, see Document 4, pp. 21–23.

27. DW to Charles Miner, Mar. 24, 1827, 2:173–74.

28. DW to Henry Clay, Mar. 25, 1827, 2:175–77. See Document 5, p. 24.

29. DW to Ezekiel Webster, Apr. 4, 1827, 2:182–83.

30. DW to Samuel Jaudon, June 23, 1840, 5:41–43. See Document 22, p. 55. "I begin to wonder about these Conventions. But the People, I suppose, must have their own way." DW to Robert C. Winthrop, June 24, 1840, 5:43.

31. DW to Charles H. Warren, Aug. 15, 1840, 5:54.

32. DW, speech at Saratoga, N.Y., Aug. 19, 1840, *The Works of Daniel Webster* (5th ed.; 6 vols.; Boston, 1853), 2:29–30.

33. DW to Henry Clay, Nov. 6, 1826, 2:139.

34. DW to Henry Clay, May 7, 1827, 2:197–99. See Document 8, p. 32.
35. Henry Shaw to DW, Feb. 8, 1837, 4:187–88.
36. DW to Robert C. Winthrop, Feb. 23, 1837, 4:195–96.
37. David Sears to DW, Jan. 27, 1844, 6:21–22.
38. DW to John P. Healy, Feb. 1, 1844, 6:26–27.
39. Isaac Parker to DW, Feb. 21, 1825, 2:30.
40. DW to Biddle, Dec. 24, 1840, 5:72–73.
41. DW to Everett, Feb. 2, 1841, 5:84–86.
42. DW to Thomas Ewing, Mar. 20, 1841, 5:96–97.
43. DW to John Davis, Apr. 16, 1841, 5:108–9.
44. DW to Thomas Ewing, Mar. 28 [?], 1841, 5:99–100.
45. Biddle to DW, July 4, 1841, 5:133.
46. DW to Washington Irving, Mar. 16, 1841; Moses H. Grinnell to DW, Feb. 10, 1842; DW to J. C. Spencer, Apr. 5, 1842; and editorial notes, 5:87–88, 95–96, 189, 198–99.
47. Everett to DW, June 26, 1848, 6:300–301.
48. DW to Richard M. Blatchford, Feb. 16, 1849, 6:315–17. See Document 29, p. 65.
49. DW to Franklin Haven, July 21, 1850, 7:130–31.
50. Editorial note, 2:79.
51. William Sullivan to DW, Mar. 30, 1830, 3:37–38.
52. DW to Nathaniel F. Williams, Oct. 20, 1830, 3:85–86.
53. *Boston Atlas*, Dec. 17, 1834, 3:380–81.
54. March to DW, Apr. 2, 1848, 6:280–81.
55. Edward Everett to DW, Sept. 13, 1850, 7:146–48.
56. Webb to DW, Feb. 8, 1852, 7:302–3.
57. DW to Webb, Feb. 11, 1852, 7:304.
58. Moses H. Grinnell and others to DW, Sept. 24, 1852, 7:356–57. See Document 35, pp. 73–75.
59. DW to Grinnell and others, Oct. 12, 1852, 7:357–58. See Document 36, p. 76.
60. Bryce, *American Commonwealth*, 1:75.
61. *Boston Journal*, May 27, 1848, quoting the *Courier and Enquirer*, 6:289. See Document 27, pp. 62–63.
62. John Davis to George Bancroft, Jan. 29, 1826, 2:80–82.
63. Charles Miner to DW, Dec. 17, 1835, 4:73–74. See Document 16, p. 46.
64. DW to Caleb Cushing, Dec. 6, 1835, 4:71. See also DW to J. H. Bingham, Oct. 24, 1835, 4:49–50; and to Charles W. Cutter, Sept. 28, 1840, 5:57–58.
65. Charles M. Wiltse and Alan R. Berolzheimer, eds., *The Papers of Daniel Webster: Speeches and Formal Writings* (2 vols.; Hanover, N.H., and London, England, 1986–1988), 1:30. Hereafter cited as *Speeches and Formal Writings*.
66. DW to Edward Everett, Dec. 11, 1834, 3:372.
67. DW to James Brooks, Aug. 5, 1834, 3:359.
68. DW to John Bolton, May 17, 1833, 3:252–53.
69. DW to Nicholas Biddle, May 9, 1835, 4:44–45.
70. Clay to DW, Jan. 29, 1845. 6:71–72.
71. DW to Daniel Fletcher Webster, Apr. 18, 1847, 6:227–28.
72. DW to Edward Everett, May 22, 1848, 6:286–87.
73. *Speeches and Formal Writings*, 2:515.
74. Waddy Thompson to DW, Mar. 2, 1850, 7:21.
75. William G. Jones to DW, Mar. 17, 1850, 7:35–37. See Document 30, p. 67.
76. Everett to DW, Apr. 3, 1850, 7:51–52.
77. Thomas Handasyd Perkins and others to DW, Mar. 25, 1850, 7:44–45.
78. Everett to DW, June 22, 1852, 7:333–34. See Document 34, p. 72.

Document 1
Text from *Correspondence* 1: 101–02.

To Samuel Smith[1]

Dear Smith,   Portsmo[uth]. March 6. [1808]
    We have felt a good deal of alarm here about the Election—& are
taking some pains to wake up our folks. I am requested to write to
you, & most devoutly to solicit your attention to the subject. The
Federalists must be roused, or we shall lose the Election. *You must see
to all the Towns around you.*

    Send the accompanying letters to New Ipswich at once. We should
write to [James] Wilson,[2] but suppose he is at Keene. You see what a
pickle we should be in, if thro negligence this Election should go
wrong. This State, under such a Govt. as we should have, would not
be fit for an honest man to live in. I am requested to urge the importance of this Election upon your consideration in the most urgent
manner. Ever yrs

                                                            D. Webster

    1. Smith (c. 1767–1842), one of Peterborough's leading entrepreneurs, invested in
retail, manufacturing, and building enterprises.
    2. Wilson (1766–1839; Harvard 1789), New Hampshire lawyer, state legislator, and
congressman (1809–1811).

Document 2
Text from *Correspondence* 1: 102–03.

To Samuel Ayer Bradley[1]

Dear Sir,   Portsmouth June 28. 1808
    As your desire is to do good, I suppose you will be willing to assist
your friends, in this State, in the ensuing August election. I write you,
therefore, to stir you up, on that occasion. In the first place, I promise
that I address you by no authority—there is, I believe somebody in
the County of Strafford, who will request your services, in a more
formal manner—I am merely one of the people. The Federalists have
agreed on a Ticket for Reps—Nathl. A. Haven, Wm. Hale, Jas. Wilson,
Jno. C. Chamberlain & Daniel Blasdel.[2]
    This list is the result of long & mature meditation—& consultation—
.& if there are men on it, as I hope there [are] none, that you do not

like, be assured they are the very best men, who could be persuaded to be candidates. For electors, the choice of whom is in Novr. a list will be seasonably formed.

The Demos have had some difficulty in their ticket. At a first Caucus, the result was that C[harles] Cutts, [Daniel Meserve] Durell [Jedediah K.] Smith, [Francis] Gardner & Obed Hall should be the men. At this [Clement] Storers[3] friends were enraged—they said he must go— Cutts friends said *he should go.* At length they broke Obeds neck, & put both Storer & Cutts on the Ticket. So it now stands Storer, Durell, Smith, Gardner & Cutts. Grafton & Coos are left without any representation—to the great lamentation of all the good Demos that way, more especially of the aforesaid Obed. Your situation will enable you to look after Conway, Eaton, Chatham, &c. A single vote will be of consequence, for it is thought the election will run very even. Pray . . . do all you can for us. . . . Your ob ser

D. Webster

1. Bradley (1774–1844; Dartmouth 1799), a close friend of Webster.

2. Nathaniel Appleton Haven (1762–1831; Harvard 1779) was a Portsmouth physician and merchant, and U.S. congressman 1809–11. Hale (1765–1848), also of Portsmouth, was a merchant and shipowner, and U.S. congressman 1809–11, 1813–17. John Chamberlain (1772–1834; Harvard 1793) was a Cheshire County lawyer, New Hampshire legislator, and U.S. congressman 1809–11. Daniel Blaisdell (1762–1833) was a schoolteacher, farmer, lawyer, New Hampshire legislator, and U.S. congressman 1809–11. In the 1808 campaign, Haven and the full slate of Federalist candidates were elected to the 11th Congress.

3. Cutts (1769–1846; Harvard 1789) was a lawyer, New Hampshire lawmaker, and United States senator 1810–13. Durell (1769–1841; Dartmouth 1794) was a Dover lawyer, judge, and state legislator. Smith (1770–1828), Amherst lawyer, was also a New Hampshire legislator, and U.S. congressman 1807–09. Gardner (1771–1835; Harvard 1793), was a Walpole and Keene lawyer and U.S. congressman 1807–09. Hall (1757–1828) was a Bartlett farmer and innkeeper, state legislator, and U.S. congressman 1811–13. Storer (1760–1830), a Portsmouth physician and merchant, was also a state legislator and U.S. congressman (1807–09) and Senator (1817–19).

Document 3
Text from *Correspondence* 1: 105–06.

To Samuel Ayer Bradley

Dear Sir,   Portsmouth Octr. 20. 1808

I have recd yours of the 15th, & am obliged to you for it. We are well aware, that every effort is making to carry the Madison Ticket, & are preparing to meet these efforts, & prevent their effects wherever we can. Of the occurrences hinted at in your letter, we shall make such use, as may be—Conway, Bartlett, Adams, Eaton, Burton, & Chatham,[1] are very much out of our way. We should be very glad if any thing could be done for them. Conway did better than we expected, on the late election, & we thank our Fryeburg Friends for it. Pray help us again, as much as you can, for we shall need your *help, more than ever.* If any thing can be done, in those Towns, you *must do it.* I fear the next election will run much closer than the last. Our adversaries are now more busy, & more cunning, than they were then.

I hope, & believe, that we shall carry our Ticket, but it will require great industry, & exertion.

I shall take the liberty of sending you a few Oracles,[2] by mail, to be used as you think best.

Sir Richard [Evans][3] is now at Concord, as Editor of the new paper. I do not well comprehend the length & depth of the project, which you mention. Sir Richard is too deep for me—but I suppose it to be a step towards the establishing of a correspondence.

In Cheshire & Grafton our zeal & our strength is in no degree diminished—I have recently come from Haverhill, & have had means of ascertaining this. I am not without fears that Rockingham & Hillsborough will not do as well as they did before—Strafford I think will.

On the whole, I am of opinion that we shall carry the Ticket, by a majority, not quite as large as the last—but this is inter nos.

In the name of all that is patriotic, I conjure you & Brother-[Judah] Dana,[4] to do all that can be done, in the Towns in your neighborhood. Yours friend and ob se

D. Webster

1. Towns on the New Hampshire-Maine border.
2. A Federalist newspaper published in Portsmouth.
3. Evans (1777–1816), a Portsmouth businessman, began publishing the *American Patriot* on October 18, 1808, in Concord. The following spring he sold the paper to Isaac Hill, who changed its name to the *New Hampshire Patriot*.
4. Dana (1772–1845; Dartmouth 1795), lawyer and politician in Fryeburg.

Document 4
Text from *Correspondence* 2: 21–22.

To Henry R. Warfield[1]

My Dear Sir   H. R. Feb. 5. 1825

I have recd your note of yesterday,[2] & reflected on its contents; and am very willing to answer it, as far as I can, without incurring the danger of misleading you, in the discharge of the delicate and important trust belonging to your present situation.

I must remark, in the first place, that my acquaintance with Mr Adams, although friendly & respectful, I hope on both sides, certainly so on mine, is not particular. I can say nothing, therefore, on the present occasion, by any authority derived from him. Being in a situation, however, not altogether unlike your own, I have naturally been anxious, like yourself, to form an opinion as to what would be his course of administration, in regard to the subject alluded to by you. For myself, I am satisfied; and shall give him my vote, cheerfully & steadily. And I am ready to say, that I should not do so, if I did not believe that he would administer the Government on liberal principles, not excluding Federalists, as such from his regard & confidence. I entertain this feeling, not because I wish to see any number of offices, or any particular office, given to those who have been called Federalists; nor because there is a number of such individuals, or any one, that I particularly desire to see employed in the public service. But because the time is come, in my opinion, when we have a right to know, whether a particular political name, in reference to former parties, is, of itself, to be regarded as cause of exclusion. I wish to see nothing like a proportioning, parcelling out, or distribution, of Offices of trust among men called by different denominations. Such a proceeding would be to acknowledge & to regard the existence of distinctions; whereas my wish is, that distinctions should be disregarded. What I think just, & reasonably to be expected, is, that by some one clear & distinct case, it may be shown, that the distinction above alluded to does not operate as cause of exclusion. Some such case will doubtless present itself, & in proper time & manner may be embraced, probably, if thought expedient to embrace it, without prejudice to the pretensions or claims of individuals. The Government will then be left at liberty to call to the public service the best ability, & the finest character. It will then be understood, that the field is open, & that men are to stand according to their individual merits. So far as this, I think it just to expect the next administration to go. At any rate, it is natural to wish to know, what may probably be expected, in this regard.

While, with these sentiments, which, My Dear Sir, are as strong in my breast as they can be in yours, I am willing to support Mr Adams, & to give him my vote & influence, I must again remind you, that my judgment is made up, not from any understanding or communication with him, but from general considerations; from what I think I know of his liberal feelings, from his good sense & judgment, & from the force of circumstances. I assure you, very sincerely, that I have a full confidence, that Mr. Adams administration, will be just and liberal, towards Federalists as towards others; and I need not say there is no individual who would feel more pain than myself if you, & the rest of our friends should ever find reason to doubt the solidity of the foundation on which this confidence rests.

Note. I read this, precisely as it now stands here, to Mr. A. on the Eve of Feb. 4. He said, when I had go[t] thro, that the letter expressed, in general sentiments, & such as he was willing to be understood, as his sentiments. There was one particular, however, on which he wished to make a remark. The letter seemed to require him—or expect him to place one Federalist in the Administration—here I interrupted him, & told him he had misapprehended the writer's meaning. That the letter did not speak of those appointments, called Cabinet appointments, particularly—but of appointments generally. With that understanding, he said the letter contained his opinions, & he should feel it his duty, by some appointment, to mark his desire of disregarding party distinctions. He said, also, that in his opinion it would be impossible for any other of the Candidates to do otherwise than to disregard party distinctions. He thought either of them if elected must necessarily act liberally in this respect.

In consequence of this conversation, I *interlined*, in this letter, the words, in proper time & manner—& made no other alteration in it.

1. Warfield (1774–1839), a representative from Maryland 1819–25.
2. Warfield to Webster, February 3, 1825, in *Correspondence* 2: 18.

Document 5
Text from *Correspondence* 2: 175–178.

To Henry Clay[1]

Private & confidential
My Dear Sir   Philadelphia Mar: 25.'27

I staid a day in Baltimore, mainly for the purpose of seeing some of our friends; & had the good fortune to fall in with many of them. Indeed some pains were taken to bring them together.

The general state of feeling, there, seems entirely satisfactory. Nobody complains of the measures of Government, & Genl [Samuel] Smith,[2] even, has few or no followers in his crooked path. Still, the state of the Press, in that City, is not quite so favorable as might be wished. The Proprietors & Editors of the Public Journals are, generally, well disposed; but they are not willing to *take a side*, & to make their papers political papers. In the mean time, engines from another quarter begin to act vigorously on the public mind. This requires counteraction; for unremitted efforts, to produce whatever convictions, will, in time, prevail if totally unresisted. You know the grievance of the *Patriot*, about the public printing. That has *neutralized* its Editor,[3] & all the rest were neutral before. I have felt it to be necessary to change this *neutrality* of the Patriot into active support; & <with> by the aid of friends measures are in train, which, I hope, may have that result. It is not necessary now to trouble you farther, on that head. I think what has been done will be satisfactory & efficient.

I wish I felt as well satisfied with the state of things here. I have now been here three days, & have heard nothing but one continued din of complaint; not at the general measures of Government, but at the disposition of the *offices* which have been recently in the gift of the Executive. I suppose there must be some, of course, who are gratified at the late Customs House appointments here, but upon my honor I have not found one such. Enemies laugh, & friends hang down their heads, whenever the subject is mentioned. Our friend [Philip Swenk] Markley is, I dare say, entirely well qualified for his Office, & was probably recommended by a great country interest:[4] but I doubt whether those recommendations came from any deeper source than mere good nature & good wishes. I doubt whether the recommenders themselves are *gratified,* still more whether any of them are *attached,* by his appointment; while it is too evident that warm & zealous friends here are, some disappointed, & others disgusted. The truth is, that there seems to be a feeling prevalent here, that to be active & prominent, in support of the Administration, *is the way to throw one's self out of the chance of promotion, & the sphere of regard.* Those who wish for Office, think the policy for them is to hold back, in the ranks of opposition until they shall be offered their price. All gratuitous support of Government, they seem to think a foolish abandonment of their own interest.

Then, again, as to the state of the Press. I cannot learn that there is any *one* paper in the City, except the Democratic Press, which may fairly be called an Administration Paper.[5] There are many neutrals— many *candid* papers—many whose devotion to good government carries them so far, that they will, occasionally, admit pieces, which others have taken the pains to write; & many others, I suppose possibly, waiting, either for *terms,* or for tokens of what is to ensue, in political affairs.

At the same time, I am persuaded, that a distinct majority of the

City is with the administration, and that if there could be a proper spirit infused, and a just degree of *confidence* excited, not only might the City return us a favorable member, but it might act also, *efficiently,* on the State.

In short things here seem to me to be precisely in that State, in which there is every thing to encourage effort, & nothing to be hoped for, without effort.

This I think the truth; tho I should be glad to write a more cheering letter.

I said something to you about the West point visitors. Since I came here, I have heard, tho probably it is without foundation, that they have been already appointed; & that the persons, or many of them, are *opposition men; so* that it would seem our friends cannot even have *feathers.* Do inquire about this. In short, all protection, all proof of regard, all patronage, which can justly be afforded by the Executive Government, must be given to friends; or otherwise it is impossible to give any general or cordial support to the Administration before the people. I speak freely, because you know I speak disinterestedly. I have neither relation, friend, or connexion, for whom I ask anything. I go solely on the grounds of the common interest of us all.

I have conversed with Gentlemen here about *a public meeting.* They think it hardly practicable, just now. Time must mollify the feeling produced by recent events, before such a meeting would be attended. I have not, however, seen Mr [Robert?] Wharton, but shall meet him today, & learn what he thinks of it.

We <took> had great difficulty, as you know, last year, to prevent the District Atty from being disgraced.[6] He must have gone, *& would have gone,* but for the President's kindness towards him. Yet, I do not believe he would now walk round one square of the City to prevent Genl Jackson from turning the President out of Office. In the meantime his 700 *ridiculous* Indictments, not only bring great expense to the Government, but what is much worse, expose it to censure & reproach. Add to this, that the whole influence of the custom house *has been, &* that much the greater part of it is *likely still to be, opposed* to the friends of the Administration, & then we see what the prospect is. In my poor judgment, the general interest of the Country, & the interest of the Administration, alike required that that custom house should <have> be thoroughly reformed. And I think, moreover, that even now <places> room should be found or *made,* to place there three or four competent & faithful men. After what the Judges of the Supreme Court felt it their duty to say, on the conduct of the officers of that Customs house, in the late *Tea case,*[7] I think public opinion would justify, & indeed that it will peremptorily require, some efficient changes in the subordinate branches of the establishment.

But I will not weary you further. In hopes of being able to make a less dolourous epistle the next time I write, I remain, My Dear Sir, with true regard Yours

Danl. Webster

Mar. 26. P.S. The rumour about the West point appointments is not, I am told, well founded. Col [Andrew M.] Prevost[8] is said to be one of the Board, which is as it ought to be. I do not know that it would now be important to ask Mr [Robert] *Walsh*[9] to be of the number. Mr. Walsh leaves here for Washington tomorrow. You will of course see him, & I hope will converse with him fully. Perhaps I may venture to write you again, on this point, before I leave the City.

1. Clay (1777–1852), U.S. senator (1806–07, 1810–11, 1831–42, 1849–52) and congressman (1811–14, 1815–21, 1823–25) from Kentucky, secretary of state under President John Quincy Adams (1825–29), and one of Websters great political rivals.

2. Smith (1752–1839), a general in the War of 1812 famous for his defense of Baltimore, U.S. representative (1793–1803, 1816–22) and senator (1803–15, 1822–33) from Maryland.

3. Clay's selection of the *Baltimore American*, upon the recommendation of many of the Maryland delegation in Congress, had alienated Isaac Munroe, publisher of the *Baltimore Patriot & Commercial Advertiser*.

4. Markley (1789–1834) a representative from Pennsylvania 1823–27. President Adams appointed Markley to the post of customs collector for the port of Philadelphia.

5. John Binns edited the Philadelphia *Democratic Press*.

6. Charles Jared Ingersoll (1782–1862), U.S. district attorney for Pennsylvania (1815–29) and congressman from Pennsylvania (1813–15, 1841–49).

7. *United States v.* 350 *Chests of Tea*, 12 Wheaton 486 (1827).

8. Prevost, born in Geneva, Switzerland, had emigrated to the United States with his parents. In the War of 1812, he commanded the first regiment of the Pennsylvania artillery.

9. Walsh (1784–1859), a prominent American author and journalist.

Document 6
Text from *Correspondence* 2: 179–181.

To John Quincy Adams

Sir,   Philadelphia March 27. 1827.

I hope you will pardon me for troubling you, once more, on a political subject. However infirm my judgment may be, in the matters about which I write, you may yet be assured that every word proceeds from entire singleness of heart, & devotion to that, which is the great immediate object of my thoughts and efforts, the support and *continuance* of the Administration.

One of the *observables,* here, is Mr [Robert] Walsh's entire neutrality, (if it be *entire,*) as to the existing contest. This is a great draw back, on the means of affecting favorably the public sentiment. It is important, as I think, and as all here think, to bring him out, in a moderate but firm manner, in support of the Administration. He circulates 4000 papers; & his Review, also, which is getting an unexpected extent of patronage, opens another field, which might be prudently and usefully occupied, for the discussion of certain principles, now becoming interesting, and on which we must hope to stand, if we stand at all, in this State.[1]

You are aware, that there are 40. or 50 thousand Electors, in Penna. who formerly belonged to the Federal Party. With these, Mr Walsh's opinions have great weight; and a majority of their votes is necessary, in any calculation, which anticipates that this State may be found in favor of the continuance of the present state of things.

I have now been here near a week, have seen very many people, & conversed with all I have seen, who are favorably disposed, whether Greek or Jew. I have learned the grievances of the Democratic Press; & what I could do or suggest, in that quarter, tending to promote satisfaction, & to ensure active exertion, has not been omitted. The present state of feeling here is certainly not the best, so far as it has been produced by the recent appointments. This I have endeavored, by all the means in my power, to mollify & satisfy; & I hope with some success.

I have endeavored also to learn the causes of Mr Walsh's coldness & to find out what might propitiate his good feelings, & secure his efforts. He sees nothing, I believe, to disapprove, in the general measures of Government, but certainly is, at present, in rather an unsatisfied mood towards the Administration. I am happy that he is going to Washington, & that you will have an opportunity to converse with him. He is an old & an attached friend of Mr [Joseph] *Hopkinson,*[2] & he feels that Mr H. as an early & true friend to the President, has been neglected, & injured. Mr Hopkinson, himself, does not talk in that way; still, if something fit for him to receive, could be offered to him, I have no doubt it would gratify Mr Walsh more than any thing else whatever. The District Judge of this District will hardly last long. It is a small office, but I presume Mr H. would take it.[3] No doubt he is entirely well qualified for it, & would probably be recommended by nearly all the bar. I am persuaded a little effort would reconcile all our other friends here, or nearly all, to this measure. Some act of patronage or kindness, performed at the same time to them, would lead them easily to acquiesce in it.

The first fruits, of such an understanding, if it were found practicable to make it, would, I am persuaded, be seen in the appearance of quite a different tone & manner in the National Gazette. It would heal, too much of the wound which is felt in N. Jersey; and would suffice, even in New England, to awaken the activity of many friends.

I know not what objections there may be, to this arrangement; but it strikes me that the good must greatly overbalance the evil. <Men> Friends here are in sections & parties; & unless union can be produced, great mischief will, or may, ensue. If things should remain in their present State, I think it more than probable, that Mr Hopkinson <would> will be run for Congress, with or against his consent, in October, *agt. Mr. [John] Sergeant.*[4]

I see not why the Nat. Gazette, & the Press might not go on, well enough, without collision. There are measures of Govt. for Mr W. to defend; steps of opposition for him to expose, & reprobate; general good principles to be enforced, &c &c.—The Press, in the mean time, may very well pursue its own course, taking care not unnecessarily to annoy its neighbors. They might thus tend to the same point, altho' they should not walk in the same road. These ideas I have endeavored, by all means in my power, to enforce on all sides.

It is proper for me to add, what you already well know, that Mr Hopkinson is my particular friend. Make as much allowance for bias, & possible error of judgment, on this account, as seems proper to yourself. Be assured only that I speak as I really think.

Again begging you to pardon me for writing on such a subject, & so long a letter, I have only to renew the assurances of my sincere & constant regard

Danl. Webster

1. *The American Quarterly Review* and the *National Gazette and Literary Register* were among the publications that Walsh edited.

2. Hopkinson (1770–1842; University of Pennsylvania 1786), lawyer and politician. He was associated with Webster in the Dartmouth College case and represented Pennsylvania in Congress from 1815 to 1819.

3. Richard Peters (1774–1828), lawyer, represented Pennsylvania in the Continental Congress in 1782–83, judge of the Eastern District of Pennsylvania from 1792 until his death. In 1828 Adams appointed Hopkinson to the post.

4. Sergeant (1779–1852; Princeton 1795), represented Pennsylvania in Congress 1815–23, 1827–29, 1837–41.

Document 7
Text from *Correspondence* 2: 184–85.

To Jeremiah Mason[1]

My dear Sir,   Boston, April 10, 1827.

You will have heard from Mary,[2] since her arrival here. We had a pleasant passage, and I was glad of her company. Since I have been at home, my attention has been occupied with various matters, private and professional. I have, nominally, some little business yet in the State courts; although my long absences have very much severed me from them. In the neighboring counties, where courts are held at seasons when I am at home, I have also an occasional engagement, and these affairs have required my attention since my return.

The business in the [Supreme] court at Washington was heavy, as you have seen; and my participation in it greater than usual. We got on with the Virginia cause famously;[3] you will see, when you see the report, that our friend Judge [Joseph] Story[4] laid out his whole strength and made a great opinion. The attorney-general [William Wirt][5] argued the cause with me. It was not one of his happiest efforts. By the aid of your brief, I got on tolerably well, and took the credit, modestly, of having made a good argument; at any rate, I got a very good fee; and although I shall not send you your just part of it, I yet enclose a draft for the least sum which I can persuade myself you deserve to receive.

I was sorry not to be able to get good materials from you, in the lottery case,[6] also. But we got along with the cause, and hope sometime to get the money.

As to political matters, I wish to say something, but hardly know where to begin. A survey of the whole ground leads me to believe, confidently, in Mr. Adams's reelection. I set down New England, New Jersey, the greater part of Maryland, and perhaps all Delaware, Ohio, Kentucky, Indiana, Missouri, and Louisiana for him.

We must then get votes enough in New York to choose him, and I think cannot fail of this. It is possible we may lose four votes in Kentucky, but I do not expect it. At the same time it is not impossible that Pennsylvania may go for Mr. Adams. Beyond doubt, public opinion is taking a very strong turn in that State, and it is not now easy to say how far the change may proceed. That there is a change, and a great change, is too clear to be questioned.

In New York, affairs wear the common complexion of New York politics. Mr. [DeWitt] Clinton and some few of his friends have the credulity to think that he has yet some chance of being President two years hence.[7] They flatter themselves that General Jackson's friends will abandon the General, and take him up. You will think none can be so weak or so ill-informed as to entertain such a hope, but, in truth, there are such men, and Mr. Clinton is himself one of them. The choice is with the people in districts, and unless some change takes place, Mr. Adams will get a majority, perhaps a large one.

You perceive how local questions have split up our good people here. You see the worst of it. In truth, right feeling very generally prevails, and nothing but prudent conduct is necessary to manifest it. Measures are in train, in relation to the ensuing choice of representatives, which I think will show that Boston is yet Boston. Care will also be taken to induce other towns to send good, and a good many, members to the general court. We shall have a Senator to elect. Our difficulty will be to find a man fit for the place, and with popularity to carry the election.

I had a great deal of conversation with Mr. [Samuel] Bell,[8] in the course of the session, respecting the state of affairs with you. I have confidence in his good dispositions, but I do not think his policy bold enough. He understands my opinion, and guesses at yours, on that point. Experience, one would think, must have taught him by this time that there is but one course; and that is to rally, as administration men, without reference to bygone distinctions.

I wish you could see and converse with him, about the 19th or 20th. I shall go up to Boscawen to see my brother.[9] If I can persuade him to accompany me, I would return by way of Portsmouth, to pass a single day with you. It seems, that without his consent or knowledge, he is chosen to the State legislature. He is so much displeased and dissatisfied with the course adopted by Mr. Adams's republican friends, in New Hampshire, that I know not whether he can be persuaded to do any thing. I have, however, thought it would be worth considering whether he should not bring forward resolutions, approving the conduct of the administration, and disapproving that of the opposition, and supporting them by a good strong speech. This would, perhaps, have two good effects; it would, in the first place, compel Mr. Adams's friends to act with him, and, in the second place, it would oblige Mr. [Isaac] Hill's[10] friends to take their side. All this, however, is for future consideration.

When you have time, not better employed, I shall be glad to hear from you. If I should not return from Boscawen by your way, I shall take another early opportunity to go to Portsmouth.

To-morrow, Thursday, I am going down to dine with the judge [Joseph Story].—Yours, always truly,

Daniel Webster

1. Mason (1768–1848; Yale 1788), a prominent lawyer and close friend of Webster, he also served as a U.S. senator from New Hampshire from 1813 to 1817.

2. Daughter of Jeremiah Mason.

3. *Bank of the United States v. Dandridge*, 12 Wheaton 64 (1827).

4. Story (1779–1845; Harvard 1798) served in the Massachusetts legislature, 1805–07, 1811, and as a U.S. congressman, 1808–09, before President James Madison appointed him to the Supreme Court in 1811. Story served on the Supreme Court until his death.

5. Wirt (1772–1834) Virginia and Maryland lawyer, served as U.S. attorney general from 1817 to 1829.

6. *Clark v. City of Washington*, 12 Wheaton 40 (1827).

7. Clinton (1769–1828; Columbia College 1786) was an unsuccessful candidate for president of the U.S. in 1812. He served as a U.S. senator from New York 1802–03, and as governor of the state 1817–21 and 1825–28.

8. Bell (1770–1850; Dartmouth 1793), governor of New Hampshire 1819–23 and a U.S. senator from New Hampshire 1823–35.

9. Ezekiel Webster (1780–1829; Dartmouth 1804), a New Hampshire farmer and lawyer.

10. Hill (1789–1851), editor of the *New Hampshire Patriot* (Concord), governor of New Hampshire 1819–23, and U.S. senator from the state 1823–35.

Document 8
Text from *Correspondence* 2: 197–200.

To Henry Clay

Private & confidential

My Dear Sir,   Boston May 7. 1827

I have to thank you for yours of the 14. & 20th of April.[1] The general information they contain, respecting the state of things in the South & West, is encouraging, & confirms what I learn from other quarters. The means agreed on, at the close of the session, & which have been partially applied, have, evidently, tended to awaken a good spirit. We cannot I think too strongly feel the conviction that public opinion is very likely to take a decisive direction between this time & the next meeting of Congress. We are all ready & willing, here, to do our part, that the direction shall be the right one.

A principal part of my present purpose is to ask your attention to a matter personal to myself. The state of Mr. [Elijah Hunt] Mills'[2] health puts his re-election to the Senate out of the question. Of course, our friends here have to find a successor, & I see pretty significant signs of an intention to offer the place to me. A similar proposition was made to me last June, when Mr [James] Lloyd resigned;[3] & repeated, with some urgency, afterwards, when an attempt was making to supply Mr Mills' place. On those occasions I was able to *get excused,* without great difficulty, & without giving offence. If the same thing should be proposed again, it will come under different circumstances, & it is necessary, therefore, to consider beforehand, what will be proper to be done. I need not trouble you with particular details of our politics: Suffice it to say, that the opposition, (for there is a little knot of Gentlemen, desiring that appellation) have seized on some local subjects,—especially a taking proposition for a *free-bridge,* by means of which they hope to strengthen their ranks. The leader of the *free-bridge* party is Mr [William C.] Jarvis, now speaker of the H. R. & who was one of the candidates for Senator last winter. He will probably be so again.[4] He *professes* friendship for Mr. Adams; but Mr. Adams' friends in the Legislature, when he is proposed for Senator, think of what happened in N. Hampshire, & *almost* happened in Vermont.[5] They do not incline to choose him. Mr. John Mills will, or may, also be thought of. I believe *he is* a very true man, but not one likely to take an active part in affairs. If Gov. [Levi] Lincoln[6] would take the appointment, it would be highly satisfactory; but I believe he is not willing, at this time, to go to the Senate, & his friends are, also, a good deal averse to his leaving the place he now fills. Beyond all these reasons, a considerable degree of new feeling is springing up, in the State, in favor of the administration; & this feeling will require that *Something be done.* The Senate is looked upon as weak, & a strong desire is felt, to do all that can be done to give the Govt. aid *there.* From these & other considerations, added to what I hear & see, I fear a strong disposition, to the effect I have intimated, may prevail, unless it be prevented, or <directed> diverted by seasonable means. I have made some attempts to this end, myself, but with no great success. I have <told> stated my own *decided wish* to stay where I am; but am told, that I have no right to my own preference, but must be disposed of as others think best. I have hinted, that my appropriate place was in the House; that my habits were made up to it; that it was accustomed to the sound of my voice—& that I could do more good there than elsewhere, &c. &c. The answer is; the House will provide for itself; it is a numerous body, & somebody will appear to supply my place,

&c. But the Senate is a small body—in which vacancies occur seldom, & which now, most woefully, requires amendment.

I need not say to you, My dear Sir, that both my *feelings & my judgement* are *against* the transfer. It would be to me a great sacrifice to make the exchange. And yet, on the other hand, as I am situated here, it would be extremely unpleasant & perhaps impossible, for me, to meet the offer if it should be made, *with a flat refusal.* I have therefore taken the liberty to write to you on the subject, for the purpose of asking you to consider of it, a little, & then to suggest what occurs to you for the use of confidential friends here. The Legislature meets the last Wednesday of the present month; & one of their first acts will probably be the choice of Senator.

You will perhaps find occasion to mention the matter to Mr Adams, & having done so, I will thank you to write a line to Mr [Nathaniel] Silsbee,[7] such as may be shown to the Govr., & other confidential friends, expressing your opinion & feeling. If it be possible to persuade the Govr. to accept the place, all will be well; but if not, I greatly fear, I shall hardly escape. Upon the whole, having distinctly expressed my feeling, & my opinion, I must now leave the matter to the decision of others. A professional engagement will call me to New York, the 25. inst.; so that I shall not be at home, probably at the election.

I conclude by repeating that for the little time I may remain in Congress, I have a strong,—a very strong—personal wish to stay in the House; Nevertheless, if *it is clearly better* that I go *elsewhere,* I must be disposed of as the common good requires.

On one or two other subjects I had intended to say something; but shall spare your patience till another post.

Have you anything new as to Mr [Louis] McLane's[8] intended course? I fear he is gone, but have thought it *possible* that the public sentiment in Del. might keep him right. Yrs always with mo[st] true regard

Danl. Webster

1. See Clay to Webster, April 14 and 20, 1827 in *Correspondence* 2:191–94.
2. Mills (1776–1829; Williams College 1797), a U.S. representative (1815–19) and senator from Massachusetts (1820–27).
3. Lloyd (1769–1831; Harvard 1787), a U.S senator from Massachusetts 1808–13 and 1822–26.
4. Jarvis represented Charlestown in the state legislature, serving as speaker of the lower house in 1826 and 1827. He advocated the construction of a toll free bridge across the Charles River.
5. Senator Levi Woodbury of New Hampshire shifted his support from Adams to Jackson in 1826, and Cornelius P. Van Ness of Vermont, a candidate for the U.S. senate, accused Adams of tampering with the Vermont election.
6. Lincoln (1782–1868; Harvard 1802) was governor of Massachusetts from 1825 to 1834.

7. Silsbee (1773–1850), a U.S. representative (1817–21) and senator (1826–35) from Massachusetts.

8. McLane (1786–1857), a U.S. representative (1817–27) and senator (1827–29) from Delaware, was in the process of shifting his political support to Andrew Jackson.

Document 9
Text from *Correspondence* 3: 25–26.

To John Hampden Pleasants[1]

Private & Confidential
Dear Sir   Washington Mar 6. 1830

Soon after I had posted a speech to you this morning, I recd yours of the 4th inst. I am glad you have written to me, on general accounts; I need not say how much I am gratified to learn there are *some* in Va. who think of my efforts without disrespect. To tell you the truth, I have sometimes felt, that while political foes have dealt to me, in yr good state, a large measure of abuse, political friends have not always interposed a shield, under circumstances, when, perhaps it might have been expected by one engaged in the same general public cause. But I have no hard feeling, in this respect. I know there were reasons, why some of us should bear abuse, without expecting to be defended. That time, I hope, has gone by. At any rate, I shd. not hope to find myself in such a condition again. I am willing to correspond with you, freely, but *in entire & sacred confidence.* Thro life, thus far, I have been as much guarded as possible agt. the accidents of the Post office & other accidents attending confidential correspondence. Nevertheless, the times require occasional confidence, & that some hazards be run. I am willing, therefore, to write you an occasional letter—knowing that I shall be safe, even if I had secrets to communicate, which will not often be the case. I shall be glad to hear from you often, you may rely on confidence on my side.

At present, there is not much to be said, growing out of the state of things here. The more objectionable nominations have not yet been acted on. It is quite uncertain how they will be disposed of. The Senate will be so nearly equally divided, that a vote or two will decide sundry nominations, & no one can say how those votes may be given. There will be close voting, certainly, in several cases. I agree with you, it is a balanced question, whether more good will flow from the rejection than from the confirmation. It wd. disappoint individuals, doubtless; but would it not, on the whole, rather strengthen the Admin to send [Isaac] Hill, [Amos] Kendall[2] &c home?

As to future operations, the general idea here seems to be this:— to bring forward no candidate this year—tho' doubtless, the general impression is that Mr C[lay] stands first & foremost in the ranks of those who wd. desire a change. I do not think there is the least abatement of the respect & confidence entertained for him. As to the other Western Gentleman, whom you mention, he must not be thought of, *for he is not with us.* Depend upon it, there is a negotiation in train to bring him out as V P. to run on the Ticket with Mr [John C.] Calhoun. In my opinion, he has very little weight or influence in the Country, & that is fast declining.[3] Our friends in the west will quit him, of course, if in that event, as he must give up their interests.

I wish now to say, that two things are not to be omitted, when we speculate on the future.

First, that Genl. Jackson will certainly be considered again, if he live & be well; I say *certainly.* I mean only that I have no doubt of it.

Second, that we cannot now foresee what events will follow from what is passing in Penna & New York, on the subject of *Anti-Masonry.* This matter, be assured, is not to be disregarded.

In the meantime, it seems to me our course must be this.

—Expose the selfishness & *pretence* of the men in power, as much as possible; taking care to let the *ministers* be made responsible, for at least their full share. The acts will be theirs, in most cases; & therefore they ought to be responsible for them, themselves.

—Show ourselves uniform, & just, by acting according to our principles; & opposing only such measures as deserve no support.

—As to *Tariff subjects,* we of the north must hold on where we are. And as to Internal Improvements, we, also, must go, temperately & cautiously for them also.

—Agree in all measures having in view the payt. of the debt.

—<Finally> To hold ourselves absolutely aloof from Mr. Van B[uren]. & Mr C[alhoun] & be ready to act for ourselves when the proper time comes—& to maintain our own men, & defend our own friends—

—Finally, cultivate a truly national spirit—go for great ends, & hold up the necessity of the Union &c.

1. Pleasants (1797–1846; William and Mary 1817), a prominent Virginia journalist who edited the Richmond *Whig* from 1824 until his death.

2. Both Hill and Kendall received appointments to the U.S. Treasury. Kendall was confirmed as fourth auditor of the Treasury, but Hill was rejected as second comptroller on April 30, 1830. In 1831, Hill was elected to the U.S. Senate. Kendall (1789–1869; Dartmouth 1811), a Kentucky journalist and an ardent supporter of Jackson, became a member of Jackson's Kitchen Cabinet and served as U.S. postmaster general from 1835–40.

3. The reference is to Associate Justice John McLean (1785–1861) of Ohio.

Document 10
Text from *Correspondence* 3: 36–37.

To Jeremiah Mason

My Dear Sir   Washington Mar. 19. 30

I return Mr. [Robert] M[ean]'s Letter. Mr. [Charles H.] A[therton] did quite as well in his letter to the Statesman, as could be expected.[1]

We have not yet acted on the N. H. nominations. I know not whether to decide to reject them, or not. [John P.] Decatur & [Samuel] Cushman are in great danger—but would they be succeeded by any body better? And if Hill should be rejected, should we not have him in the Senate?[2]

Appearances in various parts of the Country indicate dissatisfaction with the present state of things. The stock of patronage is exhausted, & many are left unprovided for; & they are looking out for other parties, & other leaders. It is admitted, I believe by most, that Mr. Clay is gaining rapidly in the west. Kentucky is doubtless strong for him, & as agt. any body but Genl Jackson, he would take nearly all the western votes. In the meantime, the *Anti masonic* party, steadily encreasing in N York, is breaking out like an Irish rebellion in Pennsylvania. It goes on with a force, that subdues all other feeling. These things put party calculation at defiance. The party here are obviously very much alarmed. The Admin Senators are understood to have held a *Caucus*, three nights ago, & endeavored to unite & rally. Something more of tone & decision has been since visible. It may become, *perhaps*, the confirmation of all the appointments. As to measures, they are irreconcilable. They can not stir agt. the Tariff. As a means of union,—& a necessary means—they seem now resolved to keep the present President in office thro a second term. He now intends to hold on, beyond all doubt. Here again, accidents to his life or health, would produce quite a new state of things. So that, on the whole, I do not think there has been a period in our time when one could see less of the future than the present.

I thank you for your civil saying abt. my speech. It has made much more *talk* than it deserves, owing to the topic, & to the times. I hope it is doing some good at the South, where, I have reason to think, it is very generally circulated & read. Yrs very sincerely

D Webster

having cut my thumb, I write even worse than usual.

1. See Mason to Webster, March 13, 1830 in *Correspondence* 3:33–34. Means (1786–1842; Bowdoin 1807) was a New Hampshire lawyer. Atherton (1773–1853; Harvard 1794) served as a congressman from New Hampshire from 1815 to 1817. His letter to the *Boston Statesman* of March 1, 1830, denied any knowledge that Webster had promoted the Hartford Convention of 1814.

2. Decatur had been nominated by President Jackson to be collector of customs of Portsmouth, and Cushman to be U.S. attorney for the district of New Hampshire. Both nominations were rejected by the Senate. As Webster anticipated, Hill was elected to the Senate. Cushman (1783–1851) later (1835–39) served as a representative from New Hampshire.

Document 11
Text from *Correspondence* 3: 78–80.

To Henry Clay

My Dear Sir   Washington May 29. 1830

We are all with the foot in the stirrup, & are not leaving in a very *composed* state. The passage of the Indian Bill[1] & the rejection of the Maysville Turnpike Bill[2] have occasioned unusual excitement. The quarrel, yesterday, between Stansbury [William Stanbery] & others, who voted for the Bill, & [James Knox] Polk, [John] Bell &c, was very warm.[3] There is more ill blood raised, I should think, than would easily be quieted again.

We think all recent occurrences have been quite favorable, & that the present prospect is cheering. We have had no *formal* meeting. After much consideration, that idea was given up. We found it difficult to assemble a *few friends*, without giving offence; or a *great number* without the danger of attracting too much notice. We have had, however, a very full & free interchange of opinions, for the last three weeks, & are all harmonious in purpose & design, and in good spirits. We incline to think no formal nomination at present advisable, tho' friends press us to such a measure from divers quarters of the country. It has seemed to me, on the whole, that a formal nomination here would not be *popular enough* in its character & origin, to do good. It would be immediately proclaimed to be the act of your friends, acting *at your instance.* It would excite jealousies, on the one hand, which are now fast dying away, &, on the other, check discontents & schisms, among our opponents, from which much is now to be hoped. Such is our view.

I am much pressed to assent to a nomination of you by the Mass. Legislature now in session. But to this, I steadily object; on the ground, that every body knows we are perfectly safe & strong in Massachusetts, & a nomination, there, would only raise the cry of *coalition revived.* It has seemed to me the proper scene for the first formal action is *Maryland.* Her Legislature is elected in October. Our friends have the utmost confidence they shall carry the State. Indeed there can be little doubt of it. In that event, the Maryland Legislature, next Decr, will occupy a position, from which they can speak to advantage. Without detail, you will see, I think, at once, many advantages in a nomination from this quarter. None could be more favorable, unless it be N York, or Penna, neither of which, I fear, is as likely to be so soon ready for it.

I hope you will think that under all circumstances, we have done wisely, in doing nothing.

If you run agt. Genl Jackson, there will be an election, by the Electors—; &, as you justly state, Gen J. will be chosen, unless either Va. Penna. or New York can be detached from him. Of the three, I have, at present, most hope of N York, & least of Va. Late occurrences will strengthen Gen J. in Va & weaken him, much, in Penna, & perhaps also in New York. I am in hopes that working men, Anti Masons, &Anti-Auction men[4] &c &c &c will break down the Regency. This we shall know in October. If it should turn out so, N. Y. will then open a very fair field. For myself, I recon on recent events as having *ensured* us Maryland, Ohio, Kentucky, & Indiana. This is one very good *breadth.* South of it, I looked for nothing but Louisiana; every thing north of it is worth a contest.

I hope your friends at the west keep a steady regard for Missouri. I am told there is good chance, or some chance, of Mr [David] Barton's reelection.[5] This is matter of very great importance; nothing, indeed, is more momentous to the country, than the approaching election of Senators to the next Congress.

On the whole, My Dear Sir, I think a crisis is arriving, or rather *has arrived.* I think you cannot be kept back from the contest. The *people* will bring you out, *nolens volens. Let them do it.* I advise you, as you will be much watched, *to stay at home;* or, if you wish to travel, visit your old friends in Va. We should all be glad to see you, at the North, *but not now.* You will hear from the north,—every town & village in it—on the *4th. of July.* Parties must, now necessarily, be sorted out, anew; & the great ground of difference will be Tariff & Int. Improvements. You are necessarily at the head of one party, & Gen J. will be, if he is not already, identified with the other. The question will be put to the Country. Let the Country decide it.

I had intended to say a word about myself, but it would be to make a long letter still longer. When I came here, it was my purpose to follow your example, (parva componere magnis) & to vacate my seat, at the end of this session. Events have suspended the execution of that purpose. How I shall think of it when I get home, I do not know. I pray kind remembrance to Mrs Clay, & beg to assure you of my unaltered regard & attachment.

Danl Webster

1. The Senate had concurred with House amendments to the Indian Bill on May 26.

2. President Jackson vetoed the Maysville and Lexington Turnpike Road Bill on May 27. Stanbery (1788–1873) a representative from Ohio 1827–33. Bell (1797–1869; University of Pennsylvania 1814) a representative (1827–41) and a senator (1847–59) from Tennessee.

3. See *Register of Debates,* 21st Cong., 1st sess., p. 1140.

4. The Anti-Auction men were those who opposed the system of disposing of imported goods at auction, which they believed favored foreign over American merchants.

5. Barton (1783–1837) had served as a senator from Missouri from 1821 to 1831, but he was not reelected in 1830.

Document 12
Text from *Correspondence* 3: 119–120.

To [Charles Miner][1]

My Dear Sir   Boston Aug. 28. 1831

I wish I could say any thing encouraging on the highly important Subjects mentioned in your letter of the 20th. The Kentucky election has not turned out to be *quite so bad* as it appeared to be, at the date of your letter; but, still, it is unsatisfactory, & has produced an unfavorable impression in this quarter. Speaking to you in the most confidential manner, I must say, that I concur with you, in the opinion that there is very little chance of electing Mr Clay. I believe we may hope for the vote of Kentucky, yet; but even with that, I do not perceive where we are to find enough others to make a majority. My present impression is, *there is but one chance left to save the country from further & worse misrule;* & that is, to bring forward some man, in whose favor the National Republicans & Anti Masons of Pennsylvania & New York could be induced to unite, so as to secure the votes of those States. With *them,* Ohio, New England, New Jersey, Delaware, Maryland would be able to elect a President. But I fear there is very little prospect of finding such a candidate. You say, that you believe the Anti Masons are intent on pushing Judge [John] McLean. It will never do. Our friends in N. England, & elsewhere, *will never be brought to support him.* As against him, the election of Genl Jackson would be certain. A Gentleman, writing from Philadelphia, says, Let us put up a candidate, if we make a choice, in whom we have perfect confidence, & if we fail, still, a minority, united on principle, & with a sound head, is a better security to the country than success, in behalf of moderate talents, or doubtful principles. I agree to all this; at the same time that I see the difficulty in finding the man. I confess I do not know him. You are pleased to say, that I possess a portion of the confidence of the conflicting parties. Perhaps it may be so; but I cannot think the country is inclined to bring me forward, & it is certain, that I shall do nothing to bring myself forward. I have little experience in public affairs, & have not been long enough before the Country to produce great general confidence. My only merit is an ardent attachment to the Country, & its constitution of Government; & I am already more than paid for all my efforts, if you, & other good men, think I have done any thing to defend the Constitution, & promote the welfare of the Country. In the favor which those efforts have attracted towards me, I see proofs of a real, substantial, fixed attachment among the People to the Constitution. The great body of the Community is quite sound, on that point. And that is the feeling which we ought to cultivate, & on which we must rely. *If we bring about a change, it will be done by us as a Union Party.*

And now, My Dear Sir, will you tell me, whether, in your judgment, there is any individual, who could so unite the Anti Masonic & Nat. Repub. votes of Penna. as to carry the State agt. Genl. Jackson? I should like much to know your present impressions, on that vital question.

The Anti Masonic Convention, at Baltimore, will have a most responsible part to act. The prosperity of the Country, perhaps the fate of its Government, hangs on their decision. God give them true wisdom, & disinterested patriotism!

I shall be glad to hear from you, at your earliest leisure. Yrs truly
D. Webster

You will of course consider this letter as in the strictest sense confidential. . . .

1. Miner (1780–1865) a representative from Pennsylvania from 1825 to 1829.

Document 13
Text from *Correspondence* 4: 4–5.

To Jeremiah Mason

Dear Sir: Washington, January 1, 1835.

Whether it is or will be best for Massachusetts to act at all on the subject of a nomination, is a question which I leave entirely to the judgment of others. I cannot say that I have any personal wishes about it, either one way or the other. A nomination by Massachusetts would certainly be one of the highest proofs of regard which any citizen can receive. As such, I should most undoubtedly esteem it. But, in the present condition of things, and with the prospects which are before us, a nomination is a questionable thing to one who is more desirous of preserving what little reputation he has than anxious to grasp at further distinction. I have made up my mind, however, to be passive, and shall be satisfied with any result.

But I have a clear opinion on one point; and, as I promised you to communicate my sentiments freely, I will state that opinion frankly. It is, that if Massachusetts is to act at all, *the time has come.* I think the proceeding, if one is to be had, should be one of the first objects of attention when the Legislature assembles. In Ohio, Mr. [John] McLean is already nominated, I presume, according to late accounts.[1] Many Whigs, who do not prefer him, fall into the measure (in Ohio) simply because they have no other choice. It is expected, or at least hoped, that New Jersey will second this nomination. Movements are in preparation in other places; but, as far as I know, nothing is yet proposed anywhere in which there could be a general union, or in which Massachusetts would be likely to agree.

If a resolution to make a movement in Massachusetts should be adopted, not only should the thing itself be done as soon as practicable, but in the mean time notice of the intention should be given to friends in the neighboring States, and especially in New York, that they may prepare for it. Let us know *here* the moment any thing is determined on.[2]

It looks at present as if Mr. [Henry] Clay would not do or say any thing. He declares himself in nobody's way; but still it is evident that his particular friends are not prepared to act heartily and efficiently for anybody else.[3]

Be sure to *burn* this letter, and assure yourself also that I write such letters to nobody else. Your truly,

D. Webster. . . .

1. McLean received the Ohio nomination in December 1834 but withdrew his candidacy in August 1835.

2. Webster received the formal nomination for the presidency by the Massachusetts legislature on January 21, 1835.

3. Clay withdrew from the presidential race on December 26, 1835.

Document 14
Text from *Correspondence* 4: 24–26.

To Jeremiah Mason

My Dear Sir,   Washington, February 1, 1835.

I received your letter yesterday, and the mail of to-day brings intelligence verifying your prediction that Mr. [John] Davis would be elected Senator.[1] So far as regards the filling up the vacant seat in the Senate, nothing could be better. I hope all the evil will not happen, which is expected or feared, arising from the difficulty of finding him a successor in the administration of the executive government of the State. I do not think Mr. [John Quincy] Adams will ever again consent to be [a] candidate; certainly not against Mr. [Edward] Everett;[2] and Mr. Everett and Mr. [Isaac Chapman] Bates[3] are not men to suffer the harmony of the State to be disturbed by a controversy among their personal friends. I am still most anxious that all fair means should be used to settle this masonic and anti-masonic quarrel in Massachusetts. You have little idea how much it retards operations elsewhere. The reported debate in the Whig Caucus, on the subject of the Bristol Senators, is industriously sent to every anti-masonic quarter of the Union, and has excited much unkind feeling, and thereby done mischief. We are endeavoring here to make the best of [Nathaniel Briggs] Borden.[4] Our anti-masonic friends in Congress will write to him, advising him not to commit himself to any course of public conduct, till he shall come here and see the whole ground. The nomination appears to have been done as well as it could be. I mean, of course, in the manner of it. No fault is found with it by our friends, so far as I know. Measures are in train to produce a correspondent feeling and action, in New York, Vermont, and some other States. The Legislature of Maryland is now in session, and I have seen a letter to-day, which says, that if Mr. Clay were fairly out of the way, that Legislature would immediately second the Massachusetts nomination. Mr. Clay does nothing, and will do nothing, at present. He thinks—or perhaps it is his friends who think—that *something* may yet occur, perhaps a war, which may, in *some* way, cause a general rally round him. Besides, sundry of the members of Congress from Kentucky, in addition to their own merits, rely not a little on Mr. Clay's popularity, to insure their reelection next August. They have been, therefore, altogether opposed to bringing forward any other man at present. Public opinion will, in the end, bring out these things straight. If Massachusetts stands steady, and our friends act with prudence, the union of the whole Whig and anti-masonic strength is certain. Everything indicates that result. Judge McLean already talks of retiring. His nomination seems coldly received everywhere. Unless Indiana should come out for him, I see no probability of any other movement in his favor. Mr. [Hugh Lawson] White's nomination is likely to be persisted in.[5] Neither you nor I have ever believed it would be easy to get Southern votes for *any* Northern man; and I think the prospect now is, that Mr. Van Buren will lose the whole South. This schism is calculated to give much additional strength to our party. If Mr. W[hite] appear likely to take the South, it will be seen that Mr. Van Buren cannot be chosen by the people; and as it will be understood that Mr. White's supporters are quite as likely to come to us, in the end, as to go to Van Buren, his course will lose the powerful support which it derives, or has derived, from an assured hope of success. The effect of those apprehensions is already visible. The recent attempt to shoot the President is much to be lamented. Thousands will believe there was plot in it; and many more thousands will see in it new proof, that he is especially favored and protected by Heaven.[6] He keeps close as to the question between White and Van Buren. I have omitted to do what I intended, that is, to say a few words upon that part of your letter which relates to myself, more directly. In a day or two I will make another attempt to accomplish that purpose. Mr. [Roger B.] Taney's case is not yet decided.[7] A movement is contemplated to annex Delaware and Maryland to Judge [Henry] Baldwin's circuit,[8] and make a circuit in the West for the judge now to be appointed. If we could get rid of Mr. Taney, on this ground, well and good; if not, it will be a close vote. We shall have a warm debate on the Post Office Report,[9] the Alabama resolutions,[10] and other matters; but I think my course is to take no prominent part in any of them. I may say something against expunging the Journal. Yours truly,

D. Webster

1. Davis (1787–1854; Yale 1812) a representative (1825–34) and a senator (1835–41, 1845–53) from Massachusetts. Davis also served as governor of Massachusetts from 1834 to 1835 and again from 1841 to 1843.

2. Everett (1794–1865; Harvard 1811, and later president of Harvard), one of Webster's closest friends, was elected governor of Massachusetts in 1836. In addition to serving as governor of Massachusetts from 1836 to 1840, Everett also served as a representative (1825–35) from Massachusetts, U.S. minister to Great Britain (1841–45), secretary of state (1852–53), and as a U.S. senator (1853–54).

3. Bates (1779–1845; Yale 1802) a representative (1827–35) and a senator (1841–45) from Massachusetts.

4. Borden (1801–65), a representative from Massachusetts (1835–39, 1841–43).

5. White (1773–1840), a senator from Tennessee (1825–40), was nominated for the presidency by the legislature of his state.

6. On January 29, Richard Lawrence attempted to assassinate President Jackson by firing two pistol shots at him. Miraculously, both shots misfired.

7. Taney (1777–1864) had been nominated to the Supreme Court on January 19, and Webster was among those who blocked his confirmation. Later, in March 1836, Taney was renominated and confirmed as chief justice of the Supreme Court.

8. Baldwin (1780–1844; Yale 1797), associate justice of the Supreme Court from 1830 to 1844.

9. This report by Senator Thomas Ewing of Ohio (1789–1871; Ohio University 1816) contended that approximately 30 percent of the Post Office funds were unaccounted for.

10. The Alabama legislature had passed resolves instructing its senators to expunge from the Senate Journal the resolutions of the previous session censuring President Jackson for the removal of deposits from the Bank of the United States.

Document 15
Text from *Correspondence* 4: 26–27.

To Jeremiah Mason

Private
My Dear Sir,   Washington Feb. 6. 1835

It is true that I have looked forward to the events which the approaching election might bring about, as likely to furnish a fit occasion for my retirement from the Senate. I have fixed on no particular time, nor made, indeed, any such determination as may not be changed, by the advice or the wishes of friends. As I am now placed, I shall certainly not leave my place, till the time arrives when I may think that its relinquishment will not be unsatisfactory to *Massachusetts*.

I do not affect, My Dear Sir, to desire to retire from public life, & to resume my profession. My habits, I must confess, & the nature of my pursuits for some years, render it more agreeable to me to <follow> attend to political than to professional subjects. But I have not lost all relish for the bar; I can still make something by the practice, & by remaining in the Senate, I am making sacrifices which my circumstances do not justify. My residence here so many months every year greatly increases my expenses, & greatly reduces my income. You know the charge of living here, with a family; & I cannot leave my wife & daughter at home,[1] & come here & go into a mess, at 10 Dollars a week.

I find it inconvenient to push my practice in the Supreme Court, while a member of the Senate; & am inclined, under any view of the future, to decline engagements hereafter, in that Court, unless under special circumstances. These are the reasons that have led me to *hope* for a fit occasion of leaving the Senate; & when I can quit, with the approbation of friends, I shall eagerly embrace the opportunity. In the meantime, I shall say nothing about it.

I ought, this Spring to go to the West, as far at least as Ken. & Indiana. I am fully persuaded it would be a highly useful thing. My friends urge it upon me, incessantly; & I hold back from promising compliance with their wishes only from an unwillingness to lose six weeks more, after the session closes. On this point, however, as nothing is decided, I say nothing at present. There will be no cause in Court, I think, to detain me after the 3rd of March.

We have nothing new here. A base attempt has been made to ascribe the *madness* of [Richard] Lawrence to the Speeches &c of the Senate. An inquisition, if it may be so called, has been had upon Lawrence, by two physicians, who have signed a report, & returned it to the Marshall. It proves a clear case of insanity. The Report will not be published, so long as the publication can be withheld.

We shall pass thro' the Senate, a pretty good Bill for reorganizing the Post Office.

I saw lately a strange letter from Washington in the Boston Gazette, about an express from the N.Y. Whigs, & a coldness between Mr W[ebster] & Mr. Clay. Both stories are equally & entirely groundless. There has been no express here, from N.Y. On the contrary, *all* the Whig papers of the City, (except [Mordecai M.] Noah)[2] will soon be out, (or we are misinformed) in the direction you would desire. Yrs truly

D. Webster

1. Caroline LeRoy (1797–1882) married Webster in 1829. Julia Webster (1818–48), Webster's daughter by his first marriage to Grace Fletcher (1781–1828).

2. Noah (1785–1851), journalist, lawyer, and playwright, edited the New York *Evening Star.*

Document 16
Text from *Correspondence* 4: 73–74.

From Charles Miner

My Dear Sir,   Harrisburg Decr. 17 1835

The Anti-Masonic Convention has just nominated Major Gen. W. H. Harrison 80 to about 20. The Alleghenny Delegation, Mr. [Thaddeus] Stevens and some others having, last night, withdrawn.[1]

Our Convention, which has done nothing but wait the movement of our Rev[ere]d and most excellent master's balance, will receive and register their edict to night.[2] What a farce! All agree, Mr. Webster is my first choice, but we cannot carry him. Why? It seems strange that he who is the *first* choice of every one should be *less* popular than the man who is only the *second* choice, & confessedly his inferior. Ah, but he was a Federalist? Damning sin! Never to be forgiven: But he was opposed to the war! Let no statesman or patriot hereafter, dare to interpose his voice to save his Country from the Horrors of war! Let no one dare raise his voice against men in power, however rich, who have sacrificed the Peace of the Country. Let no Representative withhold his vote for appropriations however wicked or foolish, in time of war. Condemn Chatham and Fox[3] to infamy; and disfranchise Webster. General Harrison cannot be made President; His nomination only increases the chances of Mr. V. B. and Judge White.

Perhaps a time-serving wisdom would persuade to submission, but neither my honest principles nor my proud spirit can allow me to advise it. I say in coolness to day at noon what I said last evening—you are *sacrificed,* and that not temporarily but on grounds & principles that affect you with this mongrel party now and forever. I am faithfully your friend

Charles Miner

1. Stevens (1792–1868; Dartmouth 1814), a Pennsylvania Antimason and a sup-

porter of Webster. Stevens served as a representative from Pennsylvania from 1849 to 1853 and from 1859 to 1868.

2. The Pennsylvania Whig convention nominated Harrison over Webster by a vote of 98–29.

3. William Pitt (1708–1778), first Earl of Chatham, and Charles James Fox (1749–1806) had opposed the use of force against the North American colonies.

Document 17
Text from *Correspondence* 4: 87–88.

[Memorandum by Levi Lincoln of a Meeting with Webster Re His Presidential Nomination]

Memo. Feb 19. 1836.

A Meeting of the Delegates from Massachusetts in the Senate and House, with the exception of Mr Webster, Mr Adams, and Mr [Nathaniel Briggs] Borden, having been had at the instance of Mr Webster, for the purpose of considering his position before the Nation, as a Candidate for the Presidency;—after consultation, Mr [Levi] Lincoln, Mr [John] Davis, and Mr [Abbott] Lawrence[1] were appointed a Committee to communicate to Mr W. the results.

On the morning of the 19th of Feby. the above named Gentlemen waited upon Mr W., when Mr Lincoln stated to Mr W., in substance, that in the meeting which had been held, the Gentlemen present, had assembled *at his instance,* and *as his personal Friends,* and in their discussions and in this communication, they, as well as this Committee, expressly disclaimed any authority or pretence for representing the opinions, feelings, or wishes of others. That they regarded their relation to the subject of his nomination to the Presidency, as one only of common interest to those with whom they were accustomed politically to act, and who had delegated no discretionary or advisory power over this subject. Mr L. further stated to Mr W., that the Gentlemen who attended the Meeting, were of opinion, that as his Nomination proceeded from a Convention of Members of the Legislature, it belonged more appropriately to Gentlemen standing in the same relation to him, and to the same party in the State Government, to hold the correspondence and give the advice which might be needed. Still, with the above disclaimer, responding to his recognition of them *as his personal and political friends,* they had regarded with equal interest & concern, the unlooked for arrangements and circumstances which now greatly embarrassed this position in which, by the agency of others, he was placed. That the nomination made by the Whig Party in the State, gave him a claim to the continued support of that Party—that this was due to their own principles, their own consistency of conduct, and their obligations to him, and that it was by no means the desire of the Delegation here, that at this time he should withdraw. This was a matter for his own consideration and decision, upon such views of public duty, and upon such knowledge of political events and prospects, as with better, or the same means of information, he might have. In fine, that the delegation were of the opinion, that, inasmuch, as circumstances had materially changed in reference to the probability of success, since his nomination, this change of circumstances left him at liberty to consult his own judgment, and either to meet, or withdraw from, the canvass as his own sense of propriety should hereafter dictate, and that the members of the Delegation individually, would hold him justified accordingly.

LL.

A.L.

1. Lawrence (1792–1855), a representative from Massachusetts 1835–37, 1839–40.

Document 18
Text from *Correspondence* 4: 182–85.

To Hiram Ketchum[1]

My Dear Sir   Washington Jan. 28. 1837.
    Professional & other engagements have delayed, until now, an answer to your friendly letter of the 14th of this month.
    I am glad if my friends think well of my remarks on the Treasury Circular, & obliged to you & others for the pains you take to distribute copies.[2]
    As to a collection & publication of my Speeches on Constitutional questions, if it be thought that such a thing would do good, I would aid in the selection, make any necessary revision, & promote the general object, so far as might be in my power.

    The frankness & kindness of your letter, however, seem to require a free expression of my opinions, & feelings, & even of personal wishes & purposes. I shall therefore, in this letter, speak without any reserve, while you will consider me as speaking in entire confidence.
    On the past, I have little to observe. Certainly, things have occurred,

that I did not expect; & of the utter impolicy of the course adopted by our friends, I held a clear opinion, at all times; but my situation necessarily shut my mouth. The result has weakened us, & distracted us; & whether we shall again obtain the character of a strong, united, patriotic party, is a question of some doubt, with me. I am willing, however, to hope for the best, & act with friends, whether few or many, who will stand on ground which they can defend.

My present purpose is to relinquish my seat in the Senate, at the close of this Session. I am aware there may be some objections to that course, but I think, too, there are some political reasons for it, & I am sure there are many personal ones. I have two years yet to serve, & no more, & the Legislature of Massachusetts is so composed, that a good appointment would now be made, in my place. In the course of the next two years, we shall see something of the developments of Mr Van Buren's policy, in regard to Texas, the Tariff, & other great questions; & although we may be sure, that it will not be such as you & I are likely to approve, it may be more or less acceptable, or unacceptable, to the Country. We are to consider, too, that the *Southern* opposition to Mr. V. B. is likely to be founded in principles, to which we must always be as much opposed, as to Mr. V. B. himself.

I do not mean by this, that our friends ought to wait, & hold back from bringing forward any man of our own. That cannot be done. Somebody will move. You see already indications of another attempt to support Genl. Harrison. If there be, therefore, a body of friends, determined, at all events, to maintain some other candidate, they ought, in my judgment undoubtedly to make that purpose early known.

What I have said above, in reference to the probable developments of two years, has regard only to another question; & that is, my return to the Senate, two years hence. If our friends in Mass should then have the power, & the inclination to send me back, & it should be thought proper, on the whole, for me to resume my labours here, I should not object. The two years I propose, (subject to these casualties which belong to human life & human things) to pass, partly in some necessary attention to my own affairs, a good deal in visiting various parts of the Country, &, by possibility, finally in a *very short* visit to Europe.

If my friends should come to a resolution to place my name before the public, I should, of course, act in conformity to their wishes, & their judgment, in whatever might be supposed likely to influence the result. My only request would be, that whatever is agreed on, should be *adhered to*.

Our strength lies in the great Central States, & in the North. New York & Pa. are key stones. Whatever candidate is agreed on, in those States, will receive the support of the party, thro. the U.S. Pa., as we know, is liable to impulses, & to strange & sudden changes; yet there is a great deal of true principle, & true worth in Pa. But my opinion is, that it is among the Whigs of New York, (& beginning in the City, & beginning immediately) that a first, decisive, & *determined* step should be taken. A resolute occupying of the ground, in that quarter, will, assuredly, bring about compliance, in other quarters. Massa. & all the Whigs in the Eastern States, would, of course, if properly addressed, immediately respond to the Whigs of New York. Those of Philadelphia would do the same, with promptness; & the rest of Pa. would not be likely to keep long aloof. Delaware & Maryland, if I am rightly informed, are ready to unite in the object.

It will be easy to open communications with other States, & Cities. For the present, if you have occasion to write to Boston, address R. C. Winthrop Esqr. Albert Fearing Esqr. and H. W. Kinsman Esqr.[3]

In the Village Record, a paper published at West Chester, Chester Co., Pa. I see a large & general meeting of the Whigs, Anti Masons &c., is called for the 7th. of next month. Now this is just one of those meetings, which, if unattended to, are so likely to commit our friends. The County of Chester, one of the largest in the State, was opposed to the nomination ultimately made at Harrisburg. What their views may be, now, I cannot tell. The leading man is Henry S. Evans Esqr. of West Chester.[4] He is a warm personal friend of mine, but has not written me, on this occasion. He heads the Comm[itt]ee. which makes the call. It is of importance, doubtless, that nothing wrong should be done at this meeting; & I think a confidential letter should be written from your City, to Mr Evans, expressing your opinions, & giving a word of friendly caution in regard to any premature movement, for a Presidential nomination. I think a friendly letter would be recd. by him, in the best spirit.

Of the propriety of all this, however, you & others will judge. I only allude to the expected meeting, as one of these local meetings, which make candidates for our party, without due reference to the state of feeling in other parts of the Country. The day of meeting, you perceive, is near at hand. I have thus, my Dear Sir, spoken very freely, as your friendship required I should do. In conclusion, I have only to request, that you will use these suggestions <prudently &> confidentially, & that you & your friends will suffer no considerations of personal kindness to induce you to adopt any course, which in your judgment, the good of the whole may require. Yours very truly

Danl Webster

Mr. Evans address, is Henry S. Evans Esqr.
West Chester, Chester Co.
Pa.

1. Ketchum (c. 1792–1870) was a New York City attorney, a close personal friend of Webster, and a leader of the Webster Whigs in the city.

2. For Webster's speech on the Specie Circular see *W & S*, 8:3–26.

3. Winthrop (1809–94; Harvard 1828) studied law with Webster and served as a representative (1840–50) and a senator (1850–51) from Massachusetts. Fearing (1798–1875), a Boston businessman who was active in Whig politics. Kinsman (1803–59; Dartmouth 1822) an associate in Webster's law office represented Boston in the Massachusetts legislature.

4. Evans (1813–72), a journalist and state legislator, was owner and editor of the West Chester *Village Record*.

Document 19
Text from *Correspondence* 4: 275–276.

To Richard Haughton[1]

My Dear Sir,   Washington Feb. 23. 1838

I wrote you some time since, & friends here, I am informed, have since addressed other Gentlemen near you.

Late movements appear to me to be breaking up the Whig party entirely, unless a determined stand be taken somewhere. There is information here this morning of an intended nomination in Maine. I presume you know, if any such thing be in contemplation. A very great effort has been made at Albany, but without effect. A letter now before me, recd. last Evening, says New York will make no nomination at present. The last account from Trenton gives the same assurance of New Jersey; but not with as much positiveness as the letters from Albany speak of New York. The origin of these sudden movements is in the proceeding in R. I.

As to the course proper to be adopted by Massachusetts, I have nothing to add to what was contained in my former letter; except that the opinions therein expressed are greatly strengthened. Nothing but a fair, *deliberative*, & upright Convention, *can save the Whig cause*. I trust, therefore, that Mass. will show that she understands this.

Having made a nomination, on a former occasion, it is proper she should say that, the confidence, which led to that expression of her preference, has not been withdrawn or diminished; but that in the actual state of things, she sees the absolute necessity of Union, & regards the assembling of a Convention as the only means of effecting that object; but that a Convention, to be useful & competent to its end, must be free, & deliberative, its members acting upon their convictions of the preferences of their constituents, & combining all the considerations which naturally belong to the occasion;—that the Convention should not be held earlier than the fall of 1839;—I think this point of *the greatest importance,* & that Massachusetts ought, by all means to state the *time;*—& that the members should be chosen, in their respective States & Districts, shortly before the time of holding the Convention. All this ought to be put forth, distinctly, & strongly.[2] If there be not that in the Whig *cause,* which can hold us together, there is nothing in any one *name* that can hold us together. It is astonishing to me, that our friends, especially our Northern friends, do not see the difficulty which there will be in supporting the candidate nominated, in these recent proceedings; & the present condition of things leads me to express, in entire & sacred confidence, an opinion, which I fully & completely entertain; & that is, supposing no Mass. candidate to be in the field, I do not believe, that in Novr. 1840, the vote of Massachusetts *can be given* for Mr Clay; nor the vote of any other State, north of Maryland.

I have thought it my duty to speak, thus freely & decidedly, to my friends—& leave the whole matter cheerfully with them. If they entertain my views, they will see the importance of even communicating, *instantly,* with friends in Maine. . . . Yrs

D Webster

1. Haughton was editor and publisher of the *Boston Atlas.*
2. On March 1, 1838, the *Boston Atlas* carried an editorial that emphasized the points made by Webster and implied that he remained Massachusetts' choice for the presidency.

Document 20
Text from *Correspondence* 5: 22–23.

To Nathaniel F. Williams[1]

My Dear Sir,   Washington Mar. 24.'40
I thank you for the No. of the Log Cabin Advocate.[2] It is a paper of good appearance, & its contents well written, or well selected. I wish it circulation & success.

I verily believe, My Dear Sir, that a political revolution is in progress.

It seems to me the evidences are plain that Genl Harrison will be elected President, if he live to see Novr. No man can rejoice in this prospect more than I do; for I think the preservation of interests, most valuable to the Country, entirely depend upon it. There is a very bad & reckless spirit abroad; a spirit of disorganization, of hostility to property, of disregard to engagements & contracts; & a spirit quite too indifferent to the obligations of morality & religion.

So far as this is political, a reformed & honest Government would tend to correct it. Our Government, like all other popular Governments, produces a great effect upon the opinions, & modes of thinking of men, by its example & its influence. A honest, upright, Free Govt. is among the greatest of human blessings. I really hope, that we are about to see some stay put, to the rage of party, & a return to the doctrines & the feelings of *honest politics,* and true patriotism.

Is there any thing I can send to you? You have been in the habit, sometimes, of reading my Speeches, when I make any; but at present I do not trouble my friends in that way. We have had a world of *discussion;* the time for *action* among the People has, I think, arrived. Yours always truly

D. Webster

1. Williams (1780–1864) was a Baltimore merchant and lifelong supporter of Webster. In 1841, through Webster's influence, President John Tyler appointed Williams collector of customs for the Port of Baltimore, and in 1851, again through Webster's influence, President Millard Fillmore appointed him appraiser for the same port.

2. *The Log Cabin Advocate* was a Whig campaign newspaper published in Baltimore, March 21–December 15, 1840.

Document 21
Text from *Correspondence* 5: 23–25.

To Joshua Bates[1]

My Dear Sir   Washington Mar. 26:'40
I must not omit writing you by the B[ritish] Q[ueen]—and as I have a half hour's leisure this morning, I may as well enjoy that pleasure now, as to postpone it to a period, nearer to her departure, since you will have all the news from other sources. We arrived, safe & well, in the Mediator, after a voyage of 35 days, the latter part of it rough, & the approach to the land a little difficult from thick weather. . . .[2]

Our political affairs wear a very different aspect, from that which I expected, when I left England. There is certainly a popular outbreak, for Genl Harrison, and, at this moment, at least an equal chance for his Election. Genl Jackson's personal weight is felt no more; Mr [Martin] V[an] B[uren] never had any personal popularity, & the power of party cohesion is very much weakened, by the state of the times, & by a sort of enthusiasm for a retired old Genl. One is hardly willing to acknowledge any national connexion, between the *fall* of cotton & wheat, & the *rise* of patriotism. But it is certain, nevertheless, that low prices make us a good deal more enthusiastic in our Country's cause. Genl Harrison is an honest man, & an amiable man; & would be likely, I think, to bring good men about him; & if he should be elected, tho' he has something of the self respect of an old soldier, will exhibit nothing of the obstinacy & ignorant presumption, of his *penult* predecessor. The Whigs all go for him, heartily, and, as I have said, his chance is at least an even one. . . . Yours truly & faithfully,

Danl. Webster

1. Bates (1788–1864), a prominent Massachusetts merchant and banker who spent much of his life in Europe.
2. Webster had visited England and France for six months in 1839, returning to the United States on December 29, 1839.

Document 22
Text from *Correspondence* 5: 41–43.

To Samuel Jaudon[1]

My Dear Sir,   Washington June 23. 1840
    I duly recd your kind letter of the 15 May, by the Unicorn, and I write you now, mainly to say a few words of our political affairs.
    The prospect is now very strong that Genl Harrison will be elected. Indeed, we have no doubt of it. We are more deceived than ever men were before if there be not a state of feeling which will bring him in, by a large majority. We have had no elections since that in Virginia, of which you know the result.[2] Louisiana has an election in July, & several important states in August; & others, as you know in October. So that before the actual voting for President, in Novr. we shall see, probably, what result may be expected. My own confidence is great & entire. No pains will be spared on either side, & we shall have a busy summer of it. And now, My Dear Sir, let me say, that if this event shall take place, it will change my condition, though I cannot say exactly

how. Indeed, some change—a change—will take place, let the election go either way. If Mr. V. Buren should be re-elected, I shall go back to the Bar—leaving the Senate—& go to work with all my might. If Genl Harrison should be chosen, I shall equally leave the Senate, & you can judge, as well as I, perhaps, whether I shall thence forward have any thing to do with the Government or not. But I have made these remarks, & introduced this subject, for the purpose of expressing to you a hope, that you will return to your own Country, & connect yourself with its affairs. You have capacity to be highly useful to the Government, in either of various situations. All you need is residence for a year or two among us, a re-integration, so to say, of yr national character, & some acquaintance with public men, who as yet may not have seen or known you. I wish to say, that my regard for you is unabated, & my disposition to serve you perfect. I have thought it not impossible, looking to the future, that we might be mutually useful to each other. If you come over soon, as I earnestly wish you may, we can converse on all these things more at length. In the mean time, I pray you, meditate upon them.

Perhaps I ought to add, that I have no present expectation of going abroad.

I write you this letter confidentially, of course, & only for the purpose of calling your attention to a probable state of things, if Genl. Harrison should be elected.

Yr Brother [Charles Baucker Jaudon][3] will have informed you that he authorized my draft on you for £1000 on security to be given.

I expect to leave Washington in a few days on a visit to Mass. July 4th. I am to meet the People, in Worcester County. July 7, I expect to be in Vermont, & July 15 on the Eastern shore of Maryland. Great conventions of the People, as you see, are all the rage. Thus far they have had powerful effect, & there is yet no abatement of spirit & zeal. We make a business of political addresses, &c. & I shall do little else till fall. If, under the present circumstances of the Country, & with the advantages we now have we cannot change the Administration, it will be useless to renew the attempt hereafter. But we shall change it. . . . always truly Yr friend

D. Webster

1. Jaudon (1796–1874; Princeton 1813) was formerly cashier of the Bank of the United States. Since 1837, he had headed the Pennsylvania Bank's agency in London.

2. The Virginia elections, concluded on April 23, gave the Whigs 87 out of 166 seats in the state legislature. On the basis of this Whig plurality, many Whigs predicted that they would carry the state for Harrison in November.

3. Jaudon (1802–1882) was a physician, but he devoted much of his time to banking and finance.

Document 23
Text from *Correspondence* 5: 244–45.

From Jacob Harvey[1]

Private

My dear Sir,   New York Sept. 27th. 1842

I regretted very much my absence from town when you passed through from Washington. I wished, at least, to have taken you by the hand, & to have rejoiced with you over the admirable Treaty it has been your good fortune to conclude.[2] I wanted also to tell you that Lord Ashburton[3] in his private conversation did ample justice to your exertions, without which, he freely admitted, the Treaty could not have been made. The *proof* of its equity toward both Countries, is found in the fact, that *ultra* politicians on both sides, condemn it equally—whilst the great body of the people here & in the Provinces are satisfied with it! And I will venture to say, that our grumbling Sister—Maine—could not be tempted *now* to give up the Treaty for a very large bribe!

My object in writing you today however, is to repeat the wish I expressed one year ago—viz—that neither the abuse of the party press, nor the solicitations of your personal friends may induce you to surrender the post you have so ably filled in the Cabinet. There are some other questions of importance to be settled, and as you have hitherto received about as much abuse as can possibly be heaped upon you, there is nothing very alarming in the prospect of having to endure it a little longer. I *know* that R[obert] B[owne] Minturn & M[oses] H[icks] Grinnell[4] wish you to remain, & so do many others also, who would tell you, however, that the *Whig party* would prefer your resignation, if you were to consult them individually!! I am so disgusted with mere party proceedings, I pay no regard whatever to the opinions of any man as a *politician*—but I do think in your position just now, you are bound to look to the interests of your Country *first*, & not to be frightened by any effects upon yourself *politically*, just at this moment. After the rage of party has spent itself, you will receive the credit due to your exertions, & people will then rejoice that you had firmness enough to remain in the path of duty, however annoying the company you have met or may meet with may be. Whig *politicians* ask: What good can Mr Webster do in such a Cabinet? I reply—how can any one tell, how much evil he may prevent. Some of the very men who would tell you to resign as a *Whig,* would be much better pleased to see you remain in, as a *Conservative.* Besides, your department is—foreign affairs—& in the management of these great Concerns, the President has certainly given you full power & left everything to yourself. At the very time that *he* confided in you—how much abuse & detraction did you receive from leading *Whig* presses & from Whig speakers? Therefore, so far as any claim on your feeling is concerned, I really think Mr Tyler has the best of the argument. But I put it to you on the ground of *patriotism* solely, irrespective of mere party, & if I have taken an improper liberty with you my motive must be my excuse. I write in great haste & with the full concurrences of our mutual friend Minturn. Yours very truly

Jacob Harvey

1. Harvey was a merchant in New York City and a close friend of several English politicians.
2. The Webster-Ashburton Treaty, signed on August 9, 1842.
3. Alexander Baring, Lord Ashburton (1774–1848), financier and special envoy to the United States in 1841–42.
4. Minturn (1805–1866), a prominent New York merchant; Grinnell (1803–1877), a merchant and a representative from New York (1839–41).

Document 24
Text from *Correspondence* 6: 4–6.

To John Haven et al.[1]

Gentlemen: Washington, January 3, 184[4]

I have received your letter, requesting permission to present my name to the People, as a Candidate for the office of President of the United States, subject to the future wise, deliberate action of the Whig National Convention of 1844.[2]

It would be disingenuous to withhold an expression of the grateful feelings awakened by a letter, containing such a request, so very numerously signed, and coming from among those who have known me through life. No one can be insensible to the distinction of being regarded, by any respectable number of his fellow-citizens, as among those from whom a choice of President might be made, with honor and safety to the country.

The office of President is an office, the importance of which cannot be too highly estimated. He who fills it, necessarily exercises a great influence, not only on all the domestic interests of the country, on its foreign relations, and the support of its honor and character among the nations of the earth, but on that, which is of the very highest import to the happiness of the people, the maintenance of the Constitution itself, and the prosperous continuance of the government under it. Our systems are peculiar; and while capable, as experience has shown, of producing the most favorable results, under wise and cautious administration, they are, nevertheless, exposed to peculiar dangers. We have six and twenty states, each possessing within itself powers of government, limited only by the Constitution of the United States; and we have a general government, to which are confided high trusts, to be exercised for the benefit of the people of all the States. It is obvious, that this division of powers, itself the result of a novel and most delicate political operation, can be preserved only by the exercise of wisdom and pure patriotism. The Constitution of the United States stands on the basis of the people's choice. It must remain on that basis, so long as it remains at all. The veneration and love, which are entertained for it, will be increased, by every instance of wise, prudent, impartial and parental administration. On the other hand, they will be diminished by every administration, which shall cherish local divisions, devote itself to local interests, seek to bend the influence of the Government to personal or partizan purposes, or which shall forget that all patriotism is false and spurious, which does not look with equal eye to the interests of the whole country, and all its parts, present and to come. I hardly know what an American statesman should so much deprecate, on his own account, as well as on account of his country, as that the Constitution of the United States, now the glory of our country and the admiration of the world, should become weakened in its foundations, perverted in its principles, or fallen and sunk, in a nation's regard and a nation's hopes, by his own follies, errors, or mistakes. The Constitution was made for the good of the country; this the people know. Its faithful administration promotes that good; this the people know. The people will themselves defend it against all foreign power, and all open force; and they will rightfully hold to a just and solemn account, those, to whose hands they commit it, and in whose hands it shall be found to be shorn of a single beam of its honor or deprived of a particle of its capacity for usefulness. It was made for an honest people, and they expect it to be honestly administered. At the present moment, it is an object of general respect, confidence and affection. Questions have arisen, however, and are likely to arise again, upon the extent of its powers, or upon the line which separates the functions of the General Government from those of the State Governments; and these questions will require, whenever they may occur, not only firmness, but much discretion, prudence and impartiality in the Head of the National Executive. Extreme counsels or extreme opinions on either side, would be very likely, if followed or adopted, to break up the well-adjusted balance of the whole. And he who has the greatest confidence in his own judgment, or the strongest reliance on his own good fortune, may yet be well diffident of his ability to discharge the duties of this trust, in such a manner as shall promote the public prosperity, or advance his own reputation.

But, gentlemen, while the office of President is quite too high to be sought by personal solicitation, or for private ends and objects, it is not to be declined, if proffered by the voluntary desire of a free people.

It is now more than thirty years since you and your fellow-citizens of New Hampshire, assigned me a part in political affairs. My public conduct, since that period, is known. My opinions on the great questions, now most interesting to the country, are known. The constitutional principles which I have endeavored to maintain, are also known. If these principles and these opinions, now not likely to be materially changed, should recommend me to further marks of public regard and confidence, I should not withhold myself from compliance with the general will. But I have no pretensions of my own to bring forward, and trust that no friends of mine would at any time use my name for the purpose of preventing harmony among those, whose general political opinions concur, or for any cause whatever, but a conscientious regard to the good of the country.

It is obvious, gentlemen, that at the present moment the tendency of opinion among those to be represented in the Convention is generally and strongly set in another direction. I think it my duty, therefore, under existing circumstances, to request those, who may feel a preference for me, not to indulge in that preference, nor oppose any obstacle to the leading wishes of political friends, or to united and cordial efforts for the accomplishment of those wishes.

The election of the next autumn must involve, in general, the same principles, and the same questions, as belonged to that of 1840. The cause, I conceive, to be the true cause of the country, its permanent prosperity, and all its great interests; the cause of its peace, and its honor; the cause of good government, true liberty, and the preservation and integrity of the Constitution; and none should despair of its success. I am, gentlemen, with sentiments of sincere regard, your obliged and obedient servant,

Daniel Webster.

1. Haven (1766–1845) was a Portsmouth merchant.

2. Haven's letter to Webster was published in the *Boston Courier* on February 4, 1844. Printed copies of the letter were circulated and signed by over one thousand New Hampshire Whigs.

Document 25
Text from *Correspondence* 6: 63–64.

To Edward Everett

My Dear Sir   Boston Decr. 15. 1844

The last Boat carried you the news of Mr [James K.] Polks election. Mr [Henry] Clay has been a candidate, since 41. Partly by the force of circumstances, & more, perhaps, by the course adopted by his friends, all alternatives, & indeed all deliberation, on that point have been excluded.

I wrote you, I think, in 42. or 43, that I was persuaded Mr Clay could never be President. That has been my prevailing feeling, ever since we tried his popularity, in 1832. But since May last, there have been periods, in which <he> I thought his election highly probable; & he certainly came near success. Five thousand more votes in N.Y. wd. have made him President. But here was the very difficulty. He was not popular in N.Y. Any other respectable Whig candidate would have recd. a large majority. His friends complain, & with justice, of the calumny & abuse of his enemies. But he would have triumphed over all these things, but for two causes;—his Alabama letter,[1]—& a general feeling throughout many parts of the Country, & especially in Western N.Y.—that his temper was bad—resentful, violent, & unforgiving.

We have all felt sad. I confess I never experienced so much depression, in consequence of any one political occurrence.

It mortifies my pride of Country, to see how the great office of President may be disposed of.

Appearances already indicate a warm session in Congress, & what will be [the] result I cannot conjecture. Possibly annexation may be postponed; & that is the best thing we may hope for.

I take it Mr Polks administration will be a strict party administration; as much so as Genl. Jackson's. How courteous he may incline to be towards the Diplomatic Gentlemen abroad, I know not; but I presume he has no favor, too great or too small, to be the subject of clamorous importunity. In a fortnight, the introduction of the Genl Appropriation Bill may show, perhaps, what *outfits* are expected to be necessary; that is, if Mr Tyler shall be advised of Mr Polk's intentions. I will by the next opportunity let you know all the gossip & guessing there is, on this subject. Mr. [Rufus] Choate[2] is expected to decline a re-election. There is some disposition, among our people, I believe, to make me his successor; but I feel little inclined to return to that area of strife; & I find a still stronger objection, in the necessity of attending to my own affairs.

If you come home, we must confer upon the future. The Country is yet worth saving. The Whig Party is strong, but it wants good direction. The mere hangers-on upon it—persons without character, or influence, of their own—have really caused it its chief misfortunes. We need your counsel, & we need your pen.

Pray make our best love to your family. We are spending a few weeks at Tremont House, & then I go to the Court, at Washington. Yrs always faithfully

Danl Webster

1. In the so-called Alabama Letters of 1844, Clay straddled the issue of the annexation of Texas. He stated that he would like to see Texas a part of the Union, but not at the expense of increased sectional strife or war with Mexico.
2. Choate (1799–1859; Dartmouth 1819) was chosen to fill Webster's vacant seat in the Senate when Webster became secretary of state in 1841. In 1845, Choate withdrew from politics, and Webster was reelected to the U.S. Senate.

Document 26
Text from *Correspondence* 6: 286–87.

To Edward Everett

Boston, Monday morning.
My Dear Sir   May 22.'48
I can think of nothing to help you, in the little project suggested in your last note.[1] The thing itself seems quite desirable; but as soon as I attempt to do any thing with it, I find myself dealing with matters, which have too much of a personal bearing.

Nothing can be better than a resumé, of what you yourself have already written.

—The members [of the Whig Convention] might be profitably reminded, that their decision is to affect the future, as well as the present;

—That if they intend to preserve the integrity and strength of the

Whig Party, they must show a disposition to be just towards the North, where the main strength of the party lies;

—That they must be ready to trust a Northern man, fully disposed, & fully pledged, to maintain all the constitutional rights of the South;

—That a persistence in the purpose of setting up a Southern Candidate, in the present state of public feeling, cannot but threaten the worst consequences to the Party, and to the Country:—&c. &c. &c.

You and Mr. H[iram] K[etchum] can, I am quite sure, get up something which will *tell*. Yrs always truly

D. W. . . .

1. Everett's note has not been found, but he may have suggested that Webster send a message to the Whig convention which was scheduled to meet in Philadelphia in June.

Document 27
Text from *Correspondence* 6: 289.

Editorial from the *Boston Journal*,
May 27, 1848

The N. Y. Courier and Enquirer in an article respecting the Whig nomination to the Presidency, says:—

"If Mr. Webster could be elected, his nomination would give joy to the hearts of the intelligent Whigs of the country, and reflect honor upon our people and our institutions."

This remark is undoubtedly true to the letter.—The Whigs in all parts of the country say the same. Why then, does the Courier and Enquirer manifest so much zeal to lay Daniel Webster upon the shelf, and urge the claims of the "Independent candidate" to the support of the whole Whig party? The answer is a hacknied one. "He is not available."

This is a left-handed compliment to the Whigs of the Union. The man whose nomination would give joy to the hearts of the intelligent Whigs, and reflect honor upon our people and our institutions, must not receive the nomination of the Whigs, because he is not available!

The Democrats are already in the field. They have made their nomination—and harmony will be restored to their ranks. Some of them may make wry faces—but they will be constrained to swallow the dose and all will unite upon General [Lewis] Cass[1]—and the immense influence of the administration, with its official patronage—an inexhaustible source of bribery and corruption, never contemplated by the framers of the Constitution—will be with them. To contend successfully against this well-organized and powerful party, the Whigs must abandon neither their principles nor their men. To ensure a glorious victory at the next election, the Whigs must nominate a WHIG—a firm, undeviating Whig—known as such by his political opinions and acts throughout the course of his life. The great struggle in the approaching political campaign will be between the Whigs and the Locofocos. It will be a struggle for principle, and the most "available" candidate of the Whig party will be—not the man whose political views in relation to the great questions of the day are yet to be developed—but the man whose whole political course is an embodiment of Whig principles; and "whose nomination would give joy to the hearts of the intelligent Whigs of the country, and reflect honor on our people and our institutions."

1. Cass (1782–1866), the presidential candidate of the Democratic party, was a senator from Michigan from 1845–48 and again from 1849–57. He also served as secretary of war (1831–36), minister to France (1836–42), and secretary of state (1857–60).

Document 28
Text from *Correspondence* 6: 299.

To Daniel Fletcher Webster[1]

Washington
My Dear Son,   June 19.'48
I am sorry that I cannot see my way clear to follow your advice, entirely. It appears to me necessary, that I should express, publicly, either acquiescence, or dissatisfaction, with the nomination. I have certainly said, often that I should not recommend Genl [Zachary] Taylor; but I have said, too, always, at the same time, that I should not oppose his election if nominated. Beyond that, I propose to say nothing, except in favor of the general Whig cause.
These Northern proceedings can come to nothing useful, to you or to me. The men are all low, in their objects. The abolitionists will adhere to Mr [John Parker] Hale.[2] The Barn-burners will nominate Mr [John Milton] Niles.[3] If the conscience men, at Worcester, were to ask to put me on their Ticket, what wd. it all come to?—I could not consent to that, with as little show of strength as they now put forth. On the other hand, suppose I acquiesce in Genl Taylor's nomination.
He will, or will not, be chosen. If chosen, (as I incline to think he

will be) it may be for *your* interest, not to have opposed him. As to *mine,* it is quite indifferent. I have, for myself, no object whatever.

If he is not chosen, things can stand no worse.

Then, on the general ground; it seems to me I must not, in consistency, abandon the support of Whig principles. My own reputation will not allow of this. I cannot be silent, without being reproached, when such as [Lewis] Cass is pressed upon the Country.

I agree, it is a difficult & doubtful question; but I think the safest way is, to overlook the nomination, as not being the main thing, & to continue to maintain the Whig cause.

We shall see; but I think we shall come out right. Yrs affectionately,

Danl Webster

I take the cars with this.
Take care of these letters, & *keep them private.*

1. Webster (1813–62; Harvard 1833), Daniel Webster's elder son.
2. Hale (1806–73; Bowdoin 1827), a representative (1843–45) and a senator from New Hampshire (1847–53, 1855–65), received the presidential nomination of the Liberty party in 1848 but withdrew his candidacy when antislavery groups established the Free Soil party and chose Martin Van Buren as its presidential candidate. In 1852, Hale became the presidential nominee of the Free Soil party.
3. Niles (1787–1856), a senator from Connecticut 1835–39, 1843–49. The Barnburners, radical antislavery and anti-bank Democrats, supported Van Buren rather than Niles.

Document 29
Text from *Correspondence* 6: 315–17.

To Richard Milford Blatchford,[1] With Enclosure

In the Senate, February 16, 1849,
My Dear Sir: Friday, Two o'clock

I hear nothing from you since your excursion to Boston, but hope you are safe at home.

I have been at home all the morning, trying to bring up my correspondence, and waiting for the sun to warm the air a little. The morning is exceedingly cold; the mercury, I believe, eight or nine above zero at sunrise.

The ice, it would seem, is likely to keep General Taylor away from Pittsburg, and to delay his arrival here. I have no news, except that

Mr. T[ruman] S[mith][2] thinks it may be his duty, after all, to go into the Treasury; at least, so says the rumor of the hour.

We are on the Diplomatic Bill, Washington Canal,[3] etc. Nothing important. Yours,

D. W.

Enclosure

Private

It is not General Taylor's present purpose to offer me a place in his Cabinet, but rather the contrary. It is possible that, after he comes here, he may alter his mind, but not probable; and I hope he will remain as he is.

I could not accept the offer, if made; and, having come to a resolution on that subject, I think it due to you to settle your mind on it by a private and confidential letter. You know the *general* reason growing out of my own condition and circumstances, and the confining and irksome nature of the duties of the office which have weighed with me when we have conversed on the matter. There are one or two other *general* reasons to which I have not frequently adverted. The first of the *general* reasons is, that I cannot help feeling some apprehension as to what the real character of the Administration is to be. Many things look very well; but, on the other hand, there is some reason to fear that the *tone* of character called into the Cabinet will not be high. If appointments should run as some of the various speculations indicate, I should have little confidence of a useful or honorable result. All may come right; I hope it will; but I cannot but entertain some doubt. Another *general* reason is, that although I would not yield myself to any undue feelings of self-respect, yet it is certain that I am senior, in years, to General Taylor; that I have been thirty years in public civil life, and have had some few friends who have thought that, for the administration of civil and political affairs, my own qualifications entitled me to be considered a candidate for nomination for the office to which General Taylor has been chosen.

Acquiescing, therefore, most cheerfully in the result of things which has flowed from honest and intelligent Whig counsels, and perfectly disposed to render all the aid in my power to the support of the new Whig Administration, I yet feel that I shall best consult my own dignity by declining to fill a subordinate place in the Executive Government.

So much for general reasons. In addition to these there is one *peculiar* reason, growing out of my peculiar relations, and that of my friends, to General Taylor's election. In Massachusetts, New York, and other States, there will be candidates for office, who have been my friends, and who opposed General Taylor's nomination to the last.

There will be other candidates for the same offices, who distinguished themselves as *early* and *zealous* friends of General Taylor's nomination, and who will naturally think themselves entitled to his regard. Cast your eyes over your own city, and you will see that questions of this kind, and several of them, must, in all probability, arise at once. And these questions would create a degree of embarrassment that I could not meet. I could not abandon my own friends; on the other hand, I could not act with any want of fidelity to General Taylor and his friends. It is clear, therefore, that my true position is a position of respect, friendship, and support of the incoming Administration; but not a position in which I should be called upon to take part in the distribution of its offices and patronage.

1. Blatchford (1798–1875; Union College 1815), a New York lawyer and financier and an intimate friend of Webster.

2. Smith (1791–1884; Yale 1815), a representative (1839–43, 1845–49) and a senator from Connecticut (1849–54), declined the appointment of secretary of interior in the cabinet of President Zachary Taylor.

3. The appropriations bill for civil and diplomatic expenses of the government included an amendment to provide for the deepening of the Washington Canal.

Document 30
Text from *Correspondence* 7: 35–37.

From William Giles Jones[1]

                                        Greensboro Alabama
Dear Sir,   March 17th. 1850

I take pleasure as a Southern man in tendering to you my most heartfelt thanks for the noble firm & patriotic stand you have lately taken in the U.S. Senate in behalf of our common Country. It is a source of much consolation to every honest man & sincere friend of freedom to know that we yet have statesmen like yourself whose souls are expansive enough to feel themselves American citizens & to look far above the little local jealousies so common with the most of our underling politicians of the day whose great & sole object seems to be to foster unpleasant sentiments between the North & South. What are we but brothers of the same great confederacy closely united by ties of blood & interest? The good of one section like the members of the human system is necessarily felt by the whole body & our intercourse & commerce is constant & reciprocal that the prosperity of one section cannot fail to extend its influence to all. Before this event you had many devoted admirers in the South but Sir the man who does not now [k]now the name of Daniel Webster living South of Pennsylvania deserves not the name of an American & allow me to say that it is my ardent hope & opinion that the people of this Country will do that justice to you which you so highly deserve of electing you to the Presidency of the U. States. There is one only reason why you have not been already elevated to that office & that is simply that others aspiring to that place & their expectants have from the dread of your talents labored constantly to impress our people that you were a Northern man a federalist &c and have prevented your nomination thereby. I know well that many of the Whigs here popular as Mr [Henry] Clay has been would have preferred your nomination to his. But if you are never called to fill that place rest assured (& it should be a proud consolation to you) that if it were left to the intelligence & worth of the people to decide you would be chosen by acclamation.

A peaceable seperation of the States is too great an absurdity for a sane mind to embrace. Where could we make a line of division. How could we divide the Navy & Army. How apportion the public property at Washington & elsewhere. It does seem to me when Mr. [John Caldwell] Calhoun talks of peaceable secession he is either (mad) deranged or wishes to be President of the South. But let us once seperate & never will such another Government be organised in this World. I sincerely trust your life may be long spared & your future days be prosperous & happy as they have been usefull.

In June 1841 while on my way to Europe I stopped at Washington & then in company with Mr. [Kenneth] Rayner of N Carolina & Mr. [Caleb] Cushing of your State[2] while you were Secretary of State was made acquainted with you in your office. I never shall forget the easy & agreeable manner I was received & noticed by you nor the warmth & cordiality with which you insisted on my calling again to see you on leaving you to go into Mr. [Horatio?] Jones[3] room to get my Passport a pleasure I did not again allow myself because I knew too well the value of time to men of business to make myself obtrusive.

Col W[illia]m R[ufus de Vane] King our Senator[4] is the only member of Congress with whom I am well acquainted. He can tell you who I am as you most likely have forgotten our short interview. With sentiments of the highest regard I am sir Your obedt Humble Sert

William Jones

1. Jones (1808–83) was an Alabama lawyer and politician who served in the state senate.

2. Rayner (1808–84) was a representative from North Carolina from 1839 to 1845. Cushing (1800–79; Harvard 1817), a wealthy Massachusetts shipowner and merchant and a friend of Webster who served in Congress as a Whig from 1835 to 1843.

3. Horatio Jones was a clerk in the Department of State.

4. King (1786–1853; University of North Carolina 1803), a representative from North Carolina (1811–16), a senator from Alabama (1819–44, 1848–52), and vice president under President Franklin Pierce.

Document 31
Text from *Correspondence* 7: 154–55.

To [Edward Everett]

My Dear Sir   Washington Sep. 26.'50

I think you might do good, if you could see your friend [George] Morey,[1] before his Com[mitt]ee get up their Resolutions & address for the Whig Convention, next week. This Central State Com[mitt]ee for some years past has entertained very narrow notions, & pursued a miserable course. They are one half inclined to abolit[ion]ism, & when you deduct that, & also what belongs to them of other *isms*, there is very little of true, broad, just & liberal Whig principles left in them. The [Boston] Atlas has been their exponent, type, leader or interpreter; & that paper has brought the Whig party in Massachusetts to the very brink of utter separation from all other Whigs. There is no estimating the mischief produced by the Atlas, & the Albany Evening Journal, & by the insane conduct of Northern men in Congress.

Let me give you a specimen. Three days ago, certain members of the H of R came to me, desiring that I would speak to three members,[2] Whigs, from N[orth] C[arolina] on the *Tariff* subject. These three members have always voted for protection, & are in all respects good men. But they have become soured. They say, the Northern men, Whigs & all, have done little else for the last nine months than to make assaults on *their* rights, their property, & their feelings; & now, they say, Northern *protection* must look out for itself. These three votes would have decided the fate of Mr [George] Ashmun's motion.[3] I have taken care to use what influence I have with these Gentlemen, & they will [do] right, but perhaps too late.

I am out of all patience with the littleness, the bigotry, the stupidity,—but as I find myself growing angry, I will stop here. Yrs truly
Danl Webster

I wish you would go to Worcester,[4] & make a Speech, & *nationalize* the Whig Party.

1. Morey (1789–1866; Harvard 1811), a Boston lawyer, was for many years chairman of the Massachusetts Whig Central Committee.
2. Probably Joseph P. Caldwell, Edmund Deberry, and David Outlaw.
3. Ashmun (1804–70; Yale 1823), a representative from Massachusetts from 1845 to 1851. In 1850, he unsuccessfully sponsored legislation to increase duties on iron and manufactured products.
4. Massachusetts Whigs were scheduled to meet in Worcester on October 1.

Document 32
Text from *Correspondence* 7: 155–56.

To Peter Harvey[1]

Private

My Dear friend;   Washington, Oct. 2, '50

I feel well, & in good spirits. My cold is going off, & although it leaves me weak, my eye[s] and head are clear, & that awful depression, which accompanies the disease has disappeared. It will return, occasionally, for a fortnight, perhaps; but not for long visits.

My main relief, however is, that Congress got thro' so well. I can now sleep anights. We have gone thro' the most important crisis, which has occurred since the foundation of the Government; & what ever party may prevail, hereafter, the Union stands firm. Faction, Disunion, & the love of mischief are put under, at least, for the present, & I hope for a long time.

Another effect of recent occurrences is the softening of political animosities. Those who have acted together, in this great crisis, can never again feel sharp asperities towards one another. For instance, it is impossible that I should entertain hostile feelings, or political acrimony towards Genl [Lewis] Cass, [Daniel Stevens] Dickinson, [James] Shield[s], [Jesse David] Bright, [Thomas Jefferson] Rusk,[2] &c. &c. in the Senate. We have agreed, that as we are never likely to be called on to act in a matter of so much moment to the Country, again, so we will not mar the joy, or the honor of the past, by any unnecessary quarrels for the future.

Another thing is not altogether improbable. And that is, a remodelling of Parties. If any considerable body of the Whigs of the North should act in the spirit of the majority of the recent Convention in N. York,[3] a new arrangement of Parties is unavoidable. There must be a Union Party, & an opposing Party under some name, I know not what, very likely the Party of Liberty. Many good men among our Whig friends of the North could not make up their minds to renounce their old ideas, & support the great measures. Very well; & if, now that the measures are adopted, & the questions settled, they will support things as they now are, & resist all further attempts at agitation & disturbance, & make no efforts for another change, they ought still to be regarded as Whigs. But those who act otherwise, or shall act otherwise, & continue to talk about Wilmot Provisos, and to resist, or seek to repeal, the Fugitive Slave Bill, or use any other means to disturb the quiet of the Country, will have no right to consider themselves either as Whigs, or as friends to this Administration. Because there is one thing that is fixed, & settled; & that is, that the present Administration will not recognize one set of Whig Principles for the North, & another for the South.

In regard to the great questions of Constitutional Law, & Public Policy, upon which the Whig Party is founded, we must all be of one faith, & that can be regarded as no Whig Party, in N. York, or Mass., which espouses doctrines, & utters sentiments, hostile to the just, & Constitutional rights of the South, and therefore such as Southern Whigs cannot agree to.

You will be glad that I have reached the bottom of the 4th page. Yrs truly

Danl Webster

1. Harvey (c. 1810–77) was a prominent Massachusetts businessman and legislator and one of Webster's closest friends.

2. Dickinson (1800–66) a Democratic senator from New York 1844–51; Shields (c. 1806–79), a Democratic senator from Illinois 1849–55; Bright (1812–75), a Democratic senator from Indiana 1845–62; Rusk (1803–57), a Democratic senator from Texas 1846–57.

3. At a divisive state convention in September, a majority of New York Whigs was critical of the Compromise of 1850.

Document 33
Text from *Correspondence* 7: 244–45.

To Peter Harvey

Private & confidential
My Dear Sir   Washington May 4th 51.

I wrote a short note to Mr [Albert] Fearing[1] yesterday and have since recd yours of the 2d. I have no hesitation of opinion upon the subject of which you write. I would not wish to dictate to others what course it may be proper for them to pursue, but for myself I am quite resolved not to commit any interest of mine to the management of The Whig State Com[mi]ttee of Mass. The leading object of that Com[mi]ttee will be to reestablish a Whig Government in Mass. And if we may judge by the past, we may fear that to effect this object, they will be ready to sacrifice high National Considerations, and to court as they have courted free soilers, and semi freesoilers, abolitionists, and semi abolitionists. The truth is that sound Whigs and sound Union men, in other states, very strongly suspect the Whig party of Mass. of these tendencies. They are not likely therefore to be willing to cooperate with that party in Mass. The Union Whigs, Tariff Whigs, Internal Improvement Whigs, and Constitutional Whigs are afraid, all over the South, to connect themselves with us; because they say, that on the question of all others, the most important to them, they have as little, indeed less, to expect from Mass. Whigs, than from Mass. Democrats. They think Gov. [George S.] Boutwell a better Union man, for example, than Gov [George Nixon] Briggs;[2] they think no worse votes are to be expected from Mr [Charlesl Sumner,[3] on the point most interesting to them, than would have been to be expected from Mr. [Robert Charles] Winthrop: they think they have no more to hope from Mr Jno [John] Davis, and Mr O[rin] Fowler[4] than from any members of the Democratic party who might succeed to their places. I speak to the fact, those sentiments may be just or unjust; but they do exist and they will influence men[']s conduct.

Besides, there is a growing opinion that the present organization of the Whig Party can not be continued throughout the United States. Georgia you perceive, has already adopted the new distinction of a

Union party, and a State Rights party. Other important Southern States are on the eve of making similar demonstrations.

Under these circumstances, it appears to me that the course of the real friends of the Union in Mass. is plain enough; that is to call a meeting of Union men of all parties. Perhaps few Gentlemen of the Democratic party would attend but never mind that. If the Idea spreads and gains ground, many of that party may come in; and New Hampshire is not unlikely to follow the example.

My dear Sir, I say all these things with diffidence, and would not say them at all, if it did not seem to be necessary to let my opinion be known to my friends in Boston. Although I have marked this private & Confidential, yet I have no wish that you should conceal its contents . . . Yours always truly

Danl Webster. . . .

1. Fearing (1798–1875) was a merchant, active in Massachusetts Whig politics.

2. Boutwell (1818–1905), a Democrat, was governor of Massachusetts 1851–52; Briggs (1796–1861), a Whig, was governor of the state from 1844 to 1851.

3. Sumner (1811–74; Harvard 1830), one of the founders of the Free Soil party in 1848, was a senator from Massachusetts from 1851 until his death in 1874.

4. Fowler (1791–1852; Yale 1814), a Whig representative from Massachusetts 1849–52.

Document 34
Text from *Correspondence* 7: 333–34.

From Edward Everett

Dear Sir,   Boston 22 June 1852

I hope you will not allow yourself to be greatly disturbed by the disappointment of our hopes at Baltimore.[1] However desirable success may have been for the Country at large or your friends, you are the individual who has least reason to regret it. Assuming that election would have followed nomination, what could the Presidency add to your happiness or fame? Even before the office had been let down by second rate and wholly incompetent persons, the example of Mr [James] Madison shows that even repeated election to the office is of very little moment to a great constitutional statesman.

He had a powerful majority in Congress;—this will be the reverse with any whig who may be chosen for the next President; and few things I should think would be more annoying than to carry on the government in face of a powerful, and what would be not less certain, a spiteful opposition at the Capitol.

It would have given me the utmost pleasure to have taken part in the proceedings of the Convention, as your friend;—but I foresaw— what the event abundantly exhibited,—a state of things entirely beyond my present state of health.

It is a source of some satisfaction to your friends here,—amidst so much to grieve and disgust them,—that so many of the delegates who voted for you did so to the last.

Upon the whole, I hope you will bear in mind that if there is no one in the Country (as your friends think) who could have filled the office so much to the public interest and honor, there is, and for that reason, no one who is so little dependent upon office, even the highest,—for influence or reputation.

Praying my kindest remembrance to Mrs W. I remain, my dear Sir, as ever Sincerely & affectionately yours,

Edward Everett

1. Webster did not even come close to obtaining the presidential nomination at the Whig National Convention which met in Baltimore from June 16 to 21. In the balloting, he ran a very distant third to Winfield Scott and Millard Fillmore. The final count was 159 for Scott, 112 for Fillmore, and 21 for Webster.

Document 35
Text from *Correspondence* 7: 356–57.

From Moses Hicks Grinnell, With Enclosure

My Dear Sir,   October 9, 1852
I enclose a communication from some of your friends in this [New York] City, it breathes the sentiments of your friends here. I send it to you with a heart full of interest and solicitude for your happiness. Sincerely your friend

M. H. Grinnell

Enclosure: From Moses Hicks Grinnell et al.

Dear Sir,   September 24, 1852
After much consideration we have thought it not improper to address to you a few words on the present aspect of political affairs with the Whig party. We venture to do this in the confidence that you will

receive this from us, as prompted only by our sincere interest in whatever affects your position before the Country, now as ever regarded by us as that of our most eminent Citizen.

Of the ill success which attended the efforts to promote the honor and safety of the Country, by presenting you as the Candidate of the great Whig party for the Presidency, we can only say, that it has occasioned to us, at least as much sorrow and chagrin as to any others of your friends political or personal, and the more that every day adds to the conviction which we expressed always and every where before the nomination, that the triumph of the Whig party would be assured under the auspices of your great name.

With all these feelings, however, we confess that we have observed with much solicitude the movements made by many of your friends, in various parts of the Country to connect your name with the impending Canvas for the Presidency. We can anticipate no result from them at all suitable to your dignity, or at all likely to correspond with their wishes. If the matter should come to the point of a nomination and the formation of electoral tickets, we can see no prospect of any other issue, than a most false record of the state of feeling in the Country towards you, an issue most unfortunate for the Country, and gratifying only to that faction whom your patriotism and great public services have made your enemies.

Nor do we think it unworthy of notice that all the best considered and effective efforts in your behalf before the meeting of the Convention took the shape of presenting your name to the ordeal of that body's selection from the candidates proposed by the Whig party, a shape suggested, as we then believed, no less by a wise policy than by a just sense of political fidelity. In the disaster which has fallen upon our hopes and plans, we do not find any warrant to disregard the observance of that good faith towards the successful competitor, which in a different result we should rightfully, have claimed from his friends.

The best reflections we have been able to give to this whole subject, have induced us to think that sound and sober public opinion, which should never be lightly regarded, deems a public disclaimer from you of any favor towards movements further connecting your name with the coming Presidential election, as required by your past and present eminent position whether as a Whig or a Statesman; that such is our own feeling we respectfully submit to you, and beg you to consider that whatever may be your decision, we shall never cease to acknowledge the great obligations which the Country and the Whig Party have always owed to you, and shall ever remain your sincere friends and obedient Servants,

M[oses] H[icks] Grinnell
W[illia]m M[axwell] Evarts
A[mbrose] C Kingsland
T[homas] Tileston
James S. Thayer
J[ames] Watson Webb
C[harles] A[ugustus] Stetson[1]

1. Evarts (1818–1901; Yale 1837) was an assistant U.S. district attorney from 1849–53; Kingsland (1804–78) was a New York Whig; Tileston (1793–1864) was a prominent merchant and shipowner who named one of his vessels *Webster*; Thayer (1818–81; Amherst 1838) was a lawyer and businessman; Webb (1802–84) was the editor of the *Morning Courier and New-York Enquirer;* Stetson (1810–88) was the proprietor and host of the Astor House. He always held a suite of rooms in reserve for Webster, who once commented that if he could not stay in the Astor House he would never again go to New York City.

Document 36
Text from *Correspondence* 7: 357–58.

To Moses Hicks Grinnell, With Enclosure[1]

My dear Mr. Grinnell,   Marshfield Oct 12 1852
   I received your note of the 9th inst., only yesterday with its enclosure; to which enclosure you will herewith receive an answer Yours with constant regard.

                                        Daniel Webster

Enclosure: To Moses Hicks Grinnell et al.

Gentlemen,   Marshfield, Oct. 12. 1852
   I received only yesterday your communication of the 24th of September; and among a great number of similar letters, it is the only one I answer.
   There is no equal number of Gentlemen in the United States, who possess more of my deep attachment and regard than the signers of your letter, I would do almost anything to comply with your request.

But if I were to do what you suggest, it would gratify not only you and your friends, but that great body of implacable enemies, who have prevented me from being elected President of the United States. You all know this; and, how can I be called upon to perform any act of humiliation for their gratification, or the promotion of their purposes?

But, Gentlemen, I do not act from personal feeling. It is with me a matter of principle and character, and I have now to State to you that no earthly consideration could enduce me to say anything or do anything from which it might be inferred directly or indirectly that I concur in the Baltimore nomination, or that, I should give it, in any way the sanction of my approbation. If I were to do such act, I should feel my cheeks already scorched with shame by the reproaches of posterity.

As to the proceedings of my friends, I encourage nothing, I discourage nothing. I leave them entirely free to judge of their own course. Probably they think they see indications that within a fortnight the Whig party in the United States will have become merely Historical. With the highest respect and the warmest attachment I remain, Gentlemen, Most truly Yours

D.W.

1. Webster dictated this letter, but he never signed it or sent it to Grinnell.

Irving H. Bartlett

DANIEL WEBSTER

The Orator and Writer

M Y SEARCH for Daniel Webster began more than twenty-five
years ago when I was writing about the New England abolitionists who hated him. I was struck by the fact that men of literary talent
and great moral sensitivity like Theodore Parker, John Greenleaf
Whittier, Wendell Phillips, and Ralph Waldo Emerson could not attack
Webster after he supported the Fugitive Slave Law in 1850 without
confessing how enormously they had once admired him. Insisting that
no living man had done so much "to debauch the conscience of the
nation," Parker said that Webster had once ranked with Charlemagne
as one of the grandest figures "in all Christendom." Whittier's famous
poem of denunciation, "Ichabod," likened Webster to a fallen angel,
and Phillips called him one of the greatest men "God ever let the devil
buy."[1] Emerson, who had followed Webster throughout his career and
was fascinated by every detail of the great man's life, reacted to his
vote for the Fugitive Slave Law by writing in his journal that "the word
liberty in the mouth of Mr. Webster" sounded like love in the mouth
of a whore, and he later announced that "every drop of his blood has
eyes that look downward." Two years later, Emerson stood on the
beach at Plymouth looking out toward Marshfield where thousands of
devout New Englanders had assembled to pay their last respects to
Webster as he lay in an open coffin in front of his house. Recalling his
impressions at that moment, Emerson wrote, "The sea, the rocks, the
woods, gave no sign that America and the world has lost the completest
man. Nature had not in our days, or not since Napoleon, cut out such
a masterpiece. . . . He was a man *in equilibrio*; a man within and without.
. . . He held undiminished the power and terror of his strength, the
majesty of his demeanour."[2]

These men turned on Webster in anger and in sorrow because in their youth he had wondrously touched them as a leader larger than life—as the godlike Daniel Webster—and their god had fallen. "The Anglo Saxon race never knew such a calamitous ruin," Theodore Parker said. "His downfall shook the continent. Truth fell prostrate in the street."[3]

When I began my research on Webster, it was the godlike image of the man that interested me the most. That image was kept alive in this century by Stephen Vincent Benet's famous story, for only a godlike man would undertake to argue down the Devil. Every biographer begins his work with some central questions about his subject; I wanted to discover why Daniel Webster's contemporaries thought he was so great. I began my research in conventional scholarly fashion by reading Webster's speeches and correspondence. I went to Faneuil Hall in Boston, stood before the enormous painting of the Webster-Hayne debate, and tried to imagine how Webster had worked his magic on the Americans of his generation. I visited the old Senate chamber in Washington, studied every Webster portrait and statue I could locate, and read practically everything in the Dartmouth archives written about Webster by his contemporaries. I learned a great deal about Webster's private and public life—about his appetite for good wine and food, about his large legal fees and his chronic inability to pay his debts, and about the numerous allegations that he was a politician in the pay of merchants, manufacturers, and the Bank of the United States—none of which helped much in understanding the godlike phenomenon.

As my research proceeded, however, I began to appreciate the solid base of accomplishments on which Webster's reputation rested. Over that forty-year period, from 1812 until his death in 1852, no American was better known. Webster's versatility was extraordinary. As a young man he regularly wrote for one of the country's leading literary journals. Henry Wadsworth Longfellow once said Webster was the only American he could imagine creating a work like Dante's *Inferno*.[4] As a professional man, he earned renown for his spectacular success in criminal trials as well as his historic appearances before John Marshall's court. As a public man, he served more than thirty years as congressman and senator, was twice secretary of state, was a perennial presidential prospect, and was generally acclaimed as America's most famous ceremonial orator.

Webster's high visibility depended not only on ability, ambition, and energy but on extraordinary personal qualities. Like other symbolic leaders and heroes, Webster was a charismatic figure. It was charisma that inspired Thomas Carlyle to compare Webster's heavily black-browed, blazing eyes to anthracite furnaces, and that made the fashionable journalist, Fanny Fern, admit that when Webster kissed the forehead of her grown daughter, she considered it "a sort of baptism." It was charisma that forced people to stop their horses or stick their heads out of windows whenever Webster walked down the street in Boston.[5]

A difficult concept to analyze, charisma is frequently related to a person's physical appearance, and it is important to understand the impression Webster made as a man of flesh and blood. The various Webster statues and busts do not, I think, do justice to the man. He was no more than average height but, in his prime, gave the impression of great size, partly because of his massive chest (bellows to the famous Webster voice) and his enormous head. The head was key. "His brow," someone said, "was to common brows" what the dome of St. Peter's was to the cupolas of small town halls and churches. This period, of course, was the age of phrenology, when intellectual power was equated with head size. Webster's head was measured at 25 inches around, compared to 23¼ for Henry Clay and 23½ for John Quincy Adams. How huge was the great Webster's brain? After he died, it was solemnly weighed, and Webster admirers were gratified to learn that it weighed 63¾ ounces, whereas an average brain weight is 50 ounces. It was one of the largest brains ever measured.[6]

Charismatic power resembles the power of drama. The charismatic agent performs; he does something or says something that establishes a transcendent bond with his audience, a bonding very similar to that achieved through religious experience. In public life, leaders become charismatic actors when they take on ceremonial or symbolic roles vital to the salvation or identity of a people. They become founders like George Washington, liberators like Mahatma Gandhi, revolutionaries like Vladimir Lenin, national restorationists like Adolf Hitler, spiritual leaders like St. Joan, or guardian figures like Daniel Webster.[7]

According to anthropologists, guardian figures play a crucial role in both traditional and modern societies. "The guardians express the ideals of the community. In art drama, celestial choric groups of angels, spirits, or gods are solemn, majestic, and sublime. In community celebrations the guardians address individuals struggling to make sense out of conflicting loyalties, they speak with deep conviction and power, because they speak as the conscience of the community."[8]

The need for guardians in antebellum America is suggested by the many historical monographs that contend that Americans were anxious about the geographic, economic, political, and social changes sweeping their country during this period. On the one hand, they were exhilarated by the possibilities of building a democratic society in a new world. On the other hand, they feared the rush into an uncertain future in which they might lose their vital connection with historic American values. Webster's ability, through his ceremonial speeches, to minister to the psychic needs of Americans growing up in the post–War of 1812 years lifted him out of the ranks of ordinary politics and into the pantheon of cultural heroes. As a guardian figure, he was perceived as a godsend; he became the "Godlike man."[9]

It is significant that Webster never tried to shed his godlike image. Despite notorious fallibilities displayed in his personal life, and his vulnerability in a profession that specializes in cutting all practitioners down to size, he was comfortable with the image. One is tempted to explain this in terms of Webster's ego, which like the Webster brain was one of the largest on record, but we can find a better explanation in the following passage written by Webster himself in 1826.

> When public bodies are to be addressed on momentous occasions, when great interests are at stake, and strong passions excited, nothing is valuable in speech farther than as it is connected with high intellectual and moral endowments. Clearness, force, and earnestness are the qualities which produce conviction. True eloquence, indeed, does not consist in speech. It cannot be brought from far. Labor and learning may toil for it, but they will toil in vain. Words and phrases may be marshalled in every way, but they cannot compass it. It must exist in the man, in the subject, and in the occasion. . . . It comes, if it comes at all, like the outbreaking of a fountain from the earth, or the bursting forth of volcanic fires, with spontaneous, original, native force. . . . This, this is eloquence; or rather it is something greater and higher than all eloquence, it is action, noble, sublime, godlike action.[10]

True eloquence is not an ordinary occurrence; it demands the right person, the right subject, and the right occasion—but when it breaks out, it is godlike. The statement is remarkably self-revealing. It explains why Webster prepared and rehearsed his formal addresses so carefully, and why he was so anxious to perform on the ceremonial occasions that some of his famous contemporaries, like Calhoun, disdained. Webster knew that a godlike reputation was neither a fraud nor a matter of luck. It was something to be earned, and by 1830 he had every right to believe that he had earned his reputation.

Webster delivered his first published oration on July 4 in Hanover when he was eighteen years old, and in it he took up the guardian themes he would return to throughout his career. It would have been an auspicious occasion for any orator, let alone an eighteen-year-old undergraduate student. The Declaration of Independence had been signed only one generation earlier, and Washington, the man whom Webster said "never felt a wound but when it pierced his country, who never groaned but when fair freedom bled," was still fresh in his grave. Like other Fourth of July orators, young and old throughout the country, Webster challenged his listeners to be true to their revolutionary legacy. In those days, and later as a New Hampshire congressman, Webster tended to equate the guardianship of the American tradition with the Federalist party, and after moving to Boston he continued to guard the old ways as a delegate to the Massachusetts Constitutional Convention by successfully fighting off attempts to democratize the state Senate.[11]

Webster made his first great national success as an orator on December 22, 1820, at the First Church in Plymouth, Massachusetts, when the two hundredth anniversary of the landing of the Pilgrims was celebrated. It is difficult to imagine a more historic occasion or a more historic site for an American audience. The symbolism must have been overpowering. George Ticknor, a young Harvard professor who had traveled widely and met most of the great literary men in England and on the Continent, recorded his impressions of that day. Before Webster spoke, Ticknor stood on Plymouth Rock and visited the hill where the Pilgrims had starved and suffered during their first winter. He saw the unmarked burial ground and the mound where the Pilgrims had conferred with Massasoit. Ticknor had previously visited Westminster Abbey and the Colosseum, but the kinship he felt for the simple setting in Plymouth was far more powerful than anything he had felt abroad. As a New Englander and as an American, he knew he stood on consecrated ground.

Inside the crowded church, Ticknor heard Webster appeal directly to the sense of history that was so pervasive on the occasion.

> We have come to this Rock, to record here our homage for our Pilgrim Fathers; our sympathy in their sufferings; our gratitude for their labors; our admiration of their virtues; our veneration for their piety; and our attachments to those principles of civil and religious liberty, which they encountered the dangers of the ocean, the storms of heaven, the violence of savages, disease, exile, and famine, to enjoy and to establish. . . .

Building on his appeal to the audience to reunite themselves to a living past, Webster urged his listeners to recreate the primal scene in their imagination—the fearful voyage, the landing, the deliberations, the suffering, the fortitude, "the mild dignity of Carver and of Bradford, the decisive and soldierlike air and manner of Standish; the devout Brewster, . . . the general firmness and thoughtfulness of the whole band. . . . All of these seem to belong to this place, and to be present upon this occasion, to fill us with reverence and admiration."

But there was a great deal more to Webster's speech than pious obeisance to the Pilgrims. Webster contrasted the first New England colonists with other colonizing people intent on trade and empire. The founders of New England had come to the New World to stay, and they brought with them a way of life based on religious faith and basic republican principles. "They left behind the whole feudal policy of the other continent," Webster said, and they laid the foundation in the New World for a new kind of polity and society in which the widespread distribution of property would support the widespread distribution of power and lead to the development of the most extensive republic in history, as the descendants of the Pilgrims founded new settlements in the American West.[12]

It was the intellectual substance in Webster's remarks as well as the invocations to the sacredness of place that helped overwhelm Ticknor—and there was Webster's eloquence. It is difficult to believe that another talented orator (an Edward Everett perhaps) could have had the same effect. Still, it is not easy to describe Webster's speaking style in great detail. We know that he differed in style from his great Senate adversaries Henry Clay and John C. Calhoun. Webster showed little of Clay's slashing sarcasm and wit, and his style was much less predictable than Calhoun's intense, rapid fire delivery, which piled argument on argument with the regularity of passing freight cars. One close observer said that Webster had three separate styles: the first was slow, deliberate, factual, and didactic; the second, more various and animated; and a third and most powerful style surfaced when he poured out "a perfect torrent of words, his voice loud on a high key, his emphasis sharp and almost screeching, his gesture perpetual and violent, his face alternately flushed and pale."[13]

This last description closely parallels what Webster himself had to say about eloquence, and if we can believe the testimony of his listeners he achieved "true eloquence" at several points in his Plymouth address. This eloquence was most notable, perhaps, in the memorable passage wherein he denounced the continuation of the slave trade "with a power of indignation" Ticknor claimed never to have seen before.

Those who heard Webster at Plymouth never forgot the experience. For the moment, at least, Webster made them forget their worries about a society that seemed to be careening into an uncharted future. He assured them that the legacy of the Pilgrim fathers was solid as the rock, and if they clung to it, their future would be secure. Thousands of Americans never heard Webster at Plymouth, but they read the speech when it was published in revised form a year later. Former President John Adams spoke for many of them when he said the address should be read "every year forever and ever." Neither John Adams nor his son, John Quincy, would ever have thought of Webster as godlike, but George Ticknor, as intellectually sophisticated a young man as you could find in the United States, had seen, heard, and felt the full force of Webster's power. "I was never so excited by public speaking before in my life," he wrote upon leaving the Plymouth Church. "Three or four times I thought my temples would burst with the pulse of blood. . . . When I came out, I was almost afraid to stand near him. It seemed to me he was like the mount that might not be touched and that burned with fire. I was beside myself and am so still."[14]

Five years after Plymouth, Webster was asked to speak at the laying of the cornerstone for the Bunker hill monument on the fiftieth anniversary of that historic battle. Marquis de Lafayette, whose triumphant tour of the United States that year has been likened to the "second coming of Washington," would be present along with surviving Bunker Hill veterans. The occasion offered a magnificent opportunity for the orator of the day, and Webster again made the most of the occasion. Demosthenes had prepared for his great speeches by practicing with pebbles in his mouth. Webster, according to his son, rehearsed for Bunker Hill in the middle of a Cape Cod trout stream, one hand attached to a fishing pole, the other extended to greet his imaginary audience. One the appointed day, Webster was at his charismatic best. As he began to speak, the crowd, numbering in the tens of thousands, began to surge against the platform, threatening to send Lafayette and the Bunker Hill veterans tumbling to the ground and to plunge the ceremony into chaos and hysteria. Upon hearing one of the committee members say it would be impossible to restore order, Webster strode forward and in a voice that seemed to come out of the heavens like a clap of thunder said, "Nothing is impossible sir. Be silent yourself and the people will obey!" And, true to his prediction, the tumult quieted and Webster continued with his speech.

Webster's first Bunker Hill Address is considered one of his best, and generations of schoolboys would commit it to memory. Webster recreated the Battle of Bunker Hill and the entire revolutionary experience. He spoke directly to Lafayette, surrogate son to the immortal Washington, and to the veterans who had fought and bled on that very ground. Under his spell, the past once again came alive to men and women who needed to be reassured that they were commonly bound to a noble and heroic tradition. The time, the place, and the participants offered a resonance for Daniel Webster's words that few American orators have ever enjoyed. A perceptive reporter for the *National Intelligencer* captured the drama of the occasion when he wrote:

> The oration at Bunker Hill was literally delivered to the world. In the open air, exposed to sun and winds, stood an orator ripe with the thoughts of manhood, before all the impressions and glow of early days had gone; myriads of listeners were around him, among them the representatives of other hemispheres; holy men who were just entering eternity . . . the bones of friends & enemies were shaking in their graves beneath the feet of new & old generations, and passing time was announcing that half a century had elapsed since the roar of battle had broke over the sacred ground; the corner stone of a time-defying monument was then resting at his feet, and a hundred thousand bosoms in his sight were swelling and heaving with patriotism and republican pride; how sublime the scene! what a moment for "thoughts that breathe, and words that burn"; and is it not enough to say that all were satisfied.[15]

Not quite one year after the Bunker Hill celebration, Thomas Jefferson and John Adams died on the same day, July 4, 1826, and Daniel Webster was invited to give the memorial service on August 2. Once again he was presented with a unique historic occasion freighted with symbolism. The death of the second and third presidents of the United States within hours of each other on the anniversary of the Declaration of Independence was obviously providential, and there was no more sacred place in the country to memorialize it than Faneuil Hall. Boston businesses were closed on August 2 as a solemn procession led by the governor, the president of the United States, John Quincy Adams, and Daniel Webster proceeded from the State House to a Faneuil Hall draped in black, jammed with an audience that had seized all available seats hours earlier, and surrounded by thousands of other spectators from Boston and far beyond.

In his address to the assemblage, Webster recreated the debates that accompanied the writing of the Declaration of Independence and quoted at length the words he thought John Adams might have spoken. "Sink or swim, live or die, survive or perish, I give my hand and my heart to this vote. It is true, indeed, that in the beginning we aimed not at independence. But there's a Divinity that shapes our ends." Thousands of Americans never realized that this was Webster's language, his dramatic reconstruction of the event. For them, Webster's John Adams and the John Adams of history had fused as one.[16]

Webster's impact on his audiences at Plymouth, Bunker Hill, and Faneuil Hall and on his far greater reading audience (he was read far more widely than any other public man of his time) is difficult for modern Americans to appreciate, partly because oratory has lost its lustre in the age of electronic media and partly because the historical situation and the audiences that he addressed could only occur once in American history. His was an oratory for great occasions.

Daniel Webster's guardianship role, which had grown steadily in the 1820's, especially for New Englanders, became a national phenomenon after his debate with Robert Y. Hayne of South Carolina in the United States Senate in January 1830. Americans at that time had plenty to worry about—their boom and bust economy, lawlessness in their cities and on the frontier, the retreat from religious orthodoxy, the expansion of slavery, and above all the viability of the federal Union. Webster's crowning achievement was to reassure Americans on this last point, and his greatest moment occurred in the encounter with Hayne. The debate, instigated by a partisan political issue, soon ascended to a higher level involving the relative power of the federal government over individual states under the Constitution. Although Webster's nominal opponent in the debate was Senator Hayne, a proud, eloquent, florid-faced Charlestonian, everyone knew that his real adversary was the presiding officer in the Senate, Vice President John C. Calhoun, who had supplied Hayne with his main arguments. For several years southern political leaders, led by Carolinians, had protested vainly about tariff legislation that they believed enriched states in the Northeast at their expense. Responding to this situation, Calhoun had developed a theoretical and constitutional defense for the South that argued for the right of individual states to nullify federal laws contrary to their vital interests. The argument, which followed to a considerable extent the reasoning in the Virginia and Kentucky Resolutions of 1789, was based on the assumption that the United States under the Constitution was not a national community of citizens but a compact of sovereign communities, each of which retained the right to withdraw its consent to federal laws or to secede from the Union.

Following an able presentation of Calhoun's ideas by Hayne, Webster argued that the people of the United States, rather than the states themselves, had created the Constitution and had given separate powers to the state and federal governments. There should therefore be no conflict between states' rights and federal power.

> I hold it to be a popular government, erected by the people; those who administer it, responsible to the people; and itself capable of being amended and modified, just as the people may choose it should be. It is as popular, just as truly emanating from the people, as the State

governments. It is created for one purpose; the State governments for another. It has its own powers, they have theirs. There is no more authority with them to avert the operation of a law of Congress, than with Congress to arrest the operation of their laws. We are here to administer a Constitution emanating immediately from the people, and trusted by them to our administration.

If it became necessary to decide on the constitutionality of a given law, Webster said, the remedy was clear, for the framers of the Constitution had made the Constitution itself "the supreme law of the land." They had extended federal judicial power "to all cases arising under the Constitution and laws of the United States."

These two provisions cover the whole ground. They are, in truth, the keystone of the arch! With these it is a government; without them it is a confederation. In pursuance of these clear and express provisions, Congress established, at its very first session, in the judicial act, a mode for carrying them into full effect, and for bringing all questions of constitutional power to the final decision of the Supreme Court. It then, Sir, became a government. It then had the means of self-protection; and but for this, it would, in all probability, have been now among things which are past.

To proceed on the contrary assumption, as Hayne did, and argue that sovereign states had created the Constitution and remained at liberty to disobey federal laws at their pleasure was to invite anarchy and civil war. This was the moral Webster wanted to leave with the Senate and with the hundreds of thousands of Americans who would soon read his words.

Webster's most famous speech during the debate with Hayne was delivered from twelve pages of notes over a period of two days. A published version revised from the stenographic records appeared in late February and became almost instantly "the most widely read and most influential utterance of its time." To memorize the peroration would become a standard schoolboy exercise.

When my eyes shall be turned to behold for the last time the sun in heaven, may I not see him shining on the broken and dishonored fragments of a once glorious Union; on States dissevered, discordant, belligerent; on a land rent with civil feuds, or drenched, it may be, in fraternal blood! Let their last feeble and lingering glance rather behold the gorgeous ensign of the republic, now known and honored throughout the earth, still full high advanced, its arms and trophies streaming in their original lustre, not a stripe erased or polluted, nor a single star obscured, hearing for its motto, no such miserable interrogatory as "What is all this worth?" nor those other words of delusion and folly,

"Liberty first and Union afterwards"; but everywhere, spread all over in characters of living light, blazing on all its ample folds, as they float over the sea and over the land, and in every wind under the whole heavens, that other sentiment, dear to every true American heart— Liberty *and* Union, now and for ever, one and inseparable![17]

I do not know how many American students could recite those words today. I do know how difficult it is for them to recapture the importance of Webster's argument and rhetoric. Students tend to take the message about liberty and Union for granted, and Webster's language seems overdone, almost baroque. What they and too many of us have forgotten is that Americans in all fifty states identify liberty with Union today largely because Webster made that speech. What did it mean to be an American in 1830? Many of Webster's countrymen were troubled and confused by the question, so fraught with implication for their own identity. Webster in his finest act as a godlike guardian enabled them to identify with a new nation rooted in constitutional order and liberty. To be an American meant believing in the supremacy of the Constitution and the Union. It was a stupendous accomplishment, which Webster made possible by repeatedly living up to his own definition of eloquence—by bringing great gifts and great convictions to great occasions.

For a politician to have a reputation for godlikeness in the rough and tumble democratic culture of young America was a mixed blessing at best. In some ways, the last twenty years of Webster's public career were anticlimactic. Never a serious candidate for the presidency despite his continued visibility, he was drawn increasingly into the bitter political infighting that accompanied the birth of a new party system, and most of his celebrated speeches in the 1830s and early 1840s were in defense of whiggery. In 1843 he returned to Bunker Hill where the monument was now complete. The occasion compared favorably to the earlier ceremony eighteen years earlier, except that Lafayette was not there and President John Tyler was. Tyler had succeeded to his high post upon William Henry Harrison's death and had immediately split the ranks of the victorious Whigs by refusing to support Henry Clay's proposal for a national bank. As secretary of state, Webster had stuck with Tyler long after the other Whig cabinet members had resigned, and inevitably many of these who heard or read his second Bunker Hill oration were more disposed to think of him as a tired politician than as a symbolic leader. In the 1820s Americans had been captured by solemn occasions that recovered the past and reaffirmed their sense of destiny, but the national mood had changed. Now the symbols that counted were log cabins, hard cider, and coonskin caps. Webster had loyally done his part to help put a Whig in the White House in 1840, but the new democratic style would always be alien to him. He did his best the second time around at Bunker Hill, but he stood his ground with the disaffected Whigs. Gracefully acknowledging Tyler's presence, Webster sternly rebuked anyone in attendance who might let partisan concerns intrude on the sacred occasion. "Woe betide the man who brings to this day's worship feeling less than wholly American," he warned, "this column stands on Union."[18]

Although Webster's speech in 1843 did not have the dramatic impact of his earlier address, Emerson could report, "There was the Monument and here was Webster, . . . and the whole occasion was answered by his presence." But there were others in the audience who had begun to sour on Webster, and John Quincy Adams probably spoke for them when he accused Webster of trying to turn Bunker Hill into "a gull trap for popularity, both for himself and for Tyler, by which he hopes to whistle back his Whig friends, whom he had cast off, as a huntsman his pack."[19]

By 1850 the partisan battling of the previous two decades, based largely around economic policy and the giant personalities of leaders like Jackson, Clay, Calhoun, and Webster, had been swallowed up by a crisis at least as dangerous as nullification. An organized antislavery movement, still waiting to be born when Webster had debated Hayne, now threatened to tip the political balance, and the question of what to do about slavery in the new territories acquired through the war with Mexico was threatening to tear the nation apart.

Although Webster had been unwilling to compromise with nullifiers in 1829, he took a different path in 1850. When Henry Clay laid a bill before the Senate that sought to win over the North by admitting California to the Union as a free state while appeasing the South by making it a federal offense to harbor escaped slaves, Webster threw the full weight of his influence and eloquence behind the proposal.

The famous speech of March 7, 1850, was a plea for reconciliation. In his debate with Hayne, Webster had appealed to the past to tie Americans from different parts of the Union together. Now he pleaded for a common understanding of why the slavery issue threatened to destroy the nation. He reminded his listeners that slavery had been accepted by the civilized world for centuries, that it had been a fact of life when the Constitution was ratified, and that the founders of the Union had expected it to disappear as the nation grew. But history had taken a different turn, and earnest, religiously motivated citizens in the North with no economic need for it now found slavery immoral, while Southerners, just as earnest and religious, believed that slavery was both good and essential to their economic survival. Discounting the debate over extending slavery to the West, where he believed it would never be profitable, Webster argued that the real question was whether or not southern citizens should be protected in their constitutional right to hold property in slaves. He knew how strongly slaveholders felt about their inability to retrieve runaways from the North, and he knew that many of his own constituents in Massachusetts had supported personal liberty laws that prevented the return of fugitives to the South. But for Webster, it was not a moral but a constitutional issue, and he sternly rebuked all who felt otherwise. "I put it to all the sober and sound minds at the North," he asked, lumping politicians and abolitionists together, "what right have they . . . to embarrass the free exercise of the rights secured by the Constitution to the persons whose slaves escape from them? None at all; none at all." Abolitionists had been agitating for twenty years, Webster said, with no result except to force the South "not to free, but to bind faster the slave population of the South."

The March 7 speech was Webster's most complete conservative statement, and it rested on the assumption that great reforms in history are gradual, determined more by "the mysterious hand of Providence" than by agitation. When forced to choose, he found himself more sympathetic toward Southerners whose place in history tied them to slavery than toward passionate northern reformers who sought to reroute history on the basis of moral abstractions. "They deal with morals as with mathematics; and they think what is right may be distinguished from what is wrong with the precision of an algebraic equation. . . . They are impatient men; too impatient always to give heed to the admonition of St. Paul, that we are not to 'do evil that good may come'; too impatient to wait for the slow progress of moral causes in the improvement of mankind."[20]

The legislative package known as the Compromise of 1850, including the Fugitive Slave Law, was signed in September 1850. Webster, meanwhile, had become secretary of state for the second time, and in that capacity found himself faced with the responsibility of directing federal marshals to enforce the law. In April 1851, under direct orders from Webster, marshals seized the celebrated fugitive, Thomas Sims, in Boston and transported him to Savannah, Georgia, where he was whipped in a public ceremony. The impact on Webster's reputation in Massachusetts was devastating as thousands of former admirers vented their anger and despair by reciting Whittier's lines:

Of all we loved and honored, naught
Save power remains;
A fallen angel's pride of thought,
Still strong in chains

All else is gone; from those great eyes
The soul has fled:
When faith is lost, when honor dies
The man is dead![21]

Content that he had done his duty and apparently oblivious to the fact that a younger generation, which had loved him once but despised him now, would also make its claim on history, Webster sailed on above the fray. Brushing away the abolitionists as he would a swarm of annoying mosquitoes, he knew he was still a towering figure in most of the country. By far, he was the most experienced statesman to continue in high public office and certainly one of the most famous American political leaders to be denied serious consideration for the presidency. In the winter of 1852, a few weeks before his death, he made his farewell tour, stopping in New York to address the historical society there on a subject apparently far removed from the heated political squabbles of the moment. Claiming it would be a purely literary production, Webster prepared his lecture on "The Dignity and Importance of History" carefully in advance and read it to a large, friendly audience in Niblo's Saloon. The result was a rhetorical tour de force that not only showed off Webster's familiarity with classical and American political history but also revealed his remarkable intellectual curiosity by calling for a new kind of social history, which would not fully attract the attention of scholars until long after his death. Pointing out that nineteenth-century readers hardly knew how their English ancestors were fed, lodged, clothed, or made their living, Webster asked for "a history of firesides; we want to know when kings and queens exchanged beds of straw for beds of down, and ceased to breakfast on beef and beer. We wish to see more, and to know more, of the changes which took place, from age to age, in the homes of England, from the castle and the palace, down to the humblest cottage."[22]

It was Webster's last grand performance, and when he had finished his prepared text with a ringing assertion that nothing in Thucydides, Xenophon, Sallust, or Livy could rival "in its proper grandeur, or its large and lasting influence upon the happiness of mankind" the great scenes surrounding the writing and ratification of the Constitution, he paused and made one final, spontaneous plea for the Union. Now a failed god to many, Daniel Webster knew his role in history and would play it to the end.

1. Theodore Parker, *Additional Speeches, Addresses and Occasional Sermons* (2 vols.; New York, 1864), 1:288, 249; Wendell Phillips, *Speeches, Lectures, and Letters* (Boston, 1863), p. 615.

2. Bliss Perry, ed., *The Heart of Emerson's Journals* (Boston and New York, 1926), pp. 252, 261.

3. Theodore Parker, *A Discourse Occasioned By the Death of Daniel Webster* (Boston, 1853), p. 74.

4. Quoted in David B. Tyack, *George Ticknor and the Boston Brahmins* (Cambridge, Massachusetts, 1967), p. 216.

5. C. E. Norton, ed., *The Correspondence of Thomas Carlyle and Ralph Waldo Emerson* (2 vols.; Boston, 1883), 1:247. The Fanny Fern anecdote is reported among the Webster Papers in an unidentified newspaper clipping in the Princeton Library.

6. S. P. Lyman, *The Public and Private Life of Daniel Webster* (2 vols.; Philadelphia, 1859), 2:223; Nelson Singer and H. S. Drayton, *Heads and Faces and How to Study Them* (New York, 1892), pp. 47, 52.

7. See for example Hugh D. Duncan, *Symbols in Society* (New York, 1968); and Orrin E. Klapp, *Symbolic Leaders: Public Dramas and Public Men* (Chicago, 1964).

8. Duncan, *Symbols in Society*, p. 96.

9. For a good example of the uneasiness of Americans in the 1820, especially in New England, see Fred Somkin, *Unquiet Eagle: Memory and Desire in the Idea of American Freedom, 1815–1860* (Ithaca, 1967).

10. Charles M. Wiltse and Alan R. Berolzheimer, eds., *The Papers of Daniel Webster: Speeches and Formal Writings* (2 vols.; Hanover, N.H. and London, England, 1986–1988), 1:255–56; hereafter cited *Speeches and Formal Writings*. See Document 40, pp. 109–110.

11. Irving H. Bartlett, *Daniel Webster* (New York, 1978), pp. 24, 81–82. For Webster's July 4, 1800, oration, see Document 37, pp. 92–94.

12. This oration, which appears in countless editions, can be conveniently found in James W. McIntyre, ed., *The Writings and Speeches of Daniel Webster* (18 vols.; Boston and New York, 1903), 1:181–226; hereafter cited *Writings and Speeches of Daniel Webster*. See Document 38, pp. 94–99.

13. John Ware, *Memoir of the Life of Henry Ware Jr.* (Boston, 1846), p. 144.

14. George Ticknor Curtis, *Life of Daniel Webster* (2 vols.; New York, 1870), 1:194; Bartlett, *Daniel Webster*, pp. 83–85.

15. *Writings and Speeches of Daniel Webster*, 1:235–54; Bartlett, *Daniel Webster*, pp. 109–11; *The National Intelligencer*, July 17, 1850. For Webster's address at Bunker Hill, see Document 39, pp. 99–104.

16. *Speeches and Formal Writings*, 1:257. See Document 40, pp. 104–113.

17. Both the stenographic and the revised version of Webster's "Second Reply to Hayne" can be found in *Speeches and Formal Writings*, 1:285–395. For a fuller discussion of the debate, see Bartlett, *Daniel Webster*, pp. 108–22. See Document 41, pp. 113–21.

18. *Writings and Speeches of Daniel Webster*, 1:265.

19. Ralph Waldo Emerson, *The Writings of Ralph Waldo Emerson* (New York, 1940), p. 863; Charles Francis Adams, ed., *Memoirs of John Quincy Adams* (12 vols.; Philadelphia, 1874–1877), 11:383.

20. *Speeches and Formal Writings*, 2:513–33. See Document 42, pp. 121–30.

21. The denigration of Webster after the March 7 speech and the return of Sims is analyzed at length in Bartlett, *Daniel Webster*, pp. 254–70.

22. *Speeches and Formal Writings*, 2:627–66. See Document 43, pp. 130–37.

Document 37
Text from *W & S* 15: 475–84.

Oration at Hanover, N.H.,
July 4, 1800.

COUNTRYMEN, BRETHREN, AND FATHERS, We are now assembled to celebrate an anniversary, ever to be held in dear remembrance by the sons of freedom. Nothing less than the birth of a nation, nothing less than the emancipation of three millions of people, from the degrading chains of foreign dominion, is the event we commemorate.

Twenty four years have this day elapsed, since United Columbia first raised the standard of Liberty, and echoed the shouts of Independence!

Those of you, who were then reaping the iron harvest of the martial field, whose bosoms then palpitated for the honor of America, will, at this time, experience a renewal of all that fervent patriotism, of all those indescribable emotions, which then agitated your breasts. As for us, who were either then unborn, or not far enough advanced beyond the threshold of existence, to engage in the grand conflict for Liberty, we now most cordially unite with you, to greet the return of this joyous anniversary, to hail the day that gave us Freedom, and hail the rising glories of our country!

On occasions like this, you have heretofore been addressed, from this stage, on the nature, the origin, the expediency of civil government. The field of political speculation has here been explored, by persons, possessing talents, to which the speaker of the day can have no pretensions. Declining therefore a dissertation on the principles of civil polity, you will indulge me in slightly sketching on those events, which have originated, nurtured, and raised to its present grandeur the empire of Columbia. . . .

The conclusion of the revolutionary war did not conclude the great achievements of our countrymen. Their military character was then, indeed, sufficiently established; but the time was coming, which should prove their political sagacity.

No sooner was peace restored with England, the first grand article of which was the acknowledgment of our Independence, than the old system of confederation, dictated, at first, by necessity, and adopted for the purposes of the moment, was found inadequate to the government of an extensive empire. Under a full conviction of this, we then saw the people of these States engaged in a transaction, which is, undoubtedly, the greatest approximation towards human perfection the political world ever yet experienced; and which, perhaps, will forever stand in the history of mankind, without a parallel. A great Republic, composed of different States, whose interest in all respects could not be perfectly compatible, then came deliberately forward, discarded one system of government and adopted another, without the loss of one man's blood.

There is not a single government now existing in Europe, which is not based in usurpation, and established, if established at all, by the sacrifice of thousands. But in the adoption of our present system of jurisprudence, we see the powers necessary for government, voluntarily springing from the people, their only proper origin, and directed to the public good, their only proper object.

With peculiar propriety, we may now felicitate ourselves, on that happy form of mixed government under which we live. The advantages, resulting to the citizens of the Union, from the operation of the Federal Constitution, are utterly incalculable; and the day, when it was received by a majority of the States, shall stand on the catalogue of American anniversaries, second to none but the birthday of Independence. . . .

With hearts penetrated by unutterable grief, we are at length constrained to ask, where is our Washington? where the hero, who led us to victory—where the man, who gave us freedom? Where is he, who headed our feeble army, when destruction threatened us, who came upon our enemies like the storms of winter; and scattered them like leaves before the Borean blast? Where, O my country! is thy political saviour? where, O humanity! thy favorite son?

The solemnity of this assembly, the lamentations of the American people will answer, alas, he is now no more—the Mighty is fallen!

Yes, Americans, your Washington is gone! he is now consigned to dust, and sleeps in dull, cold marble. The man, who never felt a wound, but when it pierced his country, who never groaned, but when fair freedom bled, is now forever silent! . . .

It becomes us, on whom the defence of our country will ere long devolve, this day, most seriously to reflect on the duties incumbent upon us. Our ancestors bravely snatched expiring liberty from the grasp of Britain, whose touch is poison; shall we now consign it to France, whose embrace is death? We have seen our fathers, in the days of Columbia's trouble, assume the rough habiliments of war, and seek the hostile field. Too full of sorrow to speak, we have seen them wave a last farewell to a disconsolate, a woe-stung family! We have seen them return, worn down with fatigue, and scarred with wounds; or we have seen them, perhaps, no more! For us they fought! for us they bled! for us they conquered! Shall we, their descendants, now basely disgrace our lineage, and pusillanimously disclaim the legacy bequeathed us? Shall we pronounce the sad valediction to freedom, and immolate liberty on the altars our fathers have raised to her? No! The response of a nation is, "No!" Let it be registered in the archives of Heaven!—Ere the religion we profess, and the privileges we enjoy, are sacrificed at the shrines of despots and demagogues, let the pillars of creation tremble! let world be wrecked on world, and systems rush to ruin! Let the sons of Europe be vassals; let her hosts of nations be a vast congregation of slaves; but let us, who are this day free, whose hearts are yet unappalled, and whose right arms are yet nerved for war, assemble before the hallowed temple of Columbian Freedom, and swear, to the God of our Fathers, to preserve it secure, or die at its portals!

Document 38
Text from *W & S* 1: 181–226.

The Plymouth Oration,
December 22, 1820.

Standing in this relation to our ancestors and our posterity, we are assembled on this memorable spot, to perform the duties which that relation and the present occasion impose upon us. We have come to this Rock, to record here our homage for our Pilgrim Fathers; our sympathy in their sufferings; our gratitude for their labors; our admiration of their virtues; our veneration for their piety; and our attachment to those principles of civil and religious liberty, which they encountered the dangers of the ocean, the storms of heaven, the violence of savages, disease, exile, and famine, to enjoy and to establish. And we would leave here, also, for the generations which are rising up rapidly to fill our places, some proof that we have endeavored to transmit the great inheritance unimpaired; that in our estimate of public principles and private virtue, in our veneration of religion and piety, in our devotion to civil and religious liberty, in our regard for whatever advances human knowledge or improves human happiness, we are not altogether unworthy of our origin.

There is a local feeling connected with this occasion, too strong to be resisted; a sort of *genius of the place*, which inspires and awes us. We feel that we are on the spot where the first scene of our history was laid; where the hearths and altars of New England were first placed; where Christianity, and civilization, and letters made their first lodgement, in a vast extent of country, covered with a wilderness, and peopled by roving barbarians. We are here, at the season of the year at which the event took place. The imagination irresistibly and rapidly draws around us the principal features and the leading characters in the original scene. We cast our eyes abroad on the ocean, and we see where the little bark, with the interesting group upon its deck, made its slow progress to the shore. We look around us, and behold the hills and promontories where the anxious eyes of our fathers first saw the places of habitation and of rest. We feel the cold which benumbed, and listen to the winds which pierced them. Beneath us is the Rock, on which New England received the feet of the Pilgrims. We seem even to behold them, as they struggle with the elements, and, with toilsome efforts, gain the shore. We listen to the chiefs in council; we see the unexampled exhibition of female fortitude and resignation; we hear the whisperings of youthful impatience, and we see, what a painter of our own has also represented by his pencil,[1] chilled and shivering childhood, houseless, but for a mother's arms, couchless, but for a mother's breast, till our own blood almost freezes. The mild dignity of [John] CARVER and of [William] BRADFORD; the decisive and soldierlike air and manner of [Miles] STANDISH; the devout [William] BREWSTER; the enterprising [Isaac] ALLERTON; the general firmness and thoughtfulness of the whole band; their conscious joy for dangers escaped; their deep solicitude about dangers to come; their trust in Heaven; their high religious faith, full of confidence and anticipation; all of these seem to belong to this place, and to be present upon this occasion, to fill us with reverence and admiration. . . .

The nature and constitution of society and government in this country are interesting topics, to which I would devote what remains of the time allowed to this occasion. Of our system of government the first thing to be said is, that it is really and practically a free system. It originates entirely with the people, and rests on no other foundation than their assent. To judge of its actual operation, it is not enough to look merely at the form of its construction. The practical character of government depends often on a variety of considerations, besides the abstract frame of its constitutional organization. Among these are the condition and tenure of property; the laws regulating its alienation and descent; the presence or absence of a military power; an armed or unarmed yeomanry; the spirit of the age, and the degree of general intelligence. In these respects it cannot be denied that the circumstances of this country are most favorable to the hope of maintaining the government of a great nation on principles entirely popular. In the absence of military power, the nature of government must essentially depend on the manner in which property is holden and distributed. There is a natural influence belonging to property, whether it exists in many hands or few; and it is on the rights of property that both despotism and unrestrained popular violence ordinarily commence their attacks. Our ancestors began their system of government here under a condition of comparative equality in regard to wealth, and their early laws were of a nature to favor and continue this equality.

A republican form of government rests not more on political constitutions, than on those laws which regulate the descent and transmission of property. Governments like ours could not have been maintained, where property was holden according to the principles of the feudal system; nor, on the other hand, could the feudal constitution possibly exist with us. Our New England ancestors brought hither no great capitals from Europe; and if they had, there was nothing productive in which they could have been invested. They left behind them the whole feudal policy of the other continent. They broke away at once from the system of military service established in the Dark Ages, and which continues, down even to the present time, more or less to affect the condition of property all over Europe. They came to a new country. There were, as yet, no lands yielding rent, and no tenants rendering service. The whole soil was unreclaimed from barbarism. They were themselves, either from their original condition, or from the necessity of their common interest, nearly on a general level in respect to property. Their situation demanded a parcelling out and division of the lands, and it may be fairly said, that this necessary act *fixed the future frame and form of their government.* The character of their political institutions was determined by the fundamental laws respecting property. The laws rendered estates divisible among sons and daughters. The right of primogeniture, at first limited and curtailed, was afterwards abolished. The property was all freehold. The entailment of estates, long trusts, and the other processes for fettering and tying up inheritances, were not applicable to the condition of society, and seldom made use of.

The true principle of a free and popular government would seem to be, so to construct it as to give to all, or at least to a very great majority, an interest in its preservation; to round it, as other things are rounded, on men's interest. The stability of government demands that those who desire its continuance should be more powerful than those who desire its dissolution. This power, of course, is not always to be measured by mere numbers. Education, wealth, talents, are all parts and elements of the general aggregate of power; but numbers, nevertheless, constitute ordinarily the most important consideration, unless, indeed, there be a *military force* in the hands of the few, by which they can control the many. In this country we have actually existing systems of government, in the maintenance of which, it should seem, a great majority, both in numbers and in other means of power and influence, must see their interest. But this state of things is not brought about solely by written political constitutions, or the mere manner of organizing the government; but also by the laws which regulate the descent and transmission of property. The freest government, if it could exist, would not be long acceptable, if the tendency of the laws were to create a rapid accumulation of property in few hands, and to render the great mass of the population dependent and penniless. In such a case, the popular power would be likely to break in upon the rights of property, or else the influence of property to limit and control the exercise of popular power. Universal suffrage, for example, could not long exist in a community where there was great inequality of property. The holders of estates would be obliged, in such case, in some way to restrain the right of suffrage, or else such right of suffrage would, before long, divide the property. In the nature of things, those who have not property, and see their neighbors possess much more than they think them to need, cannot be favorable to laws made for the protection of property. When this class becomes numerous, it grows clamorous. It looks on property as its prey and plunder, and is naturally ready, at all times, for violence and revolution.

It would seem, then, to be the part of political wisdom to found government on property; and to establish such distribution of property, by the laws which regulate its transmission and alienation, as to interest the great majority of society in the support of the government. This is, I imagine, the true theory and the actual practice of our republican institutions. . . .

I deem it my duty on this occasion to suggest, that the land is not yet wholly free from the contamination of a traffic, at which every feeling of humanity must for ever revolt,—I mean the African slave-trade. Neither public sentiment, nor the law, has hitherto been able entirely to put an end to this odious and abominable trade. At the moment when God in his mercy has blessed the Christian world with a universal peace, there is reason to fear, that, to the disgrace of the Christian name and character, new efforts are making for the extension of this trade by subjects and citizens of Christian states, in whose hearts there dwell no sentiments of humanity or of justice, and over whom neither the fear of God nor the fear of man exercises a control. In the sight of our law, the African slave-trader is a pirate and a felon; and in the sight of Heaven, an offender far beyond the ordinary depth of human guilt. There is no brighter page of our history, than that which records the measures which have been adopted by the government at an early day, and at different times since, for the suppression of this traffic; and I would call on all the true sons of New England to cooperate with the laws of man, and the justice of Heaven. If there be, within the extent of our knowledge or influence, any participation in this traffic, let us pledge ourselves here, upon the rock of Plymouth, to extirpate and destroy it. It is not fit that the land of the Pilgrims should bear the shame longer. I hear the sound of the hammer, I see the smoke of the furnaces where manacles and fetters are still forged for human limbs. I see the visages of those who by stealth and at midnight labor in this work of hell, foul and dark, as may become the artificers of such instruments of misery and torture. Let that spot be purified, or let it cease to be of New England. Let it be purified, or let it be set aside from the Christian world; let it be put out of the circle of human sympathies and human regards, and let civilized man henceforth have no communion with it. . . .

The hours of this day are rapidly flying, and this occasion will soon be passed. Neither we nor our children can expect to behold its return. They are in the distant regions of futurity, they exist only in the all-creating power of God, who shall stand here a hundred years hence, to trace, through us, their descent from the Pilgrims, and to survey, as we have now surveyed, the progress of their country, during the lapse of a century. We would anticipate their concurrence with us in our sentiments of deep regard for our common ancestors. We would anticipate and partake the pleasure with which they will then recount the steps of New England's advancement. On the morning of that day, although it will not disturb us in our repose, the voice of acclamation and gratitude, commencing on the Rock of Plymouth, shall be transmitted through millions of the sons of the Pilgrims, till it lose itself in the murmurs of the Pacific seas.

We would leave for the consideration of those who shall then occupy our places, some proof that we hold the blessings transmitted from our fathers in just estimation; some proof of our attachment to the cause of good government, and of civil and religious liberty; some proof of a sincere and ardent desire to promote every thing which may enlarge the understandings and improve the hearts of men. And when, from the long distance of a hundred years, they shall look back upon us, they shall know, at least, that we possessed affections, which, running backward and warming with gratitude for what our ancestors have done for our happiness, run forward also to our posterity, and meet them with cordial salutation, ere yet they have arrived on the shore of being.

Advance, then, ye future generations! We would hail you, as you rise in your long succession, to fill the places which we now fill, and to taste the blessings of existence where we are passing, and soon shall have passed, our own human duration. We bid you welcome to this pleasant land of the fathers. We bid you welcome to the healthful skies and the verdant fields of New England. We greet your accession to the great inheritance which we have enjoyed. We welcome you to the blessings of good government and religious liberty. We welcome you to the treasures of science and the delights of learning. We welcome you to the transcendent sweets of domestic life, to the happiness of kindred, and parents, and children. We welcome you to the immeasurable blessings of rational existence, the immortal hope of Christianity, and the light of everlasting truth!

1. The reference is to a large painting of the landing of the Pilgrims at Plymouth by Henry Sargent.

Document 39
Text from *W & S* 1: 235–54.

The Bunker Hill Monument,
June 17, 1825.

This uncounted multitude before me and around me proves the feeling which the occasion has excited. These thousands of human faces, glowing with sympathy and joy, and from the impulses of a common gratitude turned reverently to heaven in this spacious temple of the firmament, proclaim that the day, the place, and the purpose of our assembling have made a deep impression on our hearts.

If, indeed, there be any thing in local association fit to affect the mind of man, we need not strive to repress the emotions which agitate us here. We are among the sepulchres of our fathers. We are on ground, distinguished by their valor, their constancy, and the shedding of their blood. We are here, not to fix an uncertain date in our annals, nor to draw into notice an obscure and unknown spot. If our humble purpose had never been conceived, if we ourselves had never been born, the 17th of June, 1775, would have been a day on which all subsequent history would have poured its light, and the eminence where we stand a point of attraction to the eyes of successive generations. But we are Americans. We live in what may be called the early age of this great continent; and we know that our posterity, through all time, are here to enjoy and suffer the allotments of humanity. We see before us a probable train of great events; we know that our own fortunes have been happily cast; and it is natural, therefore, that we should be moved by the contemplation of occurrences which have guided our destiny before many of us were born, and settled the condition in which we should pass that portion of our existence which God allows to men on earth.

We do not read even of the discovery of this continent, without feeling something of a personal interest in the event; without being reminded how much it has affected our own fortunes and our own existence. It would be still more unnatural for us, therefore, than for others, to contemplate with unaffected minds that interesting, I may say that most touching and pathetic scene, when the great discoverer of America stood on the deck of his shattered bark, the shades of night falling on the sea, yet no man sleeping; tossed on the billows of an unknown ocean, yet the stronger billows of alternate hope and despair tossing his own troubled thoughts; extending forward his harassed frame, straining westward his anxious and eager eyes, till Heaven at last granted him a moment of rapture and ecstasy, in blessing his vision with the sight of the unknown world.

Nearer to our times, more closely connected with our fates, and therefore still more interesting to our feelings and affections, is the settlement of our own country by colonists from England. We cherish every memorial of these worthy ancestors; we celebrate their patience and fortitude; we admire their daring enterprise; we teach our children to venerate their piety; and we are justly proud of being descended from men who have set the world an example of founding civil institutions on the great and united principles of human freedom and human knowledge. To us, their children, the story of their labors and sufferings can never be without its interest. We shall not stand unmoved on the shore of Plymouth, while the sea continues to wash it; nor will our brethren in another early and ancient Colony forget the place of its first establishment, till their river shall cease to flow by it. No vigor of youth, no maturity of manhood, will lead the nation to forget the spots where its infancy was cradled and defended.

But the great event in the history of the continent, which we are now met here to commemorate, that prodigy of modern times, at once the wonder and the blessing of the world, is the American Revolution. In a day of extraordinary prosperity and happiness, of high national honor, distinction, and power, we are brought together, in this place, by our love of country, by our admiration of exalted character, by our gratitude for signal services and patriotic devotion. . . .

VENERABLE MEN! you have come down to us from a former generation. Heaven has bounteously lengthened out your lives, that you might behold this joyous day. You are now where you stood fifty years ago, this very hour, with your brothers and your neighbors, shoulder to shoulder, in the strife for your country. Behold, how altered! The same heavens are indeed over your heads; the same ocean rolls at your feet; but all else how changed! You hear now no roar of hostile cannon, you see no mixed volumes of smoke and flame rising from burning Charlestown. The ground strowed with the dead and the dying; the impetuous charge; the steady and successful repulse; the loud call to repeated assault; the summoning of all that is manly to repeated resistance; a thousand bosoms freely and fearlessly bared in an instant to whatever of terror there may be in war and death;—all these you have witnessed, but you witness them no more. All is peace. The heights of yonder metropolis, its towers and roofs, which you then saw filled with wives and children and countrymen in distress and terror, and looking with unutterable emotions for the issue of the combat, have presented you to-day with the sight of its whole happy population, come out to welcome and greet you with a universal jubilee. Yonder proud ships, by a felicity of position appropriately lying at the foot of this mount, and seeming fondly to cling around it, are not means of annoyance to you, but your country's own means of distinction and defence. All is peace; and God has granted you this sight of your country's happiness, ere you slumber in the grave. He has allowed you to behold and to partake the reward of your patriotic toils; and he has allowed us, your sons and countrymen, to meet you here, and in the name of the present generation, in the name of your country, in the name of liberty, to thank you! . . .

The great wheel of political revolution began to move in America.

Here its rotation was guarded, regular, and safe. Transferred to the other continent, from unfortunate but natural causes, it received an irregular and violent impulse; it whirled along with a fearful celerity; till at length, like the chariot-wheels in the races of antiquity, it took fire from the rapidity of its own motion, and blazed onward, spreading conflagration and terror around.

We learn from the result of this experiment, how fortunate was our own condition, and how admirably the character of our people was calculated for setting the great example of popular governments. The possession of power did not turn the heads of the American people, for they had long been in the habit of exercising a great degree of self-control. Although the paramount authority of the parent state existed over them, yet a large field of legislation had always been open to our Colonial assemblies. They were accustomed to representative bodies and the forms of free government; they understood the doctrine of the division of power among different branches, and the necessity of checks on each. The character of our countrymen, moreover, was sober, moral, and religious; and there was, little in the change to shock their feelings of justice and humanity, or even to disturb an honest prejudice. We had no domestic throne to overturn, no privileged orders to cast down, no violent changes of property to encounter. In the American Revolution, no man sought or wished for more than to defend and enjoy his own. None hoped for plunder or for spoil. Rapacity was unknown to it; the axe was not among the instruments of its accomplishment; and we all know that it could not have lived a single day under any well-founded imputation of possessing a tendency adverse to the Christian religion.

It need not surprise us, that, under circumstances less auspicious, political revolutions elsewhere, even when well intended, have terminated differently. It is, indeed, a great achievement, it is the master-work of the world, to establish governments entirely popular on lasting foundations; nor is it easy, indeed, to introduce the popular principle at all into governments to which it has been altogether a stranger. It cannot be doubted, however, that Europe has come out of the contest, in which she has been so long engaged, with greatly superior knowledge, and, in many respects, in a highly improved condition. Whatever benefit has been acquired is likely to be retained, for it consists mainly in the acquisition of more enlightened ideas. And although kingdoms and provinces may be wrested from the hands that hold them, in the same manner they were obtained; although ordinary and vulgar power may, in human affairs, be lost as it has been won; yet it is the glorious prerogative of the empire of knowledge, that what it gains it never loses. On the contrary, it increases by the multiple of its own power; all its ends become means; all its attainments, helps to new conquests. Its whole abundant harvest is but so much seed wheat, and nothing has limited, and nothing can limit, the amount of ultimate product.

Under the influence of this rapidly increasing knowledge, the people have begun, in all forms of government, to think, and to reason, on affairs of state. Regarding government as an institution for the public good, they demand a knowledge of its operations, and a participation in its exercise. A call for the representative system, wherever it is not enjoyed, and where there is already intelligence enough to estimate its value, is perseveringly made. Where men may speak out, they demand it; where the bayonet is at their throats, they pray for it. . . .

And, now, let us indulge an honest exultation in the conviction of the benefit which the example of our country has produced, and is likely to produce, on human freedom and human happiness. Let us endeavor to comprehend in all its magnitude, and to feel in all its importance, the part assigned to us in the great drama of human affairs. We are placed at the head of the system of representative and popular governments. Thus far our example shows that such governments are compatible, not only with respectability and power, but with repose, with peace, with security of personal rights, with good laws, and a just administration.

We are not propagandists. Wherever other systems are preferred, either as being thought better in themselves, or as better suited to existing condition, we leave the preference to be enjoyed. Our history hitherto proves, however, that the popular form is practicable, and that with wisdom and knowledge men may govern themselves; and the duty incumbent on us is, to preserve the consistency of this cheering example, and take care that nothing may weaken its authority with the world. If, in our case, the representative system ultimately fail, popular governments must be pronounced impossible. No combination of circumstances more favorable to the experiment can ever be expected to occur. The last hopes of mankind, therefore, rest with us; and if it should be proclaimed, that our example had become an argument against the experiment, the knell of popular liberty would be sounded throughout the earth.

These are excitements to duty; but they are not suggestions of doubt. Our history and our condition, all that is gone before us, and all that surrounds us, authorize the belief, that popular governments, though subject to occasional variations, in form perhaps not always for the better, may yet, in their general character, be as durable and permanent as other systems. We know, indeed, that in our country any other is impossible. The *principle* of free governments adheres to the American soil. It is bedded in it, immovable as its mountains.

And let the sacred obligations which have devolved on this generation, and on us, sink deep into our hearts. Those who established our liberty and our government are daily dropping from among us. The great trust now descends to new hands. Let us apply ourselves to that which is presented to us, as our appropriate object. We can win no laurels in a war for independence. Earlier and worthier hands have gathered them all. Nor are there places for us by the side of Solon, and Alfred, and other founders of states. Our fathers have filled them. But there remains to us a great duty of defence and preservation, and there is opened to us, also, a noble pursuit, to which the spirit of the times strongly invites us. Our proper business is improvement. Let our age be the age of improvement. In a day of peace, let us advance the arts of peace and the works of peace. Let us develop the resources of our land, call forth its powers, build up its institutions, promote all its great interests, and see whether we also, in our day and generation, may not perform something worthy to be remembered. Let us cultivate a true spirit of union and harmony. In pursuing the great objects which our condition points out to us, let us act under a settled conviction, and an habitual feeling, that these twenty-four States are one country. Let our conceptions be enlarged to the circle of our duties. Let us extend our ideas over the whole of the vast field in which we are called to act. Let our object be, OUR COUNTRY, OUR WHOLE COUNTRY, AND NOTHING BUT OUR COUNTRY. And, by the blessing of God, may that country itself become a vast and splendid monument, not of oppression and terror, but of Wisdom, of Peace, and of Liberty, upon which the world may gaze with admiration for ever!

Document 40
Text from *Speeches and Formal Writings* 1: 237–71.

Adams and Jefferson,
August 2, 1826.

This is an unaccustomed spectacle. For the first time, fellow-citizens, badges of mourning shroud the columns and overhang the arches of this hall. These walls, which were consecrated, so long ago, to the cause of American liberty, which witnessed her infant struggles and rung with the shouts of her earliest victories, proclaim, now, that distinguished friends and champions of that great cause have fallen. It is right that it should be thus. The tears which flow, and the honors that are paid, when the founders of the republic die, give hope that the republic itself may be immortal. It is fit that, by public assembly and solemn observance, by anthem and by eulogy, we commemorate the services of national benefactors, extol their virtues, and render thanks to God for eminent blessings, early given and long continued, through their agency, to our favored country.

ADAMS and JEFFERSON are no more; and we are assembled, fellow-citizens, the aged, the middle-aged and the young, by the spontaneous impulse of all, under the authority of the municipal government, with the presence of the chief magistrate of the Commonwealth, and others its official representatives, the University, and the learned societies, to bear our part in those manifestations of respect and gratitude which pervade the whole land. ADAMS and JEFFERSON are no more. On our fiftieth anniversary, the great day of national jubilee, in the very hour of public rejoicing, in the midst of echoing and reechoing voices of thanksgiving, while their own names were on all tongues, they took their flight together to the world of spirits.

If it be true that no one can safely be pronounced happy while he lives, if that event which terminates life can alone crown its honors and its glory, what felicity is here! The great epic of their lives, how happily concluded! Poetry itself has hardly terminated illustrious lives, and finished the career of earthly renown, by such a consummation. If we had the power, we could not wish to reverse this dispensation of the Divine Providence. The great objects of life were accomplished, the drama was ready to be closed. It has closed; our patriots have fallen; but so fallen, at such age, with such coincidence, on such a day, that we cannot rationally lament that that end has come, which we knew could not be long deferred.

Neither of these great men, fellow-citizens, could have died, at any time, without leaving an immense void in our American society. They have been so intimately, and for so long a time, blended with the history of the country, and especially so united, in our thoughts and recollections, with the events of the Revolution, that the death of either would have touched the chords of public sympathy. We should have felt that one great link, connecting us with former times, was broken; that we had lost something more, as it were, of the presence of the Revolution itself, and of the act of independence, and were driven on, by another great remove from the days of our country's early distinction, to meet posterity and to mix with the future. Like the mariner, whom the currents of the ocean and the winds carry along till he sees the stars which have directed his course and lighted his pathless way descend one by one, beneath the rising horizon, we should have felt that the stream of time had borne us onward till another great luminary, whose light had cheered us and whose guidance we had followed, had sunk away from our sight.

But the concurrence of their death on the anniversary of Independence has naturally awakened stronger emotions. Both had been Presidents, both had lived to great age, both were early patriots, and both were distinguished and ever honored by their immediate agency in the act of independence. It cannot but seem striking and extraordinary, that these two should live to see the fiftieth year from the date of that act; that they should complete that year; and that then, on the day which had fast linked for ever their own fame with their country's glory, the heavens should open to receive them both at once. As their lives themselves were the gifts of Providence, who is not willing to recognize in their happy termination, as well as in their long continuance, proofs that our country and its benefactors are objects of His care?

ADAMS and JEFFERSON, I have said, are no more. As human beings, indeed, they are no more. They are no more, as in 1776, bold and fearless advocates of independence; no more, as at subsequent periods, the head of the government; no more, as we have recently seen them, aged and venerable objects of admiration and regard. They are no more. They are dead. But how little is there of the great and good which can die! To their country they yet live, and live for ever. They live in all that perpetuates the remembrance of men on earth; in the recorded proofs of their own great actions, in the offspring of their intellect, in the deep-engraved lines of public gratitude, and in the respect and homage of mankind. They live in their example; and they live, emphatically, and will live, in the influence which their lives and efforts, their principles and opinions, now exercise, and will continue to exercise, on the affairs of men, not only in their own country but throughout the civilized world. A superior and commanding human intellect, a truly great man, when Heaven vouchsafes so rare a gift, is not a temporary flame, burning brightly for a while, and then giving place to returning darkness. It is rather a spark of fervent heat, as well as radiant light, with power to enkindle the common mass of human kind; so that when it glimmers in its own decay, and finally goes out in death, no night follows, but it leaves the world all light, all on fire from the potent contact of its own spirit. Bacon died; but the human understanding, roused by the touch of his miraculous wand to a perception of the true philosophy and the just mode of inquiring after truth, has kept on its course successfully and gloriously. Newton died; yet the courses of the spheres are still known, and they yet move on by the laws which he discovered, and in the orbits which he saw, and described for them, in the infinity of space.

No two men now live, fellow-citizens, perhaps it may be doubted whether any two men have ever lived in one age, who, more than those we now commemorate, have impressed on mankind their own sentiments in regard to politics and government, infused their own opinions more deeply into the opinions of others, or given a more lasting direction to the current of human thought. Their work doth not perish with them. The tree which they assisted to plant will flourish, although they water it and protect it no longer; for it has struck its roots deep, it has sent them to the very centre; no storm, not of force to burst the orb, can overturn it; its branches spread wide; they stretch their protecting arms broader and broader, and its top is destined to reach the heavens. We are not deceived. There is no delusion here. No age will come in which the American Revolution will appear less than it is, one of the greatest events in human history. No age will come in which it shall cease to be seen and felt, on either continent, that a mighty step, a great advance, not only in American affairs, but in human affairs, was made on the 4th of July, 1776. And no age will come, we trust, so ignorant or so unjust as not to see and acknowledge the efficient agency of those we now honor in producing that momentous event.

We are not assembled, therefore, fellow-citizens, as men overwhelmed with calamity by the sudden disruption of the ties of friendship or affection, or as in despair for the republic by the untimely blighting of its hopes. Death has not surprised us by an unseasonable blow. We have, indeed, seen the tomb close, but it has closed only over mature years, over long-protracted public service, over the weakness of age, and over life itself only when the ends of living had been fulfilled. These suns, as they rose slowly and steadily, amidst clouds and storms, in their ascendant, so they have not rushed from their meridian to sink suddenly in the west. Like the mildness, the serenity, the continuing benignity of a summer's day, they have gone down with slow-descending, grateful long-lingering light; and now that they are beyond the visible margin of the world, good omens cheer us from "the bright track of their fiery car"!

There were many points of similarity in the lives and fortunes of these great men. They belonged to the same profession, and had pursued its studies and its practice for unequal lengths of time indeed, but with diligence and effect. Both were learned and able lawyers. They were natives and inhabitants, respectively of those two of the Colonies which at the Revolution were the largest and most powerful and which naturally had a lead in the political affairs of the times. When the Colonies became in some degree united by the assembling of a general Congress, they were brought to act together in its deliberations, not indeed at the same time but both at early periods. Each had already manifested his attachment to the cause of the country, as well as his ability to maintain it, by printed addresses, public speeches, extensive correspondence, and whatever other mode could be adopted for the purpose of exposing the encroachments of the British Parliament, and animating the people to a manly resistance. Both were not only decided, but early, friends of Independence. While others yet doubted, they were resolved; where others hesitated they pressed forward. They were both members of the committee for preparing the Declaration of Independence, and they constituted the sub-committee appointed by the other members to make the draft. They left their seats in Congress, being called to other public employments at periods not remote from each other, although one of them returned to it afterwards for a short time. Neither of them was of the assembly of great men which formed the present Constitution, and neither was at any time a member of Congress under its provisions. Both have been public ministers abroad, both Vice-Presidents and both Presidents of the United States. These coincidences are now singularly crowned and completed. They have died together; and they died on the anniversary of liberty. . . .

And now, fellow-citizens, without pursuing the biography of these illustrious men further, for the present let us turn our attention to the most prominent act of their lives, their participation in the DECLARA-TION OF INDEPENDENCE. . . .

It has sometimes been said, as if it were a derogation from the merits of this paper, that it contains nothing new; that it only states grounds of proceeding and presses topics of argument, which had often been stated and pressed before. But it was not the object of the Declaration to produce any thing new. It was not to invent reasons for independence, but to state those which governed the Congress. For great and sufficient causes, it was proposed to declare independence; and the proper business of the paper to be drawn was to set forth those causes, and justify the authors of the measure, in any event of fortune, to the country and to posterity. The cause of American independence, moreover, was now to be presented to the world in such manner; if it might so be, as to engage its sympathy, to command its respect, to attract its admiration; and in an assembly of most able and distinguished men, THOMAS JEFFERSON had the high honor of being the selected advocate of this cause. To say that he performed his great work well, would be doing him injustice. To say that he did excellently well, admirably well, would be inadequate and halting praise. Let us rather say, that he so discharged the duty assigned him, that all Americans may well rejoice that the work of drawing the title-deed of their liberties devolved upon him. . . .

The Congress of the Revolution, fellow-citizens, sat with closed doors, and no report of its debates was ever made. The discussion, therefore, which accompanied this great measure, has never been preserved, except in memory and by tradition. But it is, I believe, doing no injustice to others to say, that the general opinion was, and uniformly has been, that in debate, on the side of independence, JOHN ADAMS had no equal. The great author of the Declaration himself has expressed that opinion uniformly and strongly. JOHN ADAMS, said he, in the hearing of him who has now the honor to address you, JOHN ADAMS was our colossus on the floor. Not graceful, not elegant, not always fluent, in his public addresses, he yet came out with a power, both of thought and of expression, which moved us from our seats.
. . . [1]

The eloquence of Mr. Adams resembled his general character, and formed, indeed, a part of it. It was bold, manly, and energetic; and such the crisis required. When public bodies are to be addressed on momentous occasions, when great interests are at stake, and strong passions excited, nothing is valuable in speech farther than as it is connected with high intellectual and moral endowments. Clearness, force, and earnestness are the qualities which produce conviction. True eloquence, indeed, does not consist in speech. It cannot be brought from far. Labor and learning may toil for it, but they will toil in vain. Words and phrases may be marshalled in every way, but they cannot compass it. It must exist in the man, in the subject, and in the occasion. Affected passion, intense expression, the pomp of declamation, all may aspire to it; they cannot reach it. It comes, if it comes at all, like the outbreaking of a fountain from the earth, or the bursting forth of volcanic fires, with spontaneous, original, native force. The graces taught in the schools, the costly ornaments and studied contrivances of speech, shock and disgust men, when their own lives, and the fate of their wives, their children, and their country, hang on the decision of the hour. Then words have lost their power, rhetoric is vain, and all elaborate oratory contemptible. Even genius itself then feels rebuked and subdued, as in the presence of higher qualities. Then patriotism is eloquent; then self-devotion is eloquent. The clear conception, outrunning the deductions of logic, the high purpose, the firm resolve, the dauntless spirit, speaking on the tongue, beaming from the eye, informing every feature, and urging the whole man onward, right onward to his object this, this is eloquence; or rather it is something greater and higher than all eloquence, it is action, noble, sublime, godlike action. . . .

Let us, then, bring before us the assembly, which was about to decide a question thus big with the fate of empire. Let us open their doors and look in upon their deliberations. Let us survey the anxious and care-worn countenances, let us hear the firm-toned voices, of this band of patriots.

HANCOCK presides over the solemn sitting; and one of those not yet prepared to pronounce for absolute independence is on the floor, and is urging his reasons for dissenting from the declaration.

"Let us pause! This step, once taken, cannot be retraced. This resolution, once passed, will cut off all hope of reconciliation. If success attend the arms of England, we shall then be no longer Colonies, with charters and with privileges; these will all be forfeited by this act; and we shall be in the condition of other conquered people, at the mercy of the conquerors. For ourselves, we may be ready to run the hazard; but are we ready to carry the country to that length? Is success so probable as to justify it? Where is the military, where the naval power, by which we are to resist the whole strength of the arm of England, for she will exert that strength to the utmost? Can we rely on the constancy and perseverance of the people? or will they not act as the people of other countries have acted and, wearied with a long war, submit, in the end, to a worse oppression? While we stand on our old ground, and insist on redress of grievances, we know we are right, and are not answerable for consequences. Nothing, then, can be imputed to us. But if we now change our object, carry our pretensions farther, and set up for absolute independence, we shall lose the sympathy of mankind. We shall no longer be defending what we possess, but struggling for something which we never did possess, and which we have solemnly and uniformly disclaimed all intention of pursuing, from the very outset of the troubles. Abandoning thus our old ground, of resistance only to arbitrary acts of oppression, the nations will believe the whole to have been mere pretence, and they will look on us, not as injured, but as ambitious subjects. I shudder before this responsibility. It will be on us, if, relinquishing the ground on which we have stood so long, and stood so safely, we now proclaim independence, and carry on the war for that object, while these cities burn, these pleasant fields whiten and bleach with the bones of their owners, and these streams run blood. It will be upon us, it will be upon us, if, failing to maintain this unseasonable and ill-judged declaration, a sterner despotism, maintained by military power, shall be established over our posterity, when we ourselves, given up by an exhausted, a harassed, misled people, shall have expiated our rashness and atoned for our presumption on the scaffold."

It was for Mr. Adams to reply to arguments like these. We know his opinions, and we know his character. He would commence with his accustomed directness and earnestness.

"Sink or swim, live or die, survive or perish, I give my hand and my heart to this vote. It is true, indeed, that in the beginning we aimed not at independence. But there's a Divinity which shapes our ends. The injustice of England has driven us to arms; and blinded to her own interest for our good, she has obstinately persisted, till independence is now within our grasp. We have but to reach forth to it, and it is ours. Why, then, should we defer the Declaration? Is any man so weak as now to hope for a reconciliation with England, which shall leave either safety to the country and its liberties, or safety to his own life and his own honor? Are not you, Sir, who sit in that chair, is not he, our venerable colleague near you, are you not both already the proscribed and predestined objects of punishment and of vengeance? Cut off from all hope of royal clemency, what are you, what can you be, while the power of England remains, but outlaws? If we postpone independence, do we mean to carry on, or to give up, the war? Do we mean to submit to the measures of Parliament, Boston Port Bill and all? Do we mean to submit, and consent that we ourselves shall be ground to powder, and our country and its rights trodden down in the dust? I know we do not mean to submit. We never shall submit. Do we intend to violate that most solemn obligation ever entered into by men, that plighting, before God, of our sacred honor to Washington, when, putting forth to incur the dangers of war, as well as the political hazards of the times, we promised to adhere to him, in every extremity, with our fortunes and our lives? I know there is not a man here, who would not rather see a general conflagration sweep over the land, or an earthquake sink it, than one jot or tittle of that plighted faith fall to the ground. For myself, having, twelve months ago, in this place, moved you, that George Washington be appointed commander of the forces raised, or to be raised, for defence of American liberty, may my right hand forget her cunning, and my tongue cleave to the roof of my mouth, if I hesitate or waver in the support I give him. . . ."

And now, fellow-citizens, let us not retire from this occasion without a deep and solemn conviction of the duties which have devolved upon us. This lovely land, this glorious liberty, these benign institutions, the dear purchase of our fathers, are ours; ours to enjoy, ours to preserve, ours to transmit. Generations past and generations to come hold us responsible for this sacred trust. Our fathers, from behind, admonish us, with their anxious paternal voices; posterity calls out to us, from the bosom of the future; the world turns hither its solicitous eyes; all, conjure us to act wisely, and faithfully, in the relation which we sustain.

We can never, indeed pay the debt which is upon us; but by virtue, by morality, by religion, by the cultivation of every good principle and every good habit, we may hope to enjoy the blessing, through our day, and to leave it unimpaired to our children. Let us feel deeply how much of what we are and of what we possess we owe to this liberty, and to these institutions of government. Nature has, indeed, given us a soil which yields bounteously to the hand of industry, the mighty and fruitful ocean is before us, and the skies over our heads shed health and vigor. But what are lands, and seas, and skies, to civilized man, without society, without knowledge, without morals, without religious culture; and how can these be enjoyed, in all their extent and all their excellence, but under the protection of wise institutions and a free government? Fellow-citizens, there is not one of us, there is not one of us here present, who does not, at this moment, and at every moment, experience, in his own condition, and in the condition of those most near and dear to him, the influence and the benefits, of this liberty and these institutions. Let us then acknowledge the blessing, let us feel it deeply and powerfully, let us cherish a strong affection for it, and resolve to maintain and perpetuate it. The blood of our fathers, let it not have been shed in vain; the great hope of posterity, let it not be blasted.

The striking attitude, too, in which we stand to the world around us, a topic to which, I fear, I advert too often, and dwell on too long, cannot be altogether omitted here. Neither individuals nor nations can perform their part well, until they understand and feel its importance, and comprehend and justly appreciate all the duties belonging to it. It is not to inflate national vanity, nor to swell a light and empty feeling of self-importance, but it is that we may judge justly of our situation, and of our own duties, that I earnestly urge upon you this consideration of our position and our character among the nations of the earth. It cannot be denied, but by those who would dispute against the sun, that with America, and in America, a new era commences in human affairs. This era is distinguished by free representative govemments, by entire religious liberty, by improved systems of national intercourse, by a newly awakened and an unconquerable spirit of free inquiry, and by a diffusion of knowledge through the community, such as has been before altogether unknown and unheard of America, America, our country, fellow-citizens, our own dear and native land, is inseparably connected, fast bound up, in fortune and by fate, with these great interests. If they fall, we fall with them; if they stand, it will be because we have maintained them. Let us contemplate, then, this connection, which binds the prosperity of others to our own; and let us manfully discharge all the duties which it imposes. If we cherish the virtues and the principles of our fathers, Heaven will assist us to carry on the work of human liberty and human happiness. Auspicious omens cheer us. Great examples are before us. Our own firmament now shines brightly upon our path. WASHINGTON is in the clear, upper sky. These other stars have now joined the American Constellation; they circle round their centre, and the heavens beam with new light. Beneath this illumination let us walk the course of life, and at its close devoutly commend our beloved country, the common parent of us all, to the Divine Benignity.

1. Webster had paid a five-day visit to Jefferson at Monticello in December 1824.

Document 41
Text from *Speeches and Formal Writings* 1: 285–348.

The Second Reply to Hayne,
January 26–27, 1830.

Mr. President—When the mariner has been tossed for many days in thick weather, and on an unknown sea, he naturally avails himself of the first pause in the storm, the earliest glance of the sun, to take his latitude, and ascertain how far the elements have driven him from his true course. Let us imitate this prudence, and, before we float farther on the waves of this debate, refer to the point from which we departed, that we may at least be able to conjecture where we now are. I ask for the reading of the resolution before the Senate.

The Secretary read the resolution, as follows:—

Resolved, That the Committee on Public Lands be instructed to inquire and report the quantity of public lands remaining unsold within each State and Territory, and whether it be expedient to limit for a certain period the sales of the public lands to such lands only as have heretofore been offered for sale, and are now subject to entry at the minimum price. And, also, whether the office of Surveyor-General, and some of the land offices, may not be abolished without detriment to the public interest; or whether it be expedient to adopt measures to hasten the sales and extend more rapidly the surveys of the public lands.

We have thus heard, Sir, what the resolution is which is actually before us for consideration; and it will readily occur to every one, that it is almost the only subject about which something has not been said in the speech, running through two days, by which the Senate has been entertained by the gentleman from South Carolina. Every topic in the wide range of our public affairs, whether past or present,— every thing, general or local, whether belonging to national politics or party politics,—seems to have attracted more or less of the honorable member's attention, save only the resolution before the Senate. He has spoken of every thing but the public lands; they have escaped his notice. To that subject, in all his excursions, he has not paid even the cold respect of a passing glance. . . .

Sir, let me recur to pleasing recollections; let me indulge in refreshing remembrance of the past; let me remind you that, in early times, no States cherished greater harmony, both of principle and feeling, than Massachusetts and South Carolina. Would to God that harmony might again return! Shoulder to shoulder they went through the Revolution, hand in hand they stood round the administration of Washington, and felt his own great arm lean on them for support. Unkind feeling, if it exist, alienation, and distrust are the growth, unnatural to such soils, of false principles since sown. They are weeds, the seeds of which that same great arm never scattered.

Mr. President, I shall enter on no encomium upon Massachusetts;

she needs none. There she is. Behold her, and judge for yourselves. There is her history; the world knows it by heart. The past, at least, is secure. There is Boston, and Concord, and Lexington, and Bunker Hill; and there they will remain for ever. The bones of her sons, falling in the great struggle for Independence, now lie mingled with the soil of every State from New England to Georgia; and there they will lie for ever. And Sir, where American Liberty raised its first voice, and where its youth was nurtured and sustained, there it still lives, in the strength of its manhood and full of its original spirit. If discord and disunion shall wound it, if party strife and blind ambition shall hawk at and tear it, if folly and madness, if uneasiness under salutary and necessary restraint, shall succeed in separating it from that Union, by which alone its existence is made sure, it will stand, in the end, by the side of that cradle in which its infancy was rocked; it will stretch forth its arm with whatever of vigor it may still retain over the friends who gather round it; and it will fall at last, if fall it must, amidst the proudest monuments of its own glory, and on the very spot of its origin.

There yet remains to be performed, Mr. President, by far the most grave and important duty, which I feel to be devolved on me by this occasion. It is to state, and to defend, what I conceive to be the true principles of the Constitution under which we are here assembled. I might well have desired that so weighty a task should have fallen into other and abler hands. I could have wished that it should have been executed by those whose character and experience give weight and influence to their opinions, such as cannot possibly belong to mine. But, Sir, I have met the occasion, not sought it; and I shall proceed to state my own sentiments, without challenging for them any particular regard, with studied plainness, and as much precision as possible.

I understand the honorable gentleman from South Carolina to maintain, that it is a right of the State legislatures to interfere, whenever, in their judgment, this government transcends its constitutional limits, and to arrest the operation of its laws.

I understand him to maintain this right, as a right existing *under* the Constitution, not as a right to overthrow it on the ground of extreme necessity, such as would justify violent revolution.

I understand him to maintain an authority, on the part of the States, thus to interfere, for the purpose of correcting the exercise of power by the general government, of checking it, and of compelling it to conform to their opinion of the extent of its powers.

I understand him to maintain, that the ultimate power of judging of the constitutional extent of its own authority is not lodged exclusively in the general government, or any branch of it: but that, on the contrary, the States may lawfully decide for themselves, and each State for itself, whether, in a given case, the act of the general government transcends its power.

I understand him to insist, that, if the exigency of the case, in the opinion of any State government, require it, such State government may, by its own sovereign authority, annul an act of the general government which it deems plainly and palpably unconstitutional.

This is the sum of what I understand from him to be the South Carolina doctrine, and the doctrine which he maintains. I propose to consider it, and compare it with the Constitution. Allow me to say, as a preliminary remark, that I call this the South Carolina doctrine only because the gentleman himself has so denominated it. I do not feel at liberty to say that South Carolina, as a State, has ever advanced these sentiments. I hope she has not, and never may. That a great majority of her people are opposed to the tariff laws, is doubtless true. That a majority, somewhat less than that just mentioned, conscientiously believe these laws unconstitutional, may probably also be true. But that any majority holds to the right of direct State interference at State discretion, the right of nullifying acts of Congress by acts of State legislation, is more than I know, and what I shall be slow to believe. . . .

This leads us to inquire into the origin of this government and the source of its power. Whose agent is it? Is it the creature of the State legislatures, or the creature of the people? If the government of the United States be the agent of the State governments, then they may control it, provided they can agree in the manner of controlling it; if it be the agent of the people, then the people alone can control it, restrain it, modify, or reform it. It is observable enough, that the doctrine for which the honorable gentleman contends leads him to the necessity of maintaining, not only that this general government is the creature of the States, but that it is the creature of each of the States severally, so that each may assert the power for itself of determining whether it acts within the limits of its authority. It is the servant of four-and-twenty masters, of different wills and different purposes and yet bound to obey all. This absurdity (for it seems no less) arises from a misconception as to the origin of this government and its true character. It is, Sir, the people's Constitution, the people's government, made for the people, made by the people, and answerable to the

people. The people of the United States have declared that the Constitution shall be the supreme law. We must either admit the proposition, or dispute their authority. The States are, unquestionably, sovereign, so far as their sovereignty is not affected by this supreme law. But the State legislatures, as political bodies, however sovereign, are yet not sovereign over the people. So far as the people have given power to the general government, so far the grant is unquestionably good, and the government holds of the people, and not of the State governments. We are all agents of the same supreme power, the people. The general government and the State governments derive their authority from the same source. Neither can, in relation to the other, be called primary, though one is definite and restricted, and the other general and residuary. The national government possesses those powers which it can be shown the people have conferred on it, and no more. All the rest belongs to the State governments, or to the people themselves. So far as the people have restrained State sovereignty, by the expression of their will, in the Constitution of the United States, so far, it must be admitted, State sovereignty is effectually controlled. I do not contend that it is, or ought to be, controlled farther. The sentiment to which I have referred propounds that State sovereignty is only to be controlled by its own "feeling of justice": that is to say, it is not to be controlled at all, for one who is to follow his own feelings is under no legal control. Now, however men may think this ought to be, the fact is, that the people of the United States have chosen to impose control on State sovereignties. There are those, doubtless, who wish they had been left without restraint; but the Constitution has ordered the matter differently. To make war, for instance, is an exercise of sovereignty; but the Constitution declares that no State shall make war. To coin money is another exercise of sovereign power, but no State is at liberty to coin money. Again, the Constitution says that no sovereign State shall be so sovereign as to make a treaty. These prohibitions, it must be confessed, are a control on the State sovereignty of South Carolina, as well as of the other States, which does not arise "from her own feelings of honorable justice." The opinion referred to, therefore, is in defiance of the plainest provisions of the Constitution.
. . .

I must now beg to ask, Sir, Whence is this supposed right of the States derived? Where do they find the power to interfere with the laws of the Union? Sir the opinion which the honorable gentleman maintains is a notion founded in a total misapprehension, in my judgment, of the origin of this government, and of the foundation on which it stands. I hold it to be a popular government, erected by the people; those who administer it, responsible to the people; and itself capable of being amended and modified, just as the people may choose it should be. It is as popular, just as truly emanating from the people, as the State governments. It is created for one purpose; the State governments for another. It has its own powers; they have theirs. There is no more authority with them to arrest the operation of a law of Congress, than with Congress to arrest the operation of their laws. We are here to administer a Constitution emanating immediately from the people, and trusted by them to our administration. It is not the creature of the State governments. It is of no moment to the argument, that certain acts of the State legislatures are necessary to fill our seats in this body. That is not one of their original State powers, a part of the sovereignty of the State. It is a duty which the people, by the Constitution itself, have imposed on the State legislatures; and which they might have left to be performed elsewhere, if they had seen fit. So they have left the choice of President with electors; but all this does not affect the proposition that this whole government, President, Senate, and House of Representatives, is a popular government. It leaves it still all its popular character. The governor of a State (in some of the States) is chosen, not directly by the people, but by those who are chosen by the people, for the purpose of performing, among other duties, that of electing a governor. Is the government of the State, on that account, not a popular government? This government, Sir, is the independent offspring of the popular will. It is not the creature of State legislatures; nay, more, if the whole truth must be told, the people brought it into existence, established it, and have hitherto supported it, for the very purpose, amongst others, of imposing certain salutary restraints on State sovereignties. The States cannot now make war; they cannot contract alliances; they cannot make, each for itself, separate regulations of commerce; they cannot lay imposts; they cannot coin money. If this Constitution, Sir, be the creature of State legislatures, it must be admitted that it has obtained a strange control over the volitions of its creators.

The people, then, Sir, erected this government. They gave it a Constitution, and in that Constitution they have enumerated the powers which they bestow on it. They have made it a limited government. They have defined its authority. They have restrained it to the exercise of such powers as are granted; and all others, they declare, are reserved to the States or the people. But, Sir, they have not stopped here. If they had, they would have accomplished but half their work. No definition can be so clear, as to avoid possibility of doubt; no limitation so precise, as to exclude all uncertainty. Who, then, shall construe this grant of the people? Who shall interpret their will, where it may be supposed they have left it doubtful? With whom do they repose this ultimate right of deciding on the powers of the government? Sir, they have settled all this in the fullest manner. They have left it with the government itself, in its appropriate branches. Sir, the very chief end, the main design, for which the whole Constitution was framed and adopted, was to establish a government that should not be obliged to act through State agency, or depend on State opinion and State discretion. The people had had quite enough of that kind of government under the Confederation. Under that system, the legal action, the application of law to individuals, belonged exclusively to the States. Congress could only recommend; their acts were not of binding force, till the States had adopted and sanctioned them. Are we in that condition still? Are we yet at the mercy of State discretion and State construction? Sir, if we are, then vain will be our attempt to maintain the Constitution under which we sit.

But, Sir, the people have wisely provided, in the Constitution itself, a proper, suitable mode and tribunal for settling questions of constitutional law. There are in the Constitution grants of powers to Congress, and restrictions on these powers. There are, also, prohibitions on the States. Some authority must, therefore, necessarily exist, having the ultimate jurisdiction to fix and ascertain the interpretation of these grants, restrictions, and prohibitions. The Constitution has itself pointed out, ordained, and established that authority. How has it accomplished this great and essential end? By declaring, Sir, that "*the Constitution, and the laws of the United States made in pursuance thereof, shall be the supreme law of the land, any thing in the constitution or laws of any State to the contrary notwithstanding.*"

This, Sir, was the first great step. By this the supremacy of the Constitution and laws of the United States is declared. The people so will it. No State law is to be valid which comes in conflict with the Constitution, or any law of the United States passed in pursuance of it. But who shall decide this question of interference? To whom lies the last appeal? This, Sir, the Constitution itself decides also, by declaring, "*that the judicial power shall extend to all cases arising under the Constitution and laws of the United States.*" These two provisions cover the whole ground. They are, in truth, the keystone of the arch! With these it is a government; without them it is a confederation. In pursuance of these clear and express provisions, Congress established, at its very first session, in the judicial act, a mode for carrying them into full effect, and for bringing all questions of constitutional power to the final decision of the Supreme Court. It then, Sir, became a government. It then had the means of self-protection; and but for this, it would, in all probability, have been now among things which are past. Having constituted the government, and declared its powers, the people have further said, that, since somebody must decide on the extent of these powers, the government shall itself decide; subject, always, like other popular governments, to its responsibility to the people. . . .

I have not allowed myself, Sir, to look beyond the Union, to see what might lie hidden in the dark recess behind. I have not coolly weighed the chances of preserving liberty when the bonds that unite us together shall be broken asunder. I have not accustomed myself to hang over the precipice of disunion, to see whether, with my short sight, I can fathom the depth of the abyss below; nor could I regard him as a safe counsellor in the affairs of this government, whose thoughts should be mainly bent on considering, not how the Union may be best preserved, but how tolerable might be the condition of the people when it should be broken up and destroyed. While the Union lasts, we have high, exciting, gratifying prospects spread out before us, for us and our children. Beyond that I seek not to penetrate the veil. God grant that in my day, at least, that curtain may not rise! God grant that on my vision never may be opened what lies behind! When my eyes shall be turned to behold for the last time the sun in heaven, may I not see him shining on the broken and dishonored fragments of a once glorious Union; on States dissevered, discordant, belligerent; on a land rent with civil feuds, or drenched, it may be, in fraternal blood! Let their last feeble and lingering glance rather behold the gorgeous ensign of the republic, now known and honored throughout the earth, still full high advanced, its arms and trophies streaming in their original lustre, not a stripe erased or polluted, nor a single star obscured, bearing for its motto, no such miserable interrogatory as "What is all this worth?" nor those other words of delusion and folly, "Liberty first and Union afterwards"; but everywhere, spread all over in characters of living light, blazing on all its ample folds, as they float over the sea and over the land, and in every wind under the whole heavens, that other sentiment, dear to every true American heart,—Liberty *and* Union, now and for ever, one and inseparable!

Document 42
Text from *Speeches and Formal Writings* 2: 513–51.

The Seventh of March Speech,
March 7, 1850.

Mr. President,—I wish to speak to-day, not as a Massachusetts man, nor as a Northern man, but as an American, and a member of the Senate of the United States. It is fortunate that there is a Senate of the United States; a body not yet moved from its propriety, not lost to a just sense of its own dignity and its own high responsibilities, and a body to which the country looks, with confidence, for wise, moderate, patriotic, and healing counsels. It is not to be denied that we live in the midst of strong agitations, and are surrounded by very considerable dangers to our institutions and government. The imprisoned winds are let loose. The East, the North, and the stormy South combine to throw the whole sea into commotion, to toss its billows to the skies, and disclose its profoundest depths. I do not affect to regard myself, Mr. President, as holding, or as fit to hold, the helm in this combat with the political elements; but I have a duty to perform, and I mean to perform it with fidelity, not without a sense of existing dangers, but not without hope. I have a part to act, not for my own security or safety, for I am looking out for no fragment upon which to float away from the wreck, if wreck there must be, but for the good of the whole, and the preservation of all; and there is that which will keep me to my duty during this struggle, whether the sun and the stars shall appear, or shall not appear for many days. I speak to-day for the preservation of the Union. "Hear me for my cause." I speak to-day, out of a solicitous and anxious heart for the restoration to the country of that quiet and that harmony which make the blessings of this Union so rich, and so dear to us all. These are the topics that I propose to myself to discuss; these are the motives, and the sole motives, that influence me in the wish to communicate my opinions to the Senate and the country; and if I can do any thing, however little, for the promotion of these ends, I shall have accomplished all that I expect. . . .

Now, Sir, upon the general nature and influence of slavery there exists a wide difference of opinion between the northern portion of this country and the southern. It is said on the one side, that, although not the subject of any injunction or direct prohibition in the New Testament, slavery is a wrong; that it is founded merely in the right of the strongest; and that it is an oppression, like unjust wars, like all those conflicts by which a powerful nation subjects a weaker to its will; and that, in its nature, whatever may be said of it in the modifications which have taken place, it is not according to the meek spirit of the Gospel. It is not "kindly affectioned"; it does not "seek another's, and not its own"; it does not "let the oppressed go free". These are sentiments that are cherished, and of late with greatly augmented force, among the people of the Northern States. They have taken hold of the religious sentiment of that part of the country, as they have, more or less, taken hold of the religious feelings of a considerable portion of mankind. The South, upon the other side, having been accustomed to this relation between the two races all their lives, from their birth, having been taught, in general, to treat the subjects of this bondage with care and kindness, and I believe, in general, feeling great kindness for them, have not taken the view of the subject which I have mentioned. There are thousands of religious men, with consciences as tender as any of their brethren at the North, who do not see the unlawfulness of slavery; and there are more thousands, perhaps, that, whatsoever they may think of it in its origin, and as a matter depending upon natural right, yet take things as they are, and, finding slavery to be an established relation of the society in which they live, can see no way in which, let their opinions on the abstract question be what they may, it is in the power of the present generation to relieve themselves from this relation. And candor obliges me to say, that I believe they are just as conscientious, many of them, and the religious people, all of them, as they are at the North who hold different opinions.

The honorable Senator from South Carolina [John C. Calhoun] the other day alluded to the separation of that great religious community, the Methodist Episcopal Church.[1] That separation was brought about by differences of opinion upon this particular subject of slavery. I felt great concern, as that dispute went on, about the result. I was in hopes that the difference of opinion might be adjusted, because I looked upon that religious denomination as one of the great props of religion and morals throughout the whole country, from Maine to Georgia, and westward to our utmost western boundary. The result was against my wishes and against my hopes. I have read all their proceedings and all their arguments; but I have never yet been able to come to the conclusion that there was any real ground for that separation; in other words, that any good could be produced by that separation. I must say I think there was some want of candor and charity. Sir, when a question of this kind seizes on the religious sentiments of mankind, and comes to be discussed in religious assemblies of the clergy and laity, there is always to be expected, or always to be feared, a great degree of excitement. It is in the nature of man, manifested by his whole history, that religious disputes are apt to become warm in proportion to the strength of the convictions which men entertain of the magnitude of the questions at issue. In all such disputes, there will sometimes be found men with whom every thing is absolute; absolutely wrong, or absolutely right. They see the right clearly; they think others ought so to see it, and they are disposed to establish a broad line of distinction between what is right and what is wrong. They are not seldom willing to establish that line upon their own convictions of truth and justice; and are ready to mark and guard it by placing along it a series of dogmas, as lines of boundary on the earth's surface are marked by posts and stones. There are men who, with clear perceptions, as they think, of their own duty, do not see how too eager a pursuit of one duty may involve them in the violation of others, or how too warm an embracement of one truth may lead to a disregard of other truths equally important. As I heard it stated strongly, not many days ago, these persons are disposed to mount upon some particular duty, as upon a war-horse, and to drive furiously on and upon and over all other duties that may stand in the way. There are men who, in reference to disputes of that sort, are of opinion that human duties may be ascertained with the exactness of mathematics. They deal with morals as with mathematics; and they think what is right may be distinguished from what is wrong with the precision of an algebraic equation. They have, therefore, none too much charity towards others who differ from them. They are apt, too, to think that nothing is good but what is perfect, and that there are no compromises or modifications to be made in consideration of difference of opinion or in deference to other men's judgment. If their perspicacious vision enables them to detect a spot on the face of the sun, they think that a good reason why the sun should be struck down from heaven. They prefer the chance of running into utter darkness to living in heavenly light, if that heavenly light be not absolutely without any imperfection. There are impatient men; too impatient always to give heed to the admonition of St. Paul, that we are not to "do evil that good may come"; too impatient to wait for the slow progress of moral causes in the improvement of mankind. . . .

Mr. President, in the excited times in which we live, there is found to exist a state of crimination and recrimination between the North and South. There are lists of grievances produced by each; and those grievances, real or supposed, alienate the minds of one portion of the country from the other, exasperate the feelings, and subdue the sense of fraternal affection, patriotic love, and mutual regard. I shall bestow a little attention, Sir, upon these various grievances existing on the one side and on the other. I begin with complaints of the South. I will not answer, further than I have, the general statements of the honorable Senator from South Carolina [Calhoun], that the North has prospered at the expense of the South in consequence of the manner of administering this government, in the collecting of its revenues, and so forth. These are disputed topics, and I have no inclination to enter into them. But I will allude to other complaints of the South, and especially to one which has in my opinion just foundation; and that is, that there has been found at the North, among individuals and among legislators, a disinclination to perform fully their constitutional duties in regard to the return of persons bound to service who have escaped into the free States. In that respect, the South, in my judgment, is right, and the North is wrong. Every member of every Northern legislature is bound by oath, like every other officer in the country, to support the Constitution of the United States; and the article of the Constitution[2] which says to these States that they shall deliver up fugitives from service is as binding in honor and conscience as any other article. No man fulfills his duty in any legislature who sets himself to find excuses, evasions, escapes from this constitutional obligation. I have always thought that the Constitution addressed itself to the legislatures of the States or to the States themselves. It says that those persons escaping to other States "shall be delivered up," and I confess I have always been of the opinion that it was an injunction upon the States themselves. When it is said that a person escaping into another State, and coming therefore within the jurisdiction of that State, shall be delivered up, it seems to me the import of the clause is, that the State itself, in obedience to the Constitution, shall cause him to be delivered up. That is my judgment. I have always entertained that opinion, and I entertain it now. But when the subject, some years ago, was before the Supreme Court of the United States, the majority of the judges held that the power to cause fugitives from service to be delivered up was a power to be exercised under the authority of this government.[3] I do not know, on the whole, that it may not have been a fortunate decision. My habit is to respect the result of judicial deliberations and the solemnity of judicial decisions. As it now stands, the business of seeing that these fugitives are delivered up resides in the power of Congress and the national judicature, and my friend at the head of the Judiciary Committee [James M. Mason][4] has a bill on the subject now before the Senate, which, with some amendments to it, I propose to support, with all its provisions, to the fullest extent. And I desire to call the attention of all sober-minded men at the North, of all conscientious men, of all men who are not carried away by some fanatical idea or some false impression, to their constitutional obligations. I put it to all the sober and sound minds at the North as a question of morals and a question of conscience. What right have they, in their legislative capacity or any other capacity, to endeavor to get round this Constitution, or to embarrass the free exercise of the rights secured by the Constitution to the persons whose slaves escape from them? None at all; none at all. Neither in the forum of conscience, nor before the face of the Constitution, are they, in my opinion, justified in such an attempt. Of course it is a matter for their consideration. They probably, in the excitement of the times, have not stopped to consider of this. They have followed what seemed to be the current of thought and of motives, as the occasion arose, and they have neglected to investigate fully the real question, and to consider their constitutional obligations; which, I am sure, if they did consider, they would fulfil with alacrity. I repeat, therefore, Sir, that here is a well-founded ground of complaint against the North, which ought to be removed, which it is now in the power of the different departments of this government to remove; which calls for the enactment of proper laws authorizing the judicature of this government, in the several States, to do all that is necessary for the recapture of fugitive slaves and for their restoration to those who claim them. Wherever I go, and whenever I speak on the subject, and when I speak here I desire to speak to the whole North, I say that the South has been injured in this respect, and has a right to complain; and the North has been too careless of what I think the Constitution peremptorily and emphatically enjoins upon her as a duty. . . .

Then, Sir, there are the Abolition societies, of which I am unwilling to speak, but in regard to which I have very clear notions and opinions. I do not think them useful. I think their operations for the last twenty years have produced nothing good or valuable. At the same time, I believe thousands of their members to be honest and good men, perfectly well-meaning men. They have excited feelings; they think they must do something for the cause of liberty; and, in their sphere of action, they do not see what else they can do than to contribute to an Abolition press, or an Abolition society, or to pay an Abolition lecturer. I do not mean to impute gross motives even to the leaders of these societies, but I am not blind to the consequences of their proceedings. I cannot but see what mischiefs their interference with the South has produced. And is it not plain to every man? Let any gentleman who entertains doubts on this point recur to the debates in the Virginia House of Delegates in 1832, and he will see with what freedom a proposition made by Mr. [Thomas] Jefferson Randolph for the gradual abolition of slavery was discussed in that body.[5] Every one spoke of slavery as he thought; very ignominious and disparaging names and epithets were applied to it. The debates in the House of Delegates on that occasion, I believe, were all published. They were read by every colored man who could read, and to those who could not read, those debates were read by others. At that time Virginia was not unwilling or afraid to discuss this question, and to let that part of her population know as much of the discussion as they could learn. That was in 1832. As has been said by the honorable member from South Carolina [Calhoun], these Abolition societies commenced their course of action in 1835. It is said, I do not know how true it may be, that they sent incendiary publications into the slave States; at any rate, they attempted to arouse, and did arouse, a very strong feeling; in other words, they created great agitation in the North against Southern slavery. Well, what was the result? The bonds of the slaves were bound more firmly than before, their rivets were more strongly fastened. Public opinion, which in Virginia had begun to be exhibited against slavery, and was opening out for the discussion of the question, drew back and shut itself up in its castle. I wish to know whether any body in Virginia can now talk openly as Mr. Randolph, Governor [James] McDowell,[6] and others talked in 1832 and sent their remarks to the press? We all know the fact, and we all know the cause; and every thing that these agitating people have done has been, not to enlarge, but to restrain, not to set free, but to bind faster the slave population of the South. . . .

Mr. President, I should much prefer to have heard from every member on this floor declarations of opinion that this Union could never be dissolved, than the declaration of opinion by any body, that, in any case, under the pressure of any circumstances, such a dissolution was possible. I hear with distress and anguish the word "secession," especially when it falls from the lips of those who are patriotic, and known to the country, and known all over the world, for their political services. Secession! Peaceable secession! Sir, your eyes and mine are never destined to see that miracle. The dismemberment of this vast country without convulsion! The breaking up of the fountains of the great deep without ruffing the surface! Who is so foolish, I beg every body's pardon, as to expect to see any such thing? Sir, he who sees these States, now revolving in harmony around a common centre, and expects to see them quit their places and fly off without convulsion, may look the next hour to see the heavenly bodies rush from their spheres, and jostle against each other in the realms of space, without causing the wreck of the universe. There can be no such thing as a peaceable secession. Peaceable secession is an utter impossibility. Is the great Constitution under which we live, covering this whole country, is it to be thawed and melted away by secession, as the snows on the mountain melt under the influence of a vernal sun, disappear almost unobserved, and run off? No, Sir! No, Sir! I will not state what might produce the disruption of the Union; but, Sir, I see as plainly as I see the sun in heaven what that disruption itself must produce; I see that it must produce war, and such a war as I will not describe, *in its twofold character.*

Peaceable secession! Peaceable secession! The concurrent agreement of all the members of this great republic to separate! A voluntary separation, with alimony on one side and on the other. Why, what would be the result? Where is the line to be drawn? What States are to secede? What is to remain American? What am I to be? An American no longer? Am I to become a sectional man, a local man, a separatist, with no country in common with the gentlemen who sit around me here, or who fill the other house of Congress? Heaven forbid! Where is the flag of the republic to remain? Where is the eagle still to tower? or is he to cower, and shrink, and fall to the ground? Why, Sir, our ancestors, our fathers and our grandfathers, those of them that are yet living amongst us with prolonged lives, would rebuke and reproach us; and our children and our grandchildren would cry out shame upon us, if we of this generation should dishonor these ensigns of the power of the government and the harmony of that Union which is every day felt among us with so much joy and gratitude. What is to become of the army? What is to become of the navy? What is to become of the public lands? How is each of the thirty States to defend itself? I know, although the idea has not been stated distinctly, there is to be, or it is supposed possible that there will be, a Southern Confederacy. I do not mean, when I allude to this statement, that any one seriously contemplates such a state of things. I do not mean to say that it is true, but I have heard it suggested elsewhere, that the idea has been entertained, that, after the dissolution of this Union, a Southern Confederacy might be formed. I am sorry, Sir, that it has ever been thought of, talked of, or dreamed of, in the wildest flights of human imagination. But the idea, so far as it exists, must be of a separation, assigning the slave States to one side and the free States to the other. Sir, I may express myself too strongly, perhaps, but there are impossibilities in the natural as well as in the physical world, and I hold the idea of a separation of these States, those that are free to form one government, and those that are slave-holding to form another, as such an impossibility. We could not separate the States by any such line, if we were to draw it. We could not sit down here to-day and draw a line of separation that would satisfy any five men in the country. There are natural causes that would keep and tie us together, and there are social and domestic relations which we could not break if we would, and which we should not if we could.

Sir, nobody can look over the face of this country at the present moment, nobody can see where its population is the most dense and growing, without being ready to admit, and compelled to admit, that ere long the strength of America will be in the Valley of the Mississippi. Well, now, Sir, I beg to inquire what the wildest enthusiast has to say on the possibility of cutting that river in two, and leaving free States at its source and on its branches, and slave States down near its mouth, each forming a separate government? Pray, Sir, let me say to the people of this country, that these things are worthy of their pondering and of their consideration. Here, Sir, are five millions of freemen in the free States north of the river Ohio. Can any body suppose that this population can be severed, by a line that divides them from the territory of a foreign and an alien government, down somewhere, the Lord knows where, upon the lower banks of the Mississippi? What would become of Missouri? Will she join the *arrondissement* of the slave States? Shall the man from the Yellow Stone and the Platte be connected, in the new republic, with the man who lives on the southern extremity of the Cape of Florida? Sir, I am ashamed to pursue this line of remark. I dislike it, I have an utter disgust for it. I would rather hear of natural blasts and mildews, war, pestilence, and famine, than to hear gentlemen talk of secession. To break up this great government! to dismember this glorious country! to astonish Europe with an act of folly such as Europe for two centuries has never beheld in any government or any people! No, Sir! no, Sir! There will be no secession! Gentlemen are not serious when they talk of secession. . . .

And now, Mr. President, I draw these observations to a close. I have spoken freely, and I meant to do so. I have sought to make no display. I have sought to enliven the occasion by no animated discussion, nor have I attempted any train of elaborate argument. I have wished only to speak my sentiments, fully and at length, being desirous, once and for all, to let the Senate know, and to let the country know, the opinions and sentiments which I entertain on all these subjects. These opinions are not likely to be suddenly changed. If there be any future service that I can render to the country, consistently with these sentiments and opinions, I shall cheerfully render it. If there be not, I shall still be glad to have had an opportunity to disburden myself from the bottom of my heart, and to make known every political sentiment that therein exists.

And now, Mr. President, instead of speaking of the possibility or utility of secession, instead of dwelling in those caverns of darkness, instead of groping with those ideas so full of all that is horrid and horrible, let us come out into the light of day; let us enjoy the fresh air of Liberty and Union; let us cherish those hopes which belong to us; let us devote ourselves to those great objects that are fit for our consideration and our action; let us raise our conceptions to the magnitude and the importance of the duties that devolve upon us; let our comprehension be as broad as the country for which we act, our aspirations as high as its certain destiny; let us not be pigmies in a case that calls for men. Never did there devolve on any generation of men higher trusts than now devolve upon us, for the preservation of this Constitution and the harmony and peace of all who are destined to live under it. Let us make our generation one of the strongest and brightest links in that golden chain which is destined, I fondly believe, to grapple the people of all the States to this Constitution for ages to come. We have a great, popular, constitutional government, guarded by law and by judicature, and defended by the affections of the whole people. No monarchical throne presses these States together, no iron chain of military power encircles them; they live and stand under a government popular in its form, representative in its character, founded upon principles of equality, and so constructed, we hope, as to last for ever. In all its history it has been beneficent; it has trodden down no man's liberty; it has crushed no State. Its daily respiration is liberty and patriotism; its yet youthful veins are full of enterprise, courage, and honorable love of glory and renown. Large before, the country has now, by recent events, become vastly larger. This republic now extends, with a vast breadth, across the whole continent. The two great seas of the world wash the one and the other shore. We realize, on a mighty scale, the beautiful description of the ornamental border of the buckler of Achilles:—

"Now, the broad shield complete, the artist crowned
With his last hand, and poured the ocean round;
In living silver seemed the waves to roll,
And beat the bucklers verge, and bound the whole."[7]

1. Calhoun's remarks are in the *Congressional Globe,* 31st Cong., 1st sess., pp. 451–55.
    2. Article 4, Section 2.
    3. *Prigg v. Pennsylvania,* 16 Peters 539 (1842).
    4. Mason (1798–1871; University of Pennsylvania 1818), a representative (1837–39) and a senator (1847–61) from Virginia.
    5. Randolph (1792–1875), grandson of Thomas Jefferson,was an author, financier, and Virginia state legislator. In January 1832 he introduced a bill for gradual emancipation, which lost by a narrow margin.
    6. McDowell (1795–1851; Princeton 1817), a Virginia state legislator (1831–35, 1838), governor of the state (1843–46), and a U.S. Representative from Virginia (1846–51).
    7. Alexander Pope, trans., Homer, *Iliad* (1806), Book XVIII, lines 701–04.

Document 43
Text from *Speeches and Formal Writings* 2: 627–66.

The Dignity and Importance of History,
February 23, 1852.

The object of your association [the Historical Society of New York], gentlemen, like that of others of similar character, is highly important. Historical societies are auxiliary to historical compositions. They collect the materials from which the great narrative of events is, in due time, to be framed. The transactions of public bodies, local histories, memoirs of all kinds, statistics, laws, ordinances, public debates and discussions, works of periodical literature, and the public journals, whether of political events, of commerce, literature, or the arts, all find their places in the collections of historical societies. But these collections are not history; they are only elements of history. History is a higher name, and imports literary productions of the first order.

It is presumptuous in me, whose labors and studies have been so long devoted to other objects, to speak in the presence of those whom I see before me, of the *dignity and importance* of *history,* in its just sense; and yet I find pleasure in breaking in upon the course of daily pursuits, and indulging for a time in reflections upon topics of literature, and in the remembrance of the great examples of historic art.

Well written history must always be the result of genius and taste, as well as of research and study. It stands next to epic poetry, among the productions of the human mind. If it requires less of invention than that, it is not behind it in dignity and importance. The province of the epic is the poetical narrative of real or supposed events, and the representation of real, or at least natural, characters; and history, in its noblest examples, is an account of occurrences in which great events are commemorated, and distinguished men appear as agents and actors. Epic poetry and the drama are but narratives, the former partly and the latter wholly, in the form of dialogue, but their characters and personages are usually, in part at least, the creations of the imagination.

Severe history sometimes assumes the dialogue, or dramatic form, and, without departing from truth, is embellished by supposed colloquies or speeches, as in the productions of that great master, Titus Livius, or that greater master still, Thucydides.

The drawing of characters, consistent with general truth and fidelity, is no violation of historical accuracy; it is only an illustration or an ornament.

When Livy ascribes an appropriate speech to one of his historical personages, it is only as if he had portrayed the same character in language professedly his own. Lord Clarendon's presentation, in his own words, of the character of Lord Falkland,[1] one of the highest and most successful efforts of personal description, is hardly different from what it would have been, if he had put into the mouth of Lord Falkland a speech exhibiting the same qualities of the mind and the heart, the same opinions, and the same attachments. Homer describes the actions of personages which, if not real, are so imagined as to be conformable to the general characteristics of men in the heroic ages. If his relation be not historically true, it is such, nevertheless, as, making due allowance for poetical embellishment, might have been true. And in Milton's great epic, which is almost entirely made up of narratives and speeches, there is nothing repugnant to the general conception which we form of the characters of those whose sentiments and conduct he portrays.

But history, while it illustrates and adorns, confines itself to facts, and to the relation of actual events. It is not far from truth to say, that well written and classic history is the epic of real life. It places the actions of men in an attractive and interesting light. Rejecting what is improper and superfluous, it fills its picture with real, just, and well drawn images.

The dignity of history consists in reciting events with truth and accuracy, and in presenting human agents and their actions in an

interesting and instructive form. The first element in history, therefore, is truthfulness; and this truthfulness must be displayed in a
concrete form. Classical history is not a memoir. It is not a crude
collection of acts, occurrences, and dates. It adopts nothing that is not
true; but it does not embrace all minor truths and all minor transactions. It is a composition, a production, which has unity of design, like
a work of statuary or of painting, and keeps constantly in view one
great end or result. Its parts, therefore, are to be properly adjusted
and well proportioned. The historian is an artist, as true to fact as
other artists are to nature, and, though he may sometimes embellish,
he never misrepresents; he may occasionally, perhaps, color too highly,
but the truth is still visible through the lights and shades. This unity
of design seems essential to all great productions. With all the variety
of the Iliad, Homer had the wrath of Achilles, and its consequences,
always before him; when he sang of the exploits of other heroes, they
were silently subordinated to those of the son of Thetis. Still more
remarkable is the unity in variety of the Odyssey, the character of
which is much more complicated; but all the parts are artfully adapted
to each other, and they have a common centre of interest and action,
the great end being the restoration of Ulysses to his native Ithaca.
Virgil, in the Aeneid, sang of nothing but the man, and his deeds, who
brought the Trojan gods to Italy, and laid the foundation of the walls
of imperial Rome; and Milton of nothing, but

> "Man's first disobedience, and the fruit
> Of that forbidden tree, whose mortal taste
> Brought death into the world and all our woes."[2]

And the best historical productions of ancient and of modern times
have been written with equal fidelity to one leading thought or
purpose.

It has been said by Lord Bolingbroke, that "History is Philosophy
teaching by example;"[3] and, before Bolingbroke, Shakespeare has
said:

> "There is a history in all men's lives,
> Figuring the nature of the times deceasd;
> The which observ'd, a man may prophesy,
> With a near aim, of the main chance of things
> As yet not come to life, which in their seeds,
> And weak beginnings, lie entreasured.
> Such things become the hatch and brood of time;
> And, by the necessary form of this,
> King Richard might create a perfect guess,

> That great Northumberland, then false to him,
> Would, of that seed, grow to a greater.
> Are these things, then, necessities?
> Then let us meet them like necessities." [4]

And a wiser man than either Bolingbroke or Shakespeare, has declared:

> The thing that hath been, it is that which shall be; and that which is done is that which shall be done: and there is no new thing under the sun. [5]

These sayings are all just, and they proceed upon the idea that the essential characteristics of human nature are the same everywhere, and in all ages.

This, doubtless, is true; and so far as history presents the general qualities and propensities of human nature, it does teach by example. Bolingbroke adds, with remarkable power of expression, that "the school of example is the world: and the masters of this school are history and experience. . . ." [6]

But history is not only philosophy, teaching by example; its true purpose is, also, to illustrate the general progress of society in knowledge and the arts, and the changes of manners and pursuits of men.

There is an imperfection, both in ancient and modern histories, and those of the best masters, in this respect. While they recite public transactions, they omit, in a great degree, what belongs to the civil, social, and domestic progress of men and nations. There is not, so far as I know, a good civil history of Rome, nor is there an account of the manners and habits of social and domestic life, such as may inform us of the progress of her citizens, from the foundation of the city to the time of Livy and Sallust, in individual exhibitions of character.

We know, indeed, something of the private pursuits and private vices of the Roman people at the commencement of the Empire, but we obtain our knowledge of these chiefly from the severe and indignant rebukes of Sallust, and the inimitable satires of Juvenal. Wars, foreign and domestic, the achievements of arms, and national alliances fill up the recorded greatness of the Roman Empire. . . .

It is in our day only that the history and progress of the civil and social institutions and manners of England have become the subjects of particular attention.

Sharon Turner, Lingard, and, more than all, Mr. Hallam, [7] have laid this age, and all following ages, under the heaviest obligations by their labors in this field of literary composition; nor would I separate from them the writings of a most learned and eloquent person, whose work on English history is now in progress, nor the author of the "Pictorial History of England."[8] But there is still wanting a full, thorough, and domestic, social account of our English ancestors, that is, a history which shall trace the progress of social life in the intercourse of man with man; the advance of arts, the various changes in the habits and occupations of individuals; and those improvements in domestic life which have attended the condition and meliorated the circumstances of men in the lapse of ages. We still have not the means of learning, to any great extent, how our English ancestors, at their homes, and in their houses, were fed, and lodged, and clothed, and what were their daily employments. We want a history of firesides; we want to know when kings and queens exchanged beds of straw for beds of down, and ceased to breakfast on beef and beer. We wish to see more, and to know more, of the changes which took place, down to the humblest cottage. Mr. Henry's book,[9] so far as it goes, is not without its utility, but it stops too soon, and, even in regard to the period which it embraces, it is not sufficiently full and satisfactory in its particulars.

The feudal ages were military and agricultural, but the splendor of arms, in the history of the times, monopolized the genius of writers; and perhaps materials are not now abundant for forming a knowledge of the essential industry of the country. He would be a public benefactor who should instruct us in the modes of cultivation and tillage prevailing in England, from the Conquest down, and in the advancement of manufactures, from their inception in the time of Henry IV., to the period of their considerable development, two centuries afterwards.

There are two sources of information on these subjects, which have never yet been fully explored, and which, nevertheless, are overflowing fountains of knowledge. I mean the statutes and the proceedings of the courts of law. At an early period of life, I recurred, with some degree of attention, to both these sources of information; not so much for professional purposes, as for the elucidation of the progress of society. I acquainted myself with the object and purposes and substance of every published statute in British legislation. These showed me what the legislature of the country was concerned in, from age to age, and from year to year. And I learned from the reports of controversies, in the courts of law, what were the pursuits and occupations of individuals, and what the objects which most earnestly engaged attention. I hardly know anything which more repays research, than studies of this kind. We learn from them what pursuits occupied men during the feudal ages. We see the efforts of society to throw off the chains of this feudal dominion. We see too, in a most interesting manner, the ingenious devices resorted to, to break the thraldom of personal slavery. We see the beginning of manufacturing interests, and at length bursts upon us the full splendor of the commercial age. . . .

The art of historical composition owes its origin to the institutions of political freedom. . . .

It was not until the legislation of Solon had laid the foundation of free political institutions, and these institutions had unfolded a free and powerful and active political life in the Athenian Republic; until the discussion of public affairs in the Senate and the popular Assembly had created deliberative eloquence, and the open administration of justice in the courts, and under the laws established by Solon, had applied to the transactions between the citizens all the resources of refined logic, and drawn into the sphere of civil rights and obligations the power of high forensic oratory: it is not until these *results* of the legislative wisdom of Solon had been attained, that the art of history rose and flourished in Greece. With the decline of Grecian liberty began the decline in the art of historical composition. Histories were written under the Grecian Kings of Egypt; and a long line of writers flourished under the Byzantine Emperors; but the high art of historical composition, as perfected in the master-works of Herodotus, Thucydides, and Xenophon, had perished in the death of political freedom. . . .

Other foundation is not to be laid for authentic history than well authenticated facts; but, on this foundation, structures may be raised of different characteristics, historical, biographical, and philosophical. One writer may confine himself to exact and minute narration; another, true to the general story, may embellish that story with more or less of external ornament, or of eloquence in description; a third, with a deeper philosophical spirit, may look into the causes of events and transactions, trace them with more profound research to their sources in the elements of human nature, or consider and solve, with more or less success, the more important question, how far the character of individuals has produced public events, or how far on the other hand public events have produced and formed the character of individuals.

Therefore one history of the same period, in human affairs, no more renders another history of the same period useless, or unadvisable, than the structure of one temple forbids the erection of another, or one statue of Apollo, Hercules, or Pericles should suppress all other attempts to produce statues of the same persons. . . .

Gentlemen, I must bring these desultory remarks to a close. I terminate them where perhaps I ought to have begun,—namely, with a few words on the present state and condition of our country, and the prospects which are before her.

Unborn ages and visions of glory crowd upon my soul, the realization of all which, however, is in the hands and good pleasure of Almighty God, but, under His divine blessing, it will be dependent on the character and the virtues of ourselves and of our posterity.

If classical history has been found to be, is now, and shall continue to be, the concomitant of free institutions and of popular eloquence, what a field is opening to us for another Herodotus, another Thucydides, and another Livy! And let me say, gentlemen, that if we and our posterity shall be true to the Christian religion, if we and they shall live always in the fear of God, and shall respect His commandments, if we and they shall maintain just moral sentiments and such conscientious convictions of duty as shall control the heart and life, we may have the highest hopes of the future fortunes of our country; and if we maintain those institutions of government and that political union, exceeding all praise as much as it exceeds all former examples of political associations, we may be sure of one thing, that while our country furnishes materials for a thousand masters of the historic art, it will afford no topic for a Gibbon.[10] It will have no decline and fall. It will go on prospering and to prosper. But if we and our posterity reject religious instruction and authority, violate the rules of eternal justice, trifle with the injunctions of morality, and recklessly destroy the political constitution which holds us together, no man can tell how sudden a catastrophe may overwhelm us that shall bury all our glory in profound obscurity. Should that catastrophe happen, let it have no history! Let the horrible narrative never be written! Let its fate be like that of the lost books of Livy, which no human eye shall ever read, or the missing Pleiad, of which no man can ever know more than that it is lost, and lost forever!

1. See Clarendon's *History of the Rebellion and Civil Wars of England* (Oxford, 1701–04), which Webster had in his library.
2. *Paradise Lost*, 1, lines 1–3.
3. Bolingbroke, *Letters on the Study and Use of History* (1742).
4. The quotation is from *Henry IV*, Part 2, Act 3, scene 1.

5. *Ecclesiastes,* Chapter 1, verse 9.

6. Bolingbroke, *Letters on the Study and Use of History,* Letter 11.

7. Sharon Turner (1766–1847); John Lingard (1771–1851); Henry Hallam (1777–1859).

8. The work in progress was Thomas Macaulay's (1800–1859) *History of England from the Accession of James 11* (5 vols.; London, 1849–1861); George Lillie Craik (1798–1866), *Pictorial History of England* (4 vols.; London, 1838–1841).

9. Robert Henry (1718–1790), *History of England* (5 vols.; London, 1771–1785).

10. Edward Gibbon (1737–94), *The History of the Decline and Fall of the Roman Empire* (5 vols.; 1776–88).

Maurice G. Baxter

DANIEL WEBSTER

The Lawyer

Daniel Webster started his study of law in late summer 1801, soon after his graduation from Dartmouth. An nineteen, the young man was equipped with a good general education, an invaluable long-range asset. In those days, legal training consisted of an apprenticeship in a practitioner's office instead of enrollment in a law school. Webster decided to begin at home in Salisbury, New Hampshire, as student-clerk with a neighbor, Thomas Thompson. The main reason for this choice was to be near his aging parents. Another family obligation—to his brother, a Dartmouth student—briefly interrupted that arrangement as he taught school to send a little money over to Ezekiel. Altogether, he was in Thompson's office about two years. Here he performed routine paperwork tasks and read a modest selection of treatises, such as those of Vattel, Coke, and Blackstone, with little supervision and not much more inspiration. The truth was, he had reservations about a lawyer's career: it was too materialistic yet often not especially profitable; and it could be dull intellectually.[1]

In 1804 he joined his brother, then in Boston, a broader, more interesting setting. He arranged to study with the reputable Christopher Gore. During his nine months there, he progressed rapidly. He received more guidance, had access to a greater range of materials, particularly in Gore's specialty of maritime law, and could observe New England's best attorneys in the busy state and federal courts of the Massachusetts capital. When he was admitted to the bar in the spring of 1805, the level of his training was well above average.[2]

In his consideration about where to commence practice, Webster decided he had to remain close to his family at Salisbury. A few miles down the Concord road in the village of Boscawen, he set up "shop . . . for the manufacture of Justice writs," he remarked. His office was a room that merchant Timothy Dix added to his house for that purpose; and a modest one it was, with no books and a bed in the corner.[3]

Webster traveled the circuits of county courts of common pleas, gaining the two years' experience required to practice in the Superior Court. The routine was physically taxing, often in bad weather over poor roads from one uncomfortable inn to another. Psychologically, it could also be unsatisfying, for the bulk of his activity consisted of debt collections. More often than not, he represented firms from Boston and Portsmouth that were attempting to collect payments from country merchants for goods they had bought and sold. An interesting example was his relationship with his landlord Dix. As agent of a mercantile house of Boston, Webster filed suit against Dix for overdue notes in the purchase of goods. Such actions were frequently friendly, however, the legal procedures allowing debtors some delay while respecting creditors' rights. In fact, Webster in turn represented Dix in a proceeding against his debtors.[4] Within the common law system, there were adaptations to settle disputes informally or to agree to an arbitration or a court order, almost always without jury trial. The network of credit promoted enterprise, based upon commonsense standards of fairness more than strict law. For the young lawyer, there might be ethical questions, such as dual representation in Dix's litigation; but he seemed unworried.[5]

As soon as he could, in the fall of 1807, Webster moved from the Merrimack Valley to the active seaport of Portsmouth, more attractive both professionally and personally. For a few years, the predominant number of cases continued to be note collections, though business was more lively and the income larger. The legal process was rather simple, increasingly becoming actions of assumpsit under developing rules of contracts, thus shifting emphasis from the old common law principle of fair agreement to the impersonal necessities of a market economy. All but a small number of such controversies were settled without going to a jury. Shortly after his arrival in Portsmouth, Webster handled several cases involving his landlord William Wilkins, who had to close his store below Webster's office. Some actions were against Wilkins, and some were for him against his own debtors. Occasionally, fees could be paid in a form other than cash—land or corporate stock—so obviously Webster shared the prevailing entrepreneurial outlook.[6]

There was much less work consisting of litigation on torts than on contracts. At this early stage of legal development, tort law allowed compensation for intentional damage to property or injury to person. In his first decade of practice, Webster rarely had a case involving proof of negligence, though that concept would be important later on.[7] During the War of 1812, he did bring an action of libel, of injury to the reputation of Federalist Timothy Pickering, to the federal circuit court. The suit had resulted from a derogatory comment in a Portsmouth newspaper. Whether or not he could have proved the purpose of the publication to be malicious was questionable. At any rate, he dropped the suit, although he made some political capital out of it.[8]

Webster did carry a small number of cases through to decision in the lower federal courts of New Hampshire. There was an interesting maritime case, *United States v Shapley* (1810), in which he served as co-counsel with the district attorney and prosecuted a shipmaster's violation of the embargo. This constituted a strange role for Webster, the sturdy opponent of this Jeffersonian policy, and perhaps he was not disappointed when he lost the case.[9]

Beginning in 1813, with his election to the House of Representatives, Webster was off each year to Washington for congressional sessions. Now politics affected his life as a lawyer more significantly. With his presence in the capital came the opportunity to practice before the Supreme Court. These new demands on his time led him to take on an associate, Timothy Farrar, Jr., to manage the office in New Hampshire while he was absent.

Webster now began to think about moving from that state, declining in commercial importance as it was, to a more promising place, perhaps New York City or Boston. By mid-1816 he had decided upon the Massachusetts capital and had outfitted an office on Court Street for what would be a thriving practice. Nearby were banks, mercantile houses, insurance companies, and other institutions, with their endless needs for legal services and their ample means for paying for them. As a counselor and a politician, Webster would be a leading advocate for these interests, for the rising manufacturing establishments, and for enterprise in general. His fees, until then never more than two thousand dollars annually, now climbed sharply. Despite an antiquated limit by statute on some fees—$2.50 for an appearance in the state supreme court—the more profitable advisory opinions, permanent retainers, and contingency arrangements assured a handsome income of ten to fifteen thousand dollars. And business conducted in federal courts or before claims commissions was untouched by state regulation.[10]

Central to the changing economy were the ever more numerous banks supplying indispensable capital. These institutions raised new issues for lawyers like Webster to explore, as common law rules were modified by courts and legislatures. The trend was to stimulate financial development more than to regulate it. Occasionally Webster represented parties claiming damages from banking misbehavior. For example, in *Foster v Essex Bank* (1821), he contended that a bank was liable for its cashier's theft of a special deposit of gold. Despite what seemed a plain case of the institution's laxity, the state supreme court decided that in such an instance the public must look out for itself. Similarly, Webster failed to get a remedy against the Gloucester Bank for carelessness in allowing theft and forgery of its notes. Chief Justice Isaac Parker ruled that it was not the bank's fault. Encouraged by that sympathetic decision, the Gloucester Bank then tried to get an order stipulating that Webster's client take back some of the forged notes at face value, which would have involved further loss. The attorney must have felt fortunate to prevail at least in that suit.

When he defended banking conduct, Webster seemed to fare better. For the Dedham Bank, he was able to justify circulation of bills of exchange intentionally designed to look like notes but more difficult for holders to redeem—a deception perhaps, but not illegal. Years later, in the mid-1840s, Webster was counsel for William Wyman, president of the Phoenix Bank of Charlestown, who was charged with embezzlement of over three hundred thousand dollars through massive loans to a friend's company. Strangely, the definition of embezzlement was still fuzzy. There were three Wyman trials, involving several high-paid lawyers, attracting widespread attention, and inducing emergency repair of the relevant statute by the legislature. Webster secured dismissal on the grounds that, technically, the bank president had not had "possession" of the money, an indispensable condition for embezzlement to occur. An institution's liability would be minimal if its chief officer had this much scope.[11]

Webster did take some criminal cases, though not often. The best known one concerned the brutal murder of old Joseph White, a wealthy Salem merchant, in April 1830. The prominence of the victim and the shocking circumstances of the crime caused much popular excitement, which influenced later legal proceedings. The defendants were the brothers Frank and Joe Knapp, charged with planning and assisting the murder to cover up destruction of White's will and thus allow Joe, White's relative, to inherit. At the request of the state's attorney general, Webster came into court as a special prosecutor. His prestige and golden oratory, combined with his competence in handling a jury trial resulted in convictions for both men. No doubt Webster's assets helped persuade the court to stretch the rule against self-incrimination by admitting as evidence the Knapps' confessions, which had been gained by the prosecutor's promise of immunity and then retracted by the accused. Webster's moving summations to the jury indicate how effective he might have been as a specialist in criminal law.[12]

In the area of admiralty law, Webster did handle a substantial number of cases throughout his career—a predictable occurrence during this period of flourishing foreign and coastal commerce. Some of this business concerned marine insurance, provided by corporations or groups of individuals to shipowners. A recurring question was whether the state or the national courts had jurisdiction in this area. Steadfastly, Justice Joseph Story asserted cognizance in his federal circuit, for example, *Peele v Merchants' Insurance* (1822), in which Webster represented shipowner claimants against their insurers. Despite these efforts aimed at forming a national system of rules, the Supreme Court moved quite hesitantly in that direction. One obstacle was the old English doctrine limiting admiralty jurisdiction over contracts to those made as well as executed on the sea. Story and Webster argued that the prerequisite ought to be the maritime subject matter of a contract, not the location of its formation. Another problem was the delay of settlement, dependent upon complicated determination of losses in a particular case. Story and Webster favored a standardized, actuarial basis for determining awards by underwriting companies. Eventually, these changes did occur.[13]

Webster's expertise in maritime law led to unusually profitable business before the Spanish claims commission in the early 1820s. The Florida Treaty (1819) provided that the United States assume its citizens' claims against Spain for up to five million dollars for seizure of ships during the Napoleonic wars. To administer this agreement, Congress established a commission, to which Webster and other attorneys presented memorials of claimants and received a percentage of the awards as fees. No sooner had the two countries negotiated the treaty than the lawyer had begun to look for clients. In New England and in Philadelphia, he assumed an agency for more than 225 claims, about 10 percent of what the commission considered. Documentation was time consuming and difficult so long after the seizures, with definitive proof sometimes located in foreign archives or often nonexistent. The lawyers and merchants connected with the cases actually influenced the commission's development of guidelines for decision making, for the members were not experienced in maritime law and commerce. In mid-1824, as soon as the final report appeared, Congressman Webster helped move an appropriation through the House and then collected fees of about seventy thousand dollars.[14]

Although his practice before the Supreme Court was not this

profitable, it was there that he achieved a brilliant professional reputation over a span of thirty-eight years. Soon after coming to Washington as a young Federalist congressman opposing the War of 1812, Webster advanced to the front rank of an unusually talented bar. He effected both the political culture and the constitutional law of the young republic. For the first twenty years, he appeared before the court of Chief Justice John Marshall, an unreserved nationalist and protector of property rights against state infringement. Arm in arm with the chief was Webster's intimate friend, the scholarly law professor Joseph Story. Other associate justices, even Jeffersonians such as William Johnson, normally allowed Marshall to speak for a united bench on the great questions of governmental powers. Webster's success rate in these *constitutional* cases was high, and he argued nearly all the leading ones in Marshall's day. Thereafter, from the mid-1830s until his death in 1852, Webster continued to have an extensive business in the capital, but now before a Jacksonian court. Chief Justice Roger Taney and his associates were less inclined to favor broad, exclusive national power vis-à-vis the states or to sanction special economic privilege. Now Webster lost more cases, and he deplored the judicial decline. Still, the Taney era turned out to be a time of adjustment instead of reversal of earlier decisions.[15]

It was *Dartmouth College v Woodward* that first demonstrated Webster's impressive skill as advocate in the nation's highest court. The loyal alumnus defended his alma mater from a political assault; and in doing so, he helped lay down a legal rule that would significantly shield corporations against damaging state policy for more than a century. To understand this case, one must look at the institution's history. Before the Revolution, a zealous minister, Eleazar Wheelock, moved his school for Indian instruction from Connecticut to Hanover, New Hampshire, solicited donations from England to be administered as a trust, and then in 1769 got a charter from the colonial governor to educate white students as well. Before long, Dartmouth became just another college, with little emphasis upon a specific Indian mission.

Through his will, Wheelock passed the college presidency to his son, John. John Wheelock preferred to direct affairs personally; but after a long-standing deference to this autocratic president, the trustees became independent minded. By 1815 the predominantly Federalist board had confronted Wheelock in an angry dispute, which led to his ouster and his appeal to the state's Republican politicians for redress. In the next election, William Plumer and his fellow Republicans won the governorship and control of the legislature. At the first opportunity, these politicians passed laws packing the college's board with Republicans and changing Dartmouth into a university, subject to state oversight. The old trustees contested the state statutes by suit against Secretary William Woodward, who had gone over to the university, to return the college papers he held in his possession as secretary. Such were the well-known events precipitating the litigation that brought in Webster.[16]

In the hearings before the New Hampshire Supreme Court, Webster's role was to assist Jeremiah Mason and Jeremiah Smith, both highly respected lawyers and firm Federalists. When their efforts on behalf of the old trustees failed, Webster took charge of the appeal to the federal Supreme Court at Washington, where he and Joseph Hopkinson of Pennsylvania argued the case in March 1818. The manuscript sources in Webster's hand are uncommonly full: extensive personal correspondence, the attorney's own briefs, his notes on arguments of other counsel, and his later reconstruction of the tests of all arguments, much of this expertly edited in the legal series of the *Webster Papers*. The documents show that Webster borrowed heavily from Mason and Smith, particularly on the common law status of corporations; but they also show that he was not merely presenting the research of his colleagues, as some critics have charged.[17]

Webster's strategy at the national capital had to account for the statutory provisions on the Supreme Court's jurisdiction to hear appeals from state tribunals. A constitutional question regarding individual rights or governmental power had to be involved. In this instance, Webster claimed that New Hampshire laws had impaired the obligation of a contract (the college charter) to which the state and the old trustees were parties. Since the relevant contract clause (Constitution, Article I, section 10) was a narrower basis for argument than Webster's side preferred and since the Court had only decided two contract cases previously, the lawyer sought to bring in other aspects. He did so by connecting the English common law definition of charitable trusts with the property rights of the college. The college was thus a *private* institution, not a public one as the New Hampshire Republicans claimed; and the old trustees, not the state, had supervisory rights as successors to the founder of the charity. In addition, Webster contended, the character of the federal constitutional right could be explained by reference to the *state* constitution's provision protecting liberty and property by the "law of the land." The provision was derived from the ancient Magna Carta and prohibited arbitrary interference.[18]

Although not as sober as this intricate reasoning, Webster's peroration nevertheless affected his audience deeply. While the historian cannot recover his exact words, their tenor has been credibly portrayed: "It is, Sir, as I have said, a small college. And yet *there are those who love it!* . . . I know not how others may feel, . . . but for myself, when I see my *Alma Mater* surrounded, like Caesar in the senate house, by those who are reiterating stab upon stab, I would not for this right hand have her say to me, 'And thou too, my son!' "[19]

During the year following presentation of the case up to the term of 1819, college leaders continued an attempt they had started early in the controversy to broaden their legal position: They initiated actions in federal circuit court against defendants from another state (Vermont). These so-called "cognate cases" between parties of diverse state citizenship could be appealed to the Supreme Court without having to allege violation of the Constitution. The common law doctrine on charitable trusts itself could be the basis of decision if the contract clause did not serve. Concurrently, the state's new counsel, William Pinkney, hoped to reargue the *Woodward* case at the 1819 term with new documents on the public character of the college. And both sides, to tell the truth, were pressing the limits of propriety by trying to influence justices thought to be undecided.[20] Notwithstanding, Chief Justice Marshall delivered his opinion soon after the Court reconvened. It resembled Webster's brief without some legal confections and held that the College charter was a contract and that the state had violated the contract clause. Story's concurring opinion was a detailed rationale according to common law principles.

Although the *Dartmouth* decision allowed the contract clause substantially to limit state power, many questions about its exact coverage remained for the Court to consider. During Webster's time, decisions were handed down concerning its application to particular subjects and circumstances, its relationship to other constitutional provisions, and its interplay with indispensable state powers. Characteristic of other landmark decisions, this one was a point of departure rather than an end result.

Another subject requiring judicial attention was bankruptcy. In the early nineteenth century, except for brief periods of national legislation, policy making in this field fell to the states. But during the very same term as the *Dartmouth* ruling, the Court decided in *Sturges v Crowninshield* (1819) that New York could not provide bankruptcy on debts incurred before passage of the law. The retrospective nature of the statute, said Marshall, amounted to impairment of a contract.[21]

Debts incurred *after* passage of a law was the issue in *Ogden v Saunders* (1827), which provided the occasion for Webster's argument against state bankruptcy power altogether. Coincidentally, the lawyer was pushing for a congressional enactment, albeit unsuccessfully, and he believed that the national bankruptcy power was exclusive. His brief for *Saunders* was quite broad-gauged. The obligation of a contract derived from universal natural law, he reasoned, not from a mere state enactment; thus, the relative timing of debt and statute made no difference to that contractual obligation. A state could not infringe upon a property right prospectively. This argument would have defined the contract clause, expressive of an untouchable natural right, very much like the later substantive due process doctrine under the Fifth and Fourteenth amendments. But by a division of four to three, the justices would not go that far, despite the earnest effort of the chief justice, now in the rare role of dissenter. *Ogden v Saunders* upheld a degree of state bankruptcy power and drew the contract clause's boundaries more narrowly than Marshall and Webster had hoped.[22]

The better-known *Charles River Bridge* case (1837) also limited the *Dartmouth College* decision. At Boston, a bridge spanning the river to Charlestown dated back to 1785, when subscribers had received a state charter. The project had been unusually profitable, but by the 1820s the tolls charged there had become a target of complaint. Jacksonian politicians took up the cause against the bridge company, while Federalists defended it. At last the legislature chartered the Warren Bridge Company to cross the Charles River at a location a stone's throw from the existing structure. After six years the new bridge would not collect tolls, thus promising financial disaster to the first enterprise. Like his political friends, Webster was horrified by this danger to vested rights, so he represented the corporation in the state court and carried the appeal to Washington in 1831. After the case was argued, the justices postponed a decision several times.

In 1837 counsel reargued, now before a post-Marshall Court headed by new Chief Justice Roger Taney, about whom Webster's feelings were obviously negative. The lawyer's principal position was that the state had unconstitutionally impaired a contractual obligation implied in the charter of 1785. Although the document had not specifically conferred a monopoly over this line of travel, Webster argued, the state deprived the proprietors of a specified right to take tolls when it provided for a free bridge, and the contract clause protects them from this ruinous measure.

Taney's majority opinion focused entirely on whether the Charles River Bridge charter implied an exclusive privilege. It did not, he ruled. His legal reasoning rested on some English as well as American precedents and arrived at the aphorism, "Nothing passes by implication," in interpreting a grant. Perhaps more compelling to the chief justice were economic and political considerations: Awarding a monopoly such as the old company claimed would inhibit the country's development. For example, previous grants to turnpikes must not jeopardize others to railroads and canals, for "new channels of communication are daily found necessary." To protect the rights of the community, corporate charters must be strictly construed.

Justice Story was appalled. He, too, emphasized the decision's impact upon economic growth but took the opposite view on how to promote growth. If grants became worthless as new ones superseded them, entrepreneurs would not risk capital, causing the economy to stagnate. Furthermore, Story contended in an exhaustive dissent, Taney was quite wrong about his legal precedents. It was well settled, he declared, that charters always allowed additional rights necessarily connected with those explicitly granted. Generally, Story expressed the same legal theory Webster had outlined; and, of course, the two perfectly agreed on economic and political grounds. Both also looked upon the Court's decision as destructive to the constitutional law of John Marshall.[23]

Later, still more rulings restricted the scope of the *Dartmouth* decision on the contract clause and property rights. For example, one state power that could possibly countervail that constitutional limitation was eminent domain. In the Massachusetts bridge controversy, the lawyers and judges fully discussed this point, but Taney ignored it in his opinion. It was not until 1848 in *West River Bridge v Dix* that the Supreme Court decided a case resting primarily on eminent domain (governmental acquisition of private property for public use with just compensation). By that time, the power had often been used, especially for transportation routes, indeed, sometimes by private enterprise to whom states delegated the authority to take land or water rights. But could a state employ eminent domain to cancel a corporation franchise without violating the contract clause?

Such was the question raised by Webster's client, a bridge company in Vermont whose old franchise had been revoked, it was said, to lay out a highway. The attorney argued that a corporate charter was unlike real estate; it was property that, once granted, could never be revoked for public use. No doubt realizing how advanced that argument was, Webster added a more moderate one: Even given that the state did have the power, the judicial record showed it had been abused. Vermont had taken over the bridge only in response to local complaint against tolls, had made it free, but had retained it as a part of an *existing* route despite its own law allowing eminent domain only for a *new* highway. Webster seemed to have been on better ground here than in his categorical opposition to the power in any circumstances. Nonetheless, the Court decided for the state and gave it complete discretion to define public use and just compensation. Such would be true well into the future, so as virtually to neutralize the contract clause as protection to corporate charters against eminent domain.[24]

The commerce clause would become even more important than the contract clause, and Webster had a leading role in defining it, too. Oddly, the high tribunal considered no commerce case in the first thirty-five years under the Constitution, despite the impulse commercial problems had given to framing that document in the 1780s. It is also surprising in light of the great significance this provision would have later.

Coming from New York in 1824, *Gibbons v Ogden* involved the well-known steamboat monopoly. Robert Livingston and Robert Fulton had developed an engine-powered craft to navigate the state's waters and had received an exclusive privilege to use or license others to use this new form of transportation. Aaron Ogden, one of their licensees, sought to stop an unlicensed interloper, Thomas Gibbons; and the state's courts had repeatedly decided that the monopoly was to prevail. At Washington, Webster represented Gibbons in contending that New York was unconstitutionally invading the sphere of congressional power over interstate commerce.

Ogden's counsel justified the Livingston-Fulton grant on the basis of a concurrent authority and cited numerous instances of state commercial legislation. Or, if the Court would not approve that formula, they said, then it should interpret the New York measure as merely the usual regulation of internal affairs, not interstate commerce. Either way, they could make a strong argument, for Congress had seldom acted and never specifically on steamboats carrying passengers on interior waters.

Webster's argument was one of his best. Carefully, he laid out the facts of the case and the options available to the justices. They could rule for fully concurrent state and national powers over interstate commerce, partially concurrent state power, or exclusive national power. He conceded that, in any event, a state unquestionably could regulate its purely intrastate commerce and could use its inherent police power to protect its citizens' health and safety; but at the interstate level, he urged adoption of the exclusive national option. Historically, the Constitution had aimed at removing local barriers to trade, yet several states had now reacted to the New York policy by retaliatory statutes. This disorderly circumstance was intolerable, Webster argued, because the framers had intended commerce among the states to be a unit. To be sure, Webster said, Congress had been silent about many of its aspects. Such silence, however, indicated that the national legislature meant for commerce to be free. Here was the sort of reasoning designed to appeal to Marshall, who could never forget the localism of Confederation days.

In the long run, however, Webster's alternative would be more memorable: exclusive national power over the "higher branches" of interstate commerce. The Court could judge the degree of importance of a particular commercial subject and consign it either to Congress alone or permit states to treat it until Congress had acted on it. Webster thought that interstate steamboat traffic during the transportation revolution was certainly a "higher branch," immune to New York's policy. Could he persuade the chief justice to gauge the degree of importance? Perhaps not, since Marshall preferred to classify and distribute powers separately between levels of government rather than to allow a mixture. An example was his national bank decision (*McCulloch v Maryland*) a few years earlier.

Webster allowed for that possibility and fell back on still another option, the conflict of state and national statutes. This argument led him to emphasize, though straining to do so, the federal coasting law of 1793 for licensing vessels and giving preference to American carriers in payment of tonnage duties. This national measure, he contended, must override the state legislation setting up a monopoly, because the Constitution, Article Six, declares federal statutes the supreme law of the land, state laws to the contrary notwithstanding. His client Gibbons had a coasting license.

Marshall felt caution was necessary. If he felt that congressional power was exclusive, it might alarm the slave states, and he did not wish to stir up a crisis by menacing interstate commerce in slaves with possible congressional intervention. So, bypassing all three options on classifying the commerce power—exclusive national, partial state concurrent, or full state concurrent—he moved to the safe position of statutory conflict, even though he had to read the coasting act in a dubious way. Consequently, in the decision itself, he deferred announcing any guideline for division of state and national powers while commenting favorably on a very broad congressional authority early in the opinion. In the next few years, he followed the same strategy, leaving the problem to his successors.[25]

Webster maintained a major role in this continuing saga over the next quarter century, still putting forward a nationalist formula. Like other lawyers and judges, he sometimes misrepresented Marshall's opinion in *Gibbons* as resting on an entirely exclusive rule, while others, including several Jacksonian justices, misrepresented it as opting for a fully concurrent one. Such was true in the *License Cases* (1847) and the *Passenger Cases* (1849), argued repeatedly by counsel and discussed by the judges, with a majority being unable to agree on any general statement.[26]

Finally, in *Cooley v Wardens* (1852), the Court did manage to decide a Pennsylvania pilotage case, with a sufficient number of its members united on the same guideline. It was a compromise, holding for partially concurrent state power over interstate commerce. Benjamin Curtis wrote the opinion for the majority, saying that commerce among the states was so complex that one must look at the particular subject rather than at the power as a whole. The nature of some commercial subjects required uniform national regulation, he said, while other subjects admitted concurrent state action (unless there was a statutory conflict). What Curtis did was to adopt a formula similar to that offered by Webster in the steamboat case: exclusive national authority over "higher branches." How appropriate that Curtis was the jurist to do so, since he was a protégé of Webster, who had recently urged his appointment to the bench. *Cooley* would be much more than a temporary truce among the individualists of Taney's Court. The rule would survive to the present day, nourishing constitutional nationalism but fashioning a federalism in which states could operate effectively.[27]

An assessment of Webster as a lawyer must recognize his prominence during the formative era of American legal history. His practice in state and lower federal courts often involved the adaptation of the common law to modern conditions. In the early nineteenth century, the relationship between legal and economic change was significant. The advance of corporate enterprise, the revolution in transportation, the rise of financial institutions, and the establishment of a national market all demanded large modifications of old law. Webster contributed substantially to this process, encouraging economic development in an environment where the rights of property were safe and productive. Whether he aligned himself too closely with the wealthy and powerful remains as much a debatable question as it was in his lifetime.

His unique career as a lawyer in the Supreme Court over four decades placed him at the center of constitutional development as well. Bringing to the task a keen intelligence, a remarkable eloquence, and a broad experience in politics, Webster participated in nearly all the leading constitutional cases of the day. His contract cases, despite decisions by Taney's Court, strengthened property rights and promoted economic growth. His commerce cases, notwithstanding his failure to get a full-blown nationalist rule, befitted the sort of federalism that would prove quite viable. His success in the promotion of federal judicial power, though falling short of his ideal, did not miss it by much. When his contemporaries referred to him as the expounder and defender of the Constitution, they could use the terms correctly, whether applied to the politician or to the lawyer.

1. Alfred S. Konefsky and Andrew J. King, eds., *The Papers of Daniel Webster: Legal Papers* (3 vols.; Hanover, N.H., and London, England, 1982–89), 1:9–32. Hereafter cited as *Legal Papers*.

2. Ibid., 32–58, for Webster's diary and correspondence during these months.

3. Daniel Webster to James H. Bingham, May 4, 1805, ibid., 71. See Document 49, p. 161. Daniel Webster abbreviated as DW hereafter. Maurice G. Baxter, *One and Inseparable: Daniel Webster and the Union* (Cambridge, Mass., 1984), p. 16.

4. *Legal Papers*, 1:58, 89–104, 188–89.

5. Ibid., 61–63, 72–73, 111–14.

6. Ibid., 157–63, 187, 298–99.

7. Ibid., 422–23.

8. Ibid., 530–42.

9. Ibid., 517–29.

10. Ibid., 2:119–72, for editors' discussion and for texts of DW itemized books of receipts, 1816–47.

11. Ibid., 528–64, for the bank cases. *Foster v Essex Bank*, 17 Mass. 479 (1821); *Salem Bank v Gloucester Bank*, 17 Mass. 1 (1820); *King v Dedham Bank*, 15 Mass. 447 (1819); *Commonwealth v Wyman*, in *Law Reporter*, VI (1844), 385–92, and VIII (1846), 337–44.

12. Baxter, *One and Inseparable*, pp. 158–61. An editorial comment on the case and a text of DW summations to jury are in Charles M. Wiltse, ed., *The Papers of Daniel Webster: Speeches and Formal Writings* (2 vols.; Hanover, N.H., and London, England, 1986–88), 1:395–445.

13. *Legal Papers*, 2:415–526, for the whole subject of marine insurance; ibid., 474–82, for editorial discussion of several *Peele* cases in state and lower federal courts. Story's principal decision in the United States Circuit Court of Massachusetts is in 3 Mason 27 (1822).

14. *Legal Papers*, 2:175–275, is a thorough presentation of the commission's work. For an itemized list of clients and fees, see ibid., 266–75. The commission's records are in the National Archives, RG 76, Records of the Boundary and Claims Commissions and Arbitrations. See Document 54, pp. 166–68.

15. Comprehensive informtion on all DW Supreme Court cases, 1814–52, with titles, subjects, dates argued, how reported, and names of attorneys, can be found in *Legal Papers*, 3, Appendix I, 1046–98. See also Maurice G. Baxter, *Daniel Webster and the Supreme Court* (Amherst, Mass., 1966), passim.

16. *Legal Papers*, 3:17–54. For the case as a whole, see ibid., 17–254; and Francis N. Stites, *Private Interest and Public Gain: The Dartmouth College Case, 1819* (Amherst, Mass., 1972).

17. *Legal Papers*, 3:54–175. Much of the manuscript material is in the Dartmouth College Archives and is liberally presented, with editorial annotation, in ibid.

18. DW revised draft of his argument, ibid., 119–53. Printed version is in the official Court report, 4 Wheaton 551–600 (1819). Wheaton used this draft, along with drafts of arguments of other counsel—all prepared by Webster. They appeared in a book published in the name of his former law partner, Timothy Farrar, Jr.,

Report of the Case of the Trustees of Dartmouth College against William H. Woodward (Portsmouth, N.H., 1819).

19. *Legal Papers*, 3:153–54. A spectator, Professor Chauncey Goodrich of Yale, wrote out the peroration from memory thirty-five years later, and Rufus Choate used it in his eulogy of Webster at Dartmouth in 1853. The manuscript is in the Boston Public Library. See Document 55, p. 169.

20. Stites, *Private Interest and Public Gain*, pp. 69–98.

21. In contrast to his own preference for exclusive national power over bankruptcy, Webster represented Crowninshield, relying upon the state statute in a circuit court hearing. *Legal Papers*, 3:297–99.

22. Ibid., 308–46. For DW's argument, as reported in 12 Wheaton 213 (1827), see ibid., 330–43. There was a second decision, this one for Webster's side, holding that a state's bankruptcy law could not affect debts of a citizen of another state. At a time of increasing interstate transactions, Webster therefore regained much that had seemed lost in the first decision.

23. *Legal Papers*, 3:398–646, for editorial discussion and documents; Stanley I. Kutler, *Privilege and Creative Destruction, The Charles River Bridge Case* (Philadelphia, 1971). DW manuscript brief is in *Legal Papers*, 3:600–642; but he failed to supply these notes to the Court reporter, who had to reconstruct the argument himself in 11 Peters 514–36 (1837).

24. *Legal Papers*, 3:732–38.

25. Ibid., 255–91, with DW argument, 271–87, as reported in 9 Wheaton 1 (1824). See also Maurice G. Baxter, *The Steamboat Monopoly: Gibbons v Ogden, 1824* (N.Y., 1972), pp. 37–68. See Document 60, pp. 174–91.

26. *Legal Papers*, 3:681–732. DW argument, Feb. 9, 1847, in *Passenger Cases*, ibid., 710–14. See Documents 61 and 62, pp. 191–202.

27. 12 Howard 299; Baxter, *Steamboat Monopoly*, pp. 110–15.

Document 44
Text from *Legal Papers* 1: 11–12.

To James Hervey Bingham[1]

Dear Hervey,   Salisbury, Sepr. 10th. 1801.

I can find none other method of writing to *my Hervey*, than by the circuitous journey which our friend Hutchinson[2] proposes to take. He is now here, on his way to N. Ipswich, and on his return home will lodge this at Charleston. I am now settled down in the Office where I expect to obtain a smattering of Law knowledge. With me is Mr. Abbott,[3] whom I mentioned to you at Commencement. If any one could fill the place vacated by your absence, it is he. Company, other than what occasionally falls into the Office, we have none. This you might conclude from the situation of the place. My present business is the perusal of Vattel on national [law]. I expect nextly to review Burlamaqui, & Montesquieu, [and] to read Hume,[4] before I commence an enquiry into [the p]rinciples of municipal and common law.

Thus am I, now, pray how are you? What law shop, what divinity-closet, or what medical chamber confines you? I presume, however, you are not yet engaged in either, but I apprehend you are thinking about something.

Mr. Green,[5] the attorney at Concord, communicated a wish to me, that I would give his compliments to some *respectable* young gentleman, and inform him that he expects soon to be in want of a Clerk, and that any gentleman of character and promise, who may feel disposed to read in his Office, shall be entitled to his tuition *gratis*. Mr Green is a respectable Law character, and his reputation as a private gentleman, no one, as I know, impeaches. Board, at Concord, is easily to be obtained on reasonable terms.

Now I would not advise—but suggest a few considerations.

It is not to be doubted, that you can obtain more information in four years, with the deduction of three months from every year, than by three years continued application. That is—if in those said three months, you are able to read Law, when not in School. At Concord you could probably, undoubtedly, obtain employment three months in each year, and the amount of your wages for this time would hire your board the other nine months.

Concord is a pleasant village. Mr. McFarland, Mr. Flag[g][6] and others would unite with you in harmony of sound and harmony of sentiment. The Town Library affords a field of miscellaneous reading, and, another source of improvement, the Ladies of Concord are very learned.

If it be an observation of weight that in the event of your living there we should meet often, I submit it.

Duty to Mr Green obliged me to mention his proposals, in the first instance, to *the best* man I knew, and my own feelings urge me to address the request to you with particular earnestness.

I have not heard from Hannover since I left. I hop[e the] best things for them all. Philosophy, Divinity, Hun[tingtonop]hy, Ripleyalogy, Woodwardography[7] &c all are entitled to my wishes of happiness, and here, in this written form commit those names to non-recolection. When I shall see *those plains* again I know not. You may expect me at Lempster some time this fall, but you must first write me and tell me when you shall be there.

Give my regards to your good Father, Capt. Minor, Doctor Merrill[8]
and all friends and believe me ever to be Yours

Daniel Webster

1. Bingham (1781–1859; Dartmouth 1801), a classmate and close friend of Webster,
became a New Hampshire lawyer and state legislator. When Bingham became impover-
ished, Webster secured a clerkship for him in 1851 in the Department of the Interior.
2. Perhaps Timothy Hutchinson (1777–1857; Dartmouth 1800), Bennington, New
York farmer.
3. Daniel Abbott (1777–1853; Harvard 1797), New Hampshire lawyer and state
legislator.
4. Emmerich de Vattel, *The Law of Nations* (London, 1759); Jean Jacques Burlamaqui,
The Principles of Natural and Politic Law (2 vols., London, 1752); Charles Louis de
Secondat, Baron de la Brede et de Montesquieu, *The Spirit of Laws* (2 vols., London,
1750); David Hume, *The History of England from the Invasion of Julius Caesar to the Abdication
of James the Second, 1688* (6 vols., London, 1754–62).
5. Samuel Green (1770–1851), New Hampshire lawyer and state legislator.
6. Asa McFarland (1769–1827; Dartmouth 1793), Concord clergyman, music
teacher, and Dartmouth trustee. Ebenezer Flagg, Concord clergyman.
7. Rev. Joseph Huntington (1735–94; Yale 1762), Dartmouth trustee; Sylvanus
Ripley (1749–87; Dartmouth 1771), Dartmouth professor of divinity; Bezaleel
Woodward (1745–1804; Yale 1764), Dartmouth professor of mathematics and philosophy.
8. Bingham's father, James Bingham of Lempster; probably Timothy Miner (d.
1816), Lempster tanner, currier, and shoemaker; Asa Merrill, Lempster physician and
town clerk.

Document 45
Text from *Legal Papers* 1: 24–25.

To James Hervey Bingham

Good Hervey,—   Salisbury, December 21, 1802.

Lovers, I have heard it said, are apt to write with trembling hand.
If that circumstance alone be sufficient to constitute one, I am as
valiant a lover as ever made a vow. My hand does indeed tremble, and
my brain dances with twice as much giddiness as ever. But what would
be imputed to love, if you were a lady, may now very fairly be ascribed
to the measles. This ugly disorder attacked me about a fortnight since,
and has formed a great syncope in my health and happiness. I am now
convalescent, as the faculty say, and am today just able to scrawl you
this; if it be very dull, pray do not blame me, but the measles; if
you will agree to this, I shall shift much responsibility from my own
shoulders.

The information you communicated, I will not call it an opinion, was fully anticipated. On reading the statute carefully, I found it expressly excepted specialties from its operation; and I find in Blackstone,[1] second volume, on the nature and different kinds of deeds, that a bond under seal and sign-manual, is a specialty. So in that quarter I have no loop to hang my hopes upon. Here give me leave to pronounce a wise opinion, viz: That the best way to study law is in relation to particular points. I had read the statute of limitations, I do not know how many times, nor how many times more I might have read it among others, without discovering that it did not affect a sealed instrument, unless I had looked in reference to that particular inquiry. It is very much so, I believe, with history. We read page after page, and retaining a slender thread of events, everything else glides from the mind about as fast as the eye traces the lines of the book. Yet, when we examine a particular occurrence, or search after a single date, the impression is permanent, and we have added one idea to the stock of real knowledge.

If you are entertained with politics, I will tell you for your amusement, that Mr. Thompson[2] is about to be turned out, as the phrase is, from the post-office at this place, to give room to Moses Eastman, Esq.[3] The latter gentleman has already received his appointment.

Make my compliments acceptable, pray do, to your good cousins E[nos Stevens] and P[olly Stevens].[4] I remember with joy and gratitude the kindness and hospitality with which I was treated in the family.

There is not half room enough left to enumerate all the good wishes my heart feels for you. It will save me a deal of trouble in this way, if you will only wish at once for everything you honestly can, and I will cheerfuly "second the motion." Yours,

D. Webster.

P.S. This has been delayed so long you will answer it. I mean you will write another, for there is nothing in this requiring an answer; you will write me a line, I say, soon, yes, immediately, 'twill be better than "puke or pill" to cure me of the measles.

1. William Blackstone, *Commentaries on the Laws of England* (4 vols., Oxford, 1765–69).
2. Thomas W. Thompson (1766–1821; Harvard 1786), New Hampshire lawyer, Dartmouth trustee, state legislator, and U.S. representative (1805–07) and senator (1814–17). In 1801, Webster read law in Thompson's office in Salisbury, thus making him Webster's first law teacher. From 1798 to 1803 Thompson was the postmaster of Salisbury.
3. Eastman (1770–1848; Dartmouth 1794), a New Hampshire lawyer who succeeded Thompson as postmaster of Salisbury in April 1803.
4. Enos Stevens and Polly Stevens of Charlestown.

Document 46
Text from *Legal Papers* 1: 28–30.

To James Hervey Bingham

Hervey,   Octobr. 6th 1803

One Joseph W. Brackett[1] probably handed you an *urbanic* letter
from me written at Hanover, in which I promised to send you soon
an epistle three feet long, in answer to several questions you ask
respecting my wanderings to & fro. Here then you shall have the three
feet.

And first; My Father[2] has an important suit at Law pending before
the Supreme Court of Vt. This has frequently called me into that
realm, in the course of the past Summer. Mr. Marsh[3] of Woodstock is
of counsel to us, wherefore I have made him several visits, in arranging
the necessary preliminaries to trial. This circumstance, I fancy originates the suggestion that I contemplated reading in his Office. In
reality, I have no such idea in my head at present. Heretofore I have
been inclined to think of Vt as a place of practice, & as preparatory
therefor have thought it possible that I might read a year in that State,
but I never carried my views so far as to fix on an Office, & at this time
have no views at all of that kind.

Secondly; You have heard that I contemplated finishing my studies
in Massachusetts. There is more foundation for this, than the other.
It is true I have laid many plans to enable myself to be some time in
Boston, before I go into practice, but I did not know as I had mentioned the circumstance abroad, because it is all uncertain. I believe
that some acquaintance in the Capital of New England would be very
useful to us, who expect to plant ourselves down as Country Lawyers.
But I cannot control my fortune—I must follow wherever circumstances lead. My going to Boston is therefore much more a matter of
hope, than of probability. Unless something like a miracle puts the
means in my hands, I shall not budge from here very soon. Depend
on it, however, James, that I shall sometime avail myself of more
advantages than this smoky village affords. But when, or where, you
& I know equally well. If my circumstances were like Yours, I would
by all means pass a six months in Boston. The acquaintances you would
be likely to form there, might help you to much business in the course
of life. You can pass that time there just as well as not, & I therefore
advise to it, as far as I ought to advise to anything. But some men are
born with a silver spoon in their mouths, & others with a wooden ladle!
(Would not you thank me to mend my pen?)

If you can tell what it is to read Coke[4] in black letter on a day too warm for a fire, & too cold to be without one it will save me any description of myself. When tired of old Coke, I look at Smollets continuation of Hume's history.[5] The whole of my reading, however, does not amount to much. I can hardly be called a *Student* at Law. The Law question that now puzzles us in this quarter, is, Whether Buonapartte, when he shall have gone to John Bull's palace & taken hold of the ring of the door in the name of seizin of the whole Island, will be such a king against whom it will be treason in an Englishman to fight? But they may settle this among them—you & I will not give our opinion without a *fee*.

I shall be alone here for three weeks. Why will you not just take your horse & gallop down here? do come, pray do. Twill take but just a day from your Father's. I will tell you when you must come—on the 15th Inst.—I shall be at Warner, which is not more than 25 mi[le]s from Lempster—come then & find me there—will not you be there? Say, aye, do. I shall look for you.

I am, as have been time whereof the memory of man runneth not to the contrary, Your Friend

D. Webster.

1. Joseph Warren Brackett (1775–1826; Dartmouth 1800), New York City lawyer and close friend of Webster.
2. Ebenezer Webster (1739–1806).
3. Charles Marsh (1765–1849; Dartmouth 1786), Vermont lawyer, Dartmouth trustee, and U.S. representative (1815–17) from Vermont.
4. Edward Coke, *Reports* (6 vols., 1600–15); *Institutes* (4 vols., 1628–44).
5. The continuation of Hume's history by Tobias Smollett entitled *Continuation of the Complete History of England* (5 vols., London, 1763–65).

Document 47
Text from *Legal Papers* 1: 30–32.

To James Hervey Bingham

P.S. The top of a letter is a new place for a postscript; excuse it, for its design is to beg you to give my love to your and my friends P[olly Stevens] and E[nos Stevens].

Good Hervey,   Salisbury, April 3, 1804.
I am really much obliged by your ready attention to my requests; as also by your saying, that as Mr. West[1] leaves the matter with you, I "may venture to jog on." Captain Enos is precisely the man for me; if

ever I eat bread at "No. 4,"[2] it will be at his table. The distance from the office is not too great in dry weather, and in wet times one has nothing to do in Charlestown, but just to step "the other side of the street."

I am now going, James, to give you a full survey of the "whole ground," as it respects my prospects, hopes, and wishes. The great object of a lawyer is business; but this is not, or ought not to be, his sole object. Pleasant society, an agreeable acquaintance, and a degree of respectability, not merely as a lawyer, but as a man, are other objects of importance. You and I commenced the study, you know, with a resolution which we did not say much about, of being honest and conscientious practitioners. Some part of this resolution is, I hope, still hanging about me, and for this reason I choose to settle in a place where the practice of the bar is fair and honorable. The Cheshire bar, as far as I have learned, is entitled to a preference in these respects over that of any county in the State. You know my partiality for Connecticut River folks generally. Their information and habits are far better, in my opinion, than those of the people in the eastern part of the State. These reasons compel me to say with you, "it is a goodly land," and to make it my wish to settle therein.

E contra. Many of my friends are desirous that I should make an attempt to live in Portsmouth. Mr. Thompson, my good master, knows every thing about the comparative advantages of different places, everywhere in New Hampshire, except Cheshire county. He has frequently suggested to me, that Portsmouth would be a good place for a young man, and the other evening when I hinted my inclination for Cheshire, he said he had a high esteem for the people that way, but added that he still wished me to consider Portsmouth. He says there are many gentlemen of character there, who would patronize a young lawyer, and thinks that even Mr. Attorney-General[3] would be fond of the thing.

Mr. T. will have business, on which I shall be at Portsmouth as soon as the roads are passable, and out of respect to his opinion, I shall make no certain arrangements for my future reading till that time. At present, I do not feel that Portsmouth is the place for me.

In the way of study, my present pursuit is some little knowledge of pleading. I am reading what Bacon has collected on that subject,[4] and yesterday, you will hardly believe me, I travelled through a case in Saunders of eight Latin pages.[5] Saunders inserts all the pleas, and abridges the arguments of counsel; he is therefore, I take it, very useful to those who, like myself, are a good deal ignorant of the forms of pleading. I mean to lay my hands heavily upon him, and in one month I hope to be able to give some account of him. The winter has passed away more pleasantly than any I ever before passed at Salisbury, as far, I mean, as my health, which has not been the best, would suffer it to be pleasant. Mr. T.'s sisters have been in this realm, and being very excellent folks, added much to what was before very small society in Salisbury. Miss Poor[6] is in town, yet. It would please her vastly if you would just call and play a game at backgammon with her again. She says I unreasonably monopolized your company last fall, at the expense of the folks in the house. I told you how all that matter was and would be; I don't see how I can live any longer without having a friend near me, I mean a male friend, just such a friend as one J.H.B. Yes, James, I must come; we will yoke together again; your little bed is just wide enough; we will practise at the same bar, and be as friendly a pair of single fellows as ever cracked a nut. We perhaps shall never be rich; no matter, we can supply our own personal necessities. By the time we are thirty, we will put on the dress of old bachelors, a mourning suit, and having sown all our wild oats, with a round hat and a hickory staff we will march on to the end of life, whistling as merry as robins, and I hope as innocent. Good-bye to this nonsense, and, by way of contrast, good-bye to you.

D.W.

1. Benjamin West (1746–1817; Harvard 1768), a New Hampshire lawyer, delegate to the Continental Congress (1781), and member of the Constitutional Convention (1787). Bingham read law in the office of West.
2. The original appellation of Charlestown.
3. Jeremiah Mason served as New Hampshire attorney general from 1802 to 1805.
4. Matthew Bacon, *A New Abridgment of the Law* (5th ed., 7 vols., London, 1798).
5. Edmund Saunders, *Les Reports des Divers Pleadings et Cases en le Court del Bank le Roy* (2 vols., London, 1686).
6. Emily Poor, daughter of Ebenezer Poor of Andover, Maine.

Document 48
Text from *Legal Papers* 1: 55–56.

To Thomas W. Thompson

Dear Sir,   Boston Novr 30th. 1804
Notwithstanding the rule of this Bar discriminating between Harvard scholars and others, & imposing on the latter, as a tax on their ignorance, a fourth year's study, it is pretty likely that I can be admitted

here the first of April. Mr Gore[1] has taken some interest in my favor, & in my behalf has spoken to Mr Parsons[2] & some other Gentlemen of the Bar. Mr Parsons, when informed of this *discriminating rule,* thought it a very illiberal thing, & that it must be altered. I would thank You for a Certificate of the time during which I was in your Office. To refresh your memory, I will state dates as accurately as I can. 1801 not far from the middle of July—as I think between the tenth and fifteenth—I went into your Office & tarried there until the tenth of July 1804, deducting eight months, in which I taught in the Academy at Fryeburg. You may recollect that during the two months vacation in the winter of my last College year, I was about your Office, & looking into your books. According to the custom of this place, as I understand it, these two months are to be regularly reckoned as a part of my Term. It may be otherwise in N. Hampshire. I should like to have these two months included in your Certificate if agreeable to your impressions of propriety—if not, I will nevertheless thank you to notice the circumstance. If I compute correctly on the above facts, I was with you two years and a half. My intention is to be proposed here in January—then to <pro> be at Amherst in March, & if the Hillsborough Bar <will> chuse not to admit me, I <will> can try here the first of April. Under this arrangement I am quite at rest about my admission.

An occurrence which I have no reason at all to regret, induced me, twenty five days ago, to set out on a journey, to Albany. I have just returned. At Hadley I had the pleasure of passing an hour in the family of your Brother Mr. Hopkins.[3] That was on the eleventh of this month, & the family, of whom I found Miss Isabella to be one, were then in good health. . . .

The Certificate may be enclosed, if you please, to Mr Gore. That was his suggestion. Perhaps you will find it convenient to forward it soon. I am waiting for your Commissions, with the hope of doing you some little service.

Make mention of my respects to Mrs Thompson, & assure Yourself of the affectionate regards of Your humble Servant

D. Webster

1. Christopher Gore (1758–1827; Harvard 1776), a leading Boston lawyer and Federalist politician.

2. Theophilus Parsons (1750–1813; Harvard 1769), Massachusetts lawyer and judge.

3. John Hopkins (1771–1842), brother-in-law of Thompson, a Hadley, Massachusetts merchant.

Document 49
Text from *Legal Papers* 1: 71–72.

To James Hervey Bingham

Dear Bingham,   Boscawen N.H. May 4. 1805

You must know that I have opened a shop in this village for the manufacture of Justice writs. Other mechanics do pretty well here, & I e'en determined to try my luck among others. March 25. I left Boston—with a good deal of regret, I assure you. I was then bound for Portsmouth, but I found my father extremely ill, & little fit to be left by all his sons, & therefore, partly thro' duty, partly thro' necessity & partly thro' choice, I concluded to make my stand here. Some little business is doing in the neighborhood, & of that little I hope to get a little part. This is all that I can at present say of my prospects. For one thing I ought to be thankful. If poverty brings me so near the wind that I canot stay here, *in duty to my stomach,* I have only to take my hickory & walk. The disagreeable incumbrances of houses lands & property need not delay me a moment. Nor shall I be hindered by Love, nor fastened to Boscawen by the power of Beauty. Our friend [Andrew] Lovejoy will open a store in this place next week, in which he will put Warren, his Brother, & Thomas, son of Major Taylor.[1] I shall be glad to have them here. One disaster has happened to me. With the assistance of my friends, I collected 85 Dols & sent to Boston, for the payment of a Bookseller with whom I had contracted for a few volumes. But the cash was stolen from the pocket of the bearer, after he got into Boston—& I lose all. Books, therefore, I must go without for the present.

When I have more leisure I will write you more at length. The object of this is only to tell you that I am here, & pray you to write to me. . . .

Adieu—my old—good—friend.

D. Webster

1. Andrew Lovejoy (1772–1856), a merchant; Warren Lovejoy (1784–1819); Thomas Taylor (1779–1850), a teamster.

Document 50
Text from *Legal Papers* 1: 105–06.

Writ of Attachment
[*August 22, 1805*]

Grafton—ss.] The State of New-Hampshire,
To the Sheriff of any County in this State,
or his Deputy—Greeting.
WE *command you to attach the Goods or Estate of* Samuel Butters Junior[1]
of Concord in our County of Rockingham, Trader, To *the value of*
Seven Thousand *Dollars; and for want thereof, to take the Body of the said*
Butters (*if* he *may be found in your precinct*) *and* him *safely keep, so that you*
have him *before Our Justices of Our Court of Common Pleas, to be holden at*
Plymouth *within and for Our said County of Grafton, on the* Second *Tuesday*
of September next *then and there, in Our said Court, to answer unto* Joseph
Sewall, Samuel Salisbury Jun, John Tappan and Josiah Salisbury,[2] all
of Boston in the County of Suffolk and Commonwealth of Massachusetts, Merchants, & copartners in trade, under the style and firm of
Sewall, Salisbury & Company, in a plea of the case, for that said
Butters, at Boston, to wit said Plymouth, on the nineteenth day of this
instant August, by his promissory note in writing under his hand of
that date for value received promised the Plfs, by the name of their
said Firm, to pay them or their order <Three thousand> Thirty nine
hundred and seventy three dollars, and seventy six cents, on demand
with interest from date—<Also, for that said Butters, at Boston, to
wit said Plymouth, on the same nineteenth day of August instant, by
his other promissory note under his hand in writing of that date for
value received promised the said Plaintiffs, by the name of their said
Firm, to pay them or their order Two thousand dollars, on demand
with interest from date.>

Yet, though requested said Butters hath never paid <either of the>
said notes <aforesaid>, but neglects and refuses so to do *To the Damage*
of the said Plaintiffs, *as they say the Sum of* Seven thousand *Dollars, which*
shall then and there be made to appear, with other due Damages: and have you
there this Writ, with your doings therein.—Witness, Samuel Emerson,[3] Esquire,
at Plymouth, the twenty second *day of* August *Anno Domini* 1805.

S.P. Webster[4] Clerk.

---

1. Butters (b. 1775), Concord storekeeper.
2. All partners in a Boston mercantile firm.

3. Emerson (1736–1819), prominent Plymouth farmer and chief justice of the New Hampshire Court of Common Pleas, Grafton County, 1782–1806.

4. Stephen P. Webster (1771–1841; Harvard 1792), New Hampshire lawyer, state legislator, and clerk of the Court of Common Pleas of Grafton County.

Document 51
Text from *Legal Papers* 1: 129–30.

Writ of Execution
[January 20, 1806]

Rockingham, sc. The Sate of New-Hampshire.
To the Sheriff of any County in this State,
or his Deputy, Greeting.
WHEREAS the President directors and Company of the New Hampshire Union Bank *by the consideration of our Justices of our Court of Common Pleas, holden at* Portsmouth *for and within our County of Rockingham aforesaid, on the* first *Tuesday of* January *Anno Domini,* 1806 *recovered judgment against* Timothy Dix Junior[1] of Boscawen in our County of Hillsborough Esquire *for the sum of* Six hundred and thirty dollars *Debt or Damages, and* Five dollars Seventy cents *Cost of suit, as to us appears of record, whereof Execution remains to be done. We command you therefore, that of the Goods, Chattels, or Lands of the said* Dix—*(within your precinct) you cause to be paid and satisfied unto the said* President directors & Company *at the value thereof in money, the aforesaid sums being* Six hundred thirty five dollars Seventy cents *in the whole, with* seventeen *Cents more for this Writ; and thereof to satisfy yourself for your own fees; and for want of Goods, Chattels, or lands of the said* Dix *to be by* him *shewn unto you or found within your precinct, to the acceptance of the said* President directors & Company *to satisfy the sums aforesaid, We command you to take the body of the said* Dix *and* him *commit unto either of our jails within your precinct, and detain in your custody within our said jail, until* he *pay the full sums above mentioned, with your fees, or that* he *be discharged by the said* President directors & Company *the Creditor or otherwise by order of law. Hereof fail not, and make return of this writ, with your doings therein, unto our said Court of Common Pleas, to be holden at* Exeter *in our County of Rockingham aforesaid, upon the* second *Tuesday of* August *next. Witness* Timothy Walker[2] Esq. at Exeter, the Twentieth *day of* January *Anno Domini,* 1806

N. Emery[3] *Clerk.*

Recd. the contents of this execution.

H. S. Langdon[4]
Cashier of the N.H. Union Bank

1. Dix (d. 1813), Boscawen, New Hampshire, merchant and state legislator.

2. Walker (1731–1822; Harvard 1756), a merchant and judge of the New Hampshire Court of Common Pleas, Rockingham County from 1777 to 1809.

3. Noah Emery (1748–1817), clerk of the New Hampshire Court of Common Pleas, Rockingham County, from 1787 to 1817.

4. Henry Shelburne Langdon (1766–1857; Yale 1785), Portsmouth banker and lawyer, state legislator, and cashier of the New Hampshire Union Bank from 1802 to 1815.

Document 52
Text from *Legal Papers* 1: 533.

From Timothy Pickering[1]

Dear Sir,   Salem Octr. 29th 1812.

Coming to town yesterday, my son[2] handed me your obliging letter of the 15th to him, inclosing a libellous paragraph from the New Hampshire Gazette.[3] I had before received the same paragraph thro' Captain I. Nichols of Salem, from a professed but *anonymous* friend of his. Captain N. formerly lived in Portsmouth. That friend appeared to take an interest in the matter, that the libeller might be prosecuted. But long familiarized with slander from the unprincipled agents of democracy, it excites not the slightest personal feeling; and I had concluded to let this *second-hand* libel pass unnoticed. The same slander, in substance, was uttered about two years ago, by a Dr. Josiah Smith[4] of Newbury, whom I prosecuted, & whom I forgave on his recantation which was read in open court & put on record in the office of the Clerk of the Common Pleas for this county. It was from a sense of *public duty*, that I have caused or consented to similar prosecutions; and since it has struck you that *duty* may require a prosecution in the present case, I do not hesitate to give my assent; and I request you to commence a suit against the editor of the New Hampshire Gazette, or *other* the real libeller.[5] Whatever monies you expend in the case I will re-imburse, together with your fees. You will doubtless judge it expedient to institute the action without delay; waiting no longer than to obtain the requisite evidence of the publication. Have the goodness to make your future communications directly to my son here, who probably will more speedily & regularly receive them than I should at Wenham.

I am dear sir with respectful esteem yr. obliged & obedt servt.

                                                        T. Pickering

1. Pickering (1745–1829; Harvard 1763), Federalist leader, Revolutionary War gen-

eral, postmaster general (1791–95), secretary of state (1795–1800), U.S. senator (1805–11) and representative (1812–17).

2. John Pickering (1777–1846; Harvard 1796), Massachusetts lawyer and linguist.

3. Webster's letter to John Pickering of October 15, 1812, is printed in *Correspondence* 1:133. On October 12, the *Gazette* had branded Timothy Pickering a Benedict Arnold.

4. Smith (d. 1820), Newburyport merchant and physician.

5. William Weeks was publisher of the *Gazette*, and in a libel suit the plaintiff could sue the author as well as the publisher.

Document 53
Text from *Legal Papers* 2: 201–02.

To [Peter Chardon Brooks?]¹

Dr Sir   Washington feb. 24. 1819

The Spanish Treaty will be ratified, by the Senate either today or tomorrow.² I understand it provides for the creation of a board of Commissioners with power to make compensation for Captures &c, not exceeding, in the whole five millions of Dlls. The Insurance Offices in Boston must, of course, have heavy claims of this character. The Commissioners will sit, probably, in this City. I have ventured to think, that those Offices might, usefully to themselves & me, make me their agent, in those claims. A general agency, for all or most of the Offices, would make it worth my attention, & justify me in appropriating as much time to the subject as the nature of it required. If this suggestion should meet your approbation, I hope you will communicate it to the Gentlemen at the Suffolk Office, & also to Mr. Cabot.³ If, however, any, the least, doubt, difficulty, or impropriety occurs, to you or to them, I beg you at once to forbear pursuing the suggestion. I have asked Mr [Jonathan] Mason to write to Genl. Welles' Office⁴ on the same subject. I do not remember that I ever before sought any employment with a view to pecuniary profit. No doubt I may make an awkward figure at it, now. Perhaps, too, I misjudge the importance & amount of these claims. But if it be a case in which I might render service, & receive equivalent compensation, it would suit my objects entirely to be employed in it.

I suppose Comm[issione]rs will not be appointed until the Treaty shall be ratified by Spain.

It has been suggested to me, from a pretty high source, that the persons interested in the North might have some influence, in regard to the nomination of one or more of the Comm[issione]rs. It will be in season to think of this hereafter. In the mean time I think no partial recommendation should be forwarded, if it can be avoided.

I suppose our Western boundary is fixed as follows—Beginning at the mouth of the Sabine River, following the western boundary of Louisiana to the Red River; up the Red River to the 100th deg. of W. Longitude;—thence due north to the Arkansaw; up the Arkansaw to the 42nd deg. of N. Latitude, & thence West to the Pacific—giving us about 7 Degs of Latitude on the Pacific—& the mouth of Columbia River. We also get the Floridas, in cons[ideratio]n of the 5 millions paid to our own citizens.

I am, Dr Sir, very truly Yours

Danl. Webster

1. Brooks (1767–1849), Boston merchant and marine insurance broker, president of the New England Insurance Company, and one of the Spanish claimants.

2. The Treaty of Amity, Settlement, and Limits between the United States and Spain, generally known as the Adams-Onis Treaty, was signed on February 22, 1819. It was unanimously approved by the U.S. Senate on February 24.

3. Probably George Cabot (1752–1823), Boston merchant and politician, president of the Boston Marine Insurance Company, and U.S. senator from 1791–96.

4. Jonathan Mason (1756–1831; Princeton 1774), Boston lawyer and real estate developer, state legislator, and U.S. senator (1800–03) and representative (1817–20); Arnold Welles (1761–1827; Harvard 1780), president of the Massachusetts Fire and Marine Insurance Company.

Document 54
Text from *Legal Papers* 2: 202–04.

Agreement Naming Webster
Agent for Claimants under Spanish Treaty
[*July 27, 1821*]

At a meeting of Claimants under the Spanish Treaty, in the Hall of the Massachusetts Bank, July 27th 1821, convened for the purpose of taking such measures as may be necessary in the appointment of an agent to present and manage their claims before the Commissioners under that Treaty, it was Voted

That a Committee be raised to consider what measures may be expedient under existing circumstances for promoting the purposes of the meeting.

A committee was accordingly appointed, and now Report,

That having met together they deemed it proper, in the first place, to wait upon the Hon. Mr. Webster whom it was proposed to employ as counsel. They learned from him that he would accede to the following terms; to wit, that he will give his particular attention to claims of persons whose names may be subscribed to the proposed agreement, and who reside in Massachusetts N Hampshire or Maine, provided he shall represent a sufficiently large proportion of the claims owned in those States:—that he will undertake for none whose losses happened from smuggling, illicit trade, the Slave trade, the occlusion of New Orleans, or any offence against the law of Nations, and, generally, for none whose claim is, in his judgment, inadmissible under the Treaty; but, if permitted, will oppose all such claims:—that he will act as agent & counsel for the Claimants; will inspect memorials drawn by others, or draw them himself, if desired; and, after gentlemen have put into his hands their documents & accounts stated, he will do, or cause to be done, all necessary subordinate business.

For his compensation—he will charge a commission of five per cent upon the amount paid to the claimants under the awards of the Commissioners, provided that said commission shall not exceed twenty thousand dollars. His expenses while at Washington, & in going & coming, he expects will be advanced to him from time to time, & shall be deducted from said compensation at the final settlement. Should nothing be recovered, however, on the claims to be urged by Mr Webster, he is not to refund the money so advanced to him for expenses.

The Committee further report that they deem it highly expedient that Mr. Webster should be agreed with and engaged upon these terms. They further report that a committee be appointed to make final arrangements with Mr. Webster and advance him from time to time the sums for his expenses. They further report that no gentlemen should be considered as coming within the terms and advantage of this arrangement, whose names are not subscribed to the following agreement; to wit,

We the undersigned, claimants under the late Spanish Treaty, do agree and engage to employ the Hon. Mr. Webster, as our counsel and agent, to present our claims before the Commissioners under that Treaty, and manage the business arising therefrom. And we agree to pay him, as compensation for his services proportionately to our several awards, agreeably to the terms herein by him proposed.

P[eter] C[hardon] Brooks

Gorham Parsons

Fitz William Sargent of Gloucester
   by Theophilus Parsons.

Thomas Dennie

J[ohn] Brown

Josiah Knapp

Timo[thy] Williams

John Welles for himself and
the late Firm of John &
Saml. Welles

Benja[min] Joy

For the Massa. Fire & Marine
Insurance Company—John
Welles pr order.

Stephen Higginson

William Parsons

Nathan Bridge Executor to the
late Matthew Bridge

William Davis, of Plymo[uth]
Massa.

Barnabas Hedgeby—by
William Davis

Henry Hatch administrator of
the Estate of Crowell Hatch
(dec[eased])

James & Tho[mas] H[andasyd]
Perkins

Nath[aniel] Fellowes

Benja[min] Rich

John C. Jones

Caleb Loring for the late firm
of Loring & Curtis

Tho[mas] K Jones

John Pedrick 3d

David Eckley Administrator of
the Estate of Nathaniel
Fellowes[1]

1. Webster's clients in the aggregate collected about $1,850,000 of the $5,000,000 awarded under the treaty, and Webster earned fees totaling around $70,000. For a list of the commissions Webster received for the Spanish claims cases, see *Legal Papers* 2:266–75.

Document 55
Text from *Legal Papers* 3: 153–54.

Peroration,
The Dartmouth College Case[1]
[*March 10, 1818*]

"*This, Sir, is my case!* It is the case not merely of that humble institution, it is the case of every college in our Land! It is more! It is the case of every eleemosynary institution throughout our country—of all those great charities founded by the piety of our ancestors to alleviate human misery, and scatter blessings along the pathway of life! It is more! It is, in some sense, the case of every man among us who has property of which he may be stripped, for the question is simply this, 'Shall our State Legislatures be allowed to take *that which is not their own,* to turn it from its original use, and apply it to such ends and purposes as they in their discretion shall see fit!'

Sir, you may destroy this little institution; it is weak, it is in your hands! I know it is one of the lesser lights in the literary horizon of our country. You may put it out! But if you do so, you must carry through your work! You must extinguish, one after another, all those great lights of science which for more than a century have thrown their radiance over our land! It is, Sir, as I have said, a small college. And yet *there are those who love it!* Here the feelings which he had thus far succeeded in keeping down, broke forth. His lips quivered; his firm cheeks trembled with emotion; his eyes were filled with tears; his voice choked; and he seemed struggling to the utmost, simply to gain that mastery over himself which might save him from an unmanly burst of feeling. I will not attempt to give the few broken words of tenderness in which he went on to speak of his attachment to the college. It seemed to be mingled throughout with the recollections of father, mother, brother, and all the trials and preventions through which he had made his way into life. Every one saw that it was wholly unpremeditated—a pressure on his heart which sought relief in words and tears. Recovering himself, after a few moments, and turning to Judge [John] Marshall,[2] he said, "Sir, I know not how others may feel, (glancing at the opponents of the college before him), but for myself, when I see my *Alma Mater* surrounded, like Cesar in the senate house, by those who are reiterating stab upon stab, I would not for this right hand have her to say to me, '*Et tu quoque, mi fili'[*']!*[3]

1. The following account of Webster's famous peroration derives from the recollection of Chauncey A. Goodrich (1790–1860; Yale 1810), a clergyman, lexicographer, and Yale professor who traveled to Washington in 1818 to observe Webster deliver his argument in *Dartmouth College v Woodward*.
2. Marshall (1755–1835) was chief justice of the U.S. Supreme Court from 1801 to 1835.
3. "And thou too, my son."

Document 56
Text from *Legal Papers* 3: 156–57.

To Francis Brown[1]

Dear Sir,   Washington March 11. 1818.

Our Case came on yesterday,—I opened the argument, and occupied almost the whole of the sitting in stating the burden of our complaints.

Mr. Holmes[2] followed and stated the following as his propositions.

1. This Court has no jurisdiction, because the parties do not live in different states, (we never put the jurisdiction on that ground).

2. That the grant of 1769 was not a *contract;* but the trustees merely officers of Government under the King.

3. That all Corporations, created by the King, were dissolved by the Revolution.

4. That if the Charter were a *contract,* the acts do not *impair it.* We have heard him on his three first heads. He is to take up the fourth this morning. Thus far, there is nothing new or formidable developed. (all *stuff*)

Mr. Wirt[3] is to follow Mr. Holmes. He is a man of talents, and will no doubt make the best of his case. . . .

Mr. Hopkinson[4] is to reply, and will make up for all my deficiencies, which were numerous.

Yours of the 28. Feb. I received this morning, I am glad a suit is to be brought.[5] I am very much inclined to think the Court *will not* give a judgement this term.

It is therefore most essential to have an action in which all the questions arise. Pray, therefore take care, that a proper action be properly commenced, and in the earliest season—in the Circuit Court of N. H.

All I shall at present add is, that from present appearances, I have an *increased* confidence that in the *end* Justice will be done in this Cause. Mr. Hopkinson has entered into this case with great zeal, and will do all that men can do. . . . Yours truly

D. Webster

1. Brown (1784–1820; Dartmouth 1805), minister and educator, Dartmouth tutor (1806–09), Dartmouth trustee (1810–14), president of Dartmouth College (1815–20).

2. John Holmes (1773–1843; Brown 1796), Massachusetts and Maine lawyer, U.S. representative from Massachusetts (1817–20), and U.S. senator from Maine (1820–27, 1829–33).

3. William Wirt (1772–1834), Virginia and Maryland lawyer, U.S. attorney general (1817–29), and Antimasonic presidential candidate in 1832.

4. Joseph Hopkinson (1770–1842; University of Pennsylvania 1786), Philadelphia lawyer, U.S. representative from Pennsylvania (1815–19), and U.S. district court judge (1828–42).

5. Brown's letter has not been found, but the reference is to the cognate suits.

Document 57
Text from *Legal Papers* 3: 157.

Salma Hale to William Allen[1]

Dear Sir,   H. R. March 11. 1818. evening
   This day has been occupied by Mr Holmes who closed, & by Mr. Wirt, who begun, his argument[.] Tomorrow he will close. Mr. W. was powerful. Yesterday Mr. Webster was very disingenuous, & it cost me almost the nights labor to furnish Mr. Wirt with facts & authority to put him down. I would not have had his feelings today for half his fame, yea the whole. When I have leisure I may give you a particular account of Mr. Websters positions.
   Mr. Wirt expresses great fear that the Court will not decide at this term. A question of this magnitude is almost always continued for advisement[.] Respectfully

                         S. Hale. . . .

1. Hale (1787–1866), lawyer, Dartmouth University trustee, court clerk of Cheshire County Court of Common Pleas (1812–34) and New Hampshire Superior Court of Judicature (1817–34), and U.S. representative from New Hampshire (1817–19); William Allen (1784–1868; Harvard 1802), clergyman and educator, president of Dartmouth University (1817–19).

Document 58
Text from *Legal Papers* 3: 170–71.

To Jeremiah Mason

My Dear Sir,   Washington, March 13, 1818.
   The argument in the college case terminated yesterday, having occupied nearly three days. On being inquired of by defendant's counsel whether the court would probably give a decision at this term, the chief justice answered that the court would not treat lightly an act of the legislature of a State and the decision of a State court, and that the court would not probably render any judgment at this term. The cause was opened on our side by me. Mr. Holmes followed. His propositions, as near as I recollect were, I. No jurisdiction, because both parties in same State. 2. Charter of 1769 not a contract; trustees, public officers, like judges, and sheriffs, &c.; college a part of government, &c. 3. All corporations abolished by Revolution. 4. If charter a contract, not

impaired, a great kindness to old trustees to send them new assistants, &c. Upon the whole, he gave us three hours of the merest stuff that was ever uttered in a county court. Judge Bell[1] was present, and had the pleasure of hearing him, but could not stay out his speech. Wirt followed. He is a good deal of a lawyer, and has very quick perceptions, and handsome power of argument; but he seemed to treat this case as if his side could furnish nothing but declamation. He undertook to make out one legal point on which he rested his argument, namely, that Dr. Wheelock[2] was not founder. In this he was, I thought, completely unsuccessful. He abandoned his first point, recited some foolish opinions of Virginians on the third,[3] but made his great effort to support the second, namely, that there was no contract. On this he had nothing new to say. The old story of the public nature of the use—a charter for the ultimate benefit of the people—in the nature of a public institution—like towns, &c. He made an apology for himself, that he had not had time to study the case, and had hardly thought of it, till it was called on.

Upon the whole, no new matter or reasoning was brought forward; and, in my opinion, the argument upon the law of the case on our side is not answered. Mr. Hopkinson made a most satisfactory reply, keeping to the law, and not following Holmes and Wirt into the fields of declamation and fine speaking. One pleasant thing occurred; Holmes said, that really, for his part, he could not see how nine could be a majority of twenty-one.[4] Hopkinson looked up with much good-nature, and said aloud, that he could make that out if any body could.

I believe I may say that nearly or quite all the bar are with us. How the court will be I have no means of knowing. I shall write you again before I leave the place. Ever yours,

D. Webster.

1. Samuel Bell (1770–1850; Dartmouth 1793), New Hampshire lawyer and politician, judge of New Hampshire Superior Court of Judicature (1816–19), governor of New Hampshire (1819–23), and U.S. Senator (1823–35). Bell supported the university cause.

2. Eleazar Wheelock (1711–79; Yale 1733), founder and first president of Dartmouth College (1769–79).

3. The reference is to the argument that the New Hampshire law did not impair the charter because an enlargement of the board of trustees could only improve the operations of the college.

4. Holmes's point was that since the state added only nine trustees in enlarging the twelve-member board of trustees to twenty-one, it could not be accused of having appointed a majority of the trustees.

Document 59
Text from *Legal Papers* 3: 226–27.

To Jeremiah Mason

My Dear Sir,   Washington Feb: 4. 1819

Since my arrival here I have been all the time in Court, & can therefore as yet say nothing more than I have seen & heard here.

Most of the Judges came here with opinions drawn in the College cause. On the other side a second argument, as you know was expected. Dr. Perkins[1] had been a week at Baltimore, conferring with Mr Pinkney.[2] Mr. Pinkney came up on Monday. On Tuesday Morning, he being in court, as soon as the Judges had taken their seats, the Ch. Jus. said, that, in vacation, the Judges had formed opinions in the College cause. He then immediately began reading his opinion, & of course nothing was said of a second argument. Five of the Judges concurred in the result; & I believe most or all of them will give their opinions to the Reporter. Nothing has been said in Court about the other causes.[3] Mr. Pinkney *says* he means to argue one of them; but I think he will alter his mind. There is nothing left to argue on. The Ch. J's opinion was in his own peculiar way. He reasoned along from step to step; & not referring to the cases, adopted the principles of them & worked the whole into a close, connected, & very able argument. Some of the other Judges, I am told, have drawn opinions with more reference to authorities.

Judge Bell's case, I expect to come on in two or three days.—I am alone in it, & must do as well as I can. . . .[4] Yrs truly

D. Webster

1. Cyrus Perkins (1778–1849; Dartmouth 1800), physician, professor of anatomy and surgery at Dartmouth (1810–19). Perkins sided with the university cause, and he moved to New York City following the university's demise.
2. William Pinkney (1764–1822), prominent Maryland lawyer and diplomat.
3. The cognate cases.
4. Webster argued against Pinkney in *Bullard v Bell* on February 9–11.

Document 60
Text from *Legal Papers* 3: 271–87.

Webster's Argument in
Gibbons v. Ogden
[*February 4, 1824*]

Mr. *Webster,* for the appellant, admitted, that there was a very respectable weight of authority in favour of the decision, which was sought
to be reversed. The laws in question, he knew, had been deliberately
re-enacted by the Legislature of New-York; and they had also received
the sanction, at different times, of all her judicial tribunals, than which
there were few, if any, in the country, more justly entitled to respect
and deference. The disposition of the Court would be, undoubtedly,
to support, if it could, laws so passed and so sanctioned. He admitted,
therefore, that it was justly expected of him that he should make out
a clear case; and unless he did so, he did not hope for a reversal. It
should be remembered, however, that the whole of this branch of
power, as exercised by this Court, was a power of revision. The question must be decided by the State Courts, and decided in a particular
manner, before it could be brought here at all. Such decisions alone
gave the Court jurisdiction; and therefore, while they are to be respected as the judgments of learned Judges, they are yet in the condition of all decisions from which the law allows an appeal.

It would not be a waste of time to advert to the existing state of the
facts connected with the subject of this litigation. The use of steam
boats, on the coasts, and in the bays and rivers of the country, had
become very general. The intercourse of its different parts essentially
depended upon this mode of conveyance and transportation. Rivers
and bays, in many cases, form the divisions between States; and thence
it was obvious, that if the States should make regulations for the
navigation of these waters, and such regulations should be repugnant
and hostile, embarrassment would necessarily happen to the general
intercourse of the community. Such events had actually occurred, and
had created the existing state of things.

By the law of New-York, no one can navigate the bay of New-York,
the North River [Hudson], the Sound, the lakes, or any of the waters
of that State, by steam vessels, *without a license from the grantees of New-
York,* under penalty of forfeiture of the vessel.[1]

By the law of the neighbouring State of Connecticut, no one can
enter her waters with a steam vessel *having such license.*[2]

By the law of New-Jersey, if any citizen of that State shall be *restrained*, under the New-York law, from using steam boats between the ancient shores of New-Jersey and New-York, he shall be entitled to an action for damages, *in New-Jersey*, with treble costs against, the party who thus restrains or impedes him under the law *of New-York!*[3] This act of New-Jersey is called an act of retortion against the illegal and oppressive legislation of New-York; and seems to be defended on those grounds of public law which justify reprisals between independent States.

It would hardly be contended, that all these acts were consistent with the laws and constitution of the United States. If there were no power in the general government, to control this extreme belligerent legislation of the States, the powers of the government were essentially deficient, in a most important and interesting particular. The present controversy respected the earliest of these State laws, those of New-York. On those, this Court was now to pronounce; and if they should be declared to be valid and operative, he hoped somebody would point out *where*, the State right stopped, and on what grounds the acts of other States were to be held inoperative and void.

It would be necessary to advert more particularly to the laws of New-York, as they were stated in the record. The first was passed March 19th, 1787. By this act, a sole and exclusive right was granted to *John Fitch*,[4] of making and using every kind of boat or vessel impelled by steam, in all creeks, rivers, bays, and waters, within the territory and jurisdiction of New-York, for fourteen years.

On the 27th of March, 1798, an act was passed, on the suggestion that Fitch was dead, or had withdrawn from the State, without having made any attempt to use his privilege, repealing the grant to him, and conferring similar privileges on *Robert R. Livingston*,[5] for the term of twenty years, on a suggestion, made by him, *that he was possessor of a mode of applying the steam engine to propel a boat; on new and advantageous principles.* On the 5th of April, 1803, another act was passed, by which it was declared, that the rights and privileges granted to R. R. Livingston, by the last act, should be extended to him and *Robert Fulton, for twenty years, from the passing of this act.* Then there is the act of April 11, 1808, purporting to extend the monopoly, in point of time, five years for every additional boat, the whole duration, however, not to exceed thirty years; and forbidding any and all persons to navigate the waters of the State, with any steam boat or vessel, without the license of *Livingston and Fulton*, under penalty of forfeiture of the boat or vessel. And, lastly, comes the act of April 9, 1811, for enforcing the provisions of the last mentioned act, and declaring, that the forfeiture of the boat or vessel, found navigating against the provisions of the previous acts, shall be deemed to accrue on the day on which such boat or vessel should navigate the waters of the State; and that *Livingston and Fulton* might immediately have an action for such boat or vessel, in like manner as if they themselves had been dispossessed thereof by force; and that on bringing any such suit, the defendant therein should be prohibited, by injunction, from removing the boat or vessel out of the State, or using it within the State. There were one or two other acts mentioned in the pleadings, which principally respected the time allowed for complying with the condition of the grant, and were not material to the discussion of the case.

By these acts, then, an exclusive right is given to *Livingston and Fulton,* to use *steam navigation* on all the waters of New-York, for thirty years from 1808.

It is not necessary to recite the several conveyances and agreements, stated in the record, by which *Ogden,*[6] the plaintiff below, derives title under *Livingston and Fulton,* to the exclusive use of part of these waters. The appellant being owner of a steam-boat, and being found navigating the waters between New-Jersey and the city of New-York, over which waters *Ogden,* the plaintiff below, claimed an exclusive right, under *Livingston and Fulton,* this bill was filed against him by *Ogden,* in October, 1818, and an injunction granted, restraining him from such use of his boat. This injunction was made perpetual, on the final hearing of the cause, in the Court of Chancery; and the decree of the Chancellor has been duly affirmed in the Court of Errors. The right, therefore, which the plaintiff below asserts to have and maintain his injunction, depends obviously on the general validity of the New-York laws, and, especially, on their force and operation as against the right set up by the defendant. This right he states, in his answer, to be, that he is a citizen of New-Jersey, and owner of the steam-boat in question; that the boat was a *vessel* of more than twenty tons burden, *duly enrolled and licensed for carrying on the coasting trade,* and intended to be employed by him, in that trade, between Elizabethtown, in New-Jersey, and the city of New-York; and was actually employed in navigating between those places, at the time of, and until notice of the injunction from the Court of Chancery was served on him.

On these pleadings the substantial question is raised: Are these laws such as the Legislature of New-York had a right to pass? If so, do they, secondly, in their operation, interfere with any right enjoyed under the constitution and laws of the United States, and are they, therefore, void, as far as such interference extends?

It may be well to state again their general purport and effect, and the purport and effect of the other State laws, which have been enacted by way of retaliation.

A steam vessel, of any description, going to New-York, is forfeited to the representatives of *Livingston and Fulton, unless she have their license.* Going from New-York, or elsewhere, to Connecticut, she is prohibited from entering the waters of that State, *if she have such license.*

If the representatives of *Livingston and Fulton, in New-York,* carry into effect, by judicial process, the provision of the New-York laws, against any citizen of New-Jersey, they expose themselves to a statute action, *in New Jersey,* for all damages, and treble costs.

The New-York laws extend to all steam vessels; to steam frigates, steam ferry-boats, and all intermediate classes.

They extend to public as well as private ships; and to vessels employed in foreign commerce, as well as to those employed in the coasting trade.

The remedy is as summary as the grant itself is ample; for immediate confiscation, without seizure, trial, or judgment, is the penalty of infringement.

In regard to these acts, he should contend, in the first place, that they exceeded the power of the Legislature; and, secondly, that if they could be considered valid, for any purpose, they were void, still, as against any right enjoyed under the laws of the United States, with which they came in collision; and that, in this case, they were found interfering with such rights.

He should contend, that the power of Congress to regulate commerce, was complete and entire, and, to a certain extent, necessarily exclusive; that the acts in question were regulations of commerce, in a most important particular; and affecting it in those respects, in which it was under the exclusive authority of Congress. He stated this first proposition guardedly. He did not mean to say that *all* regulations which might, in their operation, affect commerce, were exclusively in the power of Congress; but that *such power* as had been exercised in this case, did not remain with the States. Nothing was more complex than commerce; and in such an age as this, no words embraced a wider field than *commercial regulation.* Almost all the business and intercourse of life may be connected, incidentally, more or less, with *commercial regulations.* But it was only necessary to apply to this part of the constitution the well settled rules of construction. Some powers are holden to be exclusive in Congress, from the use of exclusive words in the grant; others, from the prohibitions on the States to exercise similar powers; and others, again, from the nature of the powers themselves. It has been by this mode of reasoning that the Court has adjudicated on many important questions; and the same mode is proper here. And, as some powers have been holden exclusive, and others not so, under the same form of expression, from the nature of the different powers respectively; so, where the power, on any one subject, is given in general words, like the power to regulate commerce, the true method of construction would be, to consider of what parts the grant is composed, and which of those, from the nature of the thing, ought to be considered exclusive. The right set up in this case, under the laws of New-York, is a *monopoly*. Now, he thought it very reasonable to say, that the constitution never intended to leave with the States the power of granting monopolies, either of trade or of navigation; and, therefore, that as to this, the commercial power was exclusive in Congress.

It was in vain to look for a precise and exact *definition* of the powers of Congress, on several subjects. The constitution did not undertake the task of making such exact definitions. In conferring powers, it proceeded in the way of *enumeration* stating the powers conferred, one after another, in few words; and, where the power was general, or complex in its nature, the extent of the grant must necessarily be judged of, and limited, by its object, and by the nature of the power.

Few things were better known, than the immediate causes which led to the adoption of the present constitution; and he thought nothing clearer, than that the prevailing motive was *to regulate commerce;* to rescue it from the embarrassing and destructive consequences, resulting from the legislation of so many different States, and to place it under the protection of a uniform law. The great objects were commerce and revenue; and they were objects indissolubly connected. By the confederation, divers restrictions had been imposed on the States; but these had not been found sufficient. No State, it was true, could send or receive an embassy; nor make any treaty; nor enter into any compact with another State, or with a foreign power; nor lay duties, interfering with treaties which had been entered into by Congress. But all these were found to be far short of what the actual condition of the country required. The States could still, each for itself, regulate commerce, and the consequence was, a perpetual jarring and hostility of commercial regulation.

In the history of the times, it was accordingly found, that the great topic, urged on all occasions, as showing the necessity of a new and different government, was the state of trade and commerce. To benefit and improve these, was a great object in itself; and it became greater when it was regarded as the only means of enabling the country to pay the public debt, and to do justice to those who had most effectually laboured for its independence. The leading state papers of the time are full of this topic. The New-Jersey resolutions[7] complain, that the regulation of trade was in the power of the several States, within their separate jurisdiction, in such a degree as to involve many difficulties and embarrassments; and they express an earnest opinion, that *the sole and exclusive power* of regulating trade with foreign States, ought to be in Congress. Mr. Witherspoon's motion in Congress, in 1781, is of the same general character; and the report of a committee of that body, in 1785, is still more emphatic.[8] It declares that Congress ought to possess the *sole and exclusive* power of regulating trade, as well with foreign nations, as between the States. The resolutions of Virginia, in January, 1786, which were the immediate cause of the convention, put forth this same great object.[9] Indeed, it is the *only* object stated in those resolutions. There is not another idea in the whole document. The entire purpose for which the delegates assembled at Annapolis, was to devise means for the uniform regulation of trade. They found no means, but in a general government; and they recommended a convention to accomplish that purpose. Over whatever other interests of the country this government may diffuse its benefits, and its blessings, it will always be true, as matter of historical fact, that it had its immediate origin in the necessities of commerce; and, for its immediate object, the relief of those necessities, by removing their causes, and by establishing a *uniform* and steady system. It would be easy to show, by reference to the discussions in the several State conventions, the prevalence of the same general topics; and if any one would look to the proceedings of several of the States, especially to those of Massachusetts and New-York, he would see, very plainly, by the recorded lists of votes, that wherever this commercial necessity was most strongly felt, there the proposed new constitution had most friends. In the New-York convention, the argument arising from this consideration was strongly pressed, by the distinguished person whose name is connected with the present question.[10]

We do not find, in the history of the formation and adoption of the constitution, that any man speaks of a general *concurrent power,* in the regulation of foreign and domestic trade, as still residing in the States. The very object intended, more than any other, was to take away such power. If it had not so provided, the constitution would not have been worth accepting.

He contended, therefore that the people intended, in establishing the constitution, to transfer, from the several States to a general government, those high and important powers over commerce, which, in their exercise, were to maintain an uniform and general system. From the very nature of the case, these powers must be *exclusive;* that is, the higher branches of commercial regulation must be exclusively committed to a single hand. What is it that is to be regulated? Not the commerce of the several States, respectively, but the commerce of the United States. Henceforth, the commerce of the States was to be an *unit;* and the system by which it was to exist and be governed, must necessarily be complete, entire, and uniform. Its character was to be described in the flag which waved over it, E PLURIBUS UNUM. Now, how could individual States assert a right of concurrent legislation, in a case of this sort, without manifest encroachment and confusion? It should be repeated, that the words used in the constitution, to regulate commerce, are so very general and extensive, that they might be construed to cover a vast field of legislation, part of which has always been occupied by State laws; and, therefore, the words must have a reasonable construction, and the power should be considered as exclusively vested in Congress, so far, and so far only, as the nature of the power requires. And he insisted, that the nature of the case, and of the power, did imperiously require, that such important authority as that of granting monopolies of trade and navigation, should not be considered as still retained by the States.

It is apparent, from the prohibitions on the power of the States, that the *general* concurrent power was not supposed to be left with them. And the exception, out of these prohibitions, of the *inspection laws,* proves this still more clearly.[11] Which most concerns the commerce of this country, that New-York and Virginia should have an uncontrolled power to establish their inspection for flour and tobacco, or that they should have an uncontrolled power of granting either a monopoly of trade in their own ports, or a monopoly of navigation over all the waters leading to those ports? Yet, the argument on the other side must be, that, although the constitution has sedulously guarded and limited the first of these powers, it has left the last wholly unlimited and uncontrolled.

But, although much had been said, in the discussion on former occasions, about this supposed *concurrent* power in the States, he found great difficulty in understanding what was meant by it. It was generally qualified, by saying, that it was a power, by which the States could pass laws on the subjects of commercial regulation, which would be valid, until Congress should pass other laws controlling them, or inconsistent with them, and that *then* the State laws must yield. What sort of *concurrent* powers were these, which could not exist together? Indeed, the very reading of the clause in the constitution must put to flight this notion of a general concurrent power. The constitution was formed for all the States; and Congress was to have power to regulate commerce. Now, what is the import of this, but that Congress is to give the rule—to establish the system—to exercise the control over the subject? And, can more than one power, in cases of this sort, give the rule, establish the system, or exercise the control? As it is not contended that the power of Congress is to be exercised by a *supervision* of State legislation; and, as it is clear, that Congress is to give the general rule, he contended, that this power of giving the general rule was transferred, by the constitution, from the States to Congress; to be exercised as that body might see fit. And, consequently, that all those high exercises of power, which might be considered as giving the rule, or establishing the system, in regard to great commercial interests, were necessarily left with Congress alone. Of this character he considered monopolies of trade or navigation; embargoes; the system of navigation laws; the countervailing laws, as against foreign states; and other important enactments respecting our connexion with such states. It appeared to him a most reasonable construction, to say, that in these respects, the power of Congress is exclusive, from the nature of the power. If it be not so, where is the limit, or who shall fix a boundary for the exercise of the power of the States? Can a State grant a monopoly of trade? Can New-York shut her ports to all but her own citizens? Can she refuse admission to ships of particular nations? The argument on the other side is, and must be, that she might do all these things, until Congress should revoke her enactments. And this is called concurrent legislation. What confusion such notions lead to, is obvious enough. A power in the States to do any thing, and every thing, in regard to commerce, till Congress shall undo it, would suppose a state of things, at least as bad as that which existed before the present constitution. It is the true wisdom of these governments to keep their action as distinct as possible. The general government should not seek to operate where the States can operate with more advantage to the community; nor should the States encroach on ground, which the public good, as well as the constitution, refers to the exclusive control of Congress.

If the present state of things—these laws of New-York, the laws of Connecticut, and the laws of New-Jersey, had been all presented, in the convention of New-York, to the eminent person whose name is on this record,[12] and who acted, on that occasion, so important a part; if he had been told, that, after all he had said in favour of the new government, and of its salutary effects on commercial regulations, the time should yet come, when the North River would be shut up by a monopoly from New-York; the Sound interdicted by a penal law of Connecticut; *reprisals* authorized by New-Jersey, against citizens of New-York; and when one could not cross a ferry, without transhipment; does any one suppose he would have admitted all this, as compatible with the government which he was recommending?

This doctrine of a *general* concurrent power in the States, is insidious and dangerous. If it be admitted, no one can say where it will stop. The States may legislate, it is said, wherever Congress has not made a *plenary* exercise of its power. But who is to judge whether Congress has made this *plenary* exercise of power? Congress has acted on this power; it has done all that it deemed wise; and are the States now to do whatever Congress has left undone? Congress makes such rules as, in its judgment, the case requires; and those rules, whatever they are, constitute the *system.*

All useful regulation does not consist in restraint; and that which Congress sees fit to leave free, is a part of its regulation, as much as the rest.

He thought the practice under the constitution sufficiently evinced, that this portion of the commercial power was exclusive in Congress. When, before this instance, have the States granted monopolies? When, until now, have they interfered with the navigation of the country? The pilot laws, the health laws, or quarantine laws, and various regulations of that class, which have been recognised by Congress, are no arguments to prove, even if they are to be called commercial regulations, (which they are not,) that other regulations, more directly and strictly commercial, are not solely within the power of Congress. There was a singular fallacy, as he humbly ventured to think, in the argument of very learned and most respectable persons, on this subject. That argument alleges, that the States have a concurrent power with Congress, of regulating commerce; and its proof of this position is, that the States have, without any question of their right, passed acts respecting turnpike roads, toll bridges, and ferries. These are declared to be acts of commercial regulation, affecting not only the interior commerce of the State itself, but also commerce between different States. Therefore, as all these are *commercial regulations,* and are yet acknowledged to be rightfully established by the States, it follows, as is supposed, that the States must have a concurrent power to regulate commerce.

Now, what was the inevitable consequence of this mode of reasoning? Does it not admit the power of Congress, at once, upon all these minor objects of legislation? If all these be regulations of commerce, within the meaning of the constitution, then, certainly, Congress having a concurrent power to regulate commerce, may establish ferries, turnpikes, bridges, &c. and provide for all this detail of interior legislation. To sustain the interference of the State, in a high concern of maritime commerce, the argument adopts a principle which acknowledges the right of Congress, over a vast scope of internal legislation, which no one has heretofore supposed to be within its powers. But this is not all; for it is admitted, that when Congress and the States have power to legislate over the same subject, the power of Congress, when exercised, controls or extinguishes the State power; and, therefore, the consequence would seem to follow, from the argument, that all State legislation, over such subjects as have been mentioned, is, at all times, liable to the superior power of Congress; a consequence, which no one would admit for a moment. The truth was, he thought, that all these things were, in their general character, rather regulations of police than of commerce, in the constitutional understanding of that term. A road, indeed, might be a matter of great commercial concern. In many cases it is so; and when it is so, he thought there was no doubt of the power of Congress to make it. But, generally speaking, roads, and bridges, and ferries, though, of course, they affect commerce and intercourse, do not obtain that importance and elevation, as to be deemed *commercial regulations*. A reasonable construction must be given to the constitution; and such construction is as necessary to the just power of the States, as to the authority of Congress. Quarantine laws, for example, may be considered as affecting commerce; yet they are, in their nature, *health laws*. In England, we speak of the power of regulating commerce, as in Parliament, or the King, as arbiter of commerce; yet the city of London enacts health laws. Would any one infer from that circumstance, that the city of London had concurrent power with Parliament or the Crown to *regulate commerce?* or, that it might grant a monopoly of the navigation of the Thames? While a health law is reasonable, it is a health law; but if, under colour of it, enactments should be made for other purposes, such enactments might be void.

In the discussion in the New-York Courts, no small reliance was placed on the law of that State prohibiting the importation of slaves, as an example of a commercial regulation, enacted by State authority.[13] That law may or may not be constitutional and valid. It has been referred to generally, but its particular provisions have not been stated. When they are more clearly seen, its character may be better determined.

It might further be argued, that the power of Congress over these high branches of commerce was exclusive, from the consideration that Congress possessed an exclusive admiralty jurisdiction.[14] That it did possess such exclusive jurisdiction, would hardly be contested. No State pretended to exercise any jurisdiction of that kind. The States had abolished their Courts of Admiralty, when the constitution went into operation. Over these waters, therefore, or, at least, some of them, which are the subject of this monopoly, New-York has no jurisdiction whatever. They are a part of the high sea, and not within the body of any country. The authorities of that State could not punish for a murder, committed on board one of these boats, in some places within the range of this exclusive grant. This restraining of the States from all jurisdiction, out of the bodies of their own counties, shows plainly enough, that navigation on the high seas, was understood to be a matter to be regulated only by Congress. It is not unreasonable to say, that what are called the waters of New-York, are, to purposes of navigation and commercial regulation, the waters of the United States. There is no cession, indeed, of the waters themselves, but their *use*, for those purposes, seemed to be entrusted to the exclusive power of Congress. Several States have enacted laws, which would appear to imply their conviction of the power of Congress, over navigable waters, to a greater extent.

If there be a concurrent power of regulating commerce on the high seas, there must be a concurrent admiralty jurisdiction, and a concurrent control of the waters. It is a common principle, that arms of the sea, including navigable rivers, belong to the sovereign, *so far as navigation is concerned*. Their *use* is navigation. The United States possess the general power over navigation, and, of course, ought to control, in general, the use of navigable waters. If it be admitted, that *for purposes of trade and navigation*, the North River, and its bay, are the river and bay of New-York, and the Chesapeake the bay of Virginia, very great inconveniences and much confusion might be the result.

It might now be well to take a nearer view of these laws, to see more exactly what their provisions were, what consequences have followed from them, and what would and might follow from other similar laws.

The first grant to *John Fitch*, gave him the sole and exclusive right of making, employing, and navigating, all boats impelled by fire and steam, *"in all creeks, rivers, bays, and waters, within the territory and jurisdiction of the State."* Any other person, navigating such boat, was to forfeit it, and to pay a penalty of a hundred pounds. The subsequent acts repeal this, and grant similar privileges to *Livingston and Fulton:* and the act of 1811 provides the extraordinary and summary *remedy*, which has been already stated. The river, the bay, and the marine league along the shore,[15] are all within the scope of this grant. Any vessel, therefore, of this description, coming into any of those waters, without a license, whether from another State, or from abroad, whether it be a public or private vessel, is instantly forfeited to the grantees of the monopoly.

Now, it must be remembered, that this grant is made as an exercise of *sovereign political power*. It is not an inspection law, nor a health law, nor passed by any derivative authority; it is professedly an act of sovereign power. Of course, there is no limit to the power, to be derived from the *purpose* for which it is exercised. If exercised for one purpose, it may be also for another. No one can inquire into the *motives* which influence sovereign authority. It is enough, that such power manifests its will. The motive alleged in this case is, to remunerate the grantees for a benefit conferred by them on the public. But there is no necessary connexion between that benefit and this mode of rewarding it; and if the State could grant this monopoly for that purpose, it could also grant it for any other purpose. It could make the grant for money; and so make the monopoly of navigation over those waters a direct source of revenue. When this monopoly shall expire, in 1838, the State may continue it, for any pecuniary consideration which the holders may see fit to offer, and the State to receive.

If the State may grant this monopoly, it may also grant another, for other descriptions of vessels; for instance, for all *sloops*.

If it can grant these exclusive privileges to a few, it may grant them to many; that is, it may grant them to all its own citizens, to the exclusion of every body else.

But the waters of New-York are no more the subject of exclusive grants by that State, than the waters of other States are subjects of such grants by those other States. Virginia may well exercise, over the entrance of the Chesapeake, all the power that New-York can exercise over the bay of New-York, and the waters on the shore. The Chesapeake, therefore, upon the principle of these laws, may be the subject of State monopoly; and so may the bay of Massachusetts. But this is not all. It requires no greater power, to grant a monopoly of *trade,* than a monopoly of navigation. Of course, New-York, if these acts can be maintained, may give an exclusive right of entry of vessels into her ports. And the other States may do the same. These are not extreme cases. We have only to suppose that other States should do what New-York has already done, and that the power should be carried to its full extent.

To all this, there is no answer to be given except this, that the *concurrent* power of the States, concurrent though it be, is yet *subordinate* to the legislation of Congress; and that, therefore, Congress may, when it pleases, annul the State legislation; but, until it does so annul it, the State legislation is valid and effectual. What is there to recommend a construction which leads to a result like this? Here would be a perpetual hostility; one Legislature enacting laws, till another Legislature should repeal them; one sovereign power giving the rule, till another sovereign power should abrogate it; and all this under the idea of *concurrent* legislation!

But further; under this *concurrent power,* the State does that which Congress cannot do; that is, it gives preferences to the citizens of some States over those of others.[16] I do not mean here the advantages conferred by the grant on the grantees; but the *disadvantages* to which it subjects all the other citizens of New-York. To impose an extraordinary tax on steam navigation visiting the ports of New-York, and leaving it free every where else, is giving a preference to the citizens of other States over those of New-York. This Congress could not do; and yet the State does it; so that this power, at first subordinate, then concurrent, now becomes paramount.

The people of New-York have a right to be protected against this monopoly. It is one of the objects for which they agreed to this constitution, that they should stand on an equality in commercial regulations; and if the government should not insure them that, the promises made to them, in its behalf, would not be performed.

He contended, therefore, in conclusion on this point, that the power of Congress over these high branches of commercial regulation, was shown to be exclusive, by considering what was wished and intended to be done, when the convention, for forming the constitution, was called; by what was understood, in the State conventions, to have been accomplished by the instrument; by the prohibitions on the States, and the express exception relative to inspection laws; by the nature of the power itself; by the terms used, as connected with the nature of the power; by the subsequent understanding and practice, both of Congress and the States; by the grant of exclusive admiralty jurisdiction to the federal government; by the manifest danger of the opposite doctrine, and the ruinous consequences to which it directly leads.

It required little now to be said, to prove that this exclusive grant is a law regulating commerce; although, in some of the discussions elsewhere, it had been called a law of *police.* If it be not a *regulation of commerce,* then it follows, against the constant admission on the other side, that Congress, even by an express act, could not annul or control it. For if it be not a regulation of commerce, Congress has no concern with it. But the granting of monopolies of this kind is always referred to the power over commerce. It was as arbiter of commerce that the King formerly granted such monopolies. This is a law regulating commerce, inasmuch as it imposes new conditions and terms on the coasting trade, on foreign trade generally, and on foreign trade as regulated by treaties; and inasmuch as it interferes with the free navigation of navigable waters.

If, then, the power of commercial regulation, possessed by Congress, be, in regard to the great branches of it, exclusive; and if this grant of New-York be a commercial regulation, affecting commerce, in respect to these great branches, then the grant is void, whether any case of actual collision had happened or not.

But, he contended, in the second place, that whether the grant were to be regarded as wholly void or not, it must, at least, be inoperative, when the rights claimed under it came in collision with other rights, enjoyed and secured under the laws of the United States; and such collision, he maintained, clearly existed in this case. It would not be denied that the law of Congress was paramount. The constitution has expressly provided for that.[17] So that the only question in this part of the case is, whether the two rights be inconsistent with each other. The appellant had a *right* to go from New-Jersey to New-York, in a vessel, owned by himself, of the proper legal description, and controlled and licensed according to law. This *right* belonged to him as a citizen of the United States. It was derived under the laws of the United States, and no act of the Legislature of New-York can deprive him of it, any more than such act could deprive him of the right of holding lands in that State, or of suing in its Courts. It appears from the record, that the boat in question was regularly enrolled, at Perth Amboy, and properly licensed for carrying on the coasting trade. Under this enrolment, and with this license, she was proceeding to New-York, when she was stopped by the injunction of the Chancellor, on the application of the New-York grantees. There can be no doubt that here is a collision, in fact; that which the appellant claimed as a right, the respondent resisted; and there remains nothing now but to determine, whether the appellant had, as he contends, a right to navigate these waters; because, if he had such right, it must prevail. Now, this right was expressly conferred by the laws of the United States. The first section of the act of February, 1793, c. 8. regulating the coasting trade and fisheries, declares, that all ships and vessels, enrolled and licensed as that act provides, "and no others, shall be deemed ships or vessels of the United States, entitled to the privileges of ships or vessels employed in the coasting trade or fisheries." The fourth section of the same declares, "that in order to the licensing of any ship or vessel, for carrying on the coasting trade or fisheries," bond shall be given, &c. according to the provisions of the act. And the same section declares, that the owner having complied with the requisites of the law, "it shall be the duty of the Collector to grant a license for carrying on the coasting trade;" and the act proceeds to give the form and words of the license, which is, therefore, of course, to be received as a part of the act; and the words of the license, after the necessary recitals, are, "license is hereby granted for the said vessel to be employed in carrying on the coasting trade."

Words could not make this authority more express.

The Court below[18] seemed to him, with great deference, to have mistaken the object and nature of the *license*. It seemed to have been of opinion that the *license* had no other intent or effect than to ascertain the ownership and character of the vessel. But this was the peculiar office and object of the *enrolment*. That document ascertains that the regular proof of ownership and character has been given; and the *license* is given, to confer the *right*, to which the party has shown himself entitled. It is the authority which the master carries with him, to prove his right to navigate freely the waters of the United States, and to carry on the coasting trade.

In some of the discussions which had been had on this question, it had been said, that Congress had only provided for ascertaining the ownership and property of vessels, but had not prescribed to what *use* they might be applied. But this he thought an obvious error; the whole object of the act regulating the coasting trade, was to declare what vessels shall enjoy the benefit *of being used* in the coasting trade. To secure this use to certain vessels, and to deny it to others, was precisely the purpose for which the act was passed. The error, or what he humbly supposed to be the error, in the judgment of the Court below, consisted in that Courts having thought, that although Congress *might act*, it had *not yet acted*, in such a way as to confer a *right* on the appellant: whereas, if a right was not given by this law, it never could be given; no law could be more express. It had been admitted, that supposing there was a provision in the act of Congress, that all vessels duly licensed should be at liberty to navigate, for the purpose of trade and commerce, over all the navigable harbours, bays, rivers and lakes, within the several States, any law of the States, creating particular privileges as to any particular class of vessels, to the contrary notwithstanding, the only question that could arise, in such a case, would be, whether the law was constitutional; and that if that was to be granted or decided, it would certainly, in all Courts and places, overrule and set aside the State grant.

Now, he did not see that such supposed case could be distinguished from the present. We show a provision in an act of Congress, that all vessels, duly licensed, may carry on the coasting trade; nobody doubts the constitutional validity of that law; and we show that this vessel was duly licensed according to its provisions. This is all that is *essential* in the case supposed. The presence or absence of a *non obstante* clause,[19] cannot affect the extent or operation of the act of Congress. Congress has no power of revoking State laws, as a distinct power. It legislates over *subjects;* and over those subjects which are within its power, its legislation is supreme, and necessarily overrules all inconsistent or repugnant State legislation. If Congress were to pass an act expressly revoking or annulling, in whole or in part, this New-York grant, such an act would be wholly useless and inoperative. If the New-York grant be opposed to, or inconsistent with, any constitutional power which Congress has exercised, then, so far as the incompatibility exists, the grant is nugatory and void, necessarily, and by reason of the supremacy of the law of Congress. But if the grant be not inconsistent with any exercise of the powers of Congress, then, certainly, Congress has no authority to revoke or annul it. Such an act of Congress, therefore, would be either unconstitutional or supererogatory. The laws of Congress need no *non obstante* clause. The constitution makes them supreme, when State laws come into opposition to them; so that in those cases there is no question except this, whether there be, or be not, a repugnancy or hostility between the law of Congress and the law of the State. Nor is it all material, in this view, whether the law of the State be a law regulating commerce, or a law of police, or by whatever other name or character it may be designated. If its provisions be inconsistent with an act of Congress, they are void, so far as that inconsistency extends. The whole argument, therefore, is substantially and effectually given up, when it is admitted, that Congress might, by express terms, abrogate the State grant, or declare that it should not stand in the way of its own legislation; because, such express terms would add nothing to the effect and operation of an act of Congress.

He contended, therefore, upon the whole of this point, that a case of actual collision had been made out, in this case, between the State grant and the act of Congress; and as the act of Congress was entirely unexceptionable, and clearly in pursuance of its constitutional powers, the State grant must yield.

There were other provisions of the constitution of the United States, which had more or less bearing on this question: No State shall, without the consent of Congress, lay any duty of tonnage.[20] Under colour of grants like this, that prohibition might be wholly evaded. This grant authorizes Messrs. Livingston and Fulton to *license* navigation in the waters of New-York. They, of course, license it on their own terms.

They may require a pecuniary consideration, ascertained by the tonnage of the vessel, or in any other manner. Probably, in fact, they govern themselves, in this respect, by the size or tonnage of the vessels, to which they grant licenses. Now, what is this but substantially a *tonnage* duty, under the law of the State? Or does it make any difference, whether the receipts go directly to her own treasury, or to the hands of those to whom she has made the grant?

There was, lastly, that provision of the constitution which gives Congress power to promote the progress of science and the useful arts, by securing to authors and inventors, for a limited time, an exclusive right to their own writings and discoveries.[21] Congress had exercised this power, and made all the provisions which it deemed useful or necessary. The States might, indeed, like munificent individuals, exercise their own bounty towards authors and inventors, at their own discretion. But to confer reward by exclusive grants, even if it were but a part of the use of the writing or invention, was not supposed to be a power properly to be exercised by the States. Much less could they, under the notion of conferring rewards in such cases, grant monopolies, the enjoyment of which should be essentially incompatible with the exercise of rights holden under the laws of the United States. He should insist, however, the less on these points, as they were open to counsel, who would come after him, on the same side,[22] and as he had said so much upon what appeared to him the more important and interesting part of the argument.

1. Laws, New York, c. 57 (1787), c. 55 (1798), c. 94 (1803), c. 223 (1808), c. 200 (1811).

2. Laws, Connecticut, c. 28 (1822).

3. Laws, New Jersey, pp. 223–25 (1811).

4. Fitch (1743–98), inventor who devoted himself to the development of the steamboat. Fitch obtained monopoly grants from several states and a federal patent in 1791.

5. Livingston (1746–1813; Columbia 1765), New York lawyer, judge, and statesman. In 1802 the inventor Robert Fulton (1765–1815) entered into an agreement with Livingston, who held the New York steamboat monopoly, to construct a steamboat. This resulted in the successful construction and operation of the *Clermont*.

6. Aaron Ogden (1756–1839; Princeton 1773), New Jersey lawyer and politician. Ogden entered the steamboat business in 1811.

7. The representation of the Legislative Council and the General Assembly of the State of New Jersey "On the Articles of Confederation," read at the Continental Congress on June 25, 1778, *Journals of the Continental Congress, 1774–1789* (34 vols.; Washington, D.C., 1904–1937), 11: 647–51.

8. John Witherspoon (1723–94; Edinburgh 1739), minister, president of the College of New Jersey (Princeton), state legislator, and member of the Continental Congress. Witherspoon made his motion on February 3, 1781; the report of March 28, 1785, is in *Journals of the Continental Congress*, 28:201–5.

9. "Resolution of the General Assembly of Virginia," January 21, 1786, *Documents Illustrative of the Union of the American States* (Washington, D.C., 1927), p. 38.

10. Robert Livingston in *The Debates in the Several State Conventions on the Adoption of the Federal Constitution*, Jonathan Elliot, ed. (5 vols.; Philadelphia, 1836), 2:208–16.

11. Article I, Section 10: "No state shall, without the consent of the Congress, lay any imposts or duties on imports or exports, except what may be absolutely necessary for executing its inspection laws."

12. Robert R. Livingston.

13. 17 Johnson (N.Y.) 488, 505 (1820).

14. United States Constitution, Article 111, Section 2.

15. That is, the three-mile limit.

16. Article I, Section 9: "No preference shall be given by any regulation of commerce or revenue to the ports of one state over those of another."

17. Article VI, the supremacy clause.

18. *Ogden v Gibbons*, 17 Johnson (N.Y.) 488 (1820).

19. "Notwithstanding:" a clause that implied a license to do a thing otherwise restrained.

20. Article I, Section 10.

21. Article I, Section 8.

22. William Wirt, 9 Wheaton, at pp. 165–77.

Document 61
Text from *Legal Papers* 3: 686–91.

Reported Argument: The License Cases
(*Thurlow v. Massachusetts*)

Washington, Jan. 31, 1845.

The room of the Supreme Court of the United States was crowded to-day to hear the argument of Daniel Webster on the License Law of Massachusetts.[1] It presented quite an array of beauty and intellect, compared with the usual auditory there assembled. He occupied about two hours. He commenced by saying, that the general intent of these laws is good, but there are those who believe, and I am one of them, that if Intemperance is to be put down, it must be by more powerful means than the law in question. It must be by the uses of moral, religious and persuasive means rather than by coercion. The cause of Temperance cannot be too much applauded. It is a noble and a holy cause. But there are States which have not disturbed their License Laws, where Temperance has made much more progress than where penal laws have been enacted.

If we look abroad where has the Temperance Reformation been most successful? Look to Ireland. Did Father Mathew[2] go forth, clothed with coercive powers, from British Statutes and depending on

License Laws? No. He appealed to the consciences, the understandings, the morality, the religion of the people, and where has this reformation been more successful, where has it struck deeper than in Ireland? It is this course, and this only, that can abate the evils of Intemperance. Religion and Morals, the Pulpit, the Lecture Room, the Press, the example of good men, well directed public opinion— these are the means which must work out this good and exterminate this evil.

My learned friend (Mr. Huntington[3] of Salem) has referred to statistics. I shall also refer to statistics. By the law of Massachusetts, it has been left optional with the Counties to grant licenses or to withhold them. In the Counties that have adhered to the old plan, there has been less Intemperance than in those that adopted more coercive measures.

Congress permits the importation of liquors; it may encourage or discourage such importations. Massachusetts has never asked Congress to prohibit the importation of spirits into the ports of the United States. That would have been the proper plan of proceeding; but she did not ask for any such sumptuary laws. Massachusetts, also, with all her laws, tolerates the manufacture of spirits; she does not even discourage the manufacture by taxation on distilleries.

The decision of this case in favor of the plaintiff in error would not be derogatory to the character of Massachusetts, as my learned friend hinted at. I always dislike to hear these allusions to the destruction of the character of States, if this, that, or t' other measure cannot be carried. This power to regulate commerce is clearly a prerogative of Congress; and it is not derogatory to a State to submit to the control of Congress. Massachusetts may sometimes have felt aggrieved at some decisions of this Court, but on the whole she has no cause to complain. She must forget her character and history before she complains of the National powers in regulating these affairs. It is the beneficent course of Congress that has accelerated her in her onward way. Other States have been controlled by the exercise of this power, and she has felt the benefits. The ruling in the Steamboat Monopoly[4] case of New York is one of these. She might better effect some objects, had she retained the power to control commerce, but she yielded it to Congress. It would be unjust and ungenerous to take back part of that which she yielded for the common good.

Mr. Webster then went into a history of the laws of Massachusetts on this question, pointing out the requirements of the acts of 1786, 1835, '37, '38, and '40. The act of 1835, sections 3d and 17th, provides that licenses may be granted on certain conditions. A dispute arose about the meaning of the Statute, whether it was merely optional. The act of 1837 was passed to settle this dispute, the second section providing that the County Commissioners were *empowered* not *compelled* to grant licenses.—The law of 1838 made it illegal to sell less than 15 gallons. This amounted to a prohibition, and in 1840 it was repealed, leaving the law as it was by the Statute of 1837—forbidding the retail of spirits in less than 28 gallons without license at the option of the County Commissioners.

The law against which we contend is intended for prohibition, for the abolition of sales. It is intended and effects the abolition of consumption in the State. It has been distinctly admitted by my learned friend that it is the policy of Massachusetts to abolish the consumption. The Supreme Court of Massachusetts sees nothing in the law but a regulation—her representative here boasts that it is intended for prohibition, which is not regulation.

The question then is, are State laws, intended to contravene a law of Congress, constitutional? By the laws of Congress spirits may [not] be imported in casks of less than 15 gallons and wine in bottles of less than a quart,[5] and the laws of Massachusetts say that her citizens shall not sell wine or spirits in less quantities than 28 gallons.

The case of *Brown* against *Maryland*[6] is not so strong as this. That was intended for taxation, not prohibition. The laws complained of seek no revenue which was the object of the law in the other case. In Brown's case *sale* was only *embarrassed*; here it is *prohibited*. Non-consumption is the object of this law. The Court in Brown's case decided that there is no difference between the power to admit and prohibit. If none be sold, none can be imported.

The learned Chief Justice of Massachusetts[7] says that the plaintiff is not an importer. This does not appear. For all that is on the record, Samuel Thurlow is an importer. If this was intended to be proved, it should have been stated in the indictment, not being an importer. Yet the indictment is not a bad one. The laws make no distinction between persons whether importers or retailers; yet the laws of Congress say that spirits may be imported in casks of less quantity than can be sold by retailers. This is making a distinction between persons which the law does not recognize.

This distinction is valuable in Brown's case, because the laws of Maryland were confined to importers, and because it was a tax case. It has not touched the power of Congress nor the mode in which that power shall be exercised.

The counsel admits a distinction made between importers and re-tailers. It is even said that this law may be good in part and bad in part; that it may be valid in its application to some persons and invalid in its application to others. If so, there must be some legal distinction. This act makes no distinction. No law of Congress makes any distinction. Both importer and retailer are private citizens engaged in commerce on their own account.

A word about the phraseology of the Constitution (Art. I, Sec 8). "Among the States" Congress shall have power "to regulate commerce with foreign nations and among the several States and with the Indian tribes." Among the States does not mean among the sovereignties of the States, but among the people of the States. "*Several* States" here means *all* the States. I would not dwell on this exposition of words, but would recommend it to some writer on verbal criticism.

In looking back, one now thinks it strange that New-York should have insisted on making her lakes and rivers and harbors a *mare clausum* to other States. Yet it had the sanction of such men as [Ambrose][8] Spencer. The Chief Justice[9] in his decision on this case, cut the smallest pattern possible for the work he had to do. He might have given the principle a wider application.

But this doctrine of State laws interfering with commerce among citizens cannot be maintained. If a patentee sells his patent-right to a citizen of a State in which patent-rights are not looked on favorably, can the State interfere with this transaction and say that the patent-right shall not be valid?

The power to license is clearly in the State, but where State laws conflict with the laws of Congress, the State law must yield. If it impedes a U. S. law, then it must give way. (In support of this he quoted authority in point.) Whatever State law impedes a law of Congress is unconstitutional.—Whatever tends to defeat the substantial purpose of a law impedes the law.

The law of Congress authorizes importation for the sake of consumption. The purpose of Congress is to legalize consumption. It gets duties on consumption. The learned counsel admits and proclaims that the State law is intended to prohibit—to abolish consumption.

But what is this "police power" of which we hear so much? It is not defined in the Constitution. But this case is not a law of police, but a law of commerce. A city can make police laws, but cannot make laws for the regulation of commerce. By laws of Congress spirits can be imported, or in other words purchased in casks of 15 gallons or 10 gallons; but by the laws of Massachusetts it cannot be sold in less quantities than 28 gallons except by the option of County Commissioners. If to sell or buy in less than 28 gallons is retail, then Congress imports in retail.

But I choose to take hold of this proposition by somewhat a stronger hand. Let the distinction between wholesale and retail run where it may, a State cannot control the quantity. What is the value of wholesale if retail trade is cut off? Export trade is like a river, conveying from springs and rivulets, and flowing out to the whole ocean. Import trade is like irrigation—let out by rills from a large fountain; and this large fountain must be controlled by one power, the national power. I do not deny that laws for health, &c. may be enacted by States; but laws cannot be passed to prohibit or abolish what Congress has passed laws to regulate. If retail is stopped, wholesale must stop also. If consumption is stopped, so must imports be stopped.

What would be the effect of this measure if applied to other cases? Suppose that Spirits cost one dollar a gallon. The law of Massachusetts then is that you shall not purchase less than 28 dollars worth. Now suppose this rule applied to other articles of commerce, Broadcloth for instance. The State of New York wishes to encourage her saline manufactures, and, on her Canals, gives preference to her own Salt, over foreign Salt. But could she pass a law that you should not buy a less quantity than 28 dollars worth? Suppose that the same rule now applied to other beverages. Tea, Coffee, Spices, or Tobacco, and what would be the consequence?

It is high time, your Honors, that the questions were settled, and the law established. What are we coming to? Suppose some of the Northern States should take it in a consideration to pass a law prohibiting the sale of the productions of Southern States, Sugar for instance, except in such quantities as to amount to a total prohibition. The authority of Congress over Spirits, Tea, Sugar, &c. is the same. Or on the contrary, suppose some of the Southern States should pass laws, intended to have a similar effect on the manufactures of the North imported into Southern States. These things are not so remote as to pass without notice, for threats of this kind have already been held out from high places.—Would such a state of things be desirable? I trust therefore that this question will be settled in such a way as to sustain the National authority over these cases; and show to the several States that their interest and dignity are best consulted by a ready acquiescence with the laws of Congress.

The present law of Massachusetts appears to be milder than the 15 gallon law of 1840; but here we have it openly avowed by the Counsel of the Commonwealth that its object is the same.

The several States should submit promptly to all the laws of Congress. It is derogatory to any State to hold up her own laws in opposition to those of Congress. Even when an injury is done, as some States have supposed to be the case by the operation of Tariff Laws, the States should submit with alacrity to these regulations. It is by such compromises that we maintain our nationality. They are a surrender of State privilege, given in exchange for benefits accruing from our Federal compact.

My learned friend has acknowledged, what he could not deny, that this State law is intended for prohibition. Congress has regulated this matter so as to derive a revenue from the consumption, which the State has passed a law to abolish. I have shown that when a State law conflicts with, or impedes a law of Congress, the State must yield. As therefore it is acknowledged that the present law is intended to conflict with a law of Congress regulating commerce, the State law is unconstitutional; otherwise the United States laws would be subordinate to State laws. All State laws, health laws, police laws, are subordinate to the laws of Congress and must yield to the superior if they conflict with or impede each other.

Mr. Webster then, in a low tone, submitted a few points in writing to the Court, and took his seat having occupied from 11 A.M. till 1 o'clock, P.M. in the delivery of his argument. I have merely given you some of the points, as the court room is poorly arranged for the accommodation of Reporters. Mr. Webster appears again once or twice next week.[10]

Richelieu.[11]

1. Laws, Massachusetts, c. 166, amended by Revised Statutes, 1835, c. 47, criminalized the unlicensed retail sale of alcoholic liquor in increments of less than 28 gallons. An 1837 law (c. 242) banned sales on Sundays and specified penalties for violation of c. 47. It also gave the county commissioners the authority to control the number of licenses.

2. Theobald Mathew (1790–1861), Irish priest, ordained in 1814, became leader of the Irish temperance movement in 1838.

3. Asahel Huntington (1798–1870; Yale 1819), Massachusetts lawyer.

4. *Gibbons v Ogden*.

5. 4 U.S. Statutes at Large 235 (1827) and 373 (1830).

6. 12 Wheaton (25 U.S.) 419 (1827), in which John Marshall established the original package doctrine: an article authorized by Congress to be imported continued to be part of foreign commerce while it remained in the hands of the importer in its original package; during that time states could neither tax the property nor require the importer to obtain a license to sell it. Since Samuel Thurlow, a Georgetown, Massachusetts, liquor dealer, had sold liquor purchased in its original cask from the Boston importer, Webster relied heavily on *Brown*.

7. Lemuel Shaw in *Massachusetts v Thurlow* (1837).

8. Spencer (1765–1848), New York lawyer and politician, New York attorney general (1802), justice of the New York Supreme Court (1804–19), chief justice of the New York Supreme Court (1819–23), and U.S. representative (1829).

9. John Marshall.

10. Webster did not argue any other cases that term.

11. Apparently a reporter for the *New York Tribune*, which printed Webster's argument in *Thurlow v Massachusetts* on February 3, 1845.

Document 62
Text from *Legal Papers* 3: 710–14

Reported Argument:
The *Passenger* Case[1]

Tuesday, February 9, 1847.

January Term, 1847
THE ALIEN STATE TAX CASE

Mr. D. Webster, *for the Plaintiff in Error,*

He concurred in the closing sentiment of the counsel for the defendant.[2] He too hoped that this court would preserve with sedulous care all the rights that belonged to the State of Massachusetts as well as to the National Government.

He stood here in the discharge of a not very agreeable professional duty. While he admitted that this statute of Massachusetts was in fact a commercial regulation, and in conflict with the laws of the United States, the loyalty of that State to the Government of the Union was not to be questioned. She had always distinguished herself by a determination to fulfil all her duties to the General Government, and to abstain cautiously and delicately from all infringement of the powers of Congress. He had given it as his opinion, when the act now before the court was passed, that it could not stand; that it was unconstitutional; that Massachusetts had transcended her authority in adopting it. But it is only for Massachusetts to know that it is an unconstitutional act—declared to be so by this court—and no State will submit to its decision with more gentleness than Massachusetts; for no State in the Union has found it more to her account in surrendering the power over commerce to Congress. What she is now, she owes to her participation in the benefits which have flowed out of the common Constitution to which she gave her assent.

It was the doctrine of the Milne case[3] decided here in February, 1837, which gave rise to the idea that a door had been opened thereby to the States, to enable them to raise revenue out of the exercise of the commercial power. The Massachusetts Legislature accordingly seized upon that idea, and in April, 1837, laid a tax of two dollars on all alien passengers, and devoted the proceeds exclusively to the maintenance of alien paupers, &c. The act was pronounced to be constitutional by the Supreme Court of Massachusetts.

In 1840, the Legislature directed the surplus to be paid into the State treasury; and in 1845, the State ordered that all sums received from alien passengers should be paid into the public treasury. So, the money received from this source goes to the support of alien paupers, and the excess, if any, goes into the general treasury.

This law is a pure commercial regulation. It was not adopted in the exercise of any power properly belonging to a State. The tax flowing from it is not the result of accident. It is a tax raised by a direct enactment, in a matter where the State has no right to tax at all.

The enactment is no police law. It has no features in common with any police law since the beginning of the world. A tax on goods, on tonnage, or on any of the operations of commerce, cannot be construed into a poor tax or a police tax. It is out of the nature of the subject. None of the elements necessary to constitute a poor tax or a police tax enter into the composition of commercial regulations. If a land tax was laid in Massachusetts, to raise fifty thousand pounds, would the law assessing it be called a poor law, a police law? Would it not rather be called a revenue law, for replenishing the public treasury of Massachusetts?

The importation of persons is a common expression, used both in the Constitution and in the laws of Massachusetts; and it is yet to be proved that a tax on the importation of persons is not a tax on imports.

Here are two laws, or systems of laws, over the same subject. A distinct repugnance arises between them, in principle, character, design, and general effect. The Constitution and the laws of the United States encourage the importation of all foreigners free, untaxed. This is the general scope of all the provisions of the National Government upon this subject. The State of Massachusetts claims the right to tax these foreigners at her discretion, for the benefit of her exchequer. She claims the right, if she sees fit, to exclude all foreigners from her soil; for if she can tax them two dollars, she can tax them any amount. Are not the objects and ends of the Massachusetts law repugnant to the objects and ends of the laws and Constitution of the United States?

Now, let this repugnance in principle be run out into details, and a plain, manifest collision between the agents of the two Governments will be the result.

By the laws of the United States, the master or consignee of a vessel arriving at any of the ports of the United States, from a foreign country, is required to furnish the collector of the port with a manifest of the goods and a list of the passengers imported in the ship.[4]

The 23d section of the general duty act of March 2d, 1799, requires a manifest of the goods and a list of the passengers to be furnished to the collector. By the 30th section, the arrival of the vessel is to be reported to the collector within twenty-four hours after it shall have arrived, and in forty-eight hours thereafter the manifest of the goods imported is to be handed to the collector. By the 36th section, if, within fifteen working days after the entry of the goods shall have been made at the custom-house, the goods shall remain on board, an inspector of customs shall take charge of them, and cause them to be removed to the public stores. What is this regulation but the seizure and holding by the United States, in a certain contingency, of the vessel and cargo?

Now, what does this act of Massachusetts do? By the laws of the United States, alien passengers may land when the master shall have furnished a list of them to the collector. But the law of Massachusetts prescribes another condition. It says that alien passengers shall not land until they shall have paid a tax. A boarding officer, by authority of the State, is required to go on board of the vessel and collect the State tax; and, if [it] shall not be paid, he is required to cause a pilot to conduct the vessel to some designated place, where she is anchored and detained until the tax shall be paid. What is this regulation but a seizure and holding by the State, in a certain contingency, of the vessel and cargo? The master of the vessel, on being boarded by the State officer, refuses to pay the State tax. She is accordingly seized and held by him, and prevented from finishing her voyage until the tax is paid. At the end of fifteen days, comes an officer of the United States on board the vessel, and *he* too seizes her for violation of the revenue laws. Here are two seizures by opposing parties. What is this but direct collision between the laws of the United States and the law of Massachusetts?

Much has been said of the pauper system of Massachusetts; but a tax upon commerce to support her poor never constituted a part of that system. She never, at any time, taxed her own commerce for that object, as she now proposes to tax the commerce of the United States, for the trade of Massachusetts is pre-eminently the trade of the United States. Who ever heard of a Massachusetts vessel going to England? Such a thing never has been heard of. Before the Revolution, Massachusetts ships and trade were colonial ships and trade, for they were regulated by acts of Parliament. After Massachusetts declared her independence of England, independent, sovereign Massachusetts never sent a Massachusetts vessel to England. From the peace to the formation of the Constitution, the commerce of England was shut to the shipping of the States of the Confederacy. English goods came here in English bottoms, and American goods went to England in English bottoms. It was this very inability of the States to trade with England, as independent States, that formed one of the ruling motives to the adoption of the Constitution. Commerce was in such a depressed condition at Boston, that, to give employment to the ship-builders of that town, a sum of money was subscribed to build three ships, to lie and rot where they were built. Now, the merchants of Boston, with Governor Hancock[5] at their head, proposed a nonuser of British goods imported in British vessels, until the ships of the States should be admitted to trade with England.

Massachusetts has no more right to assess a burden upon commerce in the waters of Massachusetts, geographically speaking, than New Hampshire has; for Massachusetts has no navigable waters, has no commerce. They are all United States waters, United States commerce.

Again: If Massachusetts has the right to charge foreign commerce with a burden to sustain foreign paupers coming into the port of Boston, every other State into which these foreign paupers should chance to stray would have a right to a *pro rata* division of the proceeds of this burden or tax. But Massachusetts takes all the money to sustain her system of pauperism, and then calls the law a police or pauper law! Is this fair? Is this just?

If the constitutionality of this law be affirmed, what will be said if Massachusetts, in the exercise of her sovereign discretion, shall lay a tax of ten dollars upon every alien passenger arriving in her territory? It will be called doubtless a pauper law; and as Congress cannot repeal a State pauper law, all the States will quickly follow in the steps of Massachusetts, and replenish their treasuries by a tax on aliens arriving in the United States!

The tax laid by this law of Massachusetts is levied while the ship is on the sea, her voyage not performed, the passage money of the persons taxed not earned, the insurance running; and if it is not paid, she is seized *in itinere,* holden on the sea until it is paid—though it is uncertain whether the persons who are the objects of taxation will ever touch the land. Shall such a tax be called a pauper tax? The attempt to evade the true character of such a tax, by changing its name, will not make it a poor tax.

But it is said that the right of taxation without restriction is inherent to the police system, which cannot be carried on an hour without it. How comes it, then, if this be true, that Massachusetts has never until now exercised this inherent right, by taxing aliens coming into her

territory? In all the history of the English poor laws, with their intermi-
nable provisions about settlement, &c., there is no such thing as a tax
upon the operations of commerce to raise money for the support of
the poor.

We can never lift ourselves to the elevation of this case until we
appreciate the great truth, that the commerce, the ports, the harbors,
the waters of the country belong to the United States; that the jurisdiction over them belongs to the United States for strictly commercial
purposes, and that one State has no more interest in them than another.

But it has been urged, that if the State has not a right to tax
alien passengers, it will have no power to redress the evils of foreign
pauperism. The answer to this argument is, that it belongs to Congress
to redress evils of this kind. To Congress belongs the power of regulating the admission of alien passengers, and to tax them, or not, at its
discretion. The very thing that it is said Massachusetts has a right to
do, it is proposed by Congress at the present session to do. A bill has
been introduced into Congress, at the instance of the authorities of
the city of New York, to regulate the admission of alien passengers. It
goes back to the point of embarkation in the foreign country, and
requires the alien to prove his character before the American consul.
And if the State laws upon this subject were out of the way, it is not
unreasonable to suppose that their absence would soon be supplied
by the enactment of a general system, protecting every body, and
injuring none.

There is nothing in the Milne case, no decision, no dictum, that
gives countenance to the principle proclaimed by this law. In that case,
the question raised was whether it was constitutional for a State to
compel by law the master of a vessel to report a list of his passengers,
in writing, to the State authorities. Here the question is, whether it is
constitutional for a State to make a law for taxing alien passengers
while on shipboard, and to levy it before landing. The New York law,
pronounced by this court to be constitutional, was no regulation of
commerce, as the Massachusetts law is. It neither affected nor bur-
dened any regulation of commerce or navigation. It imposed no condition on the passengers before landing. It stopped, hindered, delayed
nobody. It sought no security against the future or present pauperism
of the passengers. It was, in this view of the subject, a pure internal
police law. It had no feature in common with the law under consideration.

This court has decided that Congress possesses the exclusive power
to regulate commerce—15 *Peters*, 504, 511.[6]

Some powers were granted by the States to Congress, and some were retained. This tribunal was constituted as the surveyors of the boundary line between the two systems of government; and whenever either Government gets on the wrong side of the line, it is the duty of this court to adjudge accordingly.

1. Webster's argument was printed in the *Washington* (D.C.) *National Era*, March 4, 1847.

2. John Davis (1787–1854), counsel for the state.

3. *New York v Milne*, 11 Peters (36 U.S.) 102 (1837).

4. 1 U.S. Statutes at Large 627 (1799).

5. John Hancock (1737–93; Harvard 1754), Revolutionary statesman and first signer of the Declaration of Independence. Hancock served as governor of Massachusetts from 1780–85 and again from 1787–93.

6. *Groves v Slaughter*, Justice John McLean's concurrence: "The commercial power, as it regards foreign commerce . . . has been decided by this court to be exclusively vested in congress."

Howard Jones

DANIEL WEBSTER
The Diplomatist

D ANIEL WEBSTER'S contributions to American foreign policy
were as important as those he made to law and politics. Twice
he served as secretary of state, from March 5, 1841, to May 8, 1843,
and from July 23, 1850, until his death on October 24, 1852. During
both terms he pursued a pragmatic and realistic foreign policy based
on international law. As a sound diplomatist, he recognized the intimate relationship between domestic and foreign affairs, and he resisted intervention in the internal concerns of other nations. In the
meantime, he guarded the warmaking power of Congress, opposed
territorial expansion as injurious to national unity and conducive to
war, and sought to spread American commerce into the Far East. His
most enduring accomplishment was the Webster-Ashburton Treaty of
1842 with England, for it resolved longstanding irritants between the
nations and laid the basis for a mid-century rapprochement promoting
an Anglo-American relationship that has lasted to the present.

I

During his first tenure as secretary of state, Webster dealt with
issues such as commercial and claims litigations, the status of American
missionaries outside the country, slave mutinies, and threats to the
independence of Hawaii. In a squabble with Portugal over tariffs, he
upheld the right of his nation to levy ad valorem duties on imports.
Grievances continued with Mexico over Texas and border claims, and,
under his lead, the United States for the first time (in a case involving
Syria) extended diplomatic protection to American missionaries in
foreign lands. A dispute with Spain intensified over the *Amistad* mutiny
and the ensuing court case. Interest in maintaining Hawaii's independence led to the Tyler Doctrine, which supported the territorial rights

of a weaker people against European encroachments.[1] Webster's greatest concern, however, was a series of longstanding disputes with England: the northeastern boundary and related border issues; the African slave trade and the status of runaway American slaves in British ports; the maritime practices of search and impressment.

Webster's most immediate problem was a legacy of the presidency of Martin Van Buren: the *Caroline* crisis of 1837–1838 and the related case of Alexander McLeod. In late 1837, during the Canadian rebellions against the British Crown, Americans used the privately owned steamer *Caroline* to transport supplies and men into Canada to support the revolution. On the night of December 29, Canadian volunteers set out to destroy the vessel. Failing to find it on the Canadian side of the Niagara River, they stormed the vessel in American waters, wounding several of the crew, killing an American named Amos Durfee, and, after removing all occupants, setting it afire to sink in flames above the falls. Reaction along the Niagara frontier was electric. The Anglophobic *New York Herald* talked of war and poignantly declared that the son of the steamer's captain had been "cut down while on his knees, asking for mercy." Imaginative drawings appeared of the burning *Caroline*, hanging over the lip of the falls and about to take its terrified passengers to their deaths below. A poem made the event a legend in its own time:

> As over the shelving rocks she broke,
> And plunged in her turbulent grave,
> The slumbering genius of freedom woke,
> Baptized in Niagara's wave,
> And sounded her warning Tocsin far,
> From Atlantic's shore to the polar star.

Three days after the *Caroline* raid, American patriots in Buffalo exhibited Durfee's body in front of a hotel—his "pale forehead," according to the *Herald*, "mangled by the pistol ball, and his locks matted with his blood!" The following day they circulated coffin-shaped posters announcing a public funeral. Nearly three thousand people jammed around the coffin resting on the courthouse steps; a clergyman led a prayer, and a young attorney delivered a speech that the *Herald* called "more exciting, thrilling, and much more indignant than Mark Antony's."[2]

To halt the calls for war, President Van Buren dispatched General Winfield Scott to the scene. Armed with only a sword, the tall and ornately dressed military chieftain relied upon "rhetoric and diplomacy" by issuing a challenge that went unanswered: "I tell you, then, except it be over my body, you shall not pass this line—you shall *not* embark."[3]

Scott's activities as troubleshooter temporarily eased the furor and allowed the diplomats to take over. Van Buren's secretary of state, John Forsyth, accused the British of invading neutral American territory and demanded reparations. But the Melbourne ministry in London delayed reply: Assumption of responsibility for the action would have confirmed Britain as the aggressor and contradicted earlier reports that no one had intended to invade American territory. Foreign Secretary Lord Palmerston argued instead that the *Caroline* was a pirate and that its destruction had been an act of self-defense. Since the United States had failed to uphold neutrality along its border, the *Caroline* raid was justified by the law of nations, regardless of the vessel's location. Forsyth countered that the *Caroline* was no pirate: It was registered in Buffalo and had sailed under the American flag. The American minister in London, Andrew Stevenson, denied Britain's claim of self-defense and cited writers on international law who justified a preemptive strike only if "the necessity" was "imminent, and extreme, and involving impending destruction." Back and forth went the arguments. Finally, six months after Forsyth's initial call for reparation, Palmerston instructed his minister in Washington, Henry S. Fox, to admit that destruction of the vessel was a public act—committed under government orders. For some unexplained reason, however, Fox did not inform the United States of this position for two years. By then the *Caroline* was a source of deep resentment that needed only another incident to bring it to life again.[4]

That incident came in late 1840, when Alexander McLeod, a Canadian deputy sheriff from Niagara, was arrested in New York after allegedly bragging in a tavern in Buffalo that he had done the killing in the *Caroline* attack. Although it was a preposterous story, McLeod was charged with murder and arson. Palmerston was irate and demanded McLeod's release: Even if McLeod had participated, he said, an individual could not be held responsible for a public act. The matter belonged solely to the two governments concerned. The administration in Washington rejected Palmerston's argument, causing the fiery secretary to warm that "McLeod's execution would produce war." Forsyth, an ardent states' rightist from Georgia, contended that the *Caroline* matter fell under the jurisdiction of New York. During the controversy, Webster became secretary of state.[5]

Webster had to resolve the McLeod crisis before he could build better relations with England. He first reversed Forsyth's stand by agreeing with Palmerston that the attack on the *Caroline* was a public act; but he too encountered the insuperable obstacle of states' rights in attempting to win McLeod's freedom. In late April 1841, Webster wrote a long note to Fox setting out principles of self-defense. According to Webster (in an argument similar to that of Stevenson's), the British had failed to show "a necessity of self-defence, instant, overwhelming, leaving no choice of means, and no moment for deliberation." Webster sought to bring the case before the New York Supreme Court on a writ of habeas corpus. But the court refused to free the prisoner. Webster then prepared to bring the case before the United States Supreme Court on a writ of error; but McLeod preferred a quick trial. The secretary asked Governor William Henry Seward of New York to order a nolle prosequi (a move not to prosecute on an indictment), but he refused, though privately offering assurances that the trial would establish McLeod's innocence. Further, Seward *implied* that even if the jury voted to convict, he would pardon the defendant to prevent an execution. Despite the popular excitement and repeated threats of war, McLeod established an alibi at his trial in October, and in less than a half hour the jury returned an acquittal.[6]

Meanwhile, a change of government in England offered an opportunity to establish goodwill between the nations. The new prime minister, Sir Robert Peel, and his foreign secretary, Lord Aberdeen, had experienced the horrors of the Napoleonic Wars and were again being faced with rapidly deteriorating relations with France. Both Englishmen saw the need for maintaining peace with the United States, and Webster and President John Tyler were anxious to accommodate them. The secretary of state had earlier assured Fox that the United States would be willing to resolve the central issue—the northeastern boundary dispute—by accepting a conventional line in exchange for equivalent concessions. Yet it was the Peel ministry that took the most decisive step toward a settlement by sending a special emissary to Washington, Lord Ashburton (Alexander Baring), to resolve the differences between the nations. The aged, tall, and white-haired banking magnate from the House of Baring had married an American and was highly respected in the United States because of his outspoken opposition to British maritime practices before the War of 1812. He was also a friend of Webster's since their meeting in 1839 when the American, a longtime legal adviser to the Baring firm, visited England.[7]

Matters went awry, however, shortly after Webster and Ashburton opened discussions in the summer of 1842. Although they were confident of being able to resolve all problems within a few days, their hopes were dashed by the same obstacles that had plagued earlier negotiators. The two agreed to engage in open, honest diplomacy, but they encountered difficulties that tested each man's patience in the hot, humid weather of the nation's capital. Indeed, at one point Ashburton exclaimed that he wanted "out of this oven," and stayed only because of President Tyler's friendly intercession. The most exasperating issue was the disputed northeastern boundary between Maine and British North America. Since the end of the Revolutionary War, the United States and Britain had been embroiled in a smoldering argument over the vaguely defined border that had resulted from a flawed map drawn by American cartographer John Mitchell and used in the Paris negotiations of 1782–1783. Webster and Ashburton thought they had the solution: They would work toward a compromise and dispense with weary arguments over maps and documents purporting to delineate the Canadian-American boundary. But they found this noble objective elusive. Like earlier diplomats dealing with the boundary, they became mired in seemingly endless wrangling over land and water configurations along the frontier.[8]

Despite their grand intentions of engaging in open and straightforward discussions, both negotiators soon fell into the byzantine patterns of traditional diplomacy. Even before Ashburton's arrival in the United States in April 1842, Webster had prepared the ground for a compromise settlement of the northeastern boundary dispute. The secretary of state heeded the advice of a relatively obscure figure in Maine, Francis O. J. Smith (nicknamed "Fog"), in secretly sponsoring a newspaper campaign in the northeast designed to convince residents that a boundary compromise was the only alternative to war. Somewhat of a chameleon, Smith had been a lawyer, newspaper publisher, congressman, and a state senator. For compensation and expenses, Smith circulated editorials in late 1841 and early 1842 arguing for a peaceful resolution of the boundary controversy. As payment for Smith's services, Tyler approved Webster's request to permit drafts from the Executive Office's "secret-service fund," an annual appropriation of $30,000 established by Congress in 1810 to be used at the president's discretion "for the contingent expenses of intercourse between the United States and foreign nations." Some writers have charged Webster with an unethical propaganda campaign, but Webster himself considered Smith's efforts essential to building popular support for a compromise.[9]

Further, Webster received word of a "red-line map" that allegedly had been used in the Paris negotiations of the 1780s to mark the North American boundary. Jared Sparks, a professor of history at Harvard, wrote Webster in February 1842, explaining how he had come across the map. While doing research in the archives of the French Foreign Office earlier that year, he had discovered a letter from Benjamin Franklin, one of America's diplomats at the peace negotiations, to the Count de Vergennes, the French foreign minister. Dated December 6, 1782, the letter seemed to contain the final piece to the puzzle regarding which nation had rightful claim to the disputed territory. Franklin's words appeared conclusive: "I have the honor of returning herewith the map your Excellency sent me yesterday. I have marked with a strong red line, according to your desire, the limits of the United States as settled in the preliminaries between the British & American plenipotentiaries."[10]

Sparks asked the keeper of the archives to help him search through the sixty thousand maps and charts in the geographical collection, hoping to find Franklin's red-line map. The papers were well indexed, and Sparks soon found what he thought was the correct map: one drawn by French cartographer Jean-Baptiste d'Anville in 1746, which, unknown to Sparks, could not have been used by the Paris diplomats because they had used only Mitchell's. "Imagine my surprise," Sparks wrote Webster, "on discovering, that this line . . . [was] exactly the line now contended for by Great Britain, except that it concedes more than is claimed." Indeed, the line on the map encompassed more territory than the king of the Netherlands had awarded England in an unsuccessful arbitration in 1831. As a good historian, Sparks owed posterity the truth. As a good American, he did not want to undercut his nation's land claims and award all of the disputed territory and more to England. And so, being a person of discretion, he returned to his hotel room and, using his memory and notes, copied the red line from the archival map onto a map of Maine and forwarded it to Webster, leaving the secretary with the hard decision and the historian with a clear conscience.[11]

Sparks's revelation, however, did not surprise Webster. Another map, a Mitchell once belonging to Baron Friedrich von Steuben, had come into Webster's hands four years earlier. It also contained markings that awarded the British more territory than that previously claimed. But unlike Sparks's map, Steuben's seemed conclusive because it was a Mitchell—the type of map used in Paris. Webster's decision was not difficult: A lawyer was not bound to reveal incriminating evidence to his adversary, nor was a diplomat—or so Webster believed. He kept both maps from Ashburton.[12]

Then, a month after Ashburton's arrival, Webster engineered what he later called his "grand stroke" in the negotiations: securing the consent of Maine and Massachusetts (when Maine became a state in

1820, Massachusetts retained ownership of part of Maine's unsettled lands) to a boundary compromise. He sent Sparks to the capital of Maine at Augusta with both red-line maps on a mission, financed (like Smith's) by the president's secret-service fund, to persuade the state's leaders to accept a compromise before someone discovered another map supporting the British claim. Webster himself traveled to Massachusetts to inform the governor about the maps. Both states accepted his request to send commissioners to the negotations in Washington.[13]

Yet the backroom negotiations were not one-sided: Ashburton had likewise engaged in secret diplomacy. Without consulting London, he had privately sought the views held on the boundary in New Brunswick, the Canadian province bordering Maine. Perhaps through personal contact, combined with the weight of his powerful and prestigious position as special minister, he might convince New Brunswick's leaders of the need for compromise. To his chagrin, he found them more recalcitrant than he expected. New Brunswick secretly dispatched a delegation to Washington, which made more stringent territorial demands than the Peel ministry had authorized. Ashburton had unwittingly implanted another formidable obstacle to compromise.[14]

Patience, commitment, and the personal relationship between the diplomats ultimately prevailed, however, and in July they reached a compromise. The United States received over half the twelve thousand square miles in dispute; this allotment included the hotly contested and timber-rich Aroostook Valley and, overall, incorporated four-fifths of the assessed value of the entire region in dispute. To placate Maine and Massachusetts, each state received $150,000 compensation from Washington for land conceded to England. The United States also won free navigation of the St. John River, which winds through Maine and New Brunswick before emptying into the Atlantic Ocean; Fort Montgomery, a million-dollar American project that had been built mistakenly on the British side of the 45th parallel during the War of 1812; and Rouse's Point, an important defensive position on the north shore of Lake Champlain. The British likewise got what they wanted and, at the same time, managed to mollify New Brunswick. They received a strip of land along the border that permitted the construction of a military road below the St. Lawrence River and thus allowed access to the Canadian interior while erecting a barrier to America's northward expansion. As to the northwest section of the border from Lake Superior to the Lake of the Woods (upper Minnesota), the two negotiators drew a line awarding the United States sixty-five hundred square miles of territory (including what turned out to be vast deposits of iron ore in the Vermilion and

Mesabi ranges). In regard to the boundary of Oregon (which included territory stretching northward from Spanish California at the 42d parallel to southern Alaska at 54°40′), Webster and Ashburton agreed that more pressing matters made it advisable to postpone a settlement.[15]

Boundaries were not the only issues in the Webster-Ashburton negotiations, for the diplomats also focused on maritime concerns that, Southerners feared, might jeopardize the institution of slavery. Disagreements over the African slave trade had become entangled with slavery as well as with Britain's claims to the rights of search and impressment. The questions had become explosive because of the *Creole* mutiny of November 1841, when nineteen of 135 slaves on an American slaver moving from Virginia to New Orleans (thus legally engaged in the domestic slave trade) led a revolt near the Bahamas and took command. Afterward, the blacks steered the vessel into Nassau, where British officials eventually granted freedom to all the slaves on the basis of the Crown's emancipation legislation of the 1830s.[16]

Webster discerned a conflict of laws that could further complicate matters by thrusting slavery into the controversy. The British action was a violation of American property rights, and yet, as he explained in a dispatch meant for Aberdeen's perusal, "we well knew that when slaves get on British ground, they are free." In the interest of harmonious international relations, Webster argued, a municipal law must not violate another nation's persons or property driven into territorial waters by forces beyond their control. Since the extradition provision of Jay's Treaty of 1795 had expired, however, Webster could only appeal for the slaves' return on the basis of comity or hospitality. If the British refused, he could argue for indemnification. On the larger question of the African slave trade, even though both the United States and England had taken steps toward ending the practice, only the British had attempted to enforce them. No legitimate connection existed between the *Creole* voyage and the illegal traffic in African slaves; but in the minds of Southerners, the two had become inseparable because they both involved British threats to slavery.[17]

Thus the two diplomats had to quiet the rumbling slavery issue during the negotiations. Ashburton consented to Webster's joint-squadron proposal that called for each nation to provide a minimum of eighty guns "to enforce, separately and respectively, the laws, rights, and obligations, of each of the two countries, for the suppression of the slave trade." The squadrons would patrol West African waters independently but under orders "to act in concert and cooperation, upon mutual consultation, as exigencies may arise." Careful wording was necessary to ease American fears about British sailors boarding American ships and engaging in examinations reminiscent of search and impressment. As to the *Creole,* Ashburton convinced Webster that the issue should be referred to London. In the meantime, the envoy promised no "officious interference with American vessels driven by accident or by violence" into British ports, and he agreed to an extradition provision that, to satisfy antislavery groups in England, did not include mutiny and revolt on the list of extraditable crimes.[18]

Webster and Ashburton resolved other matters by exchanging notes that, while not officially part of the treaty, were part of the general settlement. Regarding the *Caroline,* Ashburton defended the 1837 raid by declaring that "there were grounds of justification as strong as were ever presented in such cases"; but he followed this with an assurance that the British had intended "no slight of the authority of the United States." In a statement that Webster chose to interpret as an apology, Ashburton expressed regret "that some explanation and apology for this occurrence was not immediately made" and hoped that "all feelings of resentment and ill will . . . may be buried in oblivion." Regarding McLeod, both negotiators acknowledged the principles of a public act, and Webster lamented the lengthy delay in the American judicial system. In the process of resolving the *Caroline* and McLeod affairs, Webster reiterated his earlier arguments for restraint in attempting to justify a preemptive strike as an act of self-defense.[19] To prevent another instance like that involving McLeod, Webster called for "An Act to provide further remedial Justice," which became law in 1842. It authorized federal jurisdiction over matters involving aliens charged with criminal acts committed under orders of their government. As for impressment, Webster attached to the treaty a long explanation of America's opposition to this practice. Ashburton accepted the missive, himself contributing a note claiming that impressment in peacetime had "wholly ceased" and would not be "under present circumstances renewed." Ashburton believed this a small price to pay for improved relations.[20]

II

The Webster-Ashburton Treaty, signed in Washington on August 9, 1842, was a compromise, and as such it lay vulnerable to heavy attack in both countries during the ratification debates and afterward. In the United States, opposition Democrats, led by Anglophobe Senators Thomas Hart Benton and James Buchanan, denounced the treaty as a "solemn bamboozlement" and a sacrifice of America's legitimate claims. Their herculean efforts, however, failed to undermine over-whelming Senate approval of the pact. Webster had meanwhile in-sured a controversy in England by informing Ashburton, immediately *after* he signed the treaty in Washington, of Sparks's red-line map. The British emissary declared it better for Anglo-American relations that he had not known of the map; otherwise, he would have been forced to insist on the extreme British claim. When word of the map reached England, however, Palmerston led the Whig party in a rancorous assault on Ashburton and the Tory ministry. Speaking through the *London Morning Chronicle,* Palmerston declared that the emissary had returned to England "with his finger in his mouth" after having been a "pigmy in the hands of a giant." History never recorded a more unholy tryst than that of Webster's duplicity and Ashburton's stupidity. The treaty was "Ashburton's *capitulation*."[21]

In the midst of the debate raging in Parliament—as if preordained for the sake of drama—an additional map was uncovered—a Mitch-ell—that supported the extreme American claim and thus appeared to balance off those maps held by Webster. Known as the Oswald (Richard Oswald was one of the British negotiators in Paris in 1782–1783) or King George III map, it had been found in the British Museum.[22]

Questions arose as to why, after sixty years, this map should have suddenly appeared. The answer lay in a letter from Ashburton to Senator William Cabell Rives, who was chairman of the Committee on Foreign Relations and had become a friend of Ashburton's during his stay in Washington. Two years afterward, in August 1844, Ashburton wrote Rives a revealing account of the Oswald map's discovery: "The battle of the maps may remain a vexed question to puzzle future historians. . . . [I]t is up to this moment a puzzle to me. . . . I was wholly ignorant of the existence of the British Museum map until I returned from America . . . and . . . myself discovered the existence of this map as enquiries at the Museum of which I am a Trustee."[23]

Not only had Ashburton experienced the satisfaction of discovering a map that undercut the relentless attacks on him, but he also was the chief beneficiary of an even more surprising revelation: The ministry's archcritic, Palmerston himself, had known of the Oswald map for nearly four years. In 1839, while foreign secretary, Palmerston had hidden it in the Foreign Office. Sometime during the intervening period, the map had been relocated in the British Museum where Ashburton found it.[24]

The *London Times* could not resist the temptation to launch a full-scale assault on Palmerston and the *Morning Chronicle.* The *Times* first offered a mock apology for "being like a disputant who is boring a whole dinner-table" by a tired argument with an "obstinate and somewhat stupid opponent." Yet it understood Palmerston's frustration. When he left the Foreign Office, England faced wars in China and Afghanistan and the probability of two more with the United States and France. How embarrassing that the Peel government had won the first two wars and resolved the other problems peacefully. Surely the "noble Lord's cup of humiliation was full." Then the *Times* turned on the editor of its rival newspaper: "Our contemporary is, no doubt, wise in loading his guns heavily, but before he applies the match, he would be wiser if he would take care that Lord PALMERSTON is not standing before the muzzle."[25]

The outcome in Parliament was predictable, although the aftermath was not. That body approved the treaty, and each House voted a resolution of thanks to Ashburton. The map controversy lingered, however, for all pieces of the puzzle were not yet in place. Another red-line map was found in 1843. Owned by John Jay, one of America's negotiators in Paris during the 1780s, it too was a Mitchell and supported the American claim. Further, in 1933, the Library of Congress requested a search of the archival holdings in Madrid, where authorities discovered still another map containing a red line: The map, owned by the Spanish representative in Paris, the Count de Aranda, was likewise a Mitchell and also supported the American claim.[26]

The big question remained: Which map was correct? The answer has long eluded historians and has therefore caused a stormy debate over Webster's performance during the negotiations. Indeed, his reputation as a diplomatist rests in part upon whether he sacrificed legitimate claims to the territory in dispute.

The truth is that *none* of the maps was correct. In determining the credibility of a map, one must satisfy two requirements: its authenticity (that the Paris negotiators used it in 1782–1783), and its validity (that they adopted the map as final). No map was both authentic and valid. The Sparks map had set off the controversy, yet it was a d'Anville—which had not been used in Paris. And, although the other maps were all Mitchells—used in the talks—they likewise were not credible: The Paris diplomats had accepted Franklin's suggestion during the preliminary peace discussions to resolve actual locations by joint commissions established after the war. The commissions would treat all the maps used in the Paris negotiations as mere proposals. Because of the confusion, however, Webster's critics were able to accuse him of giving away American territory. So badly did Webster want an amicable settlement that, according to the argument, he sold out his country to win favor in London, thereby smoothing the way for his winning a coveted position as minister to England. Further, Webster was charged with accepting money from Ashburton during the negotiations.[27]

These charges against Webster have been difficult to lay to rest; but they are refutable. As shown, no map established either America's or Britain's claim to the disputed territory. In addition, a series of letters between Webster and the American minister in England, Edward Everett, demonstrates that Webster had given up his interest in the London post. Finally, no evidence has appeared that Webster received money during this period; indeed, he was frantically trying to borrow.[28]

The accusations of bribery rest on circumstantial evidence. A letter written by Ashburton suggests that he and Webster were in collusion during the negotiations. Writing to Aberdeen on August 9, 1842, Ashburton declared:

> The money I wrote about went to compensate Sparkes [sic] & to send him, on my first arrival, to the Governors of Maine & Massachusetts. My informant thinks that without this stimulant Maine would never have yielded, and here it has removed many objections in other quarters. —The secret now is with the President & his Cabinet[,] the Governors of Maine & Massachusetts, seven Commissioners, four Senators, and it has this day been communicated to two more who are leading members of the Senate[']s Committee for foreign affairs. In my house it is known only by [Humphrey] Mildmay. This is a large number for keeping so singular a Secret but I must beg it may be strictly kept on your side, as my source of information would be betrayed. I am assured that it is not known by Everett. —There is one consolation to be derived from our tardy acquaintance with this fact. If I had known it before treating, in any way which would have permitted me to use it, we could not well have refrained from maintaining our undoubted right and yet we never should have got the Aroostook without fighting for it. All the evidence of angels would not have moved the Maine lumberers. This is my scrap of consolation. I have drawn on you a bill for £2998.1—90 days sight [about $14,500] for the purpose mentioned in my former private letter and you will find this put into proper form. I am not likely to want anything more.

Webster's critics have failed to realize that the "money I wrote about" referred to the funds drawn from the president's secret-service account, and have therefore run the two references to money together, erroneously making the "money I wrote about" synonymous with the funds drawn from Aberdeen. Thus, on the surface, Aberdeen seems to have paid both Sparks and Ashburton's informant. Further, some writers have surmised that the "informant" was Webster.[29]

A careful examination of this letter reveals the flaws in the critics' argument. First, Ashburton repeatedly said that he did not become aware of the maps until after the two men had signed the treaty. Surely Ashburton would not have given away so much money for something unseen. Second, Ashburton had learned that Sparks had gone to Maine for some unknown mission and that the emissary had received payment from the secret-service fund. To Aberdeen on June 14, Ashburton wrote: "I have some reason to suspect that Webster has uncovered some evidence, known at present to nobody, but favorable to our claim, and that he is using it with the Commissioners. I have some clue to this fact and hope to get at it." Perhaps this last sentence ties in with Ashburton's reference in his August 9 letter to Aberdeen pertaining to "the purpose mentioned in my former private letter." It is impossible to be sure, however, because that letter is not in the Aberdeen or Peel papers in the British Library in London. Third, a reading of the entire letter shows that Ashburton had shifted topics and that the first reference to money was to the secret-service fund and the second to money drawn from Aberdeen. Fourth, it is dangerous to guess (as one critic admits to have done) that Webster was the informant. It would be as safe to identify one of over twenty others who knew about what Ashburton called "so singular a Secret." And fifth, one has to ask what Webster could have gained from selling out to Ashburton. The secretary's chief objective remained the presidency, and a betrayal of country was not a reliable avenue to that exalted prize.[30]

Ashburton's informant will probably remain unknown. A clue to that person's identity lay in Aberdeen's letter to Ashburton of July 2, 1842. Aberdeen writes:

> The postscript to your private letter of the 14th of last month has only been communicated by me to Peel, under injunctions of the strictest secrecy, and you may rely on our desire to observe the utmost caution with respect to the matter contained in it. But this incident has, I confess, quite taken me by surprise, and opens a new view of measures which perhaps may be followed up with advantage, should there yet be time for you to do so. In order to insure success, you need not be afraid of employing the same means to a greater extent in any quarter where it may be necessary[.] —In what you have done you have been perfectly right; and indeed I look upon the proposal made to you from such a quarter, as the most certain indication we could receive of a determination to bring the negotiation to a happy issue. In any further transactions of the same kind, I have only to desire that it may be made the means of leading to success, as the condition of having recourse to it. If you can command success you need not hesitate.

Ashburton's informant was well placed and knowledgeable about the negotiations. The key to the informant's identity seemed to lie in the "postscript" to Ashburton's letter to Aberdeen of June 14. But that postscript also is not in the Aberdeen or Peel papers.[31]

Part of the reason for the lasting suspicions about the treaty is attributable to an unprecedented attempt to impeach Webster retroactively for alleged illegal activities during the negotiations. In 1846 the chairman of the House Committee on Foreign Affairs, Democrat Charles Ingersoll, accused Webster (then a senator from Massachusetts) of interfering in the McLeod trial and of warning Seward that unless the prisoner were released, New York City would be "laid in ashes." But Ingersoll was unable to prove these allegations and admitted to being "misinformed." Webster nonetheless refused to let the issue die and in the Senate unleashed a blistering attack on his accuser and longtime antagonist. Ingersoll's speech, Webster remarked, was not fit to come out of a "bar-room anywhere." Such a "series of more distinct, unalloyed falsehoods—absolute, unqualified, entire—never appeared in any publication in Christendom." Ingersoll's allegations, Webster concluded, had originated from "moral obtuseness," the inability to discern truth from falsehood. Ingersoll's mind was "grotesque—*bizarre*." Usually one says "there is a screw loose somewhere," but in "this case the screws are loose all over."[32]

Infuriated by this outburst, Ingersoll brought three new charges against the former secretary of state: illegal drafts from the president's secret-service fund; improper use of the money to "corrupt party presses" in New England; and embezzlement of over $2,000 from the State Department. A House committee heard testimonies in Webster's defense from former President John Tyler, Francis O. J. Smith of Maine, and the State Department's disbursing clerk, Edward Stubbs. Tyler undermined the first charge by testifying that he had authorized Webster to use the secret fund. Smith showed that there was nothing illegal about publication of the editorials in the New England papers. And Stubbs proved that Webster had left balanced accounts upon his departure from the State Department. The outcome of the investigation was anticipated. The committee, by vote of four to one, exonerated Webster on all counts.[33]

The Webster-Ashburton Treaty of 1842 cleared the air in Anglo-American relations and helped establish a mid-century rapprochement that has endured despite numerous threats. And, by resolving the major problems with the British in the northeast, the treaty permitted Americans to focus on expansion west.

Webster was deeply satisfied with the treaty with England, although he was not pleased that the pact had helped turn the nation's attention increasingly westward. Aberdeen, however, thought that the ensuing goodwill might encourage a settlement of the Oregon boundary, but when he suggested the idea in October 1842, Webster was not enthusiastic. He objected to Aberdeen's call for the Columbia River as a boundary because it would not afford the United States a single good harbor on the entire Pacific coast. Even though Tyler recommended a special mission to London that would focus on three matters—Oregon, Upper California, and commercial relations—neither Congress nor the British showed interest. When Webster privately proposed a tripartite arrangement whereby the British, in exchange for a settlement of the Oregon matter, would persuade Mexico to cede Upper California to the United States for enough money to satisfy American and British claims against Mexico, Britain again (as well as Mexico) expressed no interest. Texas also caused a problem. Early in the administration, Tyler had urged Webster to seek its acquisition, but the secretary feared that the move would re-open the slavery issue and argued instead for American recognition of Texas's independence. Annexation of Texas, Webster warned, would lead to sectional conflict.[34]

On another matter, Webster demonstrated his strict loyalty to the law when he confronted problems with Spain that grew out of the *Amistad* mutiny of 1839. In July of that year, a group of slaves taken earlier from Africa had revolted on board the Spanish slaver *Amistad* in Cuban waters and seized control. After ordering their white captives to steer the vessel back to Africa, the blacks were deceived into thinking that they were en route home when, in reality, they were moving up the Atlantic coast. Two months later, off Long Island, the captain of an American naval vessel seized the *Amistad*, blacks, and cargo and took them to an admiralty court for prize adjudication. Abolitionists heard of the case and, in an effort to win the blacks' freedom as "kidnapped Africans," took the matter to civil court. The case finally came before the Supreme Court, where Associate Justice Joseph Story ruled in March 1841 that the slave dealers had abducted the blacks from Africa in violation of Anglo-Spanish treaties against the slave trade. The mutiny, Story declared, was an exercise of the natural right of self-defense against unlawful detention. But once freed by the Supreme Court, the blacks became the objects of renewed damage claims by the Spanish. Webster opposed slavery but did not want to lend support to the abolitionist cause. Using the law as his refuge, he insisted that the Supreme Court had acted correctly and that the Spanish had no just claims to indemnification. But even while rejecting

218   DANIEL WEBSTER

the Spanish demands, he and President Tyler could find no law authorizing the American government to underwrite the transportation
of the blacks back to Africa. With private support, the *Amistad* captives
returned to their homes in January 1842.[35]

In regard to still another question—that of nonintervention in other
countries' concerns—Webster's actions appear inconsistent only if one
does not realize that the secretary's basic guideline was the American
national interest. He adhered to nonintervention when agents from
the Hawaiian Islands (then called Sandwich Islands) asked the United
States to extend diplomatic recognition and negotiate a treaty. Even
though American commercial groups feared that European countries
might occupy the islands, Webster did not believe that recognition
and a treaty were wise. However, in a communication to the major
European capitals, he urged respect for the integrity of Hawaii, and
the president asked Congress to authorize the dispatch of an American
commissioner. In a special message to Congress on December 30,
1842, the president used Webster's words to declare what has become
known as the Tyler Doctrine: The United States opposed "any attempt
by another power . . . to take possession of the islands, colonize them,
and subvert the native Government." Cuba was a different matter,
for it lay within the Western Hemisphere and was integral to America's
security. Fear had grown that the British were planning to instigate
a revolution on the island that would destroy slavery and leave what
Webster called "a *black Military Republic* under British protection."
Such action, he knew, would violate the no-transfer principle contained in the Monroe Doctrine. The United States made known that
if Britain used force in Cuba, Spain could depend upon American
military and naval assistance. Though the rumors of British intentions
to invade Cuba were, Webster later declared, "greatly exaggerated,"
the United States had been prepared to take military action. But when
a dispute developed between Britain and Argentina over the Falkland
Islands, Webster saw no American interests involved and argued that
the Monroe Doctrine did not apply to issues having their origins before
that pronouncement.[36]

Webster resigned from the State Department in May 1843. His
chief intention as secretary of state had been to resolve the northeastern boundary dispute with England, which he did with the treaty of
1842. But more important, Tyler's insistence upon spreading the
nation westward had combined with his interest in reelection on a
third-party ticket and the bitter division within the Whig party to make
Webster's stay in the cabinet no longer tenable. Before leaving office,
he undertook an initiative that promoted the extension of American

commercial interests in the Pacific and East Asia. On the same day that he sent instructions to Caleb Cushing as commissioner to China, May 8, 1843, Webster tendered his resignation. Acting under those instructions, in 1844 Cushing negotiated the Treaty of Wanghia, which established diplomatic relations between the United States and China and granted the United States the important concession of most favored nation status.[37]

III

Webster did not withdraw from the national scene, however. In the presidential campaign of 1844, he attempted to reestablish ties with the Whig party by campaigning for Henry Clay, who nonetheless lost to James K. Polk and the expansionist Democrats. Webster's friends in the Massachusetts legislature then reelected him to his old Senate seat in March 1845, where he became a member of the Committee on Foreign Relations and spoke out against the expansionist aims of the administration. On the Oregon question, Webster favored a compromise with England, because he thought the area in dispute was not worth a war. When the United States went to war with Mexico in 1846, he stood in staunch opposition. Although he voted with the majority in approving military appropriations, he believed that Polk had violated "the spirit of the Constitution" by starting "a Presidential war." The president, Webster allowed, could repel an invasion of America's "actual limits," but he did not have the right "to go out of our limits, and declare war for a foreign occupation of what does not belong to us." During the peace negotiations, Webster warned that territorial annexation would heighten sectional strife and ultimately destroy the Union. When the question of slavery's expansion into the new territories reached a crisis level in 1850, he worked for a compromise that would avert secession. In his "Seventh of March Speech," he supported national principles and offered assurances to those who doubted that the Union would survive, but he succeeded primarily in arousing the animosity of both North and South.[38]

With the Union in peril, President Millard Fillmore invited Webster in July 1850 to return to the office of secretary of state. Webster began his second term in the State Department during the furor over the Compromise of 1850. Indeed, his appointment was attributable more to his reputation for compromise than to his ability in shaping foreign policy. It was no surprise that his chief priority in office was to implement the terms of the Compromise and save the Union.[39]

But Webster encountered almost insurmountable problems as weak national leaders and increasing divisiveness over slavery ensured an adventurist foreign policy. The Central American republics were subject to exploitation by powers outside the hemisphere, as well as by American citizens who engaged in filibustering expeditions in Cuba and other regional areas. Unrest persisted along the Texas border, and Mexico's fears of American expansionism blocked Webster's attempt to secure railroad concessions across the isthmus of Tehuantepec. At the same time, the nation's spokesmen exemplified the aggressive mood of "Young America" in calling for commercial and territorial expansion in Latin America, direct involvement in the ongoing revolutions in Europe, and greater development of trade in the Far East. The most serious effort at expansion—the southern desire to build a Caribbean empire—repeatedly stumbled over the issue of slavery.[40]

Cuba became the focal point of Webster's second tenure as secretary of state—particularly because of filibusters such as Narciso López (a Cuban patriot) who sought to free the island from Spain. After an abortive attempt in 1848, López escaped to the United States, where he raised another expedition but failed again to topple the Cuban government in 1850. When Webster became secretary of state, he tried to maintain the nation's neutrality duties while seeking to prosecute the filibusters who were, according to the Spanish, using the United States as a base of operations and a recruiting ground. But Webster was unable to stop American participation in these ventures, largely because local juries sympathized with the accused filibusters and refused to convict them. Finally, however, Spanish authorities on the island captured López in August 1851 and, after a speedy military trial, shot fifty of his accomplices as pirates—including the United States attorney general's nephew, William Crittenden. López was soon publicly garroted in Havana, and over 150 of his cohorts were sent to Spanish mines.[41]

The filibustering problem did not end, however. Enraged Americans rioted against Spain in New Orleans and Key West, demanding retribution for the executions and liberation of the prisoners (mostly Americans) from the mines. In turn, Spain demanded an apology and reparations for property damages resulting from the riots. England and France provided another complication. Their navies patrolled Cuban waters to prevent another invasion of the island and, in so doing, stirred up ugly memories in the United States of visit-and-search. Webster thus had to stem a potential crisis with England and France, and then try to mollify the government in Madrid while seeking the Americans' freedom. He first made clear that the United States would not tolerate British or French infringements of America's sovereignty at sea. In January 1852, England and France halted these activities; but the following April, they proposed a tripartite declaration whereby the participants would permanently renounce "all intentions to obtain possession of the Island of Cuba" and agree to safeguard it in Spain's hands. Webster, however, opposed a self-denying pact regarding Cuba, which he had once called the "key to the Gulf of Mexico and the Caribbean Sea." Hoping that time might calm emotions, he expressed concern about America's traditional opposition to European encroachments in the hemisphere and delayed a reply. Sometime later, his successor in the State Department, Edward Everett, rejected the Anglo-French proposal on the grounds that Cuba was "an American question." On the issues with Spain, Webster took advantage of an implicit Spanish invitation to tie their demands for reparations with liberation of the Americans. Accordingly, he apologized and assured reparations; Spain released the prisoners.[42]

Webster's diplomacy regarding Cuba deserves more attention than it has received. He defused the filibustering activities while upholding the nation's neutrality obligations and averting a confrontation with Spain. He secured the pardon of American prisoners, who were legally in the wrong. Indeed, he accomplished all these objectives through a willingness to apologize and accept Spain's legitimate demands. And, while freeing the United States from a dangerous position, he had maintained its national interests in Cuba and safeguarded America's honor at sea by warding off potential threats from England and France. Webster's diplomacy was quiet and unobtrusive—as it should be.

In the meantime, to overcome disunionist feeling, Webster tried to rally Americans around a revolution in Hungary that had broken out against Austria in 1848. President Zachary Taylor had privately sent a special envoy to Hungary with instructions to extend recognition and negotiate commercial agreements if the rebels seemed capable of maintaining independence. But Russia aided the Hapsburg regime in putting down the revolt, and the Austrian chargé in Washington, the Chevalier Johann Georg Hülsemann, hotly protested Taylor's intentions. In 1850, after Webster became secretary of state, he criticized Austria in an effort to "make a man feel *sheepish* and look *silly* who should speak of disunion." In what has become known as the "Hülsemann Letter," Webster declared that the developments in Hungary "appeared to have their origin in those great ideas of responsible and popular governments, on which the American Constitutions themselves are wholly founded. . . . The power of this Republic . . . is spread over a region, one of the richest and most fertile on the Globe, and of an extent in comparison with which the possessions of the House of Hapsburg, are but as a patch on the earth's surface." The chargé's fury had barely abated when the exiled leader of the Hungarian rebels, Louis Kossuth, arrived in the United States in late 1851 to seek assistance in winning independence. At a bipartisan banquet held in Kossuth's honor and sponsored by Congress, Webster toasted "*Hungarian Independence.*" Webster had succeeded in temporarily uniting Americans and perhaps in drawing attention to himself as a presidential possibility, but his actions strained relations with Austria and dangerously skirted his principles of nonintervention.[43]

Webster encountered numerous other problems during his second sojourn in the State Department. A military intervention by France in the Hawaiian Islands led him to invoke the Tyler Doctrine in safeguarding their independence. Economic and strategic considerations meanwhile led him to support a deeper involvement in Latin America. After prolonged unrest in Santo Domingo endangered foreign holdings and trade, the United States broke its tradition of nonintervention and sent a special agent to work with the French and British in restoring order. Against these same two nations, however, he warily safeguarded America's interests in Cuba. And Webster again rejected Spain's continued demands for indemnification stemming from the *Amistad* affair.

Then the combination of his failing health and his futile attempt to win nomination for the presidency seems to have had an adverse effect on Webster's diplomacy. In the summer of 1852, disagreements erupted with England over the northeast fishing business. The British had turned to free trade and pushed for a reciprocal trade agreement between Canada and the United States. After negotiations stalled, the government in London barred Americans from fishing within three miles of the bays and coast between the Bay of Fundy and the Gulf of St. Lawrence—a practice allowed as a "liberty" but not as a "right" since the Anglo-American Convention of 1818. In a surprising move, Webster claimed that American negotiators in 1818 had been guilty of an "oversight," and he implicitly admitted to Britain's interpretation of "bay"—that the three-mile limit extended from "headland" to "headland" and did not follow coastal indentations. Thus Webster seemed willing to forgo American rights to fish in British bays and harbors. Informal negotiations arranged by Webster succeeded only in securing a tenuous truce.[44]

In his last piece of work as secretary of state, Webster demonstrated an uncharacteristic lack of diplomatic skill regarding a dispute with

Peru over the Lobos Islands, which were located twenty miles off its coast and were rich in guano deposits. "All my concerns in this Department," he confided to a friend, "have never given me so much disturbance, as this Lobos business." At that moment, nearly forty merchant ships, under the assurance of safety from the United States Navy, were heading toward the islands, intending to wrest $40 million of guano from Peru. It would take "almost a miracle" to prevent a war, President Fillmore declared. On the basis of thin reasoning and dubious evidence, Webster had earlier declared that neither Spain nor Peru had occupied the islands and that it seemed "quite probable" that an American had discovered them in the early 1820s. The United States government, he declared, had a "duty" to safeguard its people's interests in the fertilizer. Indeed, Webster seems to have been prepared to take the islands from Peru if the need arose.[45]

Fortunately, however, reason regained control. Word leaked out that the administration was considering force on behalf of the nation's businessmen, stimulating more interest in the guano and causing the State Department to receive numerous inquiries. When the Peruvian government vehemently protested and claimed ownership of the islands, Fillmore began to reassess the American position. It soon became clear that there was little evidence to support the American claim and that Webster would have to break his promise to protect American merchants. The secretary of state nonetheless maintained America's right to use the islands on the bases that an American had discovered the guano, that the Lobos were located more than three miles offshore and hence in international waters, and that Americans had been using the islands longer than had Peruvians. In late August he notified the government in Lima that if it would permit the entry of American vessels and alter its monopolistic practices, the Fillmore administration would recognize Peru's control over the islands. The president, however, finally realized that Peru's claims were just and brought the matter to a close by this acknowledgement. In the meantime, however, declining health had taken its toll on Webster, forcing him to spend longer periods out of Washington. He died in October.[46]

The quality of Webster's diplomacy regarding the Lobos Islands was far below that of his previous undertakings in office. In seeking to aid both American commerce and agriculture, he acted on the basis of little or no information. He did not talk with either the government in Peru or his own representative in Lima before pronouncing a policy that was built on errors. But he salvaged something respectable from the fiasco: he accepted all blame.[47]

If the greatness of a statesman is determined by the size of his shadow, Webster's shadow extended over foreign as well as domestic achievements and has earned him proper acclaim as a diplomatist. As secretary of state, he practiced a personal style of diplomacy that emphasized the spirit of compromise and advocated respect for the law in international relations. Webster was not above making apologies when his nation was in the wrong, and he was willing to make concessions in an effort to accomplish long-range objectives. Throughout his professional career, he argued that Congress had the sole power for declaring war and that the president could take the initiative only in staving off invasion or sudden attack. Further, Webster helped to spread the nation's commercial interests into the Pacific and East Asia. The Tyler Doctrine constituted the first important statement of national concern about that region of the world and was a forerunner of the Open Door Notes of 1899–1900. The Cushing mission to China resulted in the Treaty of Wanghia of 1844, which established diplomatic relations with China and won trading rights for the United States by the most-favored-nation principle. In 1851 Webster had the China market in mind when he drafted the instructions for what would become the Matthew Perry expedition that opened Japan to trade. Despite these achievements, Webster compared only the establishment of improved British relations with the accomplishments of the leading diplomatists of his age.[48] His proudest achievement was the rapprochement with England brought by the Webster-Ashburton Treaty.

1. Clyde A. Duniway, "Daniel Webster" (first term), in Samuel F. Bemis, ed., *The American Secretaries of State and Their Diplomacy* (multi-vols.; N.Y., 1928), 5:13–14, 54–56; Kenneth E. Shewmaker, "Forging the 'Great Chain': Daniel Webster and the Origins of American Foreign Policy Toward East Asia and the Pacific, 1841–1852," *Proceedings of the American Philosophical Society* 129 (1985):225–59.

2. Howard Jones, *To the Webster-Ashburton Treaty: A Study in Anglo-American Relations, 1783–1843* (Chapel Hill, 1977), pp. 23–27; Kenneth R. Stevens, *Border Diplomacy: The Caroline and the McLeod Affairs in Anglo-American-Canadian Relations, 1837–1842* (Tuscaloosa, 1989), pp. 13–17; Duniway, "Webster" (first term), p. 14. See also Howard Jones, "The *Caroline* Affair," *The Historian* 38 (May 1976):485–502; Maurice G. Baxter, *One and Inseparable: Daniel Webster and the Union* (Cambridge, Mass., 1984), pp. 320 ff.

3. H. Jones, *Webster-Ashburton Treaty*, pp. 27, 30–31; Winfield Scott, *Memoirs of Lieut.-General Scott, LL.D. Written by Himself* (2 vols., N.Y., 1864), 1:308–17; Stevens, *Border Diplomacy*, pp. 20–22.

4. H. Jones, *Webster-Ashburton Treaty*, pp. 28–30; Stevens, *Border Diplomacy*, pp. 19–

20, 22–25, 33–36. Stevens argues that destruction of the *Caroline* was not justified because it had posed no imminent threat to British sovereignty. Ibid., 35–36. According to one writer, Fox was a "withered, gray, little old man, addicted to opium, overwhelmed with debts, [who] never entertained and [whose] only entertainment was at cards." Merrill D. Peterson, *The Great Triumvirate: Webster, Clay, and Calhoun* (N.Y., 1987), p. 323.

  5. H. Jones, *Webster-Ashburton Treaty*, pp. 49–54; Stevens, *Border Diplomacy*, chap. 5; Baxter, *Webster*, pp. 322 ff.; Duniway, "Webster" (first term), pp. 14–15; Palmerston to Fox, Feb. 9, 1841, Lord Palmerston Papers, GC/FO/170, by permission of the Trustees of the Broadlands Archives, London, England. See also Alastair Watt, "The Case of Alexander McLeod," *Canadian Historical Review* 12 (June 1931):145–67; Milledge L. Bonham, "Alexander McLeod: Bone of Contention," *New York History* 18 (April 1937):189–217; Albert B. Corey, *The Crisis of 1830–1842 in Canadian-American Relations* (New Haven, 1941), p. 137.

  6. H. Jones, *Webster-Ashburton Treaty*, pp. 55–66; Stevens, *Border Diplomacy*, pp. 95, 102–4, 111–15, 120–23, 156–57; Baxter, *Webster*, p. 324; Duniway, "Webster" (first term), pp. 15–17. The New York Supreme Court eventually ruled that when no war had been declared, murder could not fit the category of a public act. Kenneth E. Shewmaker, " 'Congress only can declare war' *and* 'the President is Commander in Chief'; Daniel Webster and the War Power," *Diplomatic History* 12 (Fall 1988):389. For documentation on the McLeod crisis, see Kenneth E. Shewmaker, Kenneth R. Stevens, and Anita McGurn, eds., *The Papers of Daniel Webster, Diplomatic Papers, Volume 1 1841–1843* (Hanover, N.H., and London, England, 1983), pp. 29–153. On the *Caroline* and self-defense, see Webster to Fox, April 24, 1841, ibid., 58–68. See Document 63, pp. 229–40. Webster's arguments on self-defense have been cited in the twentieth century by various countries in justifying or criticizing military actions.

  7. H. Jones, *Webster-Ashburton Treaty*, pp. 60–61, 95–98; Wilbur D. Jones, *The American Problem in British Diplomacy, 1841–1861* (Athens, Georgia, 1974), pp. 8, 18.

  8. H. Jones, *Webster-Ashburton Treaty*, pp. 121–22, 124–25; Duniway, "Webster" (first term), pp. 18–27.

  9. Smith to Webster, June 7, 1841, in Shewmaker et al., eds., *Webster, Diplomatic Papers*, 1:94–96; H. Jones, *Webster-Ashburton Treaty*, pp. 91–94; Frederick Merk, *Fruits of Propaganda in the Tyler Administration* (Cambridge, Mass., 1971), pp. 59–64; *U.S. Statutes at Large*, 2:609. Smith eventually received $2,500 from the secret-service fund. His assistants in Maine received $500—also from the fund. See Howard Jones, "The Attempt to Impeach Daniel Webster," *Capitol Studies* 3 (Fall 1975):34–35. Critics of Webster's methods include Merk, *Fruits of Propaganda*, pp. 87–92, and Richard N. Current, "Webster's Propaganda and the Ashburton Treaty," *Mississippi Valley Historical Review* 31 (Oct. 1947):187–200. Baxter refers to Webster's "propagandizing" as "scarcely compatible with the ways of a democratic society," *Webster*, pp. 335–36. See also Richard N. Current, *Daniel Webster and the Rise of National Conservatism* (Boston, 1955), pp. 122–24.

  10. H. Jones, *Webster-Ashburton Treaty*, p. 103; Sparks to Webster, Fed. 15, 1842, in Shewmaker et al., eds., *Webster, Diplomatic Papers*, 1:513–16; Franklin to Vergennes, Dec. 6, 1782, Francis Wharton, ed., *The Revolutionary Diplomatic Correspondence of the United States* (6 vols., Wash., D.C.: Government Printing Office, 1889), 6:120. See Document 64, pp. 240–44.

  11. H. Jones, *Webster-Ashburton Treaty*, pp. 13–17, 103–4; Sparks to Webster, Feb. 15, 1842, in Shewmaker et al., eds., *Webster, Diplomatic Papers*, 1:514.

  12. H. Jones, *Webster-Ashburton Treaty*, pp. 104–7. Webster had bought the earlier map, a Mitchell that belonged to the Revolutionary War general, from Steuben's legatee and sold it to Charles Daveis, a boundary agent from Maine. Daveis immediately concealed the map. Ibid., 104. Ashburton later agreed with Webster

on the propriety of a diplomat withholding evidence from the other side. See Baxter, *Webster*, p. 356.

13. H. Jones, *Webster-Ashburton Treaty*, pp. 115–17, 131–32. Sparks received $250 from the president's fund. Ibid., 210 n. 49. Seven state commissioners arrived in mid-June, less than a week before the first boundary discussion on June 18. Ashburton, however, considered it improper for a diplomat to meet with representatives of the separate states and only reluctantly agreed to do so on an irregular basis. Ibid., 116, 124.

14. Ibid., 122–23.

15. Ibid., 132–36, 154–59; Howard Jones, "Anglophobia and the Aroostook War," *New England Quarterly* 48 (Dec. 1975):519–39; Thomas LeDuc, "The Webster-Ashburton Treaty and the Minnesota Iron Ranges," *Journal of American History* 51 (Dec. 1964):476–81; Kenneth E. Shewmaker, "Daniel Webster and the Oregon Question," *Pacific Historical Review* 51 (May 1982):195–201. A faulty survey years earlier had been responsible for the erroneous location of Fort Montgomery (or "Fort Blunder"). H. Jones, *Webster-Ashburton Treaty*, p. 12.

16. Howard Jones, "The Peculiar Institution and National Honor: The Case of the *Creole* Slave Revolt," *Civil War History* 21 (March 1975):28–50.

17. H. Jones, *Webster-Ashburton Treaty*, pp. 69 ff., 83–84; Peterson, *Great Triumvirate*, pp. 321–22; Duniway, "Webster" (first term), pp. 34–36.

18. H. Jones, *Webster-Ashburton Treaty*, pp. 142–51. The extraditable crimes were murder, assault with intent to commit murder, piracy, arson, robbery, forgery, or the issuance of forged paper. In 1853 an Anglo-American claims commission awarded compensation to the owners of the *Creole's* liberated slaves. Lewis Cass, America's minister in France, criticized the joint-cruising arrangement as a British effort to incorporate the practice of search into international law during peacetime and as a violation of George Washington's warning against "combinations upon subjects not American." Webster replied that the treaty honored Washington's counsel for limited treaties and insisted that Cass's argument rested on Thomas Jefferson's call for "entangling alliances with none." See Kenneth E. Shewmaker, "The 'War of Words': The Cass-Webster Debate of 1842–43," *Diplomatic History* 5 (Spring 1981):151–63.

19. H. Jones, *Webster-Ashburton Treaty*, pp. 152–54; Stevens, *Border Diplomacy*, pp. 165, 168. Stevens shows that the Remedial Justice Act also widened federal authority over state courts and over habeas corpus. On the *Caroline* matter, he regards Ashburton's words as an apology. Ibid., 203 n. 32. Baxter claims that Ashburton "came as close to an apology as he could," *Webster*, p. 351.

20. H. Jones, *Webster-Ashburton Treaty*, pp. 139–42, 154; Stevens, *Border Diplomacy*, pp. 160–65; Shewmaker, "Webster and War Power," p. 390; Duniway, "Webster" (first term), p. 17. For Webster's note on impressment, see Shewmaker et al., eds., *Webster, Diplomatic Papers*, 1:673–79. Remedial Justice Act in *U.S. Statutes at Large*, 5:539.

21. H. Jones, *Webster-Ashburton Treaty*, pp. 161–65, 169–70. After eleven days of debate, the Senate approved the treaty by vote of thirty-nine to nine.

22. Ibid., 107–8.

23. Ibid., 108–9; Ashburton to Rives, Aug. 26, 1844, William Cabell Rives Papers, Manuscript Division, Library of Congress, Wash., D.C.

24. H. Jones, *Webster-Ashburton Treaty*, pp. 107–9, 173. How Palmerston learned of this map remains unclear. Perhaps it came to his attention through an English geologist, George Featherstonhaugh, who had led a British survey of the boundary before returning to England in 1839. See "The 'Battle of the Maps,' " in Shewmaker et al., eds., *Webster, Diplomatic Papers*, 1:776.

25. H. Jones, *Webster-Ashburton Treaty*, pp. 171–72.

26. Ibid., 111–12, 176.

27. Ibid., 112–13, 126–27. Samuel F. Bemis concluded in his Pulitzer Prize-winning biography of John Quincy Adams that "Webster achieved a diplomatic triumph— against his own country." See Bemis's *John Quincy Adams and the Foundations of American*

Foreign Policy (N.Y., 1949), p. 481. The irony is that Bemis pointed out in an earlier study that Franklin had gotten approval for the postwar joint commissions, thereby reducing all maps to mere proposals. See Bemis, *The Diplomacy of the American Revolution* (N.Y., 1935), p. 228. See also Richard B. Morris, *The Peacemakers: The Great Powers and American Independence* (N.Y., 1965), p. 346.

28. H. Jones, *Webster-Ashburton Treaty*, pp. 127–28, 130.

29. Ibid., 128; Ashburton to Aberdeen, Aug. 9, 1842, Aberdeen Papers, British Library, 43123, London, England. Bemis wrote: "Since Ashburton did not know of Sparks's map information until near August 9, we may guess that Ashburton had handed the money over to Webster with only a general assurance that it would help out." See *Adams and Foundations of American Foreign Policy*, p. 588. Frederick Merk (Bemis's mentor) likewise treated the two sums of money as one. See Merk, *Fruits of Propaganda*, p. 71. Baxter believes that Ashburton gave Sparks "an unknown sum in addition to what the State Department paid from the secret-service fund," *Webster*, p. 343. Mildmay was Ashburton's son-in-law who worked in the Foreign Office and accompanied the emissary to the United States.

30. H. Jones, *Webster-Ashburton Treaty*, pp. 128–31; Ashburton to Aberdeen, June 14, 1842, Aberdeen Papers, British Library, 43123.

31. Aberdeen to Ashburton, July 2, 1842, Aberdeen Papers, British Library, 43123; H. Jones, *Webster-Ashburton Treaty*, pp. 128–29.

32. H. Jones, *Webster-Ashburton Treaty*, pp. 58, 66–67, 176; H. Jones, "Attempt to Impeach Webster," pp. 31–44; Baxter, *Webster*, pp. 380–86; Current, *Webster*, pp. 137–38.

33. H. Jones, *Webster-Ashburton Treaty*, pp. 176–79; H. Jones, "Attempt to Impeach Webster," pp. 33–35, 37–41; Current, *Webster*, p. 138. The House committee had consisted of two Whigs and three Democrats. The Democrats included an expansionist Ohio congressman, Jacob Brinkerhoff, who had long opposed Webster. It was Brinkerhoff who voted against exonerating Webster. Brinkerhoff condemned Webster's actions in Maine as "systematic electioneering" and raised questions about whether it was an "impeachable offence" to use federal funds to influence a state legislature. See Merk, *Fruits of Propaganda*, pp. 210–14.

34. Duniway, "Webster" (first term), pp. 57–61; Shewmaker, "Webster and Oregon Question," p. 200.

35. Howard Jones, *Mutiny on the Amistad: The Saga of a Slave Revolt and Its Impact on American Abolition, Law, and Diplomacy* (N.Y., 1987). For Webster's correspondence with Spain on the *Amistad* issue, see Shewmaker et al., eds., *Webster, Diplomatic Papers*, 1:194–229.

36. Shewmaker, "Forging the 'Great Chain,'" p. 232; Shewmaker, "Webster and War Power," pp. 393–95; Baxter, *Webster*, p. 463; Duniway, "Webster" (first term), pp. 56–57; Tyler Doctrine quoted in James D. Richardson, ed., *A Compilation of the Messages and Papers of the Presidents* (11 vols.; N.Y., 1896–1910), 4:212. The Tyler Doctrine, declared by the president in his special message of December 30, 1842, contained the same ideas and words found in Webster's letter of December 19 to Timoteo Haalilio and William Richards (commissioners of king of Hawaiian Islands). See Shewmaker et al., eds., *Webster, Diplomatic Papers*, 1:870–71. See also Haalilio and Richards to Webster, Dec. 14, 1842, ibid., 866–69. On Cuba, see Webster to Robert B. Campbell (American consul in Havana), Jan. 14, 1843, ibid., 369–72. See Document 68, pp. 257–58.

37. Duniway, "Webster" (first term), p. 62; Shewmaker, "Forging the 'Great Chain,'" p. 236; Peterson, *Great Triumvirate*, pp. 324, 331–34; editorial, "Resignation," in Shewmaker et al., eds., *Webster, Diplomatic Papers*, 1:928; Webster to Everett, April 28, 1843, ibid., 916. For Webster's note to Cushing, see ibid., 922–26, and Document 71, pp. 264–68.

38. Shewmaker, "Webster and War Power," pp. 396–97. Webster thought Polk should be charged with "an impeachable offence." See Webster's speech in James M. McIntyre, ed., *The Writings and Speeches of Daniel Webster* (18 vols.; Boston, 1903), 13:333–39.

39. Kenneth E. Shewmaker, "Daniel Webster and the Politics of Foreign Policy, 1850–1852," *Journal of American History* 63 (Sept. 1976):303–15; Current, *Webster*, p. 173.

40. Clyde A. Duniway, "Daniel Webster" (second term), in Samuel F. Bemis, ed., *The American Secretaries of State and Their Diplomacy* (multi-vols.; N.Y., 1928), 6:95–107; Baxter, *Webster*, pp. 467–70; Irving H. Bartlett, *Daniel Webster* (N.Y., 1978), pp. 278–79. See also Robert E. May, *The Southern Dream of a Caribbean Empire, 1854–1861* (Baton Rouge, 1973).

41. Angel Calderón de la Barca (Spanish minister in Washington) to Webster, Aug. 2, 1850, in Kenneth E. Shewmaker, Kenneth R. Stevens, and Alan R. Berolzheimer, eds., *The Papers of Daniel Webster, Diplomatic Papers, Volume 2 1850–1852* (Hanover, N.H., 1987), pp. 349–58; Calderón to Webster, Aug. 20, 1850, cited in ibid., 336. See Shewmaker's essay for an excellent summary of the entire affair. Ibid., 335–49.

42. Webster's assessment of Cuba in Webster to Fillmore, Oct. 4, 1851, ibid., 385; Draft Convention of Anglo-French proposal, c. April 8, 1852, encl. in John F. Crampton (British chargé in Washington) to Webster, April 23, 1852, ibid., 428–31; Everett to Eugène de Sartiges (French minister in Washington), Dec. 1, 1852, cited ibid., 348. See Document 75, pp. 287–91.

43. Webster to George Ticknor, Jan. 16, 1851, in Shewmaker et al., eds., *Webster, Diplomatic Papers*, 2:64; Hülsemann Letter, ibid., 49–61; Webster's toast and speech at Kossuth Banquet, Jan. 7, 1852, ibid., 97–105; Baxter, *Webster*, pp. 463–67; Bartlett, *Webster*, pp. 260–63; Current, *Webster*, pp. 175–76; Peterson, *Great Triumvirate*, pp. 478–79; Shewmaker, "Webster and Politics of Foreign Policy," pp. 310–11, 315. Shewmaker argues that there never was a real chance of armed hostilities between Austria and the United States, thereby making the letter more important as an attempt to stir up American support for the Compromise of 1850. Ibid., 310, 313–14. See also Donald S. Spencer, *Louis Kossuth and Young America: A Study of Sectionalism and Foreign Policy, 1848–1852* (Columbia, Missouri, 1977). For the Hülsemann Letter, see Document 72, pp. 269–81.

44. Shewmaker, "Forging the 'Great Chain,' " pp. 240–44; Baxter, *Webster*, pp. 463, 473–74; Shewmaker, "Webster and War Power," pp. 399–402, 405–7; Shewmaker, " 'Hook and line, and bob and sinker': Daniel Webster and the Fisheries Dispute of 1852," *Diplomatic History* 9 (Spring 1985):113–29; Bartlett, *Webster*, p. 280; Duniway, "Webster" (second term), pp. 108–12; H. Jones, *Mutiny on Amistad*, pp. 216–17; R. Earl McClendon, "The Amistad Claims: Inconsistencies of Policy," *Political Science Quarterly* 48 (Sept. 1933):386–412. See Document 77, pp. 293–95.

45. Kenneth E. Shewmaker, " 'Untaught Diplomacy': Daniel Webster and the Lobos Islands Controversy," *Diplomatic History* 1 (Fall 1977):321–40; Webster to Hiram Ketchum, Aug. 21, 1852, Shewmaker et al., eds., *Webster, Diplomatic Papers*, 2:760; Webster to Fillmore, Sept. 15, 1852, ibid., 774; Fillmore to Webster, Sept. 19, 1852, ibid., 775–77; Webster to Fillmore, June 5, 1852, ibid., 736–38. See Shewmaker's summary of the Lobos affair, ibid., 713–24. See Document 76, pp. 292–93.

46. Shewmaker, "Untaught Diplomacy," pp. 334–35, 337–40.

47. Fillmore to Webster, July 8, 1852, Shewmaker et al., eds., *Webster, Diplomatic Papers*, 2:742–43; Webster to Juan Ygnacio de Osma (Peruvian chargé in Washington), Aug. 21, 1852, ibid., 761–68; Webster to John P. Kennedy (secretary of the Navy), Aug. 24, 1852, ibid., 768–69; Webster to John Randolph Clay (U.S. chargé in Peru), Aug. 30, 1852, ibid., 771–74; Everett to Joaquin José de Osma (special envoy and brother of chargé), Nov. 16, 1852, ibid., 785–87. See Document 78, pp. 295–96.

48. Shewmaker, "Forging the 'Great Chain,' " pp. 236, 239, 250; Shewmaker, "Webster and War Power"; Webster to Commodore John H. Aulick, June 10, 1851, in Shewmaker et al., eds., *Webster, Diplomatic Papers*, 2:289–92 (instructions regarding Japan); Webster's "Defence of the Treaty of Washington," in Charles M. Wiltse and Alan R. Berolzheimer, eds., *The Papers of Daniel Webster: Speeches and Formal Writings* (2

vols.; Hanover, N.H., and London, England, 1986–1988), 2:379. Other contemporary diplomatists included England's Lord Castlereagh, Russia's Count Nesselrode, Austria's Prince von Metternich, and France's Charles Maurice de Talleyrand-Perigord. Webster believed that the treaty with England had kept "the peace of the world." Webster to Everett, April 27, 1843, Shewmaker et al., eds., *Webster, Diplomatic Papers*, 1:930. See Document 73 for Webster's instructions on the mission to Japan, pp. 282–84.

Document 63
Text from *Diplomatic Papers* 1: 58–68.

To Henry Stephen Fox[1]

Department of State,
Washington, 24th of April, 1841

The Undersigned, Secretary of State of the United States, has the honor to inform Mr [Henry Stephen] Fox, Envoy Extraordinary and Minister Plenipotentiary of Her Britannic Majesty, that his note of the 12th[2] of March was received and laid before the President.

Circumstances well known to Mr Fox have necessarily delayed, for some days, the consideration of that note.[3]

The Undersigned has the honor now to say, that it has been fully considered, and that he has been directed by the President to address to Mr Fox the following reply.

Mr Fox informs the Government of the United States, that he is instructed to make known to it, that the Government of Her Majesty entirely approve the course pursued by him, in his correspondence with Mr [John] Forsyth,[4] in December last, and the language adopted by him on that occasion, and that that Government have instructed him again to demand from the Government of the United States, formally, in the name of the British Government, the immediate release of Mr Alexander McLeod;[5] "that the grounds upon which the British Government make this demand upon the Government of the United States, are these: that the transaction on account of which Mr. McLeod has been arrested and is to be put upon his trial, was a transaction of a public character, planned and executed by persons duly empowered by Her Majesty's Colonial authorities to take any steps and to do any acts which might be necessary for the defence of Her Majesty's territories and for the protection of Her Majesty's subjects; and that consequently those subjects of Her Majesty who engaged in that transaction were performing an act of public duty for which they cannot be made personally and individually answerable to the laws and tribunals of any foreign country."

The President is not certain that he understands, precisely, the meaning intended by Her Majesty's Government to be conveyed, by the foregoing instruction.

This doubt has occasioned, with the President, some hesitation, but he inclines to take it for granted that the main purpose of the instruction was, to cause it to be signified to the Government of the United States, that the attack on the steamboat "Caroline" was an act of public force, done by the British Colonial authorities, and fully recognised by the Queen's Government at home, and that, consequently, no individual concerned in that transaction, can, according to the just principle of the laws of Nations, be held personally answerable in the ordinary courts of law, as for a private offence; and that upon this avowal of Her Majesty's Government Alexander McLeod, now imprisoned, on an indictment for murder, alleged to have been committed in that attack, ought to be released, by such proceedings as are usual and are suitable to the case.

The President adopts the conclusion that nothing more than this could have been intended to be expressed from the consideration, that Her Majesty's Government must be fully aware, that in the United States, as in England, persons confined under judicial process, can be released from that confinement only by judicial process. In neither country, as the Undersigned supposes, can the arm of the Executive power interfere, directly or forcibly, to release or deliver the prisoner. His discharge must be sought in a manner conformable to the principles of law, and the proceedings of Courts of judicature. If an indictment, like that which has been found against Alexander McLeod, and under circumstances like those which belong to his case, were pending against an individual, in one of the courts of England, there is no doubt, that the law officer of the crown might enter a *nolle prosequi,* or that the prisoner might cause himself to be brought up on *habeas corpus,* and discharged, if his ground of discharge should be adjudged sufficient, or that he might prove the same facts, and insist on the same defence, or exemption, on his trial.

All these are legal modes of proceeding, well known to the laws and practice of both countries. But the Undersigned does not suppose that, if such a case were to arise in England, the power of the Executive Government could be exerted in any more direct manner. Even in the case of Embassadors, and other public Ministers, whose right to exemption from arrest is personal, requiring no fact to be ascertained but the mere fact of diplomatic character, and to arrest whom is sometimes made a highly penal offence, if the arrest be actually made, it must be discharged by application to the courts of law.

It is understood that Alexander McLeod is holden as well on civil as on criminal process, for acts alleged to have been done by him, in the attack on the "Caroline;" and his defence, or ground of acquittal, must be the same in both cases. And this strongly illustrates, as the Undersigned conceives, the propriety of the foregoing observations; since it is quite clear that the Executive Government cannot interfere to arrest a civil suit, between private parties, in any stage of its progress; but that such suit must go on, to its regular judicial termination. If, therefore, any course different from such as have been now mentioned, was in contemplation of Her Majesty's Government, something would seem to have been expected, from the Government of the United States, as little conformable to the laws and usages of the English Government as to those of the United States, and to which this government cannot accede.

The Government of the United States, therefore, acting upon the presumption, which it readily adopted that nothing extraordinary or unusual was expected or requested of it, decided, on the reception of Mr Fox's note, to take such measures as the occasion and its own duty appeared to require. In his note to Mr Fox of the 26th of December last, Mr Forsyth, the Secretary of State of the United States, observes, that "if the destruction of the "Caroline" was a public act, of persons in Her Majesty's service, obeying the order of their superior authorities, this fact has not been before communicated to the Government of the United States by a person authorized to make the admission; and it will be for the court which has taken cognizance of the offence with which Mr McLeod is charged to decide upon its validity when legally established before it." And adds, "the President deems this to be a proper occasion to remind the Government of her Britannic Majesty, that the case of the "Caroline" has been long since brought to the attention of Her Majesty's Principal Secretary of State for Foreign Affairs [Lord Palmerston],[6] who up to this day, has not communicated its decision thereupon. It is hoped that the Government of Her Majesty will perceive the importance of no longer leaving the Government of the United States uninformed of its views and intentions upon a subject, which has naturally produced much exasperation and which has led to such grave consequences."

The communication of the fact, that the destruction of the Caroline was an act of public force, by the British authorities, being formally made————to the Government of the United States, by Mr Fox's note, the case assumes a decided aspect.

The Government of the United States entertains no doubt, that after this avowal of the transaction, as a public transaction, authorized and undertaken by the British authorities, individuals concerned in it ought not, by the principles of public law, and the general usage of civilized States, to be holden personally responsible in the ordinary tribunals of law, for their participation in it. And the President presumes that it can hardly be necessary to say, that the American People, not distrustful of their ability to redress public wrongs, by public means, cannot desire the punishment of individuals, when the act complained of is declared to have been an act of the Government itself.

Soon after the date of Mr Fox's note, an instruction was given to the Attorney General of the United States [John Jordan Crittenden],[7] from this Department, by direction of the President, which fully sets forth the opinions of this Government on the subject of McLeod's imprisonment, a copy of which instruction, the Undersigned has the honor herewith to enclose.

The indictment against McLeod is pending in a State Court, but his rights, whatever they may be, are no less safe, it is to be presumed, than if he were holden to answer in one of the Courts of this Government.

He demands immunity from personal responsibility, by virtue of the law of Nations, and that law, in civilized States, is to be respected in all courts. None is either so high, or so low, as to escape from its authority, in cases to which its rules and principles apply.

This Department has been regularly informed, by His Excellency the Governor of the State of New York [William Henry Seward],[8] that the Chief Justice of that State [Samuel Nelson][9] was assigned to preside at the hearing and trial of McLeod's case, but that owing to some error or mistake, in the process of summoning the jury, the hearing was necessarily deferred. The President regrets this occurrence, as he has a desire for a speedy disposition of the subject. The counsel of McLeod have requested authentic evidence of the avowal by the British Government of the attack on, and destruction of, the "Caroline" as acts done under its authority and such evidence will be furnished to them by this Department.

It is understood that the indictment has been removed into the Supreme Court of the State by the proper proceeding for that purpose, and that it is now competent for McLeod, by the ordinary process of *habeas corpus*, to bring his case for hearing before that tribunal.

The Undersigned hardly needs to assure Mr Fox, that a tribunal, so eminently distinguished for ability and learning as the Supreme Court of the State of New York, may be safely relied upon, for the just and impartial administration of the law in this, as well as in other cases; and the Undersigned repeats the expression of the desire of this Government that no delay may be suffered to take place in these proceedings, which can be avoided. Of this desire Mr Fox will see evidence in the instructions above referred to.

The Undersigned has now to signify to Mr Fox that the Government of the United States has not changed the opinion which it has heretofore expressed to Her Majesty's Government, of the character of the act of destroying the "Caroline." It does not think that that transaction can be justified by any reasonable application or construction of the right of self-defence under the laws of Nations. It is admitted that a just right of self-defence attaches always to Nations, as well as to individuals, and is equally necessary for the preservation of both. But the extent of this right is a question to be judged of by the circumstances of each particular case; and when its alleged exercise has led to the commission of hostile acts, within the territory of a Power at peace, nothing less than a clear and absolute necessity can afford ground of justification. Not having, up to this time, been made acquainted with the views and reasons, at length, which have led Her Majesty's Government to think the destruction of the "Caroline" justifiable as an act of self-defence, the Undersigned, earnestly reviewing the remonstrance of this Government against the transaction, abstains, for the present, from any extended discussion of the question. But it is deemed proper, nevertheless, not to omit, to take some notice of the general grounds of justification, stated by Her Majesty's Government, in their instruction to Mr Fox.

Her Majesty's Government have instructed Mr Fox to say, that they are of opinion, that the transaction, which terminated in the destruction of the "Caroline," was a justifiable employment of force, for the purpose of defending the British Territory from the unprovoked attack of a band of British rebels and American pirates, who, having been "permitted" to arm and organize themselves within the territory of the United States, had actually invaded a portion of the territory of Her Majesty.

The President cannot suppose that Her Majesty's Government, by the use of these terms, meant to be understood as intimating, that those acts, violating the laws of the United States, and disturbing the peace of the British Territories, were done under any degree of countenance from this Government, or were regarded by it with indifference; or, that under the circumstances of the case, they could have been prevented, by the ordinary course of proceeding. Although he regrets, that by using the term "permitted," a possible inference of that kind might be raised, yet such an inference, the President, is willing to believe, would be quite unjust to the intentions of the British Government.

That on a line of frontier, such as separates the United States from Her Britannic Majesty's North American Provinces, a line long enough to divide the whole of Europe into halves, irregularities, violences, and conflicts should sometimes occur equally against the will of both Governments, is certainly easily to be supposed. This may be more possible, perhaps, in regard to the United States, without any reproach to their Government, since their institutions entirely discourage the keeping up of large standing armies in time of peace, and their situation happily exempts them from the necessity of maintaining such expensive and dangerous establishments. All that can be expected, from either government, in these cases, is good faith, a sincere desire to preserve peace and do justice, the use of all proper means of prevention, and, that if offences cannot, nevertheless, be always prevented, the offenders shall still be justly punished. In all these respects, this Government acknowledges no delinquency in the performance of its duties.

Her Majesty's Government are pleased, also, to speak of those American citizens, who took part with persons in Canada, engaged in an insurrection against the British Government as "American pirates." The Undersigned does not admit the propriety or justice of this designation. If citizens of the United States fitted out, or were engaged in fitting out, a military expedition from the United States, intended to act against the British Government in Canada, they were clearly violating the laws of their own country, and exposing themselves to the just consequences, which might be inflicted on them, if taken within the British Dominions. But notwithstanding this, they were, certainly, not pirates, nor does the Undersigned think that it can advance the purpose of fair and friendly discussion, or hasten the accommodation of national difficulties so to denominate them. Their offence, whatever it was, had no analogy to cases of piracy. Supposing all that is alleged against them to be true, they were taking a part in what they regarded as a civil war, and they were taking a part on the side of the rebels. Surely, England herself has not regarded persons thus engaged as deserving the appellation which Her Majesty's Government bestows on these citizens of the United States.[10]

It is quite notorious, that for the greater part of the last two centuries, subjects of the British crown have been permitted to engage in foreign wars, both national and civil, and in the latter in every stage of their progress, and yet it has not been imagined that England has at any time allowed her subjects to turn pirates. Indeed, in our own times, not only have individual subjects of that crown gone abroad to engage in civil wars, but we have seen whole regiments openly recruited, embodied, armed, and disciplined in England, with the avowed purpose of aiding a rebellion against a nation, with which England was at peace; although it is true, that subsequently, an Act of Parliament was passed to prevent transactions so nearly approaching to public war without license from the crown.[11]

It may be said, that there is a difference between the case of a civil war, arising from a disputed succession, or a protracted revolt of a colony against the mother country, and the case of the fresh outbreak, or commencement of a rebellion. The Undersigned does not deny, that such distinction may, for certain purposes, be deemed well founded. He admits, that a Government, called upon to consider its own rights, interests, and duties, when civil wars break out in other countries, may decide on all the circumstances of the particular case, upon its own existing stipulations, on probable results, on what its own security requires, and on many other considerations. It may be already bound to assist one party, or it may become bound, if it so chooses, to assist the other, and to meet the consequences of such assistance. But whether the revolt be recent, or long continued, they who join those concerned in it, whatever may be their offence against their own country, or however they be treated, if taken with arms in their hands, in the territory of the Government, against which the standard of revolt is raised, cannot be denominated Pirates, without departing from all ordinary use of language in the definition of offences. A cause which has so foul an origin as piracy, cannot, in its progress, or by its success, obtain a claim to any degree of respectability, or tolerance, among nations; and civil wars, therefore, are not understood to have such a commencement.

It is well known to Mr Fox, that authorities of the highest eminence in England, living and dead, have maintained, that the general law of Nations does not forbid the citizens or subjects of one Government, from taking part in the civil commotions of another. There is some reason indeed, to think, that such may be the opinion of Her Majesty's Government at the present moment.

The Undersigned has made these remarks, from the conviction that it is important to regard established distinctions, and to view the acts and offenses of individuals in the exactly proper light. But it is not to be inferred, that there is, on the part of this Government any purpose of extenuating, in the slightest degree, the crimes of those persons, citizens of the United States, who have joined in military expeditions against the British Government in Canada. On the contrary, the President directs the Undersigned to say, that it is his fixed resolution that all such disturbers of the national peace, and violaters of the laws of their country, shall be brought to exemplary punishment. Nor will the fact, that they are instigated and led on to these excesses, by British subjects, refugees from the Provinces, be deemed any excuse or palliation; although it is well worthy of being remembered, that the prime movers of these disturbances on the borders are subjects of the Queen who come within the territories of the United States, seeking to enlist the sympathies of their citizens, by all the motives which they are able to address to them, on account of grievances, real or imaginary. There is no reason to believe that the design of any hostile movement from the United States against Canada, has commenced with citizens of the United States. The true origin of such purposes and such enterprises is on the other side of the line. But the President's resolution to prevent these transgressions of the laws is not, on that account, the less strong. It is taken, not only in conformity to his duty under the provisions of existing laws,[12] but in full consonance with the established principles and practice of this Government.

The Government of the United States has not, from the first, fallen into the doubts, elsewhere entertained, of the true extent of the duties of neutrality. It has held, that however it may have been in less enlightened ages, the just interpretation of the modern law of Nations is, that neutral States are bound to be strictly neutral; and that it is a manifest and gross impropriety for individuals to engage in the civil conflicts of other States, and thus to be at war, while their government is at peace. War and peace are high national relations, which can properly be established or changed only by nations themselves.

The United States have thought, also, that the salutary doctrine of nonintervention by one Nation with the affairs of others is liable to be essentially impaired, if, while Government refrains from interference, interference is still allowed to its subjects, individually or in masses. It may happen indeed, that persons choose to leave their country, emigrate to other regions, and settle themselves on uncultivated lands, in territories belonging to other States. This cannot be prevented by Governments, which allow the emigration of their subjects and citizens, and such persons, having voluntarily abandoned their own country, have no longer claims to its protection, nor is it longer responsible for their acts. Such cases, therefore, if they occur, show no abandonment of the duty of neutrality.

The Government of the United States has not considered it as sufficient, to confine the duties of neutrality, and non-interference, to the case of Governments, whose territories lie adjacent to each other. The application of the principle may be more necessary in such cases, but the principle itself, they regard as being the same, if those territories be divided by half the globe. The rule is founded in the impropriety and danger, of allowing individuals to make war on their own authority, or, by mingling themselves in the belligerent operations of other Nations, to run the hazard of counteracting the policy, or embroiling the relations, of their own Government. And the United States have been the first, among civilized Nations, to enforce the observance of this just rule of neutrality and peace, by special and adequate legal enactments. In the infancy of this Government, on the breaking out of the European wars, which had their origin in the French Revolution, Congress passed laws with severe penalties, for preventing the citizens of the United States from taking part in those hostilities.

By these laws, it prescribed to the citizens of the United States what it understood to be their duty, as neutrals, by the law of Nations, and the duty, also, which they owed to the interest and honor of their own country. At a subsequent period, when the American Colonies of a European Power took up arms against their Sovereign, Congress, not diverted from the established system of the Government, by any temporary considerations, not swerved from its sense of justice and of duty, by any sympathies which it might naturally feel for one of the Parties, did not hesitate, also, to pass acts applicable to the case of Colonial insurrection and civil war.[13] And these provisions of law have been continued, revised, amended, and are in full force at the present moment. Nor have they been a dead letter, as it is well known, that exemplary punishments have been inflicted on those who have transgressed them. It is known, indeed, that heavy penalties have fallen on individuals, citizens of the United States, engaged in this very disturbance in Canada with which the destruction of the "Caroline" was connected. And it is in Mr Fox's knowledge also, that the act of Congress of March 10th 1838, was passed for the precise purpose of more effectually restraining military enterprises, from the United States into the British Provinces, by authorizing the use of the most sure, and decisive preventive means. The Undersigned may add, that it stands on the admission of very high British authority, that during the recent Canadian troubles, although bodies of adventurers appeared on the border, making it necessary for the people of Canada to keep themselves in a state prepared for self-defence, yet that these adventurers were acting by no means in accordance with the feeling of the great mass of the American People, or of the Government of the United States.[14]

This Government, therefore, not only holds itself above reproach in every thing respecting the preservation of neutrality, the observance of the principle of non-intervention, and the strictest conformity, in these respects, to the rules of international law, but it doubts not that the world will do it the justice to acknowledge, that it has set an example, not unfit to be followed by others, and that by its steady legislation on this most important subject, it has done something to promote peace and good neighborhood among Nations, and to advance the civilisation of mankind.

The Undersigned trusts, that when Her Britannic Majesty's Government shall present the grounds at length, on which they justify the local authorities of Canada, in attacking and destroying the "Caroline," they will consider, that the laws of the United States are such as the Undersigned has now represented them, and that the Government of the United States has always manifested a sincere disposition to see those laws effectually and impartially administered. If there have been cases in which individuals, justly obnoxious to punishment, have escaped, this is no more than happens in regard to other laws.

Under these circumstances, and under those immediately connected with the transaction itself, it will be for Her Majesty's Government to show, upon what state of facts, and what rules of national law, the destruction of the "Caroline" is to be defended. It will be for that Government to show a necessity of self-defence; instant, overwhelming, leaving no choice of means, and no moment for deliberation. It will be for it to show, also, that the local authorities of Canada,—even supposing the necessity of the moment authorized them to enter the territories of the United States at all,—did nothing unreasonable or excessive; since the act justified by the necessity of self-defence, must be limited by that necessity, and kept clearly within it. It must be shown that admonition or remonstrances to the persons on board the "Caroline" was impracticable, or would have been unavailing; it must be shown that daylight could not be waited for; that there could be no attempt at discrimination, between the innocent and the guilty; that it would not have been enough to seize and detain the vessel; but that there was a necessity, present and inevitable, for attacking her, in the darkness of the night, while moored to the shore, and while unarmed men were asleep on board, killing some and wound[ing] others, and then drawing her into the current, above the cataract, setting her on fire, and, careless to know whether there might not be in her the innocent with the guilty, or the living with the dead, committing her to a fate, which fills the imagination with horror. A necessity for all this, the Government of the United States cannot believe to have existed.

All will see, that if such things be allowed to occur, they must lead to bloody and exasperated war; and when an individual comes into the United States from Canada, and to the very place, on which this drama was performed, and there chooses to make public and vainglorious boast of the part he acted in it, it is hardly wonderful that great excitement should be created, and some degree of commotion arise.[15]

This Republic does not wish to disturb the tranquillity of the world. Its object is peace, its policy, peace. It seeks no aggrandisement by foreign conquest, because it knows that no foreign acquisitions could augment its power and importance so rapidly as they are already advancing, by its own natural growth, under the propitious circumstances of its situation. But it cannot admit, that its Government has not both the will, and the power to preserve its own neutrality, and to enforce the observance of its own laws upon its own citizens. It is jealous of its rights, and among others, and most especially, of the right of the absolute immunity of its territory, against aggression from abroad; and these rights it is the duty and determination of this Government fully and at all times to maintain; while it will at the same time, as scrupulously, refrain from infringing on the rights of others.

The President instructs the Undersigned to say, in conclusion, that he confidently trusts, that this, and all other questions of difference between the two Governments, will be treated by both, in the full exercise of such a spirit of candor, justice, and mutual respect, as shall give assurance of the long continuance of peace between the two countries.

The Undersigned avails himself of this opportunity to assure Mr Fox of his high consideration.

Danl Webster.

1. Fox (1791–1846) served as British minister to the United States from 1835 to 1843.

2. Fox's note to Webster of March 12, 1841, is in *Diplomatic Papers*, 1:41–44.

3. President William Henry Harrison died April 4, 1841.

4. Forsyth (1780–1841; Princeton 1799), Webster's predecessor as secretary of state, served in that office from 1834 to 1841.

5. McLeod (1796–1871), a Canadian deputy sheriff, had been arrested in Lewiston, New York, on November 12, 1840, and charged with murder and arson in connection with the *Caroline* incident of 1837.

6. Henry John Temple (1784–1865), Lord Palmerston.

7. Crittenden (1787–1863; William and Mary 1806). Webster's instruction to Crittenden is in *Diplomatic Papers*, 1:45–48.

8. Seward (1801–72; Union College 1820) served as governor of New York from 1838 to 1842.

9. Nelson (1792–1873; Middlebury College 1813).

10. Under international law, piracy was defined generally as illegal acts for private ends, and insurgents usually were not treated as pirates.

11. Webster is alluding to the participation of British subjects, including soldiers and sailors acting without orders, in the Latin American revolutions in the years after 1800. Parliament forbade British participation in these revolutions in the Foreign Enlistment Act of 1819, but the law was not strictly enforced.

12. The primary American neutrality law of 1818 codified previous neutrality acts of 1794 and 1797. In response to the Canadian rebellion of 1837, Congress passed a supplementary act of 1838 designed to curtail military expeditions along the frontier.

13. Webster's reference is to the Neutrality Acts of 1817 and 1818, which were enacted in response to the Latin American wars of independence.

14. This may be a reference to a statement in Parliament on March 5, 1841, by William Ewart (1798–1869) that the mass of the American people favored peace with Britain. *Hansard's Parliamentary Debates*, 3d Series (356 vols.; London, 1830–91), 56:1356.

15. Webster's reference is to a boast allegedly made by Alexander McLeod.

Document 64
Text from *Diplomatic Papers* 1: 513–16.

From Jared Sparks[1]

Private

Dear Sir,   Cambridge, Feby, 15th 1842

I have deliberated for some time on the propriety of communicating to you the substance of this letter, but at length, believing it important that you should possess a knowledge of all the facts respecting the subject to which it alludes, I have concluded to waive the scruples that have hitherto operated on my mind.

While pursuing my researches among the voluminous papers relating to the American Revolution in the *Archives des Affaires Etrangeres* in Paris, I found in one of the bound volumes an original letter from Dr. [Benjamin] Franklin[2] to Count [Charles Gravier] de Vergennes,[3] of which the following is an exact transcript.

"Passy, 6 Dec. 1782

Sir,

I have the honor of returning herewith the map your Excellency sent me yesterday. I have marked with a strong red line, according to your desire, the limits of the United States as settled in the preliminaries

between the British & American plenipotentiaries. With great respect,
I am, &c.

B. Franklin."

This letter was written six days after the preliminaries were signed,
and if we could procure the identical map, mentioned by Franklin, it
would seem to afford conclusive evidence as to the meaning affixed
by the commissioners to the language of the Treaty on the subject of
the boundaries. You may well suppose, that I lost no time in making
inquiry for the map, not doubting that it would confirm all my previous
opinions respecting the validity of our claim. In the geographical
department of the Archives are sixty thousand maps & charts, but so
well arranged, with catalogues & indexes, that any one of them may
be easily found. After a little research in the American division, with
the aid of the keeper, I came upon a map of North America by [Jean-
Baptiste Bourguignon] D'Anville, dated 1746,[4] in size about eighteen
inches square, on which was drawn a *strong red-line* throughout the
entire boundary of the United States, answering precisely to Franklin's
description. The line is bold & distinct in every part, made with red
ink, and apparently drawn with a hair pencil, or a pen with a blunt
point. There is no other coloring on any part of the map.

Imagine my surprise on discovering, that this line runs wholly south
of the St. John's, and between the head waters of that river and those
of the Penobscot & Kennebec. In short, it is exactly the line now
contended for by Great Britain, except that it concedes more than is
claimed. The north line, after departing from the source of the St.
Croix, instead of proceeding to Mars Hill, stops far short of that point,
and turns off to the west, so as to leave on the British side all the
streams which flow into the St. John's between the source of the St.
Croix & Mars Hill. It is evident, that the line, from the St. Croix to the
Canadian highlands, is inte[n]ded to exclude *all the waters* running into
the St. John's.

There is no positive proof, that this map is actually the one marked
by Franklin, yet, upon any other supposition, it would be difficult to
explain the circumstances of its agreeing so perfectly with his description, and of its being preserved in the place where it would naturally
be deposited by Count de Vergennes. I also found another map in the
Archives, on which the same boundary was traced in a dotted red line
with a pen; apparently copied from the other.

I enclose herewith a map of Maine, on which I have drawn a strong
black line corresponding with the red one above mentioned.[5]

I also enclose the copy of a paper, which is curious as showing the views of some of the members of Congress, towards the close of the war, respecting the boundaries. It is a transcript from the original in the handwriting of Gouverneur Morris.[6] The paper seems to have been designed as an additional instruction to the Commissioners, and was probably written in the year 1781. There is no notice of it in the journals, and, from its contents, no one can wonder that it was not adopted. In the minds of some at that time, it may be presumed, the necessity of a peace was so great, that it was thought the question of boundaries ought not to be an obstacle. Morris drafted the first instructions on the subject of boundaries, as contained in the Secret Jounals for August 14th 1779.[7]

In the British offices I have read, with special care, all the correspondence of the British Commissioners with the ministry during the negotiation of the French & American treaties, which contains minute details of the conversations on every point that came under discussion. Much is of course said about the north eastern boundary. The commissioner for the American treaty first took his stand at the Kennebec, but soon retired to the Penobscot, where he maintained an obstinate defence for some time, when he retreated very reluctantly to the St. Croix. In all these discussions, however, not much light is thrown upon the difficulty now at issue. The inferences from the whole are clearly in our favor, but there is little positive or direct testimony; for the obvious reason, perhaps, that the commissioners were talking of a line which had never been surveyed, and of angles & highlands which had neither been fixed nor ascertained by observation.

In April, 1790, Dr. Franklin sent to Mr. [Thomas] Jefferson,[8] then secretary of State, that part of [John] Mitchells map[9] containing the eastern boundary as marked by himself. He died a few days afterward. Is that map now in the Department of State? If so, it cannot fail to contain important matter.

The whole weight of the controversy raised at the treaty of Ghent,[10] and since continued, rests on the single question of the north line crossing or not crossing the St. John's. Upon this point there could not possibly be any doubt in the minds of the commissioners whatever obscurity there may have been in regard to the actual position of the line in other parts; and it certainly is strange, that neither Mr. [John] Jay nor Mr. John Adams,[11] who lived several years after the controversy began to be agitated, should not have expressed and left on record, some decided opinion. This forbearance, on their part, to say the least, is suspicious.

One thing, however, is clear. The British arguments, as far as they have been carried, are equally defective in consistency & proof. Their appeals to history & ancient records leave us, at last, in a wilderness of conjecture. Confirmations, drawn from these sources, are much more favorable to the American claim than to the English; and yet, whoever reads all that has been written on the subject by both parties will find himself a good deal more perplexed and unsettled, as to the real intentions of the commissioners, than he would be by endeavoring to understand, without comment, the simple words of the treaty. The British construction, proved by maps issued under authority, and acquiesced in by Parliament while the treaty was under discussion, and while Mr. [Richard] Oswald[12] was living, is our strongest argument, and one which has neither been answered nor weakened by the labored statements on the other side.

But I did not intend to proffer opinions when I began this letter. I only meant to communicate a scrap of information, which is curious, if not valuable. I trust you will excuse the liberty I have taken, and accept the assurance of the sincere respect & regard of your most obt St.

Jared Sparks

1. Sparks (1789–1866; Harvard 1815), a professor of history at Harvard from 1839 to 1849, was a prolific editor. His works included a twelve-volume edition of *The Diplomatic Correspondence of the American Revolution* (Boston, 1829–30).

2. Franklin (1706–90) went to France as a commissioner in 1776. He became the U.S. representative at Paris in September 1778 and was named one of the peace commissioners on June 8, 1781.

3. Vergennes (1717–87) served as the French foreign minister from 1774 to 1787.

4. D'Anville (1697–1782) was a famed French cartographer.

5. Sparks's map of Maine is reproduced in Howard Jones, *To the Webster-Ashburton Treaty: A Study in Anglo-American Relations, 1783–1843* (Chapel Hill, N.C., 1977), p. 105.

6. Morris (1752–1816; Kings College 1768) was a member of the Continental Congress from 1778 to 1779. In the undated transcript, he wrote that since the eastern boundary of Maine "has never yet been ascertained, we conceive it to be open to negotiation; but not so as to be carried westward farther than the river of Kennebeck."

7. See Worthington Chauncey Ford, ed., *Journals of the Continental Congress, 1774–1789* (34 vols.; Washington, D.C., 1904–37), 14:955–66.

8. Jefferson (1743–1826; William and Mary 1762) served as secretary of state from 1790 to 1793.

9. Mitchell (d. 1768) published his map of North America in 1755. It was thereafter reissued with many changes, and it is certain that a Mitchell's map was used in the peace negotiations at Paris in 1782–83. Which edition was used at Paris, however, is not known. The map that Franklin supposedly sent to Jefferson has never been found.

10. The Treaty of Ghent, ending the War of 1812, was signed on December 24, 1814.

11. Jay (1745–1829; King's College 1764) and Adams (1735–1826; Harvard 1755) were American peace commissioners in association with Franklin and Henry Laurens (1724–92).

12. Oswald (1705–84), a British commissioner, signed the preliminary treaty of November 30, 1782.

Document 65
Text from *Diplomatic Papers* 1: 658–65.

To Lord Ashburton

Department of State,
Washington, August 1, 1842.

The President has learned with much regret, that you are not empowered by your Government to enter into a formal stipulation for the better security of vessels of the United States, when meeting with disasters in passing between the United States and the Bahama Islands, and driven, by such disasters, into British ports. This is a subject which is deemed to be of great importance, and which cannot, on the present occasion, be overlooked.

Your Lordship is aware that several cases have occurred within the last few years which have caused much complaint. In some of these cases compensation has been made by the English Government for the interference of the local authorities with American vessels having slaves on board, by which interference these slaves were set free. In other cases, such compensation has been refused.[1] It appears to the President to be for the interest of both countries that the recurrence of similar cases in future should be prevented as far as possible.

Your Lordship has been acquainted with the case of the "Creole", a vessel carried into the port of Nassau last winter by persons who had risen upon the lawful authority of the vessel, and, in the accomplishment of their purpose, had committed murder on a person on board.

The opinions which that occurrence gave occasion for this Government to express, in regard to the rights and duties of friendly and civilized maritime States, placed by Providence near to each other, were well considered, and are entertained with entire confidence. The facts in the particular case of the "Creole" are controverted: positive and officious interference by the colonial authorities to set the slaves free being alleged on one side, and denied on the other.

It is not my present purpose to discuss this difference of opinion as to the evidence in the case as it at present exists, because the rights of individuals having rendered necessary a more thorough and a judicial investigation of facts and circumstances attending the transaction, such investigation is understood to be now in progress, and its result, when known, will render me more able than at this moment to present to the British Government a full and accurate view of the whole case. But it is my purpose, and my duty, to invite your Lordship's attention to the general subject, and your serious consideration of some practical means of giving security to the coasting trade of the United States against unlawful annoyance and interruption along this part of their shore. The Bahama Islands approach the coast of Florida within a few leagues, and, with the coast, form a long and narrow channel, filled with innumerable small islands and banks of sand, and the navigation difficult and dangerous, not only on these accounts, but from the violence of the winds and the variable nature of the currents. Accidents are of course frequent, and necessity often compels vessels of the United States, in attempting to double Cape Florida, to seek shelter in the ports of these islands. Along this passage, the Atlantic States hold intercourse with the States on the Gulf and the Mississippi, and through it the products of the valley of that river (a region of vast extent and boundless fertility) find a main outlet to the sea, in their destination to the markets of the world.

No particular ground of complaint exists as to the treatment which American vessels usually receive in these ports, unless they happen to have slaves on board; but, in cases of that kind, complaints have been made, as already stated, of officious interference of the colonial authorities with the vessel, for the purpose of changing the condition in which these persons are, by the laws of their own country, and of setting them free.

In the Southern States of this Union slavery exists by the laws of the States and under the guarantee of the Constitution of the United States; and it has existed in them for a period long antecedent to the time when they ceased to be British colonies. In this state of things, it will happen that slaves will be often on board coasting vessels, as hands, as servants attending the families of their owners, or for the purpose of being carried from port to port. For the security of the rights of their citizens, when vessels having persons of this description on board are driven by stress of weather, or carried by unlawful force, into British ports, the United States propose the introduction of no new principle into the law of nations. They require only a faithful and exact observance of the injunctions of that code, as understood and practiced in modern times.

Your Lordship observes that I have spoken only of American vessels driven into British ports by the disasters of the seas, or carried in by unlawful force. I confine my remarks to these cases, because they are

the common cases, and because they are the cases which the law of
nations most emphatically exempts from interference. The maritime
law is full of instances of the application of that great and practical
rule, which declares that that which is the clear result of necessity
ought to draw after it no penalty and no hazard. If a ship be driven
by stress of weather into a prohibited port, or into an open port, with
prohibited articles on board, in neither case is any forfeiture incurred.
And what may be considered a still stronger case, it has been decided
by eminent English authority, and that decision has received general
approbation, that if a vessel be driven, by necessity, into a port strictly
blockaded, this necessity is good defence, and exempts her from
penalty.[2]

A vessel on the high seas, beyond the distance of a marine league
from the shore, is regarded as part of the territory of the nation to
which she belongs, and subjected exclusively to the jurisdiction of that
nation. If, against the will of her master or owner, she be driven or
carried nearer to the land, or even into port, those who have, or ought
to have, control over her, struggling all the while to keep her upon
the high seas, and so within the exclusive jurisdiction of her own
Government, what reason or justice is there in creating a distinction
between her rights and immunities, in a position thus the result of
absolute necessity, and the same rights and immunities before superior
power had forced her out of her voluntary course?

But, my Lord, the rule of law, and the comity and practice of
nations, go much further than these cases of necessity, and allow even
to a merchant vessel coming into any open port of another country
voluntarily, for the purposes of lawful trade, to bring with her, and
keep over her, to a very considerable extent, the jurisdiction and
authority of the laws of her own country, excluding, to this extent, by
consequence, the jurisdiction of the local law. A ship, say the publicists,
though at anchor in a foreign harbor, preserves its jurisdiction and its
laws.[3] It is natural to consider the vessels of a nation as parts of its
territory, though at sea, as the State retains its jurisdiction over them;
and, according to the commonly received custom, this jurisdiction is
preserved over the vessels, even in parts of the sea subject to a foreign
dominion.

This is the doctrine of the law of nations, clearly laid down by writers
of received authority, and entirely conformable, as it is supposed, with
the practices of modern nations.

If a murder be committed on board of an American vessel, by one
of the crew upon another or upon a passenger, or by a passenger on
one of the crew or another passenger, while such vessel is lying in a

port within the jurisdiction of a foreign State or Sovereignty, the offence is cognizable and punishable by the proper court of the United States, in the same manner as if such offence had been committed on board the vessel on the high seas. The law of England is supposed to be the same.

It is true that the jurisdiction of a nation over a vessel belonging to it, while lying in the port of another, is not necessarily wholly exclusive. We do not so consider or so assert it. For any unlawful acts done by her while thus lying in port, and for all contracts entered into while there, by her master or owners, she and they must doubtless be answerable to the laws of the place. Nor, if her master or crew, while on board in such port, break the peace of the community by the commission of crimes, can exemption be claimed for them. But, nevertheless, the law of nations, as I have stated it, and the statutes of Governments founded on that law, as I have referred to them, show that enlightened nations, in modern times, do clearly hold that the jurisdiction and laws of a nation accompany her ships, not only over the high seas, but into ports and harbors, or wheresoever else they may be water-borne, for the general purpose of governing and regulating the rights, duties, and obligations of those on board thereof, and that, to the extent of the exercise of this jurisdiction, they are considered as parts of the territory of the nation herself.

If a vessel be driven by weather into the ports of another nation, it would hardly be alleged by any one that, by the mere force of such arrival within the waters of the State, the law of that State would so attach to the vessel as to affect existing rights of property between persons on board, whether arising from contract or otherwise. The local law would not operate to make the goods of one man to become the goods of another man. Nor ought it to affect their personal obligations, or existing relations between themselves, nor was it ever supposed to have such effect, until the delicate and exciting question which has caused these interferences in the British islands arose. The local law in these cases dissolves no obligations or relations lawfully entered into or lawfully existing according to the laws of the ship's country. If it did, intercourse of civilized men between nation and nation must cease. Marriages are frequently celebrated in one country in a manner not lawful or valid in another; but did any body ever doubt that marriages are valid all over the civilized world, if valid in the country in which they took place? Did any ever imagine that local law acted upon such marriages, to annihilate their obligation, if the parties should visit a country in which marriages must be celebrated in another form?

It may be said that, in such instances, personal relations are founded in contract, and therefore to be respected; but that the relation of master and slave is not founded in contract, and therefore is to be respected only by the law of the place which recognises it. Whoever so reasons encounters the authority of the whole body of public law, from Grotius[4] down; because there are numerous instances in which the law itself presumes or implies contracts; and prominent among these instances is the very relation which we are now considering, and which relation is holden by law to draw after it mutuality of obligation.

Is not the relation between a father and his minor children acknowledged, when they go abroad? And on what contract is this founded, but a contract raised by general principles of law, from the relation of the parties?

Your Lordship will please to bear in mind, that, the proposition which I am endeavoring to support is, that by the comity of the law of nations, and the practice of modern times, merchant vessels entering open ports of other nations, for the purpose of trade, are presumed to be allowed to bring with them, and to retain, for their protection and government, the jurisdiction and laws of their own country. All this, I repeat, is presumed to be allowed; because the ports are open, because trade is invited, and because, under these circumstances, such permission or allowance is according to general usage. It is not denied that all this may be refused; and this suggests a distinction, the disregard of which may perhaps account for most of the difficulties arising in cases of this sort; that is to say, the distinction between what a State may do if it pleases, and what it is presumed to do, or not to do, in the absence of any positive declaration of its will. A State might declare that all foreign marriages should be regarded as null and void, within its territory; that a foreign father, arriving with an infant son, should no longer have authority or control over him; that, on the arrival of a foreign vessel in its ports, all shipping articles and all indentures of apprenticeship, between her crew and her owners or masters, should cease to be binding. These, and many other things equally irrational and absurd, a sovereign State has doubtless the power to do. But they are not to be presumed. It is not to be taken for granted, *ab ante*, that it is the will of the sovereign State thus to withdraw itself from the circle of civilized nations. It will be time enough to believe this to be its intention, when it formally announces that intention, by appropriate enactments, edicts, or other declarations. In regard to slavery within the British territories, there is a well-known and clear promulgation of the will of the sovereign authority; that is to say, there is a well-known rule of her law. As to England herself, that law has long existed;

and recent acts of Parliament establish the same law for the colonies. The usual mode of stating the rule of English law is, that no sooner does a slave reach the shore of England, than he is free. This is true; but it means no more than that, when a slave comes within the exclusive jurisdiction of England, he ceases to be a slave, because the law of England positively and notoriously prohibits and forbids the existence of such a relation between man and man. But it does not mean that English authorities, with this rule of English law in their hands, may enter where the jurisdiction of another nation is acknowledged to exist, and destroy those rights, obligations, and interests, lawfully existing under the authority of such other nation. No such construction and no such effect, can be rightfully given to the British law. It is true that it is competent to the British Parliament, by express statute provision, to declare that no foreign jurisdiction of any kind should exist, in or over a vessel, after its arrival voluntarily in her ports. And so she might close all her ports to the ships of all nations. A State may also declare, in the absence of treaty stipulations, that foreigners shall not sue in her courts, nor travel in her territories, nor carry away funds or goods received for debts. We need not inquire what would be the condition of a country that should establish such laws, nor in what relation they would leave her towards the States of the civilized world. Her power to make such laws is unquestionable; but, in the absence of direct and positive enactments to that effect, the presumption is that the opposites of these things exist. While her ports are open to foreign trade, it is to be presumed that she expects foreign ships to enter them, bringing with them the jurisdiction of their own Government, and the protection of its laws, to the same extent that her ships, and the ships of other commercial States, carry with them the jurisdiction of their respective Governments into the open ports of the world; just as it is presumed, while the contrary is not avowed, that strangers may travel in a civilized country, in a time of peace, sue in its courts, and bring away their property.

A merchant vessel enters the port of a friendly State, and enjoys while there the protection of her own laws, and is under the jurisdiction of her own Government, not in derogation of the sovereignty of the place, but by the presumed allowance or permission of that sovereignty. This permission or allowance is founded on the comity of nations, like the other cases which have been mentioned; and this comity is part, and a most important and valuable part, of the law of nations, to which all nations are presumed to assent until they make their dissent known. In the silence of any positive rule, affirming or denying or restraining the operation of foreign laws, their tacit adoption is presumed to the usual extent. It is upon this ground that courts of law expound contracts according to the law of the place in which they are made; and instances almost innumerable exist, in which, by the general practice of civilized countries, the laws of one will be recognised and often executed in another. This is the comity of nations; and it is upon this as its solid basis, that the intercourse of civilized States is maintained.

But while that which has now been said is understood to be the voluntary and adopted law of nations, in cases of the voluntary entry of merchant vessels into the ports of other countries, it is nevertheless true that vessels in such ports, only through an overruling necessity, may place their claim for exemption from interference on still higher principles; that is to say, principles held in more sacred regard by the comity, the courtesy, or indeed the common sense of justice of all civilized States.

Even in regard to cases of necessity, however, there are things of an unfriendly and offensive character, which yet it may not be easy to say that a nation might not do. For example, a nation might declare her will to be and make it the law of her dominions; that foreign vessels, cast away on her shores, should be lost to their owners, and subject to the ancient law of wreck. Or a neutral State, while shutting her ports to the armed vessels of belligerants, as she has a right to do, might resolve on seizing and confiscating vessels of that description, which should be driven to take shelter in her harbors by the violence of the storms of the ocean. But laws of this character, however within the absolute competence of Governments, could only be passed, if passed at all, under willingness to meet the last responsibility to which nations are subjected.

The presumption is stronger, therefore, in regard to vessels driven into foreign ports by necessity, and seeking only temporary refuge, than in regard to those which enter them voluntarily, and for purposes of trade, that they will not be interfered with; and that, unless they commit, while in port, some act against the laws of the place, they will be permitted to receive supplies, to repair damages, and to depart unmolested.

If, therefore, vessels of the United States, pursuing lawful voyages from port to port, along their own shore, are driven by stress of weather, or carried by unlawful force, into English ports, the Government of the United States cannot consent that the local authorities in those ports shall take advantage of such misfortunes, and enter them for the purpose of interfering with the condition of persons or things on board, as established by their own laws. If slaves, the property of citizens of the United States, escape into the British territories, it is not expected that they will be restored. In that case the territorial jurisdiction of England will have become exclusive over them, and must decide their condition. But slaves on board of an American vessel, lying in British waters, are not within the exclusive jurisdiction of England, or under the exclusive operation of English law, and this founds the broad distinction between the cases. If persons, guilty of crimes in the United States, seek an asylum in the British dominions, they will not be demanded until provision for such cases be made by treaty: because the giving up of criminals, fugitive from justice, is agreed and understood to be a matter in which every nation regulates its conduct according to its own discretion. It is no breach of comity to refuse such surrender.

On the other hand, vessels of the United States, driven by necessity into British ports, and staying there no longer than such necessity exists, violating no law, nor having intent to violate any law, will claim, and there will be claimed for them, protection and security, freedom from molestation, and from all interference with the character or condition of persons or things on board. In the opinion of the Government of the United States, such vessels, so driven and so detained by necessity in a friendly port, ought to be regarded as still pursuing their original voyage, and turned out of their direct course only by disaster, or by wrongful violence; that they ought to receive all assistance necessary to enable them to resume that direct course; and that interference and molestation by the local authorities, where the whole voyage is lawful, both in act and intent, is ground for just and grave complaint.

Your Lordship's discernment and large experience in affairs cannot fail to suggest to you how important it is to merchants and navigators engaged in the coasting trade of a country so large in extent as the United States, that they should feel secure against all but the ordinary causes of maritime loss. The possessions of the two Governments closely approach each other. This proximity, which ought to make us friends and good neighbors, may, without proper care and regulation, itself prove a ceaseless cause of vexation, irritation, and disquiet.

If your Lordship has no authority to enter into a stipulation by treaty for the prevention of such occurrences hereafter as have already happened, occurrences so likely to disturb that peace between the two countries which it is the object of your Lordship's mission to establish and confirm, you may still be so far acquainted with the sentiments of your Government as to be able to engage that instructions shall be given to the local authorities in the islands, which shall lead them to regulate their conduct in conformity with the rights of citizens of the

United States, and the just expectations of their Government, and in such manner as shall, in future, take away all reasonable ground of complaint. It would be with the most profound regret that the President should see that, whilst it is now hoped so many other subjects of difference may be harmoniously adjusted, nothing should be done in regard to this dangerous source of future collisions.

I avail myself of this occasion to renew to your Lordship the assurances of my distinguished consideration.

Danl Webster.

1. Webster's references are to the cases of the *Comet, Encomium,* and *Hermosa.* For information on these cases see John Bassett Moore, *A Digest of International Law* . . . (8 vols.; Washington, D.C., 1906), 2:350–52.

2. This was a doctrine pronounced by the maritime scholar and admiralty judge William Scott, Lord Stowell (1745–1836).

3. Here Webster relied on the views of the French Council of State, which had ruled thus in 1806 in two cases involving American ships. However, English, and even American, law had maintained the right of a state to extend jurisdiction over merchant vessels in their ports. See Coleman Phillipson, ed., *Wheaton's Elements of International Law* (5th ed.; London, 1916), pp. 163–65, 168.

4. Huig de Groot (1583–1645) was a Dutch-born authority on international law and author of the classic volumes *De jure praedae* (1604) and *De jure belli ac pacis* (1625).

Document 66
Text from *Diplomatic Papers* 1: 669–71.

To Lord Ashburton

Department of State,

Washington, 6th. Augt., 1842.

Your Lordship's note of the 28th of July, in answer to mine of the 27th, respecting the case of the "Caroline", has been received,[1] and laid before the President.

The President sees with pleasure that your Lordship fully admits those great principles of public law, applicable to cases of this kind, which this Government has expressed; and that on your part, as on ours, respect for the inviolable character of the territory of independent States is the most essential foundation of civilization. And while it is admitted, on both sides, that there are exceptions to this rule, he is gratified to find that your Lordship admits that such exceptions must come within the limitations stated and the terms used in a former communication from this Department to the British plenipotentiary here.[2] Undoubtedly it is just, that while it is admitted that exceptions growing out of the great law of self-defence do exist, those exceptions should be confined to cases in which the "necessity of self-defence is instant, overwhelming, and leaving no choice of means, and no moment for deliberation."

Understanding these principles alike, the difference between the two Governments is only whether the facts in the case of the "Caroline" make out a case of such necessity for the purpose of self-defence. Seeing that the transaction is not recent, having happened in the time of one of his predecessors; seeing that your Lordship, in the name of your Government, solemnly declares that no slight or disrespect was intended to the sovereign authority of the United States; seeing that it is acknowledged that, whether justifiable or not, there was yet a violation of the territory of the United States, and that you are instructed to say that your Government considers that as a most serious occurrence; seeing, finally, that it is now admitted that an explanation and apology for this violation was due at the time, the President is content to receive these acknowledgments and assurances in the conciliatory spirit which marks your Lordship's letter, and will make this subject, as a complaint of violation of territory, the topic of no further discussion between the two Governments.

As to that part of your Lordship's note which relates to other occurrences springing out of the case of the "Caroline", with which occurrences the name of Alexander McLeod has become connected, I have to say that the Government of the United States entirely adhere to the sentiments and opinions expressed in the communications from this Department to Mr. [Henry Stephen] Fox. This Government has admitted, that for an act committed by the command of his sovereign, *jure belli*, an individual cannot be responsible, in the ordinary courts of another State. It would regard it as a high indignity if a citizen of its own, acting under its authority, and by its special command, in such cases, were held to answer in a municipal tribunal, and to undergo punishment, as if the behest of his Government were no defence or protection to him.

But your Lordship is aware that, in regular constitutional Governments, persons arrested on charges of high crimes can only be discharged by some judicial proceeding. It is so in England; it is so in the colonies and provinces of England. The forms of judicial proceeding differ in different countries, being more rapid in some and more dilatory in others; and, it may be added, generally more dilatory, or at least more cautious, in cases affecting life, in Governments of a strictly limited than in those of a more unlimited character. It was a subject of regret that the release of McLeod was so long delayed. A State court, and that not of the highest jurisdiction, decided that, on summary application, embarrassed as it would appear, by technical difficulties, he could not be released by that court. His discharge, shortly afterwards, by a jury, to whom he preferred to submit his case, rendered unnecessary the further prosecution of the legal question. It is for the Congress of the United States, whose attention has been called to the subject, to say what further provision ought to be made to expedite proceedings in such cases; and, in answer to your Lordship's question towards the close of your note, I have to say that the Government of the United States holds itself not only fully disposed, but fully competent, to carry into practice every principle which it avows or acknowledges, and to fulfill every duty and obligation which it owes to foreign Governments, their citizens, or subjects.

I have the honor to be, my Lord, with great consideration, your obedient servant,

Danl Webster.

1. Webster's note to Ashburton of July 27, 1842, and Ashburton's to Webster of July 28, 1842 can be found in *Diplomatic Papers*, 1:650–56.
2. Webster to Fox, April 24, 1841. See Document 63.

Document 67
Text from *Diplomatic Papers* 1: 693–95.

Editorial:
The Treaty of Washington[1]

Monday, August 22, 1842.

The Treaty with ENGLAND, the first, we believe, ever negotiated with that Power in the United States, was RATIFIED BY THE SENATE on Saturday evening (at about nine o'clock) after a discussion of four days. The proceedings are not made public; but it is generally understood that the vote of ratification was no less strong than THIRTY-NINE *Yeas* against NINE *Nays*.

When we consider the variety of subjects which the Treaty is supposed to embrace, their magnitude, and the obvious and acknowledged difficulty of some of them; and when we consider the state of the country, and the effects of that unhappy party spirit, which, in regard to other important subjects, so much distracts our public councils, this strong and decisive majority, necessarily made up of members of all parties, reflects the highest credit upon those who have conducted the negotiation, and gives the fullest assurance that the National honor has been maintained, and all the great interests affected by the Treaty effectually upheld and promoted.

Most sincerely and cordially do we felicitate the country on this auspicious result; and we may properly congratulate the World on the event, since, if any of the difficulties, now settled, had terminated in war between the United States and England, such a war must have convulsed the globe. We cannot but indulge the hope that this favorable settlement of affairs with England is but the first, in a series of measures and events, tending to restore the country to its former prosperity. Let us hail it as the welcome harbinger of better times!

Up to the last year, the Boundary Question had lingered along, events occurring but too frequently, in the mean time, to create new exasperations, and difficulties springing up in regard to other subjects of interest and sensitiveness. Formal diplomatic correspondence seemed to do nothing towards terminating, or even allaying, these controversies. In this state of things, the new English Ministry resolved to signify at once their sense of the importance of an immediate adjustment, and their respect for the Government of the United States, by sending a Special and Extraordinary Mission. For this work of reconciliation and peace they selected Lord ASHBURTON; and surely a wiser or a better choice could not have been made. Lord ASHBURTON arrived at Washington about five months ago, and was received by the President, and Members of Congress of all parties, and by the citizens of this place, with distinguished respect and civility. To all this kindness he has made full and just return. His general intercourse in our society has been most agreeable; and now that, having accomplished his work, he has left us, probably again never to visit our city, it is but justice to say that he has left among all classes a deep and most favorable impression of his character and deportment. A man advanced in life, fully acquainted for many years with affairs between his own country and ours, always endeavoring in his public conduct to preserve amity between them, he came to this country, not to enter upon a career of showy diplomacy, or to swell the volume, already too large, of unproductive correspondence, but to sit down to existing topics, in a business-like way, to treat them frankly and fairly, to say what he could do, and what he could not, and to remove all obstacles, as far as he could. We fully believe all this to be true of his objects and purposes. As he is reported to have said of himself, he "came not to make difficulties, but to make a Treaty." We have heard the Commissioners of the States of MAINE and MASSACHUSETTS, who had necessarily much intercourse with him, speak, in terms as sincere as complimentary, of the frankness, good faith, kindness, and evenness of temper, which he invariably displayed in all their interviews with him. In a word, every voice speaks well of this "fine old English gentleman." Long may he yet live to enjoy the satisfaction of reflecting on the good he has accomplished!

It is no more than just also to say, that, from the moment of the annunciation of Lord ASHBURTON's mission, the conduct of our Government in this matter has been both wise and judicious. The first object was to settle, if possible, the long-contested Boundary question, by agreement and compromise; a settlement rendered so much more difficult than it would have been by the necessity of consulting the inclinations and wishes of two important States of the Union.

Of the industry and ability with which this important affair has been conducted, we have already expressed our opinion fully and frankly. In addition to which, we ought not to withhold from the Secretary of State the credit due for the comprehensive and business-like manner in which he commenced and prosecuted the whole negotiation. In the conduct of it he discarded all local feeling, and showed that he was governed by a truly national spirit and ambition. Whilst on a great Eastern question he consulted Eastern men and Eastern interests, on matters affecting other portions of the Union he consulted with equal sedulousness those whose feelings and interests were peculiarly involved in them.

Those who have been most opposed to Mr. WEBSTER's remaining in the Cabinet are understood to admit that it was fortunate for the country that he was there at this important juncture. We doubt whether any other citizen would have had it in his power to bring the affair to so happy an issue. Able as he has heretofore shown himself in the Senate, he has proved himself no less wise in counsel, and resolute in action. We say this, upon information upon which we rely, derived as it is from those who have been actors in the negotiation, or made acquainted with its merits.

The treaty itself, which has been ratified by this Government, cannot be published and proclaimed before it has been ratified by both Governments. It is understood, however, that it provides for the settlement, not only of the boundary question, but of other important matters, of which probably we shall be soon able to lay before our readers, though not in official form, all the material points of the adjustment.

1. The text of this unsigned editorial by Webster is from the Washington, D.C., *National Intelligencer*, August 23, 1842. Because of his friendship with William Winston Seaton (1785–1866) and Joseph Gales (1786–1860), the publishers of the *National Intelligencer*, Webster was able to place his unsigned editorials in the columns of one of the nation's most influential newspapers.

Document 68
Text from *Diplomatic Papers* 1: 870–71.

To Timoteo Haalilio and William Richards[1]

Gentlemen: Washington, December 19th 1842

I have received the letter which you did me the honor to address to me under date of 14th instant,[2] stating that you had been commissioned to represent in the United States the Government of the Hawaiian Islands, inviting the attention of this Government to the relations between the two countries and intimating a desire for a recognition of the Hawaiian government by that of the United States.

Your communication has been laid before the President and by him considered.

The advantages of your country to navigators in the Pacific, and in particular to the numerous vessels and vast tonnage of the United States frequenting that sea are fully estimated; and just acknowledgments are due to the government and inhabitants of the Islands for their numerous acts of hospitality to the citizens of the United States.

The United States have regarded the existing authorities in the Sandwich Islands as a Government suited to the condition of the people and resting on their own choice; and the President is of opinion that the interests of all the Commercial nations require that this Government should not be interfered with by foreign powers. Of the vessels which visit the Islands, it is known that a great majority belong to the United States. The United States, therefore, are more interested in the fate of the Islands and of their government, than any other Nation can be; and this consideration induces the President to be quite willing to declare as the sense of the government of the United States that the government of the Sandwich Islands ought to be respected; that no power ought either to take possession of the Islands as a conquest or for the purpose of colonization; and that no power ought to seek for any undue control over the existing Government, or any exclusive privileges or preferences in matters of commerce.

Entertaining these sentiments, the President does not see any present necessity for the negotiation of a formal Treaty, or the appointment or reception of diplomatic characters. A Consul or agent from this Government will continue to reside in the Islands. He will receive particular instructions to pay just and careful attention to any claims or complaints which may be brought against the Government or people of the Islands by citizens of the United States; and will be also instructed to receive any complaint which may be made by that Government for acts of individuals, citizens of the United States, on account of which the interference of this Government may be requested; and to transmit such complaint to this Department.

It is not improbable that this correspondence may be made the subject of a communication to Congress, and it will be officially made known to the Governments of the principal Commercial powers of Europe. I have the honor to be, Gentlemen, Your obt servt

Danl Webster

1. Haalilio (d. 1844) and Richards (1793–1847; Williams 1819) were sent on a special mission in 1842 by King Kamehameha III (1813–54) to gain recognition of Hawaiian independence from the governments of the United States, Great Britain, and France. Haalilio was the private secretary and financial advisor to the king, and Richards was an American missionary who went to Hawaii in 1822 and became an influential advisor to the king.
2. See Haalilio and Richards to Webster, December 14, 1842, in *Diplomatic Papers*, 1:866–70.

Document 69
Text from *Diplomatic Papers* 1: 841–44.

To Edward Everett[1]

Private and Confidential.
My Dear Sir: Washington, Jany 29, 1843.
Your despatch and private letter by the "Caledonia", (Jany 3d) were received yesterday,[2] and I write this hastily, as it must leave Washington to-morrow morning, in order to reach the vessel at Boston before her departure on the 1st of February.

You will have noticed that the business of the Oregon Territory is exciting a good deal of interest in Congress. A bill was introduced into the Senate by Dr [Lewis Fields] Linn,[3] not only for extending criminal jurisdiction over our citizens in that region, (after the example of the English statute,) but also making prospective regulations for granting lands to settlers. This latter part of the measure is opposed, as being inconsistent with existing arrangements between the two Governments. Mr. [John Caldwell] Calhoun, Mr. [John Macpherson] Berrien, Mr [Rufus] Choate, Mr. [George] McDuffie,[4] and others have spoken strongly in opposition to the bill, and Mr [Thomas Hart] Benton, Dr Linn, Mr [Samuel] McRoberts,[5] and other western gentlemen in favor of it. The probability is, it will not pass the Senate.[6] This new outbreak of interest and zeal for Oregon has its origin in motives and objects this side the Rocky Mountains. The truth is, there are lovers of agitation; and when most topics of dispute are settled, those which remain are fallen on with new earnestness and avidity. We feel the importance of settling this question if we can; but we fear embarrassments, and difficulties, not, perhaps, so much from the subject itself, as from the purposes of men, and of parties, connected with it. Mr. Calhoun distinguished himself by his support of the late treaty. You know his position before the country, in regard to the approaching election of President. Mr. Benton, as leader of the [Martin] Van Buren party, or at least of the more violent part of it, is disposed to make war upon every thing which Mr Calhoun supports; and seems much inclined at present to get up an anti-English feeling, whenever and wherever possible. You have read his speech on the treaty,[7] written as it is said, after the adjournment of the Senate. In the spirit of this speech he fell upon Oregon; and the treaty and the Oregon questions are now under discussion together.

I have conversed with the President since he was made acquainted with the contents of your last private letter. We gather from that, that Lord Aberdeen[8] and Lord Ashburton are, on the whole, of opinion, that a special mission would hardly be advisable. But the President still retains a strong impression that such a measure would be useful.

You know what has been said about a cession of California to the United States. England, as we learn from you, as well as from other sources, would rather favor such a transaction, if it might be the means of settling the Oregon business. It has occurred to me, therefore, to consider, whether it might not be possible to make a tripartite arrangement.

   1. Mexico to cede Upper California to the United States.

   2. United States to pay for the cession——millions of dollars.

   3. Of this sum,——millions to be paid to citizens of U.S. having claims on Mexico.

   4. The residue to English subjects, having claims, or holding bonds, against Mexico.

5. The line between U.S. and England, in Oregon, to be run pretty much as I mentioned to you.[9]

These are only thoughts, not yet shaped into opinions.

The truth is, if we negotiate about Oregon alone, I hardly know what instructions to give you; because I cannot tell what sort of a treaty two-thirds of the Senate would be sure to agree to. Here is the difficulty. My own opinion of the value of that whole country is by no means as high as that of many others. It is a poor country, in comparison with the U. States, or even with California. And if our most mischievous spirit of party could be laid, I have no doubt a proper adjustment of all disputes respecting the territory might readily be effected. But almost any treaty would be opposed; and "two-thirds" is a great majority, to be expected on any measure, in the present state of things here. If we are to treat on this question, as a distinct and unconnected matter, there would be some advantage in entering on the negotiation here, as during the session of Congress we might be able to ascertain what would be satisfactory to the Senate. But I fear that this Department and Mr. Fox would not be likely to make any very rapid progress.

I ought to say, that we do not yet know how far Mexico would listen to the idea of the cession of California. Mr. [Waddy] Thompson[10] has been instructed to sound its Government, on that particular, but we have as yet no answer. I have spoken on the subject to Genl [Juan Nepomuceno] Almonte;[11] but he has, at present, no instructions. The revolutionary state of that Government, its war with Texas, and Yucatan, may prove favorable, or unfavorable, to the cession, according to circumstances, and the interests and objects of those in power at the moment.

We hope to hear from you again before the rising of Congress; and perhaps your next communication will determine the President's mind, on the subject of the extra mission. I believe the gentlemen of the Cabinet are all in favor of the measure, and that Mr Calhoun, and his friends in the Senate, also think well of it. (As to the person who would be sent, I suppose I may say the President would probably nominate me, if I should incline to go; but it is a question I should have great doubts about. If I could see a strong probability of effecting *both* objects—California and Oregon—I should not decline the undertaking.)

You are aware that if Congress should be now called on for an appropriation for the outfit and salary of a Minister, he must be nominated to the *Senate*, at the present session, according to those ideas of the powers of the President, which Southern gentlemen (and the President himself,) have held. This may probably oblige the President to come to a conclusion on the subject, sooner than may be convenient, or might be wished.

If nothing should be heard from you before the 3d of March, either to confirm or to weaken the President's present impression, it is quite probable he may recommend provision for the mission to Congress, and nominate the Minister; and yet not despatch him till more information be received, or further consideration had. If, therefore, you should hear of a nomination, you will not infer that a mission is absolutely decided on.

On receipt of this, I wish you would hold a free and confidential conversation with Lord Aberdeen, on the various points suggested in this private letter. The President has the strongest desire to settle this Oregon dispute, as well as every other difficulty with England. We all fully believe that the English Government is animated by an equally just and friendly spirit. Both Governments, undoubtedly, would rejoice to see this object accomplished soon. The way of accomplishing it, then, becomes a subject for mutual consultation; and you may assure Lord Aberdeen of, what I hope he does not doubt, <are> the perfect sincerity, good faith, and spirit of amity, with which we shall receive and reciprocate an interchange of unofficial opinions, as to the course which the interest of both countries requires should now be adopted.

Your answer to this may be expected by the steamer which shall leave Liverpool on the 4th of March; and on its receipt here the President will make up his mind, if not done before, as to future proceedings.

No gentleman has yet been named as successor to Genl [Lewis] Cass.[12] You will see that the President has recommended to Congress to make provision for some sort of a mission to China.[13] If the provision should be ample, and you were in the country, I think I should advise the President to send you to the Celestial Empire. It would be a mission full of interest, and with your powers of application and attainments you would make great additions to your stock of ideas. I have great difficulty in fixing on a proper person.

Be kind enough to make my most friendly regards to your family, and believe me always most truly Your friend and obedt. servt,

Danl Webster

1. Everett served as U.S. minister to Great Britain from 1841 to 1845.
2. See Everett to Webster, January 2, 1843, in *Diplomatic Papers*, 1:838–41.
3. Linn (1796–1843), a Democrat from Missouri.

4. Calhoun (1782–1850; Yale 1804), a Democrat from South Carolina in 1843; Berrien (1781–1856; Princeton 1796), a Whig from Georgia; Choate (1799–1859; Dartmouth 1819), a Whig from Massachusetts; McDuffie (1790–1851; University of South Carolina 1813), a Democrat from South Carolina.

5. Benton (1782–1858), a Democrat from Missouri; McRoberts (1799–1843; Transylvania University), a Democrat from Illinois.

6. Linn's bill for the occupation and fortification of Oregon passed the Senate on February 3 but was not considered in the House of Representatives.

7. Benton's speech of August 18, 1842, is in the *Congressional Globe*, 27th Congress, 3d session, appendix, pp. 1–27.

8. George Hamilton-Gordon, Lord Aberdeen (1784–1860) was Britain's foreign minister from 1841 to 1846.

9. In a private letter to Everett dated November 28, 1842, Webster intimated that he might be willing to accept a line that followed the Columbia River to the sea but left a quadrilateral tract of land north of that river adjoining the Strait of Juan de Fuca to the United States. See Webster to Everett, November 28, 1842, in *Diplomatic Papers*, 1:834–38.

10. Thompson (1798–1868; South Carolina College 1814) served as U.S. minister to Mexico from 1842 to 1844.

11. Almonte (1803–69) served as Mexico's minister to the United States from 1842 to 1845.

12. Cass (1782–1866) served as U.S. minister to France from 1836 to 1842.

13. On December 30, 1842, President John Tyler recommended that Congress appropriate funds for a mission to China.

Document 70
Text from *Diplomatic Papers* 1: 785–87.

To Jared Sparks

Dear Sir   Washington Mar: 11. '43

In the pressure of affairs, at the close of the Session, I have not found time to consider the questions suggested by you, touching that part of the Treaty which respects the Navigation of the St. Johns.[1] I apprehend no practical difficulty on that head; because I believe all the considerable People in the Province will be entirely disposed to give every facility to the introduction of American lumber &c, into the River. It may be doubtful, therefore, whether it is worth while to discuss Mr. [George William] Featherstonehaugh's[2] budget of questions. He is a vain & light man. I hope you have read Mr [Rufus] Choate's speech.[3] On the Eastern & Western Boundary questions, he is very able, & has placed them in their true light.

I have been for some time inclined to suggest to you, whether your Review of the Treaty should not be divided into two numbers, or parts;[4] the first embracing all the agreements of boundary, with their various Equivalents; the second, the correspondence on questions of public law, especially *Impressment of Seamen.* I confess I consider this last branch of the subject as full of importance; & if it should be postponed, should much desire an interview with you, which I shall have the opportunity of holding.

As to the Boundary subject, you understand it well. What is likely to be overlooked, by superficial thinkers, is the value of Rouse's Point. England will never visit us with an army from Canada for the purpose of conquest; but if she had retained Rouse's Point, she would at all times have access to Lake Champlain, & might in two days place a force within two days March of the City of Albany. The defence of the Country, therefore, would require a large military force in that neighborhood.

As to the *conduct* of the negotiation, there is one point in which I wish to speak to you very freely, even at the hazard of a well founded imputation of some vanity. The grand stroke, was to get the *previous* consent of Maine & Massachusetts. Nobody else had attempted this; it had occurred to nobody else; it was a movement of great delicacy, & of very doubtful result. But it was made, with how much skill & judgment in the manner, you must judge; & it succeeded, & to this success the fortunate result of the whole negotiation is to be attributed. I am, Dear sir, with great regard, Yrs

Danl Webster

You notice the great majorities, with which after all the high sounding notes of opposition, the appropriations for the Treaty passed both Houses. There is, probably, no instance of a similar approach to unanimity. In the Senate, 4 votes were found against it; in the House about 40.

P. Script.   Mar. 14. 1843

As belonging to what I have considered might be the second part of the Review, I should have mentioned the Cruising Articles. Indeed they constitute a most important topic, of themselves.

You have not yet seen my correspondence with Genl. [Lewis] Cass:[5] I will send it as soon as possible. . . .

1. Sparks's letter to Webster of February 21, 1843, is in *Diplomatic Papers,* 1:782–84.
2. Featherstonehaugh (1786–1866) was a British geologist who conducted a survey of the northeastern frontier in 1839. In February 1843 he published a pamphlet entitled *Observations upon the Treaty of Washington* in which he charged Webster with withholding cartographical information that upheld British claims to the disputed northeastern boundary.
3. In a speech in the Senate on February 3, 1843, Choate maintained that Webster and Ashburton had properly directed their attention to the northeastern boundary,

leaving the "distant desert" of Oregon for later. See *Congressional Globe*, 27th Congress, 3d session, appendix, pp. 222–29.

4. Sparks published an article titled "The Treaty of Washington" in the April 1843 issue of the *North American Review*.

5. For the acrimonious correspondence between Webster and Cass over the Treaty of Washington see *Diplomatic Papers*, 1:710–75.

Document 71
Text from *Diplomatic Papers* 1: 922–26.

To Caleb Cushing[1]

No. 1.   Department of State,
Sir   Washington, May 8, 1843.

You have been appointed by the President Commissioner to China, and Envoy Extraordinary and Minister Plenipotentiary of the United States to the Court of that Empire. The ordinary general or circular letter of instructions will be placed in your hands, and another letter stating the composition or organization of the Mission, your own allowances, the allowance of the Secretary, and other matters connected with the expenditures about to be incurred under the authority of Congress.

It now remains for this Department to say something of the political objects of the Mission, and the manner in which it is hoped these objects may be accomplished. It is less necessary, than it might otherwise be, to enter into a detailed statement of the considerations which have led to the institution of the Mission, not only as you will be furnished with a copy of the President's communication to Congress, recommending provision to be made for the measure,[2] but also as your connexion with Congress has necessarily brought those considerations to your notice and contemplation.

Occurrences happening in China within the last two years have resulted in events which are likely to be of much importance as well to the United States as to the rest of the civilized world. Of their still more important consequences to China herself, it is not necessary here to speak. The hostilities which have been carried on between that Empire and England, have resulted, among other consequences, in opening four important ports to English commerce, viz: Amoy, Ning-po, Shang-hai, and Fow-chow-fow.

These ports belong to some of the richest, most productive, and most populous provinces of the Empire; and are likely to become very important marts of commerce. A leading object of the Mission in which you are now to be engaged, is to secure the entry of American ships and cargoes into these ports, on terms as favorable as those which are enjoyed by English merchants. It is not necessary to dwell, here, on the great and well known amount of imports of the productions of China into the United States. These imports, especially in the great article of tea, are not likely to be diminished. Heretofore they have been paid for in the precious metals, or, more recently, by bills drawn on London. At one time, indeed, American paper, of certain descriptions was found to be an available remittance. Latterly a considerable trade has sprung up in the export of certain American manufactures to China. To augment these exports, by obtaining the most favorable commercial facilities, and cultivating, to the greatest extent practicable, friendly commercial intercourse with China, in all its accessible ports, is matter of moment to the commercial and manufacturing, as well as the agricultural and mining, interests of the United States. It cannot be foreseen how rapidly, or how slowly, a people of such peculiar habits as the Chinese, and apparently so tenaciously attached to their habits, may adopt the sentiments, ideas, and customs of other nations. But if prejudiced and strongly wedded to their own usages, the Chinese are still understood to be ingenious, acute, and inquisitive. Experience, thus far, if it does not strongly animate and encourage efforts to introduce some of the arts and the products of other countries into China, is not, nevertheless, of a character, and such as should entirely repress those efforts. You will be furnished with accounts, as accurate as can be obtained, of the history and present state of the export trade of the United States to China.

As your Mission has in view only friendly and commercial objects, objects, it is supposed, equally useful to both countries, the natural jealousy of the Chinese, and their repulsive feeling towards foreigners, it is hoped may be in some degree removed or mitigated by prudence and address on your part. Your constant aim must be to produce a full conviction on the minds of the Government and the people that your Mission is entirely pacific; that you come with no purposes of hostility or annoyance; that you are a messenger of peace, sent from the greatest Power in America to the greatest Empire in Asia, to offer respect and good will, and to establish the means of friendly intercourse. It will be expedient, on all occasions, to cultivate the friendly dispositions of the Government and people, by manifesting a proper respect for their institutions and manners, and avoiding, as far as possible, the giving of offence, either to their pride or their prejudices. You will use the earliest, and all succeeding occasions, to signify that the Government which sends you has no disposition to encourage, and will not encourage, any violation of the commercial regulations of China, by citizens of the United States. You will state, in the fullest manner, the acknowledgment of this Government, that the commercial regulations of the Empire, having become fairly and fully known, ought to be respected by all ships, and all persons, visiting its ports; and if citizens of the United States, under these circumstances, are found violating well known laws of trade, their Government will not interfere to protect them from the consequences of their own illegal conduct. You will, at the same time, assert and maintain, on all occasions, the equality and independence of your own country. The Chinese are apt to speak of persons coming into the Empire from other nations as tribute bearers to the Emperor [Tao Kuang/Dao Guang].[3] This idea has been fostered perhaps by the costly parade embassies of England. All ideas of this kind, respecting your Mission, must, should they arise, be immediately met by a declaration, not made ostentatiously, or in a manner reproachful towards others, that you are no tribute bearer; that your Government pays tribute to none; and expects tribute from none; and that even as to presents, your Government neither makes nor accepts presents. You will signify to all Chinese authorities, and others, that it is deemed to be quite below the dignity of the Emperor of China, and the President of the United States of America to be concerning themselves with such unimportant matters as presents from one to the other; that the intercourse between the heads of two such Governments should be made to embrace only great political questions, the tender of mutual regard, and the establishment of useful relations.

It is of course desirable that you should be able to reach Pekin, and the Court and person of the Emperor, if practicable. You will accordingly at all times signify this as being your purpose and the object of your Mission; and perhaps it may be well to advance as near to the Capital as shall be found practicable, without waiting to announce your arrival in the country. The purpose of seeing the Emperor in person must be persisted in as long as may be becoming and proper. You will inform the officers of the Government that you have a letter of friendship from the President of the United States to the Emperor, signed by the President's own hand,[4] which you cannot deliver except to the Emperor himself, or some high officer of the Court in his presence. You will say, also, that you have a commission conferring on you the highest rank among representatives of your Government; and that this, also, can only be exhibited to the Emperor, or his chief officer. You may expect to encounter, of course, if you get to Pekin, the old question of the *Kotou*.

In regard to the mode of managing this matter, much must be left to your discretion, as circumstances may occur. All pains should be taken to avoid the giving of offence, or the wounding of the national pride; but, at the same time, you will be careful to do nothing which may seem, even to the Chinese themselves, to imply any inferiority on the part of your Government, or any thing less than perfect independence of all Nations. You will say that the Government of the United States is always controlled by a sense of religion and of honor; that Nations differ in their religious opinions and observances; that you cannot do any thing which the religion of your own country, or its sentiments of honor, forbid; that you have the most profound respect for His Majesty the Emperor; that you are ready to make to him all manifestations of homage which are consistent with your own sense; and that you are sure His Majesty is too just to desire you to violate your own duty; that you should deem yourself quite unworthy to appear before His Majesty as peace bearer from a great and powerful Nation, if you should do any thing against religion or against honor, as understood by the Government and people in the country you come from. Taking care thus in no way to allow the Government or people of China to consider you as tribute bearer from your Government, or as acknowledging its inferiority, in any respect, to that of China, or any other Nation, you will bear in mind, at the same time, what is due to your own personal dignity and the character which you bear. You will represent to the Chinese authorities, nevertheless, that you are directed to pay to His Majesty the Emperor the same marks of respect and homage as are paid by your Government to His Majesty the Emperor of Russia [Nicholas I],[5] or any other of the great Powers of the world.

A letter, signed by the President, as above intimated, and addressed to the Emperor, will be placed in your hands. As has been already stated, you will say that this letter can only be delivered to the Emperor, or to some one of the great officers of State, in his presence. Nevertheless, if this cannot be done, and the Emperor should still manifest a desire to receive the letter, you may consider the propriety of sending it to him, upon an assurance that a friendly answer to it shall be sent, signed by the hand of the Emperor himself.

It will be no part of your duty to enter into controversies which may exist between China and any European State; nor will you, in your communications, fail to abstain altogether from any sentiment, or any expression, which might give to other Governments just cause of offence. It will be quite proper, however, that you should, in a proper manner, always keep before the eyes of the Chinese the high character,

importance, and power of the United States. You may speak of the
extent of their territory, their great commerce spread over all seas,
their powerful navy, every where giving protection to that commerce,
and the numerous schools and institutions established in them, to
teach men knowledge and wisdom. It cannot be wrong for you to
make known, where not known, that the United States, once a country
subject to England, threw off that subjection, years ago, asserted its
independence, sword in hand, established that independence, after a
seven years' war, and now meets England upon equal terms upon the
ocean and upon the land. The remoteness of the United States from
China, and still more the fact that they have no colonial possessions
in her neighborhood, will naturally lead to the indulgence of a less
suspicious and more friendly feeling, than may have been entertained
towards England, even before the late war between England and China.
It cannot be doubted that the immense power of England in India must
be regarded by the Chinese Government with dissatisfaction, if not with
some degree of alarm. You will take care to show strongly how free the
Chinese Government may well be from all jealousy arising from such
causes towards the United States. Finally, you will signify, in decided
terms, and a positive manner, that the Government of the United States
would find it impossible to remain on terms of friendship and regard
with the Emperor, if greater privileges, or commercial facilities, should
be allowed to the subject of any other Government, than should be
granted to citizens of the United States.

It is hoped and trusted that you will succeed in making a treaty
such as has been concluded between England and China; and if one
containing fuller and more regular stipulations could be entered into,
it would be conducting Chinese intercourse one step further towards
the principles which regulate the public relations of the European and
American States. I am, Sir, very respectfully, Your obedient servant,

Danl Webster.

1. Cushing (1800–79; Harvard 1817), a wealthy Massachusetts shipowner and merchant, served in Congress as a Whig from 1835 to 1843.

2. Tyler's message of December 30, 1842, is in James D. Richardson, ed., *A Compilation of the Messages and Papers of the Presidents* . . . *1789–1897* (10 vols.; Washington, D.C., 1896–99), 4:211–14.

3. Tao Kuang, or Dao Guang (1782–1850), was emperor of China from 1821 until his death.

4. The letter from President Tyler to the emperor, dated July 13, 1843, can be found in *Senate Documents*, Serial 457, No. 138, p. 8.

5. Nicholas I (1796–1855) ruled 1825–55.

Document 72
Text from *Diplomatic Papers* 2: 49–61.

To Johann Georg Hülsemann[1]

Washington December 21st 1850.
The Undersigned, Secretary of State, of the United States, had the honor to receive, some time ago, the Note of Mr. Hülsemann, Chargé d'Affaires of His Majesty, The Emperor of Austria, of the 30th of September.[2] Causes, not arising from any want of personal regard for Mr. Hülsemann, or of proper respect for his Government, have delayed an answer until the present moment. Having Submitted Mr. Hülsemann's letter to the President, I am now directed by him, to return the following reply.

The objects of Mr. Hülsemann's note are, first, to protest by order of his Government, against the Steps, taken by the late President of the United States, to ascertain the progress and probable result of the revolutionary movements in Hungary; and, secondly, to complain of some expressions in the instructions of the late Secretary of State to Mr A[mbrose] Dudley Mann, a confidential Agent of the United States, as communicated by President [Zachary] Taylor to the Senate on the 28th of March last.[3]

The principal ground of protest is founded on the idea, or in the allegation, that the Government of the United States, by the mission of Mr. Mann and his instructions, has interfered in the domestic affairs of Austria, in a manner unjust, or disrespectful, towards that power. The President's message was a communication made by him to the Senate, transmitting a correspondence between the Executive Government and a confidential Agent of its own. This would seem to be itself a domestic transaction, a mere instance of intercourse between the President and the Senate, in the manner which is usual, and indispensable, in communications between the different branches of the Government. It was not addressed either to Austria, or Hungary; nor was it any public manifesto, to which any foreign state was called on to reply. It was an account of its transactions, communicated by the Executive Government to the Senate, at the request of that body; made public, indeed, but made public only, because such is the common and usual course of proceeding; and it may be regarded as somewhat strange, therefore, that the Austrian Cabinet did not perceive, that by the instructions given to Mr. Hülsemann, it was itself interfering with the domestic concerns of a foreign state; the very thing, which is the ground of its complaint against the United States.

This Department has, on former occasions, informed the Ministers of foreign Powers, that a communication from the President to either House of Congress, is regarded as a domestic communication, of which, ordinarily, no foreign state has cognizance; and in more recent instances, the great inconvenience of making such communications subjects of diplomatic correspondence and discussion, has been fully shown.[4] If it had been the pleasure of His Majesty, The Emperor of Austria, during the struggles in Hungary, to have admonished the Provisional Government, or the People of that Country, against involving themselves in disaster, by following the evil and dangerous example of the United States of America, in making efforts for the establishment of Independent Governments, such an admonition from your Sovereign to his Hungarian Subjects would not have originated, here, a Diplomatic correspondence. The President might, perhaps, on this ground, have declined to direct any particular reply to Mr. Hülsemann's note; but out of proper respect for the Austrian Government, it has been thought better to answer that note, at length; and the more especially as the occasion is not unfavorable for the expression of the general sentiments of the Government of the United States upon the topics which that note discusses.

A leading subject in Mr. Hülsemann's note, is that of the correspondence between Mr. Hülsemann and the predecessor of the Undersigned, in which Mr. [John M.] Clayton, by direction of the President, informed Mr. Hülsemann "that Mr. Mann's mission had no other object in view, than to obtain reliable information, as to the true state of affairs in Hungary, by personal observation." Mr. Hülsemann remarks, that "this explanation can hardly be admitted, for it says very little as to the cause of the anxiety which was felt to ascertain the chances of the revolutionists." As this, however, is the only purpose which can with any appearance of truth be attributed to the agency; as nothing whatever is alleged by Mr. Hülsemann to have been either done, or said, by the Agent inconsistent with such an object, the Undersigned conceives that Mr. Clayton's explanation ought to be deemed not only admissible, but quite satisfactory. Mr. Hülsemann states, in the course of his note, that his instructions to address his present communication to Mr. Clayton reached Washington about the time of the lamented death of the late President;[5] and that he delayed from a sense of propriety the execution of his task, until the new administration should be fully organized: "a delay which he now rejoices at, as it has given him the opportunity of ascertaining from the new President himself, on the occasion of the reception of the Diplomatic Corps, that the fundamental policy of the United States, so frequently proclaimed, would guide the relations of the American Government with other powers." Mr. Hülsemann also observes that it is in his power to assure the Undersigned "that the Imperial Government is disposed to cultivate relations of friendship and good understanding with the United States." The President receives this assurance of the disposition of the Imperial Government with great satisfaction, and in consideration of the friendly relations of the two Governments thus mutually recognized and of the peculiar nature of the incidents, by which their good understanding is supposed by Mr. Hülsemann to have been, for a moment, disturbed or endangered, the President regrets that Mr. Hülsemann did not feel himself at liberty wholly to forbear from the execution of instructions, which were of course transmitted from Vienna, without any foresight of the state of things under which they would reach Washington. If Mr. Hülsemann saw, in the address of the President to the Diplomatic Corps, satisfactory pledges of the sentiments, and the policy of this Government, in regard to neutral rights, and neutral duties, it might, perhaps, have been better not to bring on a discussion of past transactions. But the Undersigned readily admits, that this was a question fit only for the consideration and decision of Mr. Hülsemann himself; and although the President does not see that any good purpose can be answered by re-opening the enquiry into the propriety of the steps taken by President Taylor, to ascertain the probable issue of the late civil war in Hungary, justice to his memory requires the Undersigned briefly to re-state the history of those steps, and to show their consistency with the neutral policy, which has invariably guided the Government of the United States in its foreign relations, as well as with the established and well settled principles of national intercourse, and the doctrines of public law.

The Undersigned will first observe, that the President is pursuaded His Majesty, The Emperor of Austria, does not think that the Government of the United States ought to view, with unconcern, the extraordinary events which have occurred, not only in his Dominions, but in many other parts of Europe, since February, 1848. The Government and People of the United States, like other intelligent Governments and communities, take a lively interest in the movements and the events of this remarkable age, in whatever part of the world they may be exhibited. But the interest taken by the United States in those events, has not proceeded from any disposition to depart from that neutrality toward foreign powers, which is among the deepest principles, and the most cherished traditions, of the political history of the Union. It has been the necessary effect of the unexampled character

of the events, themselves, which could not fail to arrest the attention
of the contemporary world; as they will doubtless fill a memorable
page in History. But the Undersigned goes further, and freely admits,
that in proportion as these extraordinary events appeared to have their
origin in those great ideas of responsible and popular governments, on
which the American Constitutions themselves are wholly founded,
they could not but command the warm sympathy of the People of this
Country.

Well known circumstances in their History, indeed their whole
History, have made them the representatives of purely popular principles of Government. In this light they now stand, before the world.
They could not if they would, conceal their character, their condition,
or their destiny. They could not, if they so desired, shut out from the
view of mankind, the causes, which have placed them, in so short a
national career, in the station which they now hold among the civilized
States of the world. They could not, if they desired it, suppress, either
the thoughts, or the hopes, which arise in men's minds, in other
countries, from contemplating their successful example of Free Government. That very intelligent and distinguished personage, The Emperor Joseph The Second, was among the first to discern this necessary
consequence of the American Revolution, on the sentiments and opinions of the People of Europe. In a letter to his Minister in the Netherlands, in 1787, he observes that "it is remarkable that France by the
assistance which she afforded to the Americans, gave birth to reflections on freedom."[6] This fact which the sagacity of that Monarch
perceived, at so early a day, is now known and admitted, by intelligent
powers all over the World; true, indeed, it is, that the prevalence on
the other continent, of sentiments favorable to Republican Liberty, is
the result of the re-action of America upon Europe; and the source
and centre of this re-action has doubtless been, and now is, in these
United States. The position thus belonging to the United States is a
fact as inseparable from their History, their Constitutional organization, and their character, as the opposite position of the powers composing the European Alliance is, from the History and Constitutional
organization of the Governments of those powers. The Sovereigns,
who form that alliance, have, not unfrequently, felt it their right to
interfere with the political movements of foreign states; and have, in
their Manifestoes and Declarations, denounced the popular ideas of
the age, in terms so comprehensive as of necessity to include the
United States, and their forms of Government. It is well known that
one of the leading principles, announced by the allied Sovereigns after
the restoration of the Bourbons, is, that all popular, or constitutional

rights, are holden no otherwise than as grants and indulgences from crowned heads. "Useful and necessary changes in legislation and administration," says the Laybach Circular of May, 1821, "ought only to emanate from the free will and intelligent conviction, of those whom God has rendered responsible for power; all that deviates from this line necessarily leads to disorder, commotions, and evils far more insufferable than those which they pretend to remedy. And his late Austrian Majesty, Francis 11, is reported to have declared in an address to the Hungarian Diet in, 1820, that "the whole World has become foolish, and leaving their ancient laws, was in search of imaginary Constitutions."[7] These declarations amount to nothing less, than a denial of the lawfulness of the origin of the Government of the United States; since it is certain, that that Government was established in consequence of a change which did not proceed from Thrones, or the permission of crowned heads. But the Government of the United States heard these denunciations of its fundamental principles without remonstrance, or the disturbance of its equanimity. This was thirty years ago. The power of this Republic, at the present moment is spread over a region, one of the richest and most fertile on the Globe, and of an extent in comparison with which the possessions of the House of Hapsburg, are but as a patch on the earth's surface; its population, already twenty-five millions will exceed that of the Austrian Empire, within the period, during which, it may be hoped, that Mr. Hülsemann may yet remain in the honorable discharge of his duties to his Government; its navigation and commerce are hardly exceeded by the oldest and most commercial nations; its maritime means, and its maritime power, may be seen by Austria herself, in all seas where she has ports, as well as it may be seen, also, in all other quarters of the Globe; life, liberty, property and all personal rights, are amply secured to all Citizens, and protected by just and stable laws; and credit, public and private, is as well established, as in any Government of Continental Europe. And the Country in all its interests and concernes, partakes most largely in all the improvements and progress, which distinguish the age. Certainly, the United States may be pardoned, even by those who profess adherence to the principles of absolute Governments, if they entertain an ardent affection for those popular forms of political organization which have so rapidly advanced their own prosperity and happiness, and enabled them, in so short a period, to bring their Country and the Hemisphere to which it belongs, to the notice and respectful regard, not to say the admiration, of the civilized World. Nevertheless, the United States have abstained, at all times, from acts of interference with the political changes of Europe. They cannot, however, fail to cherish, always, a lively interest in the fortunes of Nations, struggling for institutions like their own. But this sympathy, so far from being necessarily a hostile feeling toward any of the parties to these great national struggles, is quite consistent with amicable relations with them all. The Hungarian People are three or four times as numerous as the inhabitants of these United States were when the American Revolution broke out. They possess in a distinct language, and in other respects, important elements of a separate nationality, which the Anglo Saxon race in this Country did not possess; and if the United States wish success to Countries contending for popular constitutions and National Independence, it is only because they regard such constitutions and such National Independence, not as imaginary, but as real blessings. They claim no right, however, to take part in the struggles of foreign powers in order to promote these ends. It is only in defence of his own Government, and its principles and character, that the Undersigned has now expressed himself on this subject. But when the United States behold the people of foreign Countries, without any such interference, spontaneously moving toward the adoption of institutions like their own, it surely cannot be expected of them to remain wholly indifferent spectators.

In regard to the recent very important occurrences in the Austrian Empire, the Undersigned freely admits the difficulty which exists in this Country, and is alluded to by Mr. Hülsemann of obtaining accurate information. But this difficulty is by no means to be ascribed to what Mr. Hülsemann calls, with little justice, as it seems to the Undersigned "the mendacious rumors propagated by the American press." For information on this subject, and others of the same kind, the American press, is, of necessity, almost wholly dependant upon that of Europe, and if "mendacious rumors" respecting Austrian and Hungarian affairs, have been anywhere propagated, that propagation of falsehoods has been most prolific on the European Continent, and in Countries immediately bordering on the Austrian Empire. But where ever these errors may have originated, they certainly justified the late President in seeking true information through authentic channels. His attention was first particularly drawn to the state of things in Hungary, by the correspondence of Mr. [William Henry] Stiles, Chargé d'Affaires of the United States at Vienna.[8] In the Autum of, 1848, an application was made to this Gentleman on behalf of Mr. [Louis] Kossuth,[9] formerly Minister of Finance for the Kingdom of Hungary, by Imperial appointment, but at the time the application was made, Chief of the Revolutionary Government. The object of this application was, to obtain the good offices of Mr. Stiles with the Imperial Government, with a view to the suspension of hostilities. This application became the subject of a conference between Prince [Felix zu] Schwarzenberg,[10] the Imperial Minister for Foreign Affairs, and Mr. Stiles. The Prince commended the considerateness and propriety, with which Mr. Stiles had acted; and so far from disapproving his interference, advised him, in case he received a further communication from the Revolutionary Government in Hungary, to have an interview with Prince [Alfred] Windischgrätz,[11] who was charged by the Emperor with the proceedings determined on, in relation to that Kingdom. A week after these occurrences, Mr. Stiles received, through a secret channel, a communication signed by L. Kossuth, President of the Committee of defense, and countersigned by Francis Pulsky,[12] Secretary of State. On the receipt of this communication, Mr. Stiles had an interview with Prince Windischgrätz who received him with the utmost kindness, and thanked him for his efforts toward reconciling the existing difficulties. Such were the incidents which first drew the attention of the Government of the United States, particularly, to the affairs of Hungary; and the conduct of Mr. Stiles, though acting without instructions in a matter of much delicacy, having been received with satisfaction by the Imperial Government, was approved by that of the United States.

In the course of the Year 1848, and the early part of 1849, a considerable number of Hungarians came to the United States. Among them were individuals representing themselves to be in the confidence of the Revolutionary Government, and by these persons the President was strongly urged to recognize the existence of that Government. In these applications, and in the manner in which they were viewed by the President, there was nothing unusual; still less was there any thing unauthorized by the Law of Nations. It is the right of every independent State to enter into friendly relations with ev[e]ry other independent State. Of course, questions of prudence naturally arise in reference to new States, brought by successful revolutions into the family of Nations; but it is not to be required of neutral powers that they should await the recognition of the new Government by the parent state. No principle of public law has been more frequently acted upon, within the last thirty years, by the great powers of the World, than this. Within that period, eight or ten new States have established independent Governments, within the limits of the Colonial Dominions of Spain, on this Continent; and in Europe, the same thing has been done by Belgium and Greece. The existence of all these Governments was recognized by some of the leading powers of Europe, as well as by the United States, before it was acknowledged by the States from which they had separated themselves.

If, therefore, the United States had gone so far, as formally to acknowledge the Independence of Hungary, although as the result has proved, it would have been a precipitate step, and one from which no benefit would have resulted to either party, it would not, nevertheless, have been an act against the law of Nations, provided they took no part in her contest with Austria. But the United States did no such thing. Not only did they not yield to Hungary any actual countenance or succor; not only did they not show their ships of War in the Adriatic with any menacing or hostile aspect, but they studiously abstained from every thing, which has not been done in other cases in times past, and contented themselves with instituting an enquiry, into the truth and reality of alleged political occurrences. Mr. Hülsemann incorrectly states, unintentionally certainly, the nature of the mission of this Agent, when he says that a "United States Agent had been despatched to Vienna, with orders to watch for a favorable moment to recognize the Hungarian Republic, and to conclude a Treaty of Commerce with the same." This indeed, would have been a lawful object, but Mr. Mann's errand was, in the first instance, purely one of enquiry. He had no power to act, unless he had first come to the conviction that a firm and stable Hungarian Government existed. "The principle object the President has in view" (according to his instructions) "is, to obtain minute and reliable information in regard to Hungary, in connection with the affairs of adjoining Countries, the probable issue of the present revolutionary movements, and the chances we may have of forming commercial arrangements with that power, favorable to the United States." Again, in the same paper it is said, "The object of the President, is to obtain information in regard to Hungary, and her resources and prospects, with a view to an early recognition of her independence, and the formation of commercial relations with her." It was only in the event that the new Government should appear, in the opinion of the Agent, to be firm and stable, that the President proposed to recommend its recognition.

Mr. Hülsemann, in qualifying these steps of President Taylor with the epithet of "hostile", seems to take for granted, that the enquiry could, in the expectation of the President, have but one result, and that favorable to Hungary. If this were so, it would not change the case. But the American Government sought for nothing but truth; it desired to learn the facts through a reliable channel. It so happened in the chances and vicissitudes of human affairs, that the result was adverse to the Hungarian Revolution. The American agent (as was stated in his instructions to be not unlikely) found the condition of Hungarian affairs less prosperous than it had been, or had been believed to be. He did not enter Hungary, nor hold any direct communication with her revolutionary leaders. He reported against the recognition of her independence, because he found that she had been unable to set up a firm and stable government. He carefully forebore, as his instructions required, to give publicity to his mission, and the Undersigned supposes that the Austrian Government first learned its existence from the communications of the President to the Senate.

Mr. Hülsemann will observe from his statement, that Mr. Mann's mission was wholly unobjectionable, and strictly within the rule of the Law of Nations, and the duty of the United States as a neutral power. He will, accordingly, feel how little foundation there is for his remark, that "those who did not hesitate to assume the responsibility of sending Mr. Dudley Mann on such an errand, should, independent of considerations of propriety, have borne in mind, that they were exposing their emissary to be treated as a spy." A spy is a person, sent by one belligerent to gain secret information of the forces and defences of the other, to be used for hostile purposes. According to practice he may use deception, under the penalty of being lawfully hanged, if detected. To give this odious name and character to a confidential agent of a neutral power, bearing the Commission of his Country, and sent for a purpose fully warranted by the Law of Nations, is not only to abuse language, but also, to confound all just ideas, and to announce the wildest and most extravagant notions, such as certainly were not to have been expected in a grave diplomatic paper; and the President directs the Undersigned to say to Mr. Hülsemann, that the American Government would regard such an imputation upon it by the Cabinet of Austria, as that it employed spies, and that in a quarrel none of its own, as distinctly offensive, if it did not presume, as it is willing to presume, that the word used in the original German, was not of equivalent meaning with "spy" in the English language or that in some other way the employment of such an opprobrious term may be explained. Had the Imperial Government of Austria subjected Mr. Mann to the treatment of a spy, it would have placed itself without the pale of civilized nations; and the Cabinet of Vienna may be assured, that if it had carried, or attempted to carry, any such lawless purpose into effect, in the case of an authorized Agent of this Government, the Spirit of the People of this Country, would have demanded immediate hostilities, to be waged by the utmost exertion of the Power of the Republic, military and naval.

Mr. Hülsemann proceeds to remark that "this extremely painful incident, therefore, might have been passed over, without any written evidence being left, on our part in the Archives of the United States, had not General Taylor thought proper to revive the whole subject, by communicating to the Senate in his message of the 18th (28th) of last March, the instructions with which Mr. Mann had been furnished on the occasion of his mission to Vienna. The publicity which has been given to that document, has placed the Imperial Government under the necessity of entering a formal protest through its official representative against the proceedings of the American Government, lest that Government should construe our silence into approbation or toleration even, of the principles which appear to have guided its action and the means it has adopted." The Undersigned re-asserts to Mr. Hülsemann, and to the Cabinet of Vienna, and in the presence of the world, that the Steps taken by President Taylor, now protested against by the Austrian Government, were warranted by the Law of Nations, and agreeable to the usages of civilized states. With respect to the communication of Mr. Mann's instructions to the Senate, and the language in which they are couched, it has already been said, and Mr. Hülsemann must feel the justice of the remark, that these are domestic affairs, in reference to which the Government of the United States, cannot admit the slightest responsibility to the Government of His Imperial Majesty. No state deserving the appellation of independent, can permit the language, in which it may instruct its own officers in the discharge of their duties to itself, to be called in question, under any pretext by a foreign power. But even if this were not so, Mr. Hülsemann is in an error in stating that the Austrian Government is called an "Iron Rule" in Mr. Mann's instructions. That phrase is not found in the paper;[13] and in respect to the honorary epithet bestowed in Mr. Mann's instructions, on the late Chief of the Revolutionary Government of Hungary, Mr. Hülsemann will bear in mind, that the Government of the United States cannot justly be expected, in a confidential communication to its own Agent, to withhold from an individual, an epithet of distinction, of which a great part of the world thinks him worthy, merely on the ground that his own Government regards him as a rebel. At an early stage of the American Revolution, while Washington was considered by the English Government as a rebel chief, he was regarded on the Continent of Europe as an illustrious hero. But the Undersigned, will take the liberty, of bringing the Cabinet of Vienna, into the presence of its own predecessors, and of citing for its consideration, the conduct of the Imperial Government itself. In the Year 1777, the War of the American Revolution was raging all over the United States; England was prosecuting that war, with a most resolute determination, and by the exertion of all her military means to the fullest extent. Germany was, at that time, at peace with England; and yet an Agent of that Congress, which was looked upon by England in no other light than that of a body in open rebellion, was not only received with great respect, by the Ambassador of the Empress Queen at Paris, and by the Minister of the Grand Duke of Tuscany, who afterwards mounted the Imperial Throne, but resided in Vienna for a considerable time; not indeed, officially acknowledged, but treated with courtesy and respect; and the Emperor suffered himself to be persuaded by that Agent, to exert himself to prevent the German Powers from furnishing troops to England, to enable her to suppress the rebellion in America.[14] Neither Mr. Hülsemann nor the Cabinet of Vienna, it is presumed, will undertake to say, that any thing said or done by this Government in regard to the recent war between Austria and Hungary, is not borne out, and much more than borne out, by this example of the Imperial Court. It is believed that the Emperor Joseph, The Second, habitually spoke in terms of respect and admiration of the character of Washington, as he is known to have done of that of Franklin; and he deemed it no infraction of neutrality, to inform himself of the progress of the Revolutionary Struggle in America; nor to express his deep sense of the merits and the talents of those illustrious men, who were then leading their country to independence and renown. The Undersigned may add, that in 1781, the Courts of Russia and Austria, proposed a diplomatic Congress of the belligerent powers, to which the commissioners of the United States should be admitted.[15]

Mr. Hülsemann thinks that in Mr. Mann's instructions improper expressions are introduced in regard to Russia, but the Undersigned has no reason to suppose that Russia, herself, is of that opinion. The only observation made in those instructions about Russia is, that she "has chosen to assume an attitude of interference, and her immense preparations for invading and reducing the Hungarians to the rule of Austria—from which they desire to be released—gave so serious a character to the contest, as to awaken the most painful solicitude in the minds of Americans." The Undersigned cannot but consider the Austrian Cabinet as unnecessarily susceptible in looking upon language like this as a "hostile demonstration." If we remember that it was addressed by the Government to its own Agent, and has received publicity only through a communication from one Department of the American Government to another, the language quoted must be deemed moderate and inoffensive. The comity of nations would hardly forbid its being addressed to the two Imperial Powers themselves. It is scarcely necessary for the Undersigned to say, that the Relations of the United States with Russia, have always been of the most friendly kind: and have never been deemed by either party to require any compromise of their peculiar views upon subjects of domestic or foreign polity, or the true origin of Governments. At any rate, the fact, that Austria in her contest with Hungary, had an intimate and faithful ally in Russia, cannot alter the real nature of the question, between Austria and Hungary, nor in any way affect the neutral rights and duties of the Government of the United States, or the justifiable sympathies of the American people. It is, indeed, easy to conceive that favor toward struggling Hungary would be not diminished, but increased, when it was seen that the arm of Austria was strengthened and upheld, by a power, whose assistance threatened to be, and which in the end proved to be, overwhelmingly destructive of all her hopes.[16]

Toward the conclusion of his Note Mr. Hülsemann remarks that "if the Government of the United States were to think it proper to take an indirect part in the political movements of Europe, American policy would be exposed to acts of retaliation, and to certain inconveniences which would not fail to affect the commerce and the industry of the two Hemispheres."

As to this possible fortune; this hypothetical retaliation, the Government and people of the United States are quite willing to take their chances, and abide their destiny. Taking neither a direct, nor an indirect part, in the domestic or intestine movements of Europe, they have no fear of events, of the nature alluded to by Mr. Hülsemann. It would be idle, now, to discuss with Mr. Hülsemann those acts of retaliation which he imagines may possibly take place at some indefinite time hereafter. Those questions will be discussed when they arise, and Mr. Hülsemann and the Cabinet at Vienna, may rest assured that in the meantime, while performing with strict and exact fidelity all their neutral duties, nothing will deter, either the Government or the people of the United States, from exercising, at their own discretion, the rights belonging to them as an independent nation, and of forming and expressing their own opinions, freely and at all times, upon the great political events which may transpire among the civilized nations of the Earth. Their own Institutions stand upon the broadest principles of civil liberty, and believing those principles, and the fundamental laws in which they are embodied to be eminently favorable to the prosperity of states—to be, in fact, the only principles of Government which meet the demands of the present enlightened age,—the President has perceived with great satisfaction, that in the Constitution recently introduced into the Austrian Empire, many of these great principles are recognized and applied,[17] and he cherishes a sincere wish that they may produce the same happy effects throughout His Austrian Majesty's extensive dominions, that they have done in the United States.

The Undersigned has the honor to repeat to Mr Hülsemann the assurance of his high consideration.

Danl Webster

1. Hülsemann served with the Austrian legation in the United States for twenty-five years. From 1838 to 1841 he was secretary of the legation; on October 13, 1841, he became chargé d'affaires *ad interim;* and from December 5, 1855, to March 11, 1863, he was minister resident.

2. Hülsemann to Webster, September 30, 1850, in *Diplomatic Papers,* 2:43–46.

3. When news of the 1848 Hungarian rebellion against Austria reached the United States, Secretary of State John M. Clayton (1796–1856; Yale 1815) sent Ambrose Dudley Mann (1801–99) on a confidential and special mission to Hungary. If he found that the Hungarians were able to maintain their independence, Mann was empowered to recognize their government and to conclude commercial treaties with them. For Mann's instructions of June 18, 1849, and President Taylor's message to the Senate, see *Senate Documents,* 31st Congress, 1st session, Serial 558, No. 43, pp. 1, 3–6.

4. Webster's reference here is to a heated public dispute carried on from 1834 to 1836 between President Andrew Jackson and France over France's refusal to pay an indemnity owed U.S. citizens under a treaty of 1831. For a detailed analysis of the claims dispute with France, see John M. Belohlavek, *"Let the Eagle Soar!" The Foreign Policy of Andrew Jackson* (Lincoln, 1985), pp. 90–126.

5. President Taylor died on July 9, 1850.

6. Joseph 11 (1741–90) wrote these words to Prince Ferdinand de Trautmansdorff (1749–1827), an Austrian diplomat, in September 1787.

7. Francis 11 (1768–1835) ruled Austria from 1792 to 1835.

8. Stiles (1808–65), of Georgia, was chargé d'affaires to Austria from 1845 to 1849.

9. Lajos Kossuth (1802–94) was the leader of the Hungarian revolution of 1848–49.

10. Schwarzenberg (1800–52) was prime minister of Austria from 1848 to 1852.

11. Windischgratz (1787–1862), Austrian field marshal.

12. Pulsky or Pulszky (1814–97) served as undersecretary of state for foreign affairs in the Hungarian government.

13. Although the phrase was deleted before President Taylor submitted Mann's instructions to the Senate, Secretary of State Clayton did refer to Austria's "iron rule" in the unaltered document. The Austrians probably surreptitiously obtained a copy of Mann's instructions through the U.S. consul in Vienna, an Austrian to whom Mann entrusted his papers.

14. In 1777 Congress named William Lee (1739–95), of Virginia, commissioner to the courts of Berlin and Vienna. Lee reported that at his request the king of Prussia had denied permission for British recruits from Hesse and Hanau to pass through his territory. See Francis Wharton, ed., *The Revolutionary Diplomatic Correspondence of the United States* (6 vols.; Washington, D.C., 1889), 2:454–55. The empress queen was Maria Theresa (1717–80). The grand duke of Tuscany was Leopold I (1747–92), who became Holy Roman Emperor Leopold 11 in 1790.

15. In 1781, Austria and Russia jointly offered to mediate between the belligerents, but Britain declined the offer.

16. At the request of Austria, in 1849 Russia sent 200,000 troops to Hungary and crushed the Hungarian revolution.

17. In 1849 the Hapsburg government introduced a constitution containing some liberal provisions. It was never put into force, however, and was abolished in 1851.

Document 73
Text from *Diplomatic Papers* 2: 289–93.

To John H. Aulick[1]

Department of State,
Sir.—   Washington, 10th June, 1851.

The moment is near, when the last link in the chain of oceanic steam-navigation is to be formed. From China and the East Indies to Egypt, thence through the Mediterranean and the Atlantic Ocean to England thence again to our happy shores, and other parts of this great Continent, from our own ports to the Southern-most part of the Isthmus, that connects the two Western Continents; and from its Pacific coast, north and southwards, as far as civilization has spread,— the steamers of other nations and of our own, carry intelligence, the wealth of the world, and thousands of travellers.

It is the President's opinion, that steps should be taken at once, to enable our enterprising merchants, to supply the last link in that great chain, which unites all nations of the world, by the early establishment of a line of steamers from California to China. In order to facilitate this enterprise, it is desirable, that we should obtain from the Emperor of Japan permission, to purchase from his subjects the necessary supplies of coal, which our steamers on their out- and inward voyages may require. The well known jealousy with which the Japanese Empire has, for the last two centuries, rejected all overtures from other nations to open its ports to their vessels,—embarasses all new attempts, to change the exclusive policy of that country.

The interests of commerce, and even those of humanity, demand, however, that we should make another appeal to the Sovereign of that country, in asking him to sell our Steamers,—not the manufactures of his artizans or the results of the toil of his husbandmen,—but a gift of Providence, deposited, by the Creator of all things in the depths of the Japanese Islands, for the benefit of the human family.

By the President's directions I now transmit to you a letter to the Emperor of Japan,[2] (with an open copy,) which you are to carry to Jeddo, his capital, in your flagship, accompanied by as many of the vessels of the Squadron under your command, as may conveniently be employed in this service. A Chinese translation of this letter will be furnished to you by the United States Legation at Canton, or sent to your anchorage at Hong Kong or Macao.

At one of the latter places you will probably meet with a national

vessel, detached by the Commodore of the Squadron in the Pacific,—
(as you will perceive by the enclosed copy of a correspondence between
this and the Navy Department,) to carry to you a number of ship-
wrecked Japanese mariners who were, some time ago, picked up at
sea by the Barque Auckland. These men you will take with you to
Jeddo, and deliver them over to the officers of the Emperor, giving
them through your interpreter the assurance, that the American Government will never fail to treat with kindness any of the Natives of
Japan, whom misfortune may bring to our shores; and that it expects
similar treatment of such of its own citizens, who may be driven on
the Coasts of Japan.[3]

The letter of the President to the Emperor of Japan, you will deliver
to such of his high officers, as he may appoint for the purpose of
receiving it. To them you will, also, explain the main object of your
visit.

Mineral coal is so abundant in Japan, that the Government of that
country can have no reasonable objection to supply our steamers, at
fair prices, with that great necessary of commerce. One of the eastern
ports of Niphon would be the most desirable place for this purpose.
Should, however, the Government of Japan persist in following out
its system of exclusiveness, you might perhaps induce them, to consent
to the transportation of the coal by their own vessels to a neighboring
island, easy of access, where the steamers could supply their wants,
avoiding thus the necessity of an intercourse with any large number
of the people of the country.

It is considered important that you should avail yourself of every
occasion to impress on those Japanese officers, with whom you will be
brought in contact, that the Government of the United States does not
possess any power over the religion of its own citizens, and that there
is therefore no cause to apprehend that it will ever interfere with the
religion of other countries.

The President, although fully aware of the great reluctance hitherto
shown by the Japanese Government to enter into treaty stipulations
with any foreign nation, a feeling which it is sincerely wished that you
may be able to overcome,—has thought it proper, in anticipation of
this latter favorable contingency, to invest you with full power to
negotiate & sign a treaty of Amity and Commerce between the United
States and the Empire of Japan.

I transmit, herewith, the Act of the President clothing you with that
Power, as also copies of the treaty between the United States and
China, with Siam and with Muscat, which may, to a certain extent,
be of use to you as precedents.[4] It is important, that you should

secure to our vessels the right to enter one or more of the ports of Japan, and there to dispose of their cargoes, either by sale or by barter, without being subjected to extravagant port-charges; and even more important is it, that the Government of Japan should bind itself to protect American sailors and property, which may be wrecked on their shores. The second Article of our Treaty with Muscat, and the 5th Article of the Treaty with Siam embrace these objects.

Every treaty has to be submitted to the Senate, for ratification, as you are aware. In consideration of the great distance between the two countries, and unforeseen difficulties, it would be prudent, should you succeed in effecting the object proposed, to fix the period for the exchange of the ratifications at three years. I am, Sir, respectfully, Your obedient servant,

Daniel Webster.

1. Aulick (1789–1873) was commander of the East India squadron. Because of charges of misconduct, Aulick was recalled in November 1851 and Commodore Matthew C. Perry appointed to undertake the mission to Japan.

2. See President Millard Fillmore to the Emperor of Japan, [May 10, 1851], in *Diplomatic Papers*, 2:289.

3. See Webster to William A. Graham, May 9, 1851, in *Diplomatic Papers*, 2:288.

4. The treaties of amity and commerce with China (July 3, 1844), Siam (March 20, 1833), and Muscat (September 21, 1833) can be found in Hunter Miller, ed., *Treaties and Other International Acts of the United States of America* (8 vols.; Washington, D.C., 1931–48), 4:559–62; 3:741–88, 789–810.

Document 74
Text from *Diplomatic Papers* 2: 277–79.

To Luther Severance[1]

Department of State,
Sir: Washington, July 14th. 1851.

I have written you a regular official despatch,[2] setting forth the principles of policy which will be pursued by the administration here, in whatever respects the government of the Hawaiian Islands.

I now write you a letter of private instructions, made necessary by suggestions contained in your communications by Lieutenant [Robert E.] Johnson.[3]

In the first place I have to say, that the war-making power in this Government, rests entirely with Congress; and that the President can authorize belligerent operations only in the cases expressly provided for by the Constitution and the laws. By these, no power is given to the Executive to oppose an attack by one independent nation, on the possessions of another. We are bound to regard both France and Hawaii as independent States, and equally independent; and though the general policy of the government might lead it to take part with either, in a controversy with the other, still, if this interference be an act of hostile force, it is not within the Constitutional power of the President; and still less is it, within the power of any subordinate Agent of Government, Civil or Military. If the "Serieuse"[4] had attacked Honolulu, and thereupon the "Vandalia" had fired upon the "Serieuse", this last act, would have been an act of violence against France, not to be justified: and in fact, if not disavowed at Washington, it would have been an act of War. In these cases, where the power of Congress cannot be exercised beforehand, all must be left to the redress which that body may subsequently authorize. This, you will constantly bear in mind. But at the same time, it is not necessary that you should enter into these explanations with the French Commissioner, or the French Naval Commander.

In my official letter of this date, I have spoken of what the United States would do in certain contingencies. But in thus speaking of the government of the United States, I do not mean the Executive power, but the government in its general aggregate, and especially that branch of the government which possesses the War making power. This distinction you will carefully observe, and you will neither direct, request or encourage any Naval officer of the United States in committing hostilities on French vessels of War.

Another leading topic in your communication is the proposed contingent surrender, by the government of the Islands, of their sovereignty to the United States, or their annexation to this country.

This is a very important question, and one which you will readily see, rises above any functions with which you are charged. It may indeed, be very proper for you in this case, as well as in all others, to communicate to your government, whatever the government to which you are accredited desires to have so communicated; but it is very important that on a question involving such deep interests, both domestic and foreign, you should, yourself, altogether forbear expressing any opinion whatever to the Hawaiian Government. You will see by my official letter, which you are at liberty to communicate to that government, the disposition of the United States to maintain its independence; beyond that you will not proceed. The act of contingent or conditional surrender, which you mention in your letter, as having been placed in your hands, you will please to return to the Hawaiian

Government.[5] In this case, the Government of the United States, acts upon principles of general policy; it will protect its own rights. It feels a deep interest in the preservation of Hawaiian independence, and all questions beyond this, should they arise, must be considered and settled here, by the competent authority.

You inform us that many American citizens have gone to settle in the Islands; if so they have ceased to be American citizens. The government of the United States must, of course, feel an interest in them, not extended to foreigners; but by the Law of Nations, they have no right further to demand the protection of this government. Whatever aid or protection might under any circumstances be given them, must be given, not as matter of right on their part, but in consistency with the general policy and duty of the government and its relations with friendly powers.

You will therefore, not encourage in them, nor indeed, in any others, any idea or expectation that the Islands will become annexed to the United States. All this, I repeat, will be judged of hereafter, as circumstances and events may require, by the Government at Washington.

I do not suppose there is any immediate danger of any new menaces from France; still less, of any actual attack on the Islands by her Naval Armament. Nevertheless, you will keep us constantly and accurately informed of whatever transpires. . . . I have the honor to be With regard Your obedient servant

Daniel Webster.

1. Severance (1797–1855), of Maine, served as commissioner to the Hawaiian Islands from June 7, 1850, to December 20, 1853.

2. See No. 4. Webster to Severance, July 14, 1851, in *Diplomatic Papers*, 2:275–77.

3. Johnson (d. 1855) was an officer on the *U.S.S. Vandalia*. On June 20, he arrived in Washington with a bundle of dispatches from Severance.

4. A French corvette.

5. On March 10, 1851, King Kamehameha III had signed a confidential proclamation transferring his sovereignty over the Hawaiian kingdom to the United States in the event of an outbreak of hostilities with France, and Severance assured the king that the United States would use its naval power to defend the islands.

Document 75
Text from *Diplomatic Papers* 2: 396–401.

To Angel Calderon de la Barca[1]

Department of State,
Washington, 13th Novbr. 1851.

The Undersigned, Secretary of State of the United States, has the honor to acknowledge the receipt of the note of Senor Don A. Calderon de la Barca, Envoy Extraordinary & Minister Plenipotentiary of Her Catholic Majesty, of the 14th of last month,[2] upon the subject of the excesses, committed at New Orleans, upon the house of the Spanish Consul, and also on the property of certain individuals, subjects of Her Catholic Majesty.

Mr. Calderon has written and acted on this occasion, as well as on others, growing out of similar occurrences, with his accustomed zeal, as well as with fidelity to his Government; and he has met, and will meet, on the part of that of the United States, an entire readiness to listen most respectfully to his representations, and to do all that honor, good faith, and the friendly relations subsisting between the United States & Spain, may appear to demand.

The first rumor of the outrage at New Orleans induced the Government of the United States to take immediate steps to become acquainted with the particulars. It was regarded as a case in which the honor of the country was involved; and, as Mr. Calderon has already been informed by this Department, the Attorney of the United States, for the District of Louisiana, was instructed to cause inquiry to be made into the circumstances attending the occurrences, and to report the same to this Department.

The report of the District Attorney has been received, and a copy of it is now communicated to Mr. Calderon, for his information. It is accompanied, as will be perceived, by a statement of the Mayor of the city of New Orleans,[3] whose duty, as well as whose inclination, led him to make himself acquainted with every thing which took place.

From these authentic sources of information, it appears, that on the morning of the 21st of August, the Steamer "Crescent City" arrived at New Orleans from Havana with intelligence of the execution of the fifty persons who were captured near the coast of Cuba.[4] Mr Brincio, the Secretary of the Spanish Consul, was a passenger in the Steamer, and was understood to have been entrusted, by the Captain General, with letters written by the persons who were afterwards executed, to their friends in the United States. Instead of putting these letters into the Post-Office at once, on his arrival, he retained them, as was alleged. This occasioned an impression that he acted with great impropriety, and a report became current, that the Consul had refused to deliver the letters, when requested. Written placards were accordingly posted up in the City, threatening an attack on the office of the Spanish newspaper, called "La Union", during the ensuing night. This attack was probably precipitated by an Extra-Sheet, issued from the office of that paper, at half past two o'clock in the afternoon, giving an account of the execution of the fifty persons at Havana, as the attack was made between three & four o'clock the same afternoon, & before the public authorities were, or could be prepared to prevent it. During the attack, however, no personal injury was offered to any one. Afterwards attacks were made upon Coffeehouses and cigar-shops, kept by Spaniards. Between five & six o'clock, the same afternoon, Mr. [Joseph] Genois the Recorder of the First Municipality, hearing that an assault was threatened on the Consul's office, situated in that Municipality, repaired thither, accompanied by some of the police. He found the streets filled with people, the doors of the office broken open, & seven or eight persons in the act of breaking & destroying the furniture. He commanded the rioters to desist and they withdrew, after obtaining possession of the Consul's sign, which they took to a public square and there burned. After the departure of the mob, the doors of the Consul's office were fastened up by the officers, and the Police retired, not apprehending that the attack would be renewed. Within an hour, however, the rioters returned; forced their way into the office; destroyed all the remaining furniture; threw the Archives into the street; defaced the portraits of the Queen of Spain, & of the Captain General of Cuba, and tore in pieces the flag which they found in the office. This is believed to be a true account of every thing material which took place.

The Undersigned has now to say that the Executive Government of the United States regards these outrages not only as unjustifiable, but as disgraceful acts, and a flagrant breach of duty & propriety; and that it disapproves them as seriously, and regrets them as deeply, as either Mr. Calderon or his Government can possibly do. The Spanish Consul[5] was in this country discharging official duties, and protected, not only by the principles of public & national law, but also by the express stipulations of treaties; and the Undersigned is directed to give to Mr. Calderon, to be communicated to his Government, the President's assurance, that these events have caused him great pain; & that he thinks a proper acknowledgment is due to Her Catholic Majesty's Government. But the outrage, nevertheless, was one perpetrated by a mob, composed of irresponsible persons, the names of none of whom are known to this Government; nor, so far as the Government is informed, to its officers or agents, in New Orleans. And the Undersigned is happy to assure Mr. Calderon, that neither any officer or agent of the Government of the United States, high or low, nor any officer of the State of Louisiana, high or low, or of the municipal government of the city of New Orleans, took any part in the proceeding, so far as appears, or gave it any degree of countenance whatever. On the contrary, all these officers & agents, according to the authentic accounts of the Mayor and District Attorney, did all which the suddenness of the occasion would allow, to prevent it.

The assembling of mobs happens in all countries, popular violences occasionally break out, every where, setting law at defiance, trampling on the rights of citizens & private men, and sometimes on those of public officers, and the Agents of foreign governments, especially entitled to protection. In these cases the public faith & national honor require, not only that such outrages should be disavowed, but also that the perpetrators of them should be punished, wherever it is possible to bring them to justice; and, further, that full satisfaction should be made, in cases in which a duty to that effect rests with the Government, according to the general principles of law, public faith & the obligation of treaties. Mr. Calderon thinks that the enormity of this act of popular violence is heightened by its insult to the flag of Spain. The Government of the United States would earnestly deprecate any indignity offered in this country, in time of peace, to the flag of a nation so ancient, so respectable, so renowned as Spain. No wonder that Mr. Calderon should be proud, and that all patriotic Spaniards of this generation should be proud, of that Castilian Ensign, which, in times past, has been reared so high, and waived so often, over fields of acknowledged and distinguished valor; and which has floated, also, without stain, on all seas, and especially, in early days, on those seas which wash the shores of all the Indies. Mr. Calderon may be assured, that the Government of the United States does not, and cannot desire, to witness the desecration or degradation of the national banner of his Country. It appears, however, that in point of fact no flag was actually flying or publicly exhibited when the outrage took place; but this can make no difference, in regard to the real nature of the offence or its enormity. The persons composing the mob knew that they were offering insult and injury to an officer of Her Catholic Majesty, residing in the United States under the sanction of laws & treaties; and therefore their conduct admits of no justification. Nevertheless Mr. Calderon & his government are aware, that recent intelligence had then been received from Havana, not a little calculated to excite popular feeling, in a great city, and to lead to popular excesses. If this be no justification, as it certainly is none, it may still be taken into view, and regarded, as showing that the outrage, however flagrant, was committed in the heat of blood, & not in pursuance of any predetermined plan or purpose of injury or insult.

The people of the United States are accustomed, in all cases of alleged crime, to slow & cautious investigation, & deliberate trial, before sentence of condemnation is passed, however apparent, or however enormous the imputed offence may be. No wonder therefore the information of the execution, so soon after their arrest, of the persons above referred to, most of whom were known in New Orleans, and who were taken, not in Cuba, but at sea, endeavoring to escape from the Island, should have produced a belief, however erroneous, that they had been executed without any trial whatever,—caused an excitement in the city, the outbreak of which the public authorities were unable, for the moment, to prevent or control.

Mr. Calderon expresses the opinion, that not only ought indemnification to be made to Mr. [Juan Ygnacio] Laborde [y Rueda], Her Catholic Majesty's Consul, for injury & loss of property, but that reparation is due, also, from the Government of the United States to those Spaniards, residing in New Orleans, whose property was injured or destroyed by the mob; and intimates that such reparation had been verbally promised to him. The Undersigned sincerely regrets that any misapprehension should have grown up out of any conversation between Mr. Calderon & officers of this Government on this unfortunate & unpleasant affair; but while this Government has manifested a willingness and determination to perform every duty, which one friendly nation has a right to expect from another, in cases of this kind, it supposes that the right[s] of the Spanish Consul, a public officer residing here under the protection of the United States' Government, are quite different from those of the Spanish subjects, who have come into the country to mingle with our own citizens and here to pursue their private business & objects. The former may claim special indemnity, the latter are entitled to such protection as is afforded to our own citizens. While, therefore, the losses of individuals, private Spanish subjects, are greatly to be regretted, yet it is understood that many American citizens suffered equal losses from the same cause. And these private individuals, subjects of Her Catholic Majesty, coming voluntarily to reside in the United States, have certainly no cause of complaint if they are protected by the same law, & the same administration of law, as native born citizens of this country.

They have in fact some advantages over citizens of the State in which they happen to be, in as much as they are enabled, until they become citizens themselves, to prosecute for any injuries done to their persons or property in the Courts of the United States, or the State Courts, at their election.

The President is of opinion, as already stated, that, for obvious reasons, the case of the Consul is different, and that the Government of the United States should provide for Mr. Laborde a just indemnity and a recommendation to that effect will be laid before Congress, at an early period of its approaching Session.[6] This is all, which it is in his power to do. The case may be a new one, but the President being of opinion, that Mr. Laborde ought to be indemnified, has not thought it necessary to search for precedents.

In conclusion the Undersigned has to say that if Mr. Laborde shall return to his post, or any other Consul for New Orleans shall be appointed by Her Catholic Majesty's Government, the officers of this Government, resident in that city, will be instructed to receive & treat him with courtesy; & with a National salute to the Flag of his ship, if he shall arrive in a Spanish Vessel, as a demonstration of respect, such as may signify to him, and to his Government, the sense entertained by the Government of the United States of the gross injustice done to his predecessor by a lawless mob, as well as the indignity and insult offered by it to a Foreign State, with which the United States are, & wish ever to remain, on terms of the most respectful & pacific intercourse. The Undersigned avails himself of this occasion to offer to Mr. Calderon renewed assurances of his most distinguished consideration.

Danl. Webster.

1. Calderon de la Barca (1790–1860) was Spain's minister to the United States from 1845 to 1853.

2. Calderon to John J. Crittenden, October 14, 1851, in *Diplomatic Papers*, 2:388–90.

3. The report of District Attorney Logan Hunton and the statement by Mayor A. D. Crossman can be found in *Executive Documents*, 32d Congress, 1st session, Serial 634, No. 2.

4. On August 16, after a summary trial, about fifty captured filibusters were executed in Cuba. Narciso López, the leader of the filibustering expedition, was garroted in a public square in Havana on September 1, and the 156 survivors of his foray were sent to work the quicksilver mines in Spain. Most of the filibusters were citizens of the United States.

5. Juan Ygnacio Laborde y Rueda, the Spanish consul in New Orleans, fled the city in fear for his life during the rioting.

6. On August 31, 1852, in response to President Fillmore's recommendation, Congress appropriated $25,000 to indemnify both the Spanish consul and the Spanish citizens who had suffered property losses in the riots.

Document 76
Text from *Diplomatic Papers* 2: 737–38.

To James C. Jewett[1]

Department of State,
Sir: Washington, 5th June, 1852.
    I have to acknowledge the receipt of your letter of the 2nd instant,[2] inquiring whether citizens of the United States can take guano from the Lobos Islands, which are situated near the coast of Peru, without infringing upon the rights of the citizens or subjects or government of any other nation?

    In reply, I have to inform you, that if those Islands should lie within the distance of a marine league from the continent, or if, being further than that distance, should have been discovered and occupied by Spain or by Peru, the Peruvian government would have a right to exclude therefrom the vessels and citizens of other nations except upon such conditions as it may think proper to prescribe. There can be no doubt that the title of Peru to the Chincha Islands, whence guano is now chiefly taken, is founded upon the basis of discovery and occupancy. That article was taken from those Islands and used as a manure by the Peruvians anterior to the conquest of Peru by Spain. It continued to be so taken and used throughout the Spanish dominion in that country, and this practice has been kept up to the present day. Although those Islands are uninhabitable, the custom of resorting to them from the neighbouring continent for the purpose of procuring guano may be said to have constituted such an occupancy of them as to give to the sovereign of the continent a right of dominion over them under the law of nations.

    This department, however, is not aware that the Lobos Islands were either discovered or occupied by Spain or by Peru or that the guano on them has ever been used for manure on the adjacent coast or elsewhere. It is certain that their distance from the continent is five or six times greater than is necessary to make them a dependency thereof pursuant to public law.[3] On the other hand it is quite probable that Benjamin Morrell, Junior, who, as Master of the Schooner Wasp, of New York, visited those Islands in September, 1823, may justly claim to have been their discoverer. He gives a full account of them in his Narrative published at New York in 1832.[4] Under these circumstances, it may be considered the duty of this government to protect citizens of the United States who may visit the Lobos Islands for the purpose of obtaining guano. This duty will be the more apparent when it is considered that the consumers of Chincha Island guano in this country might probably obtain it for half the price they now pay were it not for the charges of the Peruvian government. I shall consequently communicate a copy of this letter to the Secretary of the Navy and suggest that a vessel of war be ordered to repair to the Lobos Islands, <either for the purpose of taking possession of them on behalf of the United States in consequence of their discovery by one of their citizens, or>[5] for the purpose of protecting from molestation any of our citizens who may wish to take guano from them. I am, Sir, very respectfully, Your obedient servant,

D.W.

1. Jewett was a merchant ship captain involved in the guano trade.
2. Jewett to Webster, June 2, 1852, in *Diplomatic Papers*, 2:736.
3. The Chincha Islands are about sixteen miles off the coast of Peru; the Lobos Islands are approximately forty miles off the coast of Peru.
4. Morrell (1795–1839) made several voyages in the Southern Hemisphere, and he described the Lobos Islands in *A Narrative of Four Voyages to the South Sea* (New York, 1832).
5. The letter from Webster to Jewett printed above is a draft, and the words in angle brackets were deleted from the letter actually sent to him.

Document 77
Text from George Ticknor Curtis, *Life of Daniel Webster* (2 vols; New York, 1870), 2:644–46.

Mr. Sprague and Friends
[*July 25, 1852*[1]]

I thank you from the very bottom of my heart for this warm welcome home, which so many of you have assembled to offer to me to-day. It was unexpected. I had not looked for such a testimonial of your regard. But it draws from me, as it ought to draw, the most grateful acknowledgments of my heart. . . .

Friends and neighbors, it is now twenty years that I have been in the midst of you, passing here, on the side of the sea, all that portion of the year in which I have been able to enjoy some relaxation from the cares of my profession, or the duties of public life. Happy have they been to me and mine, for, during all this period, I know not of an unkind thing done, or word spoken to me or mine, or to any one near or dear to me.

Gentlemen, most of you are farmers, and I take a great concern in your interests, becuase I have a wish to promote the general prosperity of the whole country. Others of you have your occupations on the seas. Some of you I have found there, and have had the pleasure to mingle in your pursuits; a pleasure I hope to enjoy again. . . .[2]

Mr. Sprague has made allusion to recent occurrences, threatening disturbances on account of the fisheries.[3] It would not become me to say much on that subject until I speak officially, and under direction of the head of the Government. And then I shall speak. In the mean time, be assured that the interest will not be neglected by this Administration under any circumstances.

The fishermen shall be protected in all their rights of property, and in all their rights of occupation. To use a Marblehead phrase, they shall be protected hook and line, and bob and sinker. And why should they not? They employ a vast number. Many of our own people are engaged in that vocation. There are perhaps among you some who have been on the Grand Banks for forty successive years, and there hung on to the ropes in storm and wreck.

The most important consequences are involved in this matter. Our fisheries have been the very nurseries of our navy. If you flag-ships have conquered the enemy on the sea, the fisheries are at the bottom of it. The fisheries were the seeds from which those glorious triumphs were born and sprung. . . . The Treaty of 1818 was made with the Crown of England.[4] If a fishing-vessel is captured by one of her vessels-of-war, and brought in for adjuducation, the Crown of England is answerable, and then we know who we have to deal with. But it is not to be expected that the United States will submit their rights to be adjudicated upon in the petty tribunals of the provinces, or that they will allow our vessels to be seized by constables and other petty officers, and condemned by muncipal courts of Canada and Newfoundland, New Brunswick, or Nova Scotia!! No, no, no! [Great cheering.] Further than this, gentlemen, I do not think it expedient to remark upon this topic at present; but, you may be assured, it is a subject upon which no one sleeps at Washington. . . .

Gentlemen, I deem it a great piece of good-fortune, coming from the mountains as I did, that I came where I did; that, when I came from the mountains, I descended to the sea-shore. Many people, when they come down here, wonder what in the world could have induced Mr. Webster to come to Marshfield. I answer, partly good sense, but more good fortune. I had no particular fancy for rich lands, but I had for a kind neighborhood; and myself and friends, when I came here, had a well-understood covenant, that I would talk to them about farming, but not a word about law or politics.

You have kept your word, and I hope I have kept mine; and now, my friends and neighbors, accept from a grateful heart my warm acknowledgments that you have come here with countenances so open, so frank, to give me the assurance of your perennial regards and continued friendship.

Again I thank you with all my heart, and my prayers are that the Almighty Power will preserve you, and shower down upon you and yours the blessings of happy affection and peace and prosperity.

1. Seth Sprague, one of Webster's Marshfield neighbors, was the head of a welcoming committee that arranged a large public reception for the secretary of state on July 25, 1852. When Webster stepped from the train at Kingston, about nine miles from his home at Marshfield, he was surprised by a large assembly consisting of thousands of neighbors and well-wishers from the surrounding area. In a procession involving over 150 carriages, the welcoming committee escorted the secretary of state to his estate. Upon arrival at his home, Webster, who was very moved by the occasion, extemporaneously delivered this, his last public speech, to the crowd of friends and neighbors.

2. Webster was an avid sports fisherman.

3. On July 5, without any prior warning, the British government announced that a naval force had been deployed off the coast of British North America to prevent encroachments by American fishermen.

4. For the Convention of October 20, 1818, between Great Britain and the United States, see Miller, ed., *Treaties*, 2:658–62.

Document 78
Text from *Diplomatic Papers* 2: 774.

To Millard Fillmore

Private & Confidential
My Dear Sir,   Marshfield, Sept. 15. '52

I am glad you have returned safe to Washington, & that you left Mrs Fillmore[1] improving in health. I return Mr [Alfred G.] Bensons letter,[2] as requested. I feel concern about the Lobos business, but we will do as well as we can, & must trust to fortune. People say, that Mr Fillmore's good luck will bring him out of all trouble.

In regard to this subject, my original letter to [James C.] Jewett[3] may have been a wrong step, or a hasty step. It was taken, as you knew, in a hurried moment, and, in a great measure on confidence, first, in Mr [William] Hunter,[4] who seemed well informed, & had no doubts; &, secondly, in Mr [Hiram] Ketchums[5] strong recommendation of Mr

Jewett, & Mr Jewett's absolute, particular, & full statement,[6] as made by a man long acquainted with the whole subject, both historically, & locally. I admit, it would have been wise, to have inquired further. But what I wish, more particularly, to say, now, is, that the measure was mine, & I am responsible for it. It is true, you approved the letter to Jewett; but you, as well as myself, were, at the moment, overwhelmed with affairs; you were not able to give the subject much attention, & your approval was, doubtless, very much founded in your confidence in me.

My Dear Sir; You have, as I hope,—a future; & if, in your fortunes hereafter, it shall become necessary to say, that the Lobos proceeding was mine, say so, & use this letter as my acknowledgement of that truth.

May God preserve & bless you!

Danl Webster

1. Abigail Powers Fillmore (1798–1853).
2. Benson (1804–78), a New York shipping merchant, who imported guano on a large scale and was Jewett's silent partner.
3. See Document #76, Webster to Jewett, June 5, 1852.
4. Hunter (1805–86) served in the Department of State from 1829 until his death. In 1852, he was chief clerk, the second ranking position in the department after the secretary of state.
5. Ketchum (c. 1792–1870), a New York City lawyer, leader of the Webster Whigs in that city, and a close friend of Webster.
6. See Jewett to Webster, June 2, 1852, in *Diplomatic Papers*, 2:736.

BIBLIOGRAPHICAL ESSAY

———◆——

Those interested in exploring further the life and times of Daniel Webster have a wealth of primary sources and secondary works to draw from. With respect to primary sources, there are several important collections of Webster materials. Under the title *The Private Correspondence of Daniel Webster* (2 vols.; Boston, 1857), his son Fletcher edited with filial piety two volumes of his father's letters. Although Fletcher Webster "improved" his father's prose in places and occasionally deleted or altered words and phrases that he thought might prove to be embarrassing, the work remains a valuable primary source because many of the letters contained in it cannot be found elsewhere, having either been lost or destroyed in a fire in 1881. George Ticknor Curtis's *Life of Daniel Webster* (2 vols.; New York, 1870) is valuable for the same reason. As a close friend of Webster and one of his literary executors, Curtis assiduously collected letters and recollections from Webster's correspondents prior to composing his biography, and many of these documents have been reprinted in the two volumes. Despite his loyalty to the memory of Webster, Curtis is generally fair-minded in his well-written and carefully documented account of the life and times of Daniel Webster. Other useful works by contemporaries include Peter Harvey's *Reminiscences and Anecdotes of Daniel Webster* (Boston, 1877), Charles Lanman's *The Private Life of Daniel Webster* (New York, 1858), Samuel P. Lyman's *Life and Memorials of Daniel Webster* (2 vols.; New York, 1853), and Caroline Le Roy Webster's *"Mr. W. and I"* (Binghamton, New York, 1942). The last item, edited by Claude M. Fuess, is Mrs. Webster's diary of the trip she took with her husband to Britain and France in 1839.

Other important primary sources are C. H. Van Tyne's *The Letters of Daniel Webster* (New York, 1902), and James W. McIntyre's massive *The National Edition of the Writings and Speeches of Daniel Webster* (18 vols.; Boston, 1903). Van Tyne's large book, which is organized topically, draws primarily upon previously unpublished documents from the New Hampshire Historical Society. McIntyre's multivolume work reprints Fletcher Webster's 1857 edition of his father's correspondence and contains the most complete compilation of Daniel Webster's speeches and formal writings. *The Letters and Times of the Tylers* (3 vols.; Richmond and Williamsburg, Virginia, 1884–96), edited by Lyon G. Tyler, and the *Millard Fillmore Papers* (2 vols.; Buffalo, New York, 1907), edited by Frank H. Severance, contain, respectively, correspondence between Webster and presidents John Tyler and Millard Fillmore.

All previous collections of primary sources have been superseded by the *Microfilm Edition of the Papers of Daniel Webster* and its companion letterpress publication, both under the overall editorship of Charles M. Wiltse. Issued in forty-one reels in 1971, the microfilm edition is now the definitive compilation of primary sources relating to Daniel Webster. Wiltse's *Guide and Index to the Microfilm Edition of the Papers of Daniel Webster* (Ann Arbor, Michigan, and Hanover, New Hampshire, 1971), conveniently indexes the forty-one reels. While more selective, the companion letterpress publication offers readers the essential writings of Webster with scholarly annotation and commentary. Published by the University Press of New England between 1974 and 1989, the series consists of seven volumes of general correspondence, three of legal papers, two of diplomatic papers, two of speeches and formal writings, and a master index. More specifically, the series can be found under the following references: Charles M. Wiltse and others, eds., *The Papers of Daniel Webster, Correspondence* (7 vols.; Hanover, N.H., and London, England, 1974–86); *Volume I: 1798–1824*, Wiltse and Harold D. Moser, eds. (1974); *Volume 2: 1825–1829*, Wiltse and Moser, eds. (1976); *Volume 3: 1830–1834*, Wiltse and David G. Allen, eds. (1977); *Volume 4: 1835–1839*, Wiltse and Moser, eds. (1980); *Volume 5: 1840–1843*, Moser, ed. (1982); *Volume 6: 1844–1849*, Wiltse and Wendy B. Tilgham, eds. (1984); *Volume 7: 1850–1852*, Wiltse and Michael J. Birkner, eds. (1986). Alfred S. Konefsky and Andrew J. King, eds., *The Papers of Daniel Webster, Legal Papers* (3 vols.; Hanover, N.H., and London, England, 1982–89); *Volume 1: The New Hampshire Practice*, Konefsky and King, eds. (1982); *Volume 2: The Boston Practice*, Konefsky and King, eds. (1983); *Volume 3: The Federal Practice*, King, ed. (1989). Kenneth E. Shewmaker and others, eds., *The Papers of Daniel Webster, Diplomatic Papers* (2 vols.; Hanover, N.H., and London, England, 1983–87); *Volume 1: 1841–1843*, Shewmaker, Kenneth R. Stevens, and Anita McGurn, eds. (1983); *Volume 2: 1850–1852*, Shewmaker, Stevens, and Alan R. Berolzheimer, eds. (1987). Wiltse and Berolzheimer, eds., *The Papers of Daniel Webster, Speeches and Formal Writings* (2 vols.; Hanover, N.H., and London, England, 1986–88); *Volume 1: 1800–1833* (1986); *Volume 2: 1834–1852* (1988). Berolzheimer, ed., *The Papers of Daniel Webster, General Index* (Hanover, N.H., and London, England, 1989). In effect, the multivolume *Papers of Daniel Webster* constitutes a documentary history of the life and times of one of America's most influential statesmen.

With respect to secondary works, there are several excellent full-scale biographies of Webster. Maurice G. Baxter's *One and Inseparable: Daniel Webster and the Union* (Cambridge, Massachusetts, 1984) is the most richly detailed scholarly account. Although the book assesses all aspects of Webster's life, it is particularly strong on his legal and political careers. Baxter concludes that Webster's nationalistic vision of the Union as one and inseparable with liberty, which triumphed over the philosophy of state sovereignty, was his greatest contribution to American history. Politics is the focus of Merrill D. Peterson's *The Great Triumvirate: Webster, Clay, and Calhoun* (New York and Oxford, 1987). In this innovative collective biography, Peterson offers readers an absorbing narrative of politics and public policy from the War of 1812 to the Compromise of 1850. Seeing the triumvirs as the giants among the second generation of American leadership, he characterizes Webster as irresponsible and extravagant in his personal behavior but brilliantly successful in his public role as the tribune of American nationalism. Unlike other scholars, Irving H. Bartlett in *Daniel Webster* (New York, 1978) emphasizes the private rather than the public side of the subject. He views Webster as a talented statesman flawed by his improvidence with money, opulent lifestyle, and involvement in conflict of interest situations. Bartlett's study also stands out for its careful assessment of the content and impact of such major Webster orations as the "Second Reply to Hayne" and the "Seventh of March" speech. Richard N. Current's short, interpretive biography, *Daniel Webster and the Rise of National Conservatism* (Boston and Toronto, 1955), places Webster in the historical context of nineteenth-century conservatism and excels in analyzing Webster's activities in relation to the larger themes of American history. Current understands Webster as a spokesman for a brand of national conservatism that assumed that property and power should go together and as a politician who sought to advance that philosophy both in domestic and foreign policy. Although Claude M. Fuess's *Daniel Webster* (2 vols.; Boston, 1930) can no longer be considered the standard account, it continues to be valuable for its scope and comprehensiveness. In this admiring study, Fuess depicts Webster as an enormously gifted statesman of power and majesty.

Certain specialized secondary works that fall short of being full-scale biographies also offer valuable commentary about Webster's life and times. Taken together, Sydney Nathans's *Daniel Webster and Jacksonian Democracy* (Baltimore, 1973), and Robert F. Dalzell, Jr.'s *Daniel Webster and the Trial of American Nationalism 1843–1852* (Boston, 1973), provide a comprehensive review of Webster's political career from 1828 until his death in 1852. Both authors address the interesting question of why Webster never gained the presidency, Nathan covering the years 1828–1844 and Dalzell dealing with the last decade of Webster's life. Two monographs by Maurice G. Baxter offer incisive appraisals of Webster's legal career: *Daniel Webster and the Supreme Court* (Amherst, Massachusetts, 1966), and *The Steamboat Monopoly: Gibbons v Ogden, 1824* (New York, 1972).

Several books are particularly helpful in understanding Webster's foreign policies during his first term as secretary of state. In *To the Webster-Ashburton Treaty: A Study of Anglo-American Relations, 1783–1843* (Chapel Hill, 1977), Howard Jones skillfully assesses the complicated negotiations that led to what probably constituted Webster's greatest achievement as a diplomat; and the same author's *Mutiny on the Amistad: The Saga of a Slave Revolt and Its Impact on American Abolition, Law, and Diplomacy* (New York and Oxford, 1987) includes an account of how Webster dealt with the repercussions of that celebrated slave uprising on Spanish-American relations. Frederick Merk's *Fruits of Propaganda in the Tyler Administration* (Cambridge, Massachusetts, 1971) devotes more attention to Webster than it does to President Tyler and includes a probing analysis of the ethical dilemmas Webster confronted in his search for a lasting peace between Britain and the United States. The events that precipitated a crisis between Great Britain and the United States have been studied in detail by Kenneth

R. Stevens in *Border Diplomacy: The Caroline and McLeod Affairs in Anglo-American Relations, 1827–1842* (Tuscaloosa and London, 1989).

With respect to Webster's second term as secretary of state, several essays by Kenneth E. Shewmaker offer interpretive appraisals. "Daniel Webster and the Politics of Foreign Policy, 1850–1852," *Journal of American History* 63 (September 1976) explores the intersection between domestic and foreign affairs; "Forging the 'Great Chain': Daniel Webster and the Origins of American Foreign Policy Toward East Asia and the Pacific, 1841–1852," *Proceedings of the American Philosophical Society* 129 (September 1985) underscores Webster's seminal role in fashioning the American approach to that important region of the world; " 'Hook and line, and bob and sinker': Daniel Webster and the Fisheries Dispute of 1852," *Diplomatic History* 9 (Spring 1985), and " 'Untaught Diplomacy': Daniel Webster and the Lobos Islands Controversy," *Diplomatic History* 1 (Fall 1977) scrutinize the mistakes Webster made in 1852 in disputes with England and Peru. Shewmaker's " 'Congress only can declare war' *and* 'the President is Commander in Chief': Daniel Webster and the War Power," *Diplomatic History* 12 (Fall 1988) examines Webster's thought and record on the important question of which branch of the federal government possesses the authority to authorize hostilities against other nations; and his "Daniel Webster and American Conservatism," in *Traditions and Values: American Diplomacy, 1790–1865*, edited by Norman A. Graebner (Lanham, Maryland, 1985), analyzes Webster's conservative philosophy of international relations. Finally, Howard Jones's "The Attempt to Impeach Daniel Webster," *Capitol Studies* 3 (Fall 1975) deals with an unusual effort by Congressman Charles Ingersoll of Pennsylvania in 1846 to impeach Webster retroactively on charges of misconduct while serving as secretary of state from 1841 to 1843; and Peter J. Parish's "Daniel Webster, New England, and the West," *Journal of American History* 54 (December 1967) takes issue with the stereotype of Webster as a spokesman for the eastern establishment by investigating his attitudes toward the American West.

INDEX

Page references in italics refer to source documents.

Abbott, Daniel, *152*, 154n.3
Aberdeen, Lord (George Hamilton Gordon, Fourth Earl), 206, 210, 214, 215, 217, *259*, *261*, 262n.8
Abolitionists, xxiv, 4, 88, 89, *125–26*, 217–18
Adams, Charles Francis, xxii
Adams, John, xx, 82, *109*, *111–12*, 242, 243n.11; Webster's memorial address on Jefferson and, xx, xxi, 84, *104–13*
Adams, John Quincy, 2, 5, 6, 8, 22, *23*, 26n.4, *42*, 83, 84, 88; accused of election tampering, 33n.5; letter from Webster to, *126–28;* phrenological statistics, 79; reelection campaign, *29–30*
Adams-Onis Treaty. See Florida Treaty
Admiralty law, 142. *See also* Maritime law
Albany Evening Journal, 68
Alien tax, *197–202*
Alien vote, 4
Allen, William, 171n.1; letter from Salma Hale to, *171*
Almonte, Juan Nepomuceno, 260, 262n.11
American Patriot, 21n.3. *See also New Hampshire Patriot*
American Quarterly Review, 27, 28n.1
American Revolution, 268, 272, 278–79, 281nn.14–15
Amistad mutiny, 217–18, 222
Anglo-American Convention of 1818, 222
Anti-auction men, *38*, 39n.4
Antimasons, 2, 11, 13, *35*, *36*, *38*, *40*, *42*, *43*, *46*, *50*, 170n.3
Appointments, political, *65. See also* Patronage appointments
Aranda, Count (Pedro Pable Abarca y Bolea), 213
Argentina, 218
Articles of Confederation. *See* Confederation period
Ashburton, Lord (Alexander Baring), 3, *56*, 57n.3, 206–15 passim, 225–26nn.12–13, 226n.19, 227n.29, *255–56*, *259;* letters from Webster to, *244–54*
Ashmun, George, *69*, 69n.3

Astor House, 75n.1
Atherton, Charles, *36*, 37n.1
Aulick, John H., 284n.1; letter from Webster to, *282–84*
Australia, forensic oratory in High Court of, xi
Austria: experiments with liberal constitution, *280–81*, 281–82n.17; Hungarian uprising of 1848, 221, *269–81* passim; offers to mediate end to American Revolution, 281n.15

Bacon, Matthew, *158*, 159n.4
Baldwin, Henry, *43*, 44n.8
Baltimore American, 26n.3
Baltimore Patriot and Commercial Advertiser, 24, 26n.3
Bank, national, Clay's proposal for, 87
Bank of the United States, 14, 44n.10, 55n.1
Bank of the United States v. Dandridge, 29, 31n.3
Banking, xxv; laws, 140–41
Bankruptcy law, 146–47, 152n.22
Baring, Alexander. *See* Ashburton, Lord
Barnburners, *63*, 64n.3
Bartlett, Irving H., xix–xxvii passim, xxix(n.10)
Barton, David, *38*, 39n.5
Bates, Isaac Chapman, *42*, 44n.3
Bates, Joshua, 54n.1; letter from Webster to, *53–54*
Baxter, Maurice G., xix–xxvi passim, xxix(n.10), 227n.29
Bell, John, *37*, 39n.2
Bell, Samuel, *30*, 31n.8, *172*, 172n.1, *173*
Bemis, Samuel F., 227n.29
Benét, Steven Vincent, xxi
Benson, Alfred G., *295*, 296n.2
Benton, Thomas Hart, 211, *259*, 262n.5, 262n.7
Berrien, John Macpherson, *259*, 262n.4
Biddle, Nicholas, xxv, 3–4, 8, 9
Bingham, James Hervey, 154n.1, 159n.1; letters from Webster to, *152–59*, *154*, 154n.8, *161*
Blackstone, William, *155*, 155n.1